SO AN SHADOW

BIRTHING MOTHERWORLD

ಜಿ

THE HEALING JOURNEY OF A PRIESTESS OF AVALON

ಜಿ

Kathy Jones

ARIADNE
PUBLICATIONS

"Soul and Shadow: Birthing MotherWorld.
The Healing Journey of a Priestess of Avalon"
by Kathy Jones
Copyright ©2017 Kathy Jones. All rights reserved.
Published and copyright ©2017 by Ariadne Publications.

The right of Kathy Jones to be identified as the author of the Work has been asserted by her in accordance with the Copyright, Designs and Patents Act 1988.
No part of this publication may be reproduced or used in any form or by any means without written permission from the Publisher except for review purposes.

ISBN 978-1-872983-43-1
A CIP catalogue record for this book is available from the British Library.

Cover painting by Foosiya Miller
Design, text styling and artwork by
Bernard Chandler, Glastonbury, England.
www.graffik.co.uk

Text set in 11 on 16pt Adobe Jenson, with Centaur titling.
Decorative initials scanned from a copy of
"A Book of Alphabets Plain & Ornamental",
printed c.1900 by The Leadenhall Press, London SE1.
End of chapter "vesica" glyph adapted and drawn from details
from the iron age Battersea Shield.

Printed and bound in Great Britain by CPI Group (UK) Ltd, Croydon CR0 4YY

DEDICATION

For my lovely Mike, Iona, Torquil and Samba.

For all my sister Priestesses and Priests of Avalon.

For all who take responsibility for their personal behaviour,
bringing alive the Vision of Motherworld – the society which
places Mother Earth, mothers and the values of mothering
– love, care and support for each other,
in the centre of everything.

Contents

Introduction 1
1 Travels of a Priestess: Aveline's Hole 13
2 Travelling to Anatolia, Land of the Ancient Mothers 19
3 Breast Cancer 43
4 Surgery and Beyond 57
5 The Healing Journey – Living in Fear or in Her Confidence 73
6 The Sacred Landscape Temple of Rhandirmwyn 91
7 Soul Travel 107
8 Meeting the Wounding 123
9 Re-Membering MotherWorld 139
10 Where Are You Now, Eileen? 155
11 The Shock of Sudden Death 163
12 Falling Down a Hole into MotherWorld 177
13 The Wounded Child 193
14 Long Live the Witch! 207
15 Creating Paradise 223
16 A Small Miscommunication 233
17 Failure 245
18 The Orchard of Avalon 253
19 Sisters, Sisters 261
20 Re-Membering the Queen 269
21 The Isle of Stones 281

22	Constructive Developments, the War and all that	291
23	Ioua	313
24	The Process of Healing	323
25	The Crone	339
26	Our Wedding	353
27	The Ducking Stool	359
28	Sacrifices Made	369
29	Letting Go	379
30	Resolution	395
Finale	Gratitude	413

Introduction

I AM KATHRYN OF AVALON, daughter of Eileen, daughter of Beatrice, daughter of Mary, daughter of Madron of the lineage of Avallach. I am Priestess of Avalon, Priestess of Goddess, Priestess of the Lady of Avalon. I return from ancient times to live in the small country town of Glastonbury in southwest England. Glastonbury is a Gateway to the Paradise Isle of Avalon, the Land where Goddess is loved and adored, and always has been. Here She is known as Lady of Avalon, a new-found yet ancient Goddess, to whom many people are responding in the present day. Her earthly and energetic bodies are visible here within the physical and energetic shapes of the hills and valleys of Glastonbury's sacred landscape, which is the Outerworld counterpart to the Otherworldly Isle of Avalon.

The Lady of Avalon is an awesome and powerful Goddess of love, deep healing and transformation on all levels. She changes everything She touches. She appears here in the land and in mythical reality, as Maiden, Lover, Mother and Crone, Lady of Earth, Water, Fire, Air and the Space between all things. She is present in the physical form of Glastonbury Tor, an iconic landscape feature that rises above the flat Summerland meadows. Her familiar name is Nolava, the reflective Mirror of Avalon. Those who hear Her call must each look deeply into Her Mirror, to see and know ourselves and our beauty, as well as all that must be transformed within us. The Lady is Nolava of the Sacred Land, Black Nolava of the Under Ground and Stella Nolava of the Heavenly Realms.

My life is dedicated to bringing Goddess alive in the world from out of our human forgetting. I do this through my creativity, writing, teaching, healing, through the Goddess ceremonies and events I create and everything in my life for which I take responsibility. All these activities are within my embrace as Queen of my realm. My dedication is to bring the loving and life-affirming values of Her Motherworld back to Her Earth.

My pleasure is to love and serve the Lady of Avalon, Her land and Her people. Calling myself Her Priestess in Avalon is not a goal that I have reached, an end in itself, where I can sit back and rest on my laurels. I am always in process of becoming Her Priestess of Avalon, learning from all my experiences in this sacred place and out in the wider world. As I experience Her transforming powers working in my own life I surrender more and more to Her love. The Lady has inspired me to initiate and bring into being, with lots of amazing women and men, many Goddess-centred community adventures in Glastonbury. She blesses our lives with Her love.

I HAVE BEEN a spiritual seeker all my life and my Goddess path in this life began in Glastonbury in a women's consciousness-raising group in the late 1970s. Most of us were in our late 20s/early 30s. There we shared our experiences of life as women. We discussed in detail the seven demands of the women's liberation movement – free contraception, abortion on demand, et al. We encouraged each other to take part in political protests in support of life and against nuclear weapons. We did street theatre on market days and travelled to Greenham Common Airbase to take part in women's protests at the coming of American nuclear cruise missiles onto British soil. Our woman consciousness was awakened and stimulated.

My personal awareness of Goddess grew through strong emotional and spiritual experiences at Greenham and in Glastonbury, through reading feminist books and ancient Goddess myths. It expanded dramatically when I was inspired to write, direct and perform Sacred Dramas. I wrote these on my own or with friends, who include Leona Graham, Peter Davies and Mike Jones. Our stories redressed imbalances in patriarchal myths, bringing Goddess to the fore once again so that She could express Herself anew. Over a period of 13 years from the early 1980s onwards, inspired by different Goddesses – Persephone, Inanna, Ariadne, Green Tara, the Lady of Avalon, to name just a few, we came to know something of their many faces. These were the years of Ariadne Productions, named for the transformational Kretan Snake Goddess.

As I researched Goddess I was encouraged by the daring, intelligence, insight, courage, wisdom and humanity of my foresisters who walked these paths of awareness before me – Emily Pankhurst, Virginia Woolf, Anais Nin, Alice Bailey, Jane Roberts, Merlin Stone, Mary Daly, Violet Firth/Dion Fortune, Mary Renault, Jane Harrison, Maria Gimbutas, Maya Angelou, Starhawk and many other sparkling women. I follow in their footsteps to this day.

I learned about Goddess in the past and had direct and powerful experiences of Her in the present. I shared what I learned with others. I began teaching evening, day and weekend Goddess workshops and joined with others in celebrating the eight seasonal festivals of the year.

In 1996 with Tyna Redpath, I initiated the first annual Glastonbury Goddess Conference. Our plan was to create a three day Goddess celebration with ceremony, art, stories, music, dance, Goddess workshops of all kinds, sacred landscape walks, etc. We invited presenters from all over Britain and abroad who love Goddess to join us in celebrating Her here in Her sacred land of Avalon. The Goddess Conference is now in its 22nd year and is a nine day spiritual and cultural extravaganza for those who wish to dive deeply into the world of Goddess. A person's first Conference is often an initiatory highlight in their lives, opening hearts to Goddess, and becoming an annual pilgrimage which brings renewed inspiration and commitment to Goddess. The event has brought thousands of Goddess-seeking visitors to Glastonbury over the years, prospering the town and its people.

At the end of our second Goddess Conference I realised that we really needed properly trained Priestesses to hold our Conference ceremonial container. Up to that point people from the plays had been helping, but were not necessarily devoted priestesses. After much internal dialogue in 1998 I initiated the first Priestess/Priest of Avalon Training in Glastonbury. It seemed such a bold and scary title to claim for myself and for others, with its resonances of magic and mystery. That first year we had a big class with 35 people gathering for eight weekends in the year at the seasonal festivals to learn about the different faces of Goddess and what it might mean to be Her Priest/ess of Avalon.

As the Priestess Training developed over the years I realised that there was so much to learn about becoming Her Priestess or Priest and what that truly means. After a few years we expanded the teaching into a three year Three Spiral Priestess training with myself and Priestess Erin McCauliff, and that is only the beginning of one's life as Her Priest/ess. Twenty years experience later I believe ours is now one of the finest Priestess Trainings in the world for those who really want to embrace this spiritual path of devotion to Goddess, to the Lady of Avalon.

I FIRST MET the love of my life, Mike Jones, during our 1988 Ariadne Production of Green Tara, when he came to play music. We share a love of Goddess born in each of us before we met, and it was She who brought us together. We have a similar dedication to the exploration of consciousness, although we have different spiritual practices. One of the things we enjoy is visiting the many ancient Goddess sites in Britain, Europe and elsewhere. On our travels we often retrieve pieces of the jigsaw of our soul lives from previous incarnations, reintegrating them and helping make us whole. In 1999 after the third Goddess Conference we were on holiday in Greece. One day we took a trip to Mount Olympus. Arriving through thick mist, just like the journey to Avalon, we saw ahead the great beautiful mountain of many peaks. We visited the ruins of the town of Dion at the foot of the mountain, where there are several ancient ruined Temples dedicated to different Goddesses. Beside a small pool in the ruins of a Temple to Isis I felt such overwhelming sorrow. Here we were visiting yet another Goddess Temple in ruins. I could not bear it. I felt so sad. In that moment I made a vow that when I returned home I would create a present day living Goddess Temple in Glastonbury.

Introduction

When we got home I called people together who might be interested in creating a Goddess Temple. After many meetings and much talking we opened our first pop-up Goddess Temple for three days at the end of May 2000 in the Miracles Room in the Glastonbury Experience. We decorated the room as Her Temple with a large wicker Goddess statue from the Conference and colourful materials. We opened our Temple to the public, held Goddess ceremonies and had a blessed time. From then on we created pop-up Temples every six weeks at each seasonal festival in different rooms that we hired. In 2001 a space became available upstairs in the Courtyard of the Glastonbury Experience and we decided to rent it to be our permanent Goddess Temple dedicated to the Lady of Avalon. We opened the Temple to the public at Imbolc 2002 and have been open ever since. We are open everyday from 12noon to 4.00pm with the help of many volunteer Melissas.

We have grown organically and expanded step by step since then. The Temple is registered as a Place of Worship, the first indigenous British Goddess Temple ever to be legally recognised in Britain and Europe. Now we also own Glastonbury Goddess Hall, and recently we have taken on Goddess House, as our Goddess Healing, Wellness and Educational Centre. The transforming effects of all these Goddess activities have rippled out from this small magical town into the world, inspiring others on their Goddess paths to initiate their own Goddess activities and Temples in their own communities and lands. Goddess is alive and coming back into human awareness.

MANY PEOPLE are attracted to Glastonbury. It is a place of transformation and healing, and people's experiences of visiting and living here are often strong and challenging. Over the last twenty years or so a wonderful community of Goddess-loving people has come together in Glastonbury, supporting all the different Goddess ventures which are being created here. However it is not a simple easy process to form a Goddess community, with high ideals and big aspirations, and the reality of dealing with our individual and interpersonal wounding. There are peaks and troughs on this soul journey.

In creating any new venture there are people who are there at the beginning, who like to start things and then move on. Then there are people who are good at stabilising and continuing things, who like turning up every day. There are people who find a place to express their creativity for a while and then depart. There are those who create something and then want it to stay the same and there are those who want things to keep moving, to change. People are so varied, and creating a sustainable whole with Goddess and the Temple in the centre can be challenging.

This book describes some of my experiences in creating with others a Goddess-centred community, focused around Glastonbury Goddess Temple. It is a personal story of Soul and Shadow and the dance between them in my life. Soul is that fundamental essence we all carry, which is love. It is the conscious Presence of the Divine inside each one of us, which connects us to all other souls in all places, and to Goddess within and without. Shadow is that which is unconscious, unknown within the psyche, which provides the fuel for suffering, pain, emotional reactivity and absence from aliveness.

In my understanding the nature of the Soul is to always be moving into expression in the world through the vehicles of our personalities – our minds, emotions and physical bodies. Personality allows us to express our Soul's purpose, but it is conditioned and limited by our negative and positive experiences in life, which are built upon the karmic seeds we carry from life to life. As personalities we often identify with our wounding, but we are so much more than our conditioning.

As the Soul's loving compassionate energy moves to express itself in the world it meets resistances created from our experiences and wounding. Conflict arises inside of us between the different parts of ourselves, between that which wants to be loving, altruistic and hopeful and that which is selfish, uncaring, despairing. Such internal conflicts are usually projected outwards into the world, onto other people and into the environments in which we find ourselves. *They, that woman, that man, that situation,* becomes the battleground. Its all *their fault.*

There is a continual play between the free-flowing energies of the Soul and the more fixed forces of the Personality, often between Soul and that part of us which is Shadow. We find ourselves coming into conflict with each other, rubbing the raw places, triggering each other into meeting and dealing with wounds which lie hidden within our Shadows, within the parts of ourselves that we do not know about. The Call of the Soul is a call to consciousness, a call to healing. The Light of the Soul illuminates the hidden places in the Shadow, allowing the Jewels, the Pearls of Wisdom that lie hidden within our unconsciousness to be retrieved and re-birthed into the world.

Over the years the Lady of Avalon has brought me several times to meet my personal Shadow material and the hidden unconscious edges of my core life wounds, so that I might heal myself. These last few years I have met my own personal Shadows through dis-ease, accident and multiple personal attacks on social media and directly from mostly women. This book is about my personal Priestess journey impelled by my Soul to find some of my deeply wounded Shadow places, that they might be brought into the Light and healed.

IN THIS PROCESS the Lady speaks to me of the Re-Membering of Mother-World, and the Healing of Wounds that were inflicted on women and men, by men and women, at the endings of the Goddess Temples, thousands of years ago. The repercussions of these wounds have rippled through countless lifetimes to the present day, carried in the karmic seeds which accompany our Souls, which are expressed in our DNA and in repeating painful experiences. The Lady speaks to me of the great need for the healing of these wounds, and the placing of the caring, life-giving values of women, of mothers and mothering, back into the centre of all life on Her earth.

AT THE BEGINNING of this book you need to know that I am a storyteller, as we all are. At an early age we begin to make up stories about our lives, in which we are usually at the effect of events and circumstances, which we experience as happening to us from the outside. We often feel oppressed and victimised by our stories in life and feel we can do nothing about the things that happen to us.

These feelings continue until we become conscious that we are always the authors of our own stories, no matter how they happen to us.

Then we can move from,

'You did this to me. It's all your fault. I can't do anything about it. You must change!'

to,

'Somehow and for some reason I don't understand I have helped create this event or circumstance.'

Then perhaps we can ask,

'Why did I attract this experience? What is its purpose in my life? Why did this happen to me and not that? What is the meaning of this experience for me? What is the meaning of my life?'

Then we begin to take responsibility for our lives.

IN MY QUEST for meaning I make stories out of my experiences. Nearly everything that I write about in this book is true in that the events happened, sometimes not always exactly in the same order, as my memory can fail to be accurate, although I am writing from my diary entries. I, as writer, am the only one who knows mostly what is fact in this story and what is fiction. I have tried to become more conscious in the telling of my story, in revealing how I have co-created my story.

I am a person who is moved and inspired by Vision, especially those visions which I believe come from the Lady of Avalon. I know these visions come from Her because they are grounded in love and are always about helping create the best for the individual and for the whole. I live my life according to these inspirations that I receive from Her. I see my role in life to be a Vision-holder for my community and my journey is to bring Visions from Her into reality.

Some might say that I am just exercising my own will, what my little ego wants, but I do not think it is that. I believe that I follow the calling of my Soul. I follow the Lady's instructions to me, which I receive as an inner knowing, as words spoken or heard in my heart and mind, or which I see in scenes and images. This inner knowing can sometimes clash with the knowing of others, and who then is right or wrong, or is it the play of knowing that is important?

Introduction

IN READING this book you need to be clear that I know that this is my version of events, no-one else's. It is my expression of the amazing healing pathway with the Lady of Avalon that my life follows. I am always writing from my own personal point of view and sometimes that is a place coloured by my personal Shadow wounding, which is not a place of clarity. I try in my life to do my best for myself and for everyone around me, as everyone does, and I make mistakes. I am provocative. I can do the wrong thing while trying to do the right thing. Some things I do really well and others not so well. I am learning just like everyone else. Hopefully you will be able to recognise how I learn over time, but when our sleeping Shadows are disturbed by the Soul's calling, we often find more than we bargain for.

I try to write of my feelings and thoughts as they were happening, from the diary entries which I wrote at the time, and not from the perspective of hindsight. I hope to show how a small event, sometimes just a misplaced reactive word signals the beginning or the deepening of a healing journey. I hope to demonstrate how my learning has evolved through experience. This book is about emotions, feelings and thoughts, clarity and confusion, action and reaction, the known and the hidden, Soul and Shadow, consciousness and its development through time. It is a revelation, an unravelling of my personal patriarchal wounding and its effects in me and within our Goddess community, through experiences I shared with others.

As you read you may find that your mind will form judgements, make assumptions, criticise, empathise with different viewpoints and experiences. You may find yourself taking sides. Be-aware. Look with compassion to yourself, to me and to others in your thoughts and feelings. Look to your own wounding, your own failings and love yourself and all of us.

This is an exploration of the pitfalls of empowerment, of what it can take to be a leader in an aspirational egalitarian woman-centred world. Each woman is on her own independent, often wayward path of self-discovery, emerging slowly from her patriarchal conditioning. We talk of working with women as being like *trying to herd cats*. No-one in the Goddess world wants to be part of a homogeneous crowd, where we are all the same. No-one wants to obey anyone else. No-one wants to be part of any Cult, myself included.

Everyone wants to know themselves to be unique and special in their own way, but often the fight to prove this becomes more important than the goal of bringing Goddess back into the world. Particularly amongst women called by Goddess there are disagreements, arguments, defence of the conditioned self, of the little 'I', which rise to the fore, with harmful effects – unconscious blaming, shaming, talking behind each other's backs, undermining/subverting each other, keeping each other small, pulling each other down, attacking the teacher, the leader, the mother/father substitute authority figure, personally, publicly, anonymously, on social media, while failing to actually speak to the person with whom you have a problem. As girls we are taught to behave like this from an early age.

This is the culture we have to change.

This book is about an emotional and spiritual journey to change those old patriarchal habits and to forge a new way of living and loving each other in harmony with our Great Mother and the world around us.

The viewpoint on all events described is mine. It may be very different to yours or anyone else who is mentioned in these stories. I do not wish to attack, blame or give offense to anyone. I am expressing my personal feelings at all times, and these are not necessarily true. I am teasing out my truth from my experiences. This is my journey of expanding consciousness and awareness that lies beneath my story. I do not claim to be a fount of wisdom for you, but I hope that the descriptions of my journey may help you in yours.

MY SHADOW first makes herself strongly known to me during the long months of 2012. I have some strong emotional reactions to difficult people and difficult situations. I feel betrayed by sister priestesses who should be supporting me, and it feels like an old repeating pattern.

ACTUALLY my Shadowlands had been shaken awake the year before in December 2011. Two days before we were due to go on a Goddess Pilgrimage to modern day Turkey with Priestess Anna Osann, to explore the ancient

Goddess sites of Anatolia, Land of the Mothers, I received a letter from Taunton Hospital. They were booking me an appointment to go in for some investigation in my breast. Fear arose immediately in my body as I realised what this could mean. I did know that something was not quite right in my breast. I had ignored it, as you do. But oh no, I might have breast cancer again, for the second time, sixteen and a half years after the first awful experience!

PERHAPS the Shadow-shaking began earlier that year in April 2011 with the death of my 96 year old mother Eileen Mary Jones. The death of a parent often brings *stuff* to the surface.

OR PERHAPS it began the first time round that I had breast cancer in 1995, and although much was healed then, maybe not all of it. I wrote about that experience in *Breast Cancer: Hanging on by a Red Thread* (Ariadne Publications).

OR DID THE Shadow-making begin when I was the small sensitive daughter of an emotionally repressed, alienated and angry father, probably suffering from post-traumatic stress after the Second World War. My mother was affectionate towards me, but told me in the truth-speaking years of dementia before she died, that I was actually the last person in her family affections, after my father and my sister. My parents never knew me as I am and did not want to know me, nor did anyone else in my genetic family. They were incapable of comprehending or encouraging my wild and unorthodox nature.

OR PERHAPS my karma began in 1944 with my difficult and frightening death in my last incarnation.

OR PERHAPS the wounding all began much earlier in other lifetimes, in the times of the witch-burnings, when tens of thousands of European women and some men were betrayed by other men and women, and burned or hanged as witches. And I had been one of those, more than once.

OR PERHAPS it all began much earlier, three, four, five, six thousand years ago with the endings of Goddess Temples and Goddess cultures across the lands of Old Europe. I know from my emotional wounds and from the memories attached to those wounds, that life after life I was one of many priestesses of the ancient Goddess, who was attacked, hurt, raped, hunted down, killed, taken as a slave by patriarchal invaders, who destroyed the beauty and harmony of Her ancient MotherWorld. I was also one who fled from Her Temple out on my own into a lonely and hostile world.

WHERE do things begin?

When is the first wound made, that becomes a repeating karmic pattern echoing through many lives?

How do we find and heal these ancient wounds that can arise repeatedly in our present day lives?

This is my quest, my seeking of the truths that bring self-knowledge and healing, driven by experiences of cancer, accident and betrayal. This is the story of my healing journey as a returning Priestess of Goddess, a returning Priestess of Avalon, led by my beloved Lady.

My hope and prayer is that my healing journey may inspire you and illuminate your understanding in your life as a woman, as a man, as Her priestess, as Her priest, and by which ever spiritual path you make your return to Her.

Chapter One

TRAVELS OF A PRIESTESS: AVELINE'S HOLE

T IS NOVEMBER 2011 and we are on the first weekend of the year long Priestess Enchantress training which I teach occasionally. As part of our Samhain experience of the Dark Goddess we descend into Aveline's Hole, a cave near Burrington Coombe in the Mendip Hills in Somerset, not far from Glastonbury. This cave once held the largest collection of Mesolithic human remains in Britain. Over 70 skeletons were found here which are thought to be between 10,400 and 10,200 years old, dating from the end of the last Ice Age. A series of inscribed lines and crosses have been found on the inner walls, also believed to date from that time and to be amongst the oldest carvings found so far in Britain.

This accessible cave is a wonderful place in which to connect with the Dark Underworld Goddess and with the ancestors of our land. Here we can feel their presence still reverberating in the walls and air of the cave, although access to the inner cave has now been blocked off by metal bars, to protect the engravings. In a previous year's Enchantress Training we had created a wonderful ceremony in the complete darkness of the inner cave.

* * *

On our descent into the rocky downward sloping cave we sing,

> *"Deep into the Earth we go*
> *Deep into the Earth we know*
> *Hold my hand, sister*
> *Hold my hand,*
> *Hold my hand, brother*
> *Hold my hand"*
> ©Tarisha

I am disappointed to find a metal grill is now in place and we can't go deeper into the darkness of the cave. Then as we sit on the rocks and pray, we connect into the space. We call to the ancestors whose bones were once buried here, rhythmically clicking together stones which we find on the floor of the cave. Breathing in the energy of the earth, my consciousness changing and expanding, I see the ancient people from the times of ice and snow, those who moved with the herds of reindeer, those people whose bodies had been laid in this cave. I give my fears to the earth, to the Dark Mother of Samhain.

I remember my mother Eileen, who died in April this year, who is my closest family ancestor. I didn't really experience much grief when she died. She had had a good life and it was her time to leave the earth. She had had dementia for 10 years and it was a relief for her to leave. I journeyed with her across the threshold to make sure that she was not frightened and felt safe. She had no spiritual belief and I wanted to make sure that she was OK as she crossed the threshold.

I do not have much experience of grief at death. Not many of my close loved ones have died. It is only when deep love relationships have ended or when a beloved dog has died that I have felt strong grief. Perhaps I know that they are just there, through the gateway – not far away, still living, loving.

As I become absorbed in the space my consciousness is expanding. I feel the deep velvet peace of the earth. I look upwards and there high on the ceiling of the cave are archetypal images, self-arising in the rocks above our heads, images of goddesses, humans, animals, birds, deer, appearing out of the rock itself. The more we look the more we can see emerging from the rock. This is like the stunning Korykian Creation and Oracle Cave above Delphi in Greece, where there are many self-arising images of the Greek pantheon of Goddesses and Gods, emanating from the walls. It is also like the Western Valley at Mount Kailash in Tibet, where images of Buddhas and Dakinis, of Tibetan writing, created by the endless wind, rain, ice, snow and sunshine, are visible in the high rocky cliffs. These Creation places have a powerful numinous energy. Here divine ancestors and creators move between the worlds.

I have never noticed this ceiling here in Aveline's Hole before, as we have usually passed straight through this part of the cave into the darkness beyond. This is a Creation Cave as well as a Temple of the Dead. At the ending of the Ice Age, this is one of the places where the archetypes of life were held safe, until the ice melted and Her green life came back into Britain. In the ancient world the burial places of the ancestors are often also places of conception, places where people make love in order to conceive an honoured ancestor.

We leave the darkness and cold of the cave to sit outside on the rocky scree in the November sun. My whole body is shaking, vibrating still, a vibration that is not of the cold, although I am not warm. Goddess is shaking me gently. "*Wake up….*" She says.

THE PRIESTESS Enchantress training is one where we learn to allow the membrane between the visible and invisible worlds to become permeable, so that consciousness expands and connects into invisible energies and realities. For the duration of the year long course as I ponder and walk on the sacred land I have many visions. As I walk our dog in Bushy Coombe I have the sense that everything above sea level is permeated with a thick blancmange-like energy. I see it over-laying the land.

My dreams are more intense, more meaningful. I understand that they contain messages from my soul. Looking out over the landscape below our house I feel the surface of the land as a living skin. It ripples from the horizon towards where I am sitting. The land buckles as the earth quakes, but I am not frightened. It is Her living body moving and breathing. There are portents in my dreams, of which I have no understanding.

I read Munya Andrews's book *The Seven Sisters of the Pleiades: Stories from around the world*, in which she describes the relationship between her own aboriginal Australian people and their ancestors, who are the Seven Sisters of the Pleiades. This story is common in many indigenous cultures. For several days I think about the stories of the Circles of Nine Sisters found in Northern Europe cultures, including our own Nine Morgen Sisters who dwell in Avalon, and their relationship to the Seven Pleiadean Sisters. Then as I examine the visible stars held within a much bigger cloud of Pleiadean stars, it turns out that as well as the seven visible stars there are two more visible stars, which are often named as the parents of the seven sisters. So actually there are nine visible stars, which must have been visible to the naked eye in the clear night skies of Old Europe.

My feeling is that the Nine Sisters came to earth to dwell in the Paradise Isle of Avalon, where they are known as the Nine Morgens, of whom Morgen la Fey or Morgana is the most well known. The Pleiades, like the Morgens, are connected to weather, their rising and setting in the heavens marks the seasons of Her nature on the earth. In Avalon the Morgens create weather. They are the sunshine, heat, rain, clouds, wind, thunder, lightning, ice and snow in this land.

Now it's the third week of November and I have a routine mammogram at the mobile unit in the car park. I think nothing of it. I am healthy. I have been well for the last 16 years. I don't expect to ever have cancer again in my life. I have been feeling a little tired, but I am 64 years old. Old age is catching up with me at last. I don't like it that I don't have so much energy as I used to. I have noticed some twinges in the side of my right breast, but nothing more unusual than that. After the mammogram I forget about it and go on with life.

A week later on the 30th November I receive a letter from Taunton Hospital asking me to go for an appointment the following week, as they want to look further into my results. I am shocked. On 2nd December we are leaving to go on a Goddess Pilgrimage to Anatolia, now modern day Turkey. We are visiting sacred sites of the Goddess in a small group of English and Spanish people, led by Anna Osann and Koko Newport, who have both trained with us as Priestesses of Avalon. Anna has a strong connection to Turkey and has organised a wonderful itinerary, exploring ancient Goddess sites, which my partner Mike has long wanted to visit. I am happy to go along, but not so strongly called. I am feeling a bit tired and it's December, and maybe I'd prefer to be relaxing at home rather than jaunting around. But we are going. I postpone the hospital appointment until our return from Turkey.

Chapter Two

Travelling to Anatolia, Land of the Ancient Mothers

MIKE AND I drive to our overnight hotel near Luton through a continuous heavy rainstorm. Our pilgrimage begins. Is this a portent for our journey? Next morning we are up at 5.00am to take the car from the hotel to the parking place, then catch the bus to Luton airport, where we find Koko waiting for us. She has been travelling from Bristol all night on buses. Thousands of people are pouring into the airport like ants. It's a scene of madness.

The flight to Istanbul takes three and a half hours and then we need to change airports to catch a Turkish internal flight. We take a bus past many ugly concrete buildings into the centre of Istanbul, where we meet Anna and the Spanish pilgrims. There are eight of us, three British, four Spaniards and Anna, who speaks a multitude of languages and translates between us. The Spaniards don't speak much English and we don't speak Spanish. Sign language works for day-to-day communication, but it's not really possible to go much deeper without translation.

We catch our next flight to Sanliurfa or Urfa in south-eastern Turkey, just twenty miles from the Syrian border. When we arrive it is already dark. We have been travelling for over 14 hours. We climb into a minibus and are driven for nearly an hour along smooth and then progressively rougher roads. For our first two nights in Turkey we are staying in the Kurdish Village of Yuvacali Koyu, in Hilvan. As we bounce along through the darkness in the headlights we see piles of large boulders lining the twisting dirt track. Where are we? We seem to be moving into the past, into ancient times.

This is our Village Homestay, where we will stay in a small village with a Kurdish family. We arrive at a small concrete house, the front wall illuminated by harsh neon light. Otherwise it is pitch black all around apart from the pinpricks of a million stars in the sky. People come out to greet us and we take our shoes off and leave them outside in the freezing air – it is December. We go through a hallway into a rectangular room, which has carpets and rugs on the floor and cushions against the walls. The Kurdish family are welcoming, offering us tea and three pieces of cake each. We introduce ourselves and speak our intentions for our pilgrimage, with the Kurdish family sitting alongside us. We communicate in a mixture of English, Spanish, Kurdish, Turkish and sign language. It's the first time we pilgrims have really been able to talk to each other as a group.

After a while Mike and I, and Rosa and Gary, the Spanish couple we have just met a few hours ago, are taken by car to a second home where we are going to stay the night. Outside beautiful stars shine clearly and overhead are the Pleiades. Again we must leave our boots outside in the cold air. We enter the two-roomed house and are welcomed by a young couple who have three small children. The loo is village style, a small shed with a hole in the ground 20 metres away from the house through the darkness. My body reacts and contracts. What do I do if I want to pee in the night? Will I be able to see to get out of the house?

We are shown into the room where we two couples will sleep, one on one side of the smallish room and one on the other – we thought we would have separate rooms. All our privileged western assumptions are being challenged. This is a pilgrimage after all. We undress and climb into the freezing beds, which are wool filled mattresses on the floor, with thick eiderdowns. In the beginning they are very cold but they warm up through the night. There is a heater/air conditioner on the wall above us, which roars through the night like a dragon.

I don't sleep well the first night. I wake up with cancer fear coursing through my belly. I just lie there feeling afraid and unable to do anything with the fear. I pull on my coat and creep out of the room and out of the house to pee on the rough grass. I prefer the earth to the outside loo. Above my head is a vast night sky, shining with a billion stars. There is little light pollution here in the middle of nowhere. It is icy cold.

In the morning we wake suddenly at 6.30am, which is actually 4.30am for our bodies and minds, all four of us struggling to come to life. We must have breakfast at 7.00am to be ready for today's adventures. We dress quickly and go outside. It's our first sight of our surroundings. We are staying in a white concrete house on the edge of a small village of similar houses sloping down a hill towards a distant river. There are few trees and the vegetation is dried up since it's winter. In one direction there is a vast seemingly empty plain stretching away to a far horizon. The sky is completely clear, a winter ice blue. There is silence out there, no background mechanical noises. It's wonderful to hear the silence. I want to walk out into that peace.

Below us down the hill is something amazing – a huge prehistoric settlement mound, over 100 metres high, something I have never seen before. Dotted all over the high flat plains of central and eastern Turkey there are over 3,000 settlement mounds, which are the ancestral villages of Anatolia, where the ancient peoples once lived in mud-brick-walled homes. When the mud walls crumbled in the sunshine, rain, wind and snow, new homes were built on top of them, piling ever higher and higher. Smaller and larger groups of people, sometimes up to 10,000, lived in these villages.

The story of the peoples can be traced within these mounds from the Mesolithic people who lived at ground level, perhaps 10,000 years ago, moving through the layers of time, to the Neolithic, Chalcolithic and Roman settlements, all piled up in one mound. The mounds are large in circumference and reach up to 30-100 metres high. They were mostly abandoned 1,500 years ago, and contain a rich, often undisturbed record of ancient life in the Land of the Mothers. The celebrated Goddess site Çatal Höyük, is one such mound, which we are going to visit in a few days.

But here in the centre of this small remote village is a large undisturbed settlement mound, and the houses are clustered around one side of it. In fact the first house we went to last night nestles half way up one side the mound. I long to go look at the mound and feel the presence of the ancestors.

The land below the village is semi-arid, stretching away to the distant River Euphrates. The village's once abundant water supplies dried up with the building of the Atatürk Dam on the Euphrates. This whole area was once the Garden of Eden lying between the Euphrates and the Tigris rivers, with abundant crops and fruit trees. The village now suffers from severe water shortages, with water being brought from a depth of 100m below the surface for irrigation, while household water is piped into the area. Piped water actually only came to Yuvacali in 2007. Electricity came in 1982, but power cuts are still frequent. Further on across the Mesopotamian plains, 200 km away, we can see the snow-capped Mount Nemrut.

I pee on the ground behind a shed (I am avoiding the toilet). Mike says that he thought that this might be a Tibet-style trip, with four people sleeping in a room and an outside primitive loo. Now he tells me.

Back in the house our bedroom has been transformed into a dining room. The beds have been rolled away and on a cloth on the floor a huge breakfast is laid out for us. There is home-made salty cheese and butter, yogurt and honey, home grown tomatoes, cucumbers, fresh herbs, scrambled eggs with chillies. Mike eats a whole plateful of the latter, before realising all plates are for sharing, and mixing in a bread wrap warm from the oven. There is far more food than we can possibly eat. I feel bad about leaving so much food, but later I am assured that this is homestay food and nothing will go to waste, but will be shared with the wider village family.

Our kind hosts are Mehmet and Zaria. Mehmet eats with us, but Zaria sits at the edge of the room with her two children, waiting until we have finished eating, before she can begin. She has done all the work preparing the food and is not permitted to eat with us. Although this is not a directly Muslim culture, the Kurds have a more ancient nature-based heritage, it is definitely patriarchal. I feel very uncomfortable with this distinction between us women.

Before we came to Yuvacali Koyu we were asked to respect the traditional culture of the Kurdish people. We were asked to dress with care, and to wear long skirts rather than trousers. Shorts or short skirts are unacceptable. Loose fitting t-shirts are the best choice for tops. At least we don't have to cover our heads, except when visiting mosques or other Islamic buildings. The men in the group were asked not to wear shorts, although short sleeves are acceptable. It is winter, so we can handle this, but in summer when the temperatures rise easily to 45° Celsius, the women must bake in their long skirts.

THE MINIBUS ARRIVES and we drive to the other house, where our sister travellers stumble out, also looking sleep-deprived and a bit shell-shocked. We drive out of the village, the previous night's boulders by the roadside revealing themselves to be just that, piles of boulders which are the remnants of ancient dwellings, dotted through the village. This village is very old. As well as its peaceful prehistoric inhabitants, it has a more recent bloody past. At the beginning of the 20th century the village was occupied by Jews and Armenians. The Jews were sent away and the Armenians were murdered. Kurds have lived in this village since the early 20th century.

We drive out of the village and a few miles on to the amazing Gobekli Tepe (Belly or Womb Hill), the earliest Goddess Temple presently known, dating from 10,000 BCE. It is 7,000 years older than Stonehenge. The landscape is again one of bare, rocky folded hills and Gobekli Tepe lies on top of one of these rolling hills with a 360° view in all directions. We drive up a single track winding road to the entrance, a gate on the road. Two camels are tied near the entrance. By the stony track there is a wide stone platform with large offering basins cut into the rock and smaller mortar holes, just like the ones in Britain, Argentina and California that I have seen, where native peoples ground nuts for flour and other staples. In Argentina they are said to be laid out on the rocks as star maps, matching the star formations in the heavens. There are also two larger rectangular holes for statues or pillars, now gone.

We walk around the small hill to the excavation site. Apart from a couple of relaxed site guards our group are the only ones here in December. It's a very exciting moment as we see large T-shaped stone pillars sticking up out of the ground. Walking onto a wooden walkway, we find ourselves looking down into the centre of a large oval enclosure, perhaps 15 metres in diameter, with two tall central T-shaped limestone pillars, 5 metres high, with eight shorter side pillars facing inwards around the edges. Some have carvings on them. The spaces between the pillars are lined with rough unworked stones and there are stone benches there too. The central pillars may have held up a wooden roof, now long gone. They appear to be aligned north/south.

The large stones are between 3 and 6 metres tall, and weigh between 7 and 16 tons each. No one knows how they were carried up from the quarry several hundred metres away down the bottom of the steep hill. The stones were chiselled, smoothed and carved with flint tools. Today some of the decorated pillars have wood around the carvings to protect them from the winter weather, to which they are exposed for the first time in 12,000 years. It is an awesome place!

Around this deeper central oval of stones, there are others, a bit higher up the hill, smaller circles and more ovals. They are built right on top of each other with little space between. Many of the side and central pillars are decorated with beautiful carvings of animals, which are sometimes realistic, but mostly stylised, images. There are foxes, gazelles, snakes, wild ducks, cranes, bulls, insects, vultures, bulls, bears, scorpions, boars and lions – the animals which lived in these parts at the time.

I am fascinated by two central pillars that have stylised carvings of arms coming down from the shoulders of the pillar. There is a girdle, with a fox skin hanging down from the belly. A fox leaps across the surface of the pillar. Each wears a necklace, an early symbol for the feminine. These are Fox Women! Was this central Temple dedicated to Fox Women, those intelligent immortal beings, renowned in other cultures, who possess magical qualities, divine beings who can assume human and animal forms? They are powerful images.

It is an amazing awesome sacred site and so far the archaeologists have excavated only five per cent of it. Geomagnetic surveys indicate that there are at least 20 rings, piled together higgledy-piggledy, still under the ground. The earliest rings dating from 10,000 BCE seem to have the most elegant carvings. Every few decades it seems that the pillars and their enclosures were buried and new small circles were put inside the first. Then the whole thing was filled in with debris and new circles were created nearby. As time went by the pillars became smaller and all building work had ended by 8,200 BCE.

The whole site is a place of mystery, but the current theory is that behind the walls there are the remains of the dead, that this is a mortuary site, but they haven't yet excavated behind the walls, or beneath the floors. Another theory is that the temples are laid out in the pattern of the Pleiades, although only a few temples have been excavated so far and the placing may be much more random.

We stay at the site for a good long time, breathing in the ancestral energies as the sun rises into the sky. On the top of the hill is a wishing tree, where we tie our prayer flags. I pray for the Return of the Mother into this ancient land of the Mothers, for Her recognition by the people and Her release from the control of patriarchy. I ask for healing for myself in this ancient Mother place.

We light a flame together in memory of the Ancestors, which is the renewed Flame of Gobekli Tepe. Koko is taking this flame home to add into the Flame of Avalon. We are very happy.

WE DRIVE ON in the minibus stopping at small places on the way. We briefly visit the village of Harran with its ancient mud beehive-shaped buildings. Harran was once a prosperous caravan city in the ancient world, home to a widely renowned shrine to the moon god Sin, and a centre for pilgrimage, sacrifice, healing and fertility rites. It was inhabited from the 3rd millennium BCE. The beehive houses have been built by villagers, using bricks collected from the Harran ruins. Two or more cones are joined by an archway, and the elongated building is perfectly suited to the climate of the region, the houses providing cool shelter in the torrid Harran summer, and warmth in the winter. The people claim that in these houses hens lay more eggs, horses and other animals are more docile, onions sprout more quickly, and food stays fresh longer. The village is now more of a tourist trap.

WE DON'T STAY LONG but drive on to the ruins of Han el-Barür Caravanserai built nearly 1000 years ago, where a horde of small children appear out of the ruins to greet us. Foreigners are a good distraction in this rural area of Turkey.

THEN ON TO Sogmator and a rocky hilly moonscape where on "seven hilltops sit seven temples" with rock carvings dedicated to the sun, moon and planets. These are the ruins of an ancient pagan complex built for planetary observation and the worship of Sky Beings. In the centre of the complex is a sacred hill dedicated to the chief god/dess. It is in fact another huge ancient settlement mound set deep in a valley and enclosed by hills. The mound once had high stone walls at the top. Syriac inscriptions throughout the site describe the rituals performed at this large open-air temple.

The Temple of the Moon is a cave cut into solid rock in the hillside, a bit like some Indian temples. The Temple of the Sun is on top of the hill. There are images of a Sun Goddess and Moon Goddess carved into the rock just below the top. On top of the hill there are mortars, round basins carved into the rock, and a large sun/moon scrying pool filled with water. From the top of this hill an encircling horizon of hills with nipples and notches to mark the rising and setting of the sun, moon, planets and stars, can be seen. It's a vast astronomical and astrological observatory, a Star Temple.

On top of this hill of the Temple of the Sun we watch the sun set, the sky slowly changing colour. Sparkling Venus rises and then another planet. It is very beautiful. Down below in the small village as dusk falls the flocks of sheep are returning to their folds, herded by young boys. In the village are donkeys and dogs, which is unusual as Kurdish and Turkish villages don't usually have dogs. These dogs wear huge spiked collars, to wound any wild aggressors who might go for the throat.

We talk with a dissatisfied teacher from the local school – a concrete building in a dusty landscape. He is bored in the winter holidays when school is closed for three months while the children are sent into the fields to harvest cotton. He has no knowledge of the magnificent Star Temple in which he lives and no interest.

Back in the bus we drive through the black night along bumpy roads to Sanliurfa and the Hammam, a Turkish Bath. Here we use sign language to communicate with the Turkish women and Koko and I laugh uproariously as we share a cubicle to wash our intimate parts, and then go to get scoured and slapped on hot marble shelves. We arrive back late at the house in Yuvacali where our hosts are waiting for us with supper. Once again we feel embarrassed to have kept them all up so late and waiting with mountains of food we cannot eat. It has been a long, long day.

In the middle of the night fear wakes me and I go outside to pee under the million star sky, my solar plexus full of liquid fire, below endless space and unknown realities in galaxies beyond my comprehension. It's so mind-boggling and I who will be extinguished sooner or later, cannot get my head round it all. The contrast between the vastness of space and my tiny concerns, so big in my mind.

THE NEXT DAY we rise early again, eating breakfast on the floor and then saying goodbye to our hosts, who have been very hospitable to us. We take a walk around the village with Alison Tanik, who has organised our Homestay through Nomad Tours Turkey. Alison is the British wife of a Kurdish man and now lives in the village. Compared to life in Britain her life here is restricted. She cannot drive on her own or leave the village without a male relative. She must cover her hair and wear long skirts, but she seems happy enough. She is doing something wonderful for her adopted people, bringing life and prosperity to a poor Kurdish village through organising homestay visits for tourists from all over the world. The men of the village find it hard to get employment and until recently spent 6 months of the year working in the coastal resorts leaving behind their wives and children. Now more of them are employed in the homestay business as hosts and drivers. In the last two years they have had 200 people homestaying each month, which helps everyone. We are told that the main difference is that now the men are employed in the village and have more money they beat their wives less often!

Alison takes us around the settlement mound and explains her ideas about the different layers of the mound. There has been no excavation here, but the bottom layers are Neolithic and continue up to the Roman layers at the top. All the peoples who have lived here are represented in these layers of soil and in the stonework. Outside Alison's house is wooden shelving with finds from these layers including the broken figure of a Neolithic Goddess that just emerged from the soil one day. The village once housed 15,000 people, now there are about 1,000, but this causes inbreeding and there are damaged children. Water for drinking must be pumped from deep in the earth and irrigation pipes waiting to be dug into the dry earth litter the land. We give money to the village to plant fruit trees in people's dry gardens, where they will be looked after, an Orchard of Avalon in the Garden of Eden.

WE DRIVE in the minibus to the town of Sanliurfa to visit the small museum. It is absolutely wonderful. Stone artefacts from Gobekli Tepe, 12,000 year old carvings, are just there, mostly not enclosed in glass cases, but standing just a couple of feet away, within touching distance. I can put my hand out and touch them.... I fall to my knees before the damaged carved totem, which looks to me like a Great Bear Mother, holding in her arms a woman with a bear's head, a mother who in her turn is giving birth to a baby. This is the mythic Bear Mother, the mother of all human beings, made visible here in stone, honoured for 1000s of years in the mythologies of Europe. Tears rise to my eyes as I greet this Bear Mother once again for the first time in 12,000 years. She feels so familiar. Like a long-lost mother. I am deeply touched.

There are other carvings, animals, people embracing, and images of Goddess from these early times. Another favourite is the delicate outline of a Sheela na Gig, a naked woman, legs akimbo with labia hanging down, which was carved into one of the benches that surrounded the oval enclosures on the site. After She was found archaeologists hid Her image away, face down in a shed. It was the focus of the artist scholar Lydia Ruyle and the Friends of Çatal Höyük, that managed to get Her out of the shed and into the museum where She can now be seen by all. Sheelas are one of the oldest images of Goddess in Brigit's Isles, often carved on the walls and ceilings of churches. She is usually represented as a skinny old woman, who displays Her open vulva as a gateway, representing the source of all life and the place of return at death.

Lydia Ruyle is the creator of the wonderful Goddess Icon banners, images of Goddess from all over the world, which fly in sacred exhibitions and at important women's events, including our own Glastonbury Goddess Conference. Lydia made a banner of this Gobekli Tepe Sheela, which has flown at our Conference, so it was especially delightful to see Her in the flesh, as it were, in the stone. In patriarchy images of Sheela are often described as vulgar and pornographic as She displays Her Gig vulva. Placed on church and castle walls they are used to curse and threaten attackers of any kind. Many Sheela carvings, iconic images of female power, are still hidden away in the vaults of Irish museums. She is returning here in Sanliurfa, unearthed from 10,000 years of forgetting.

And there are so many other wonderful carvings....

IN THE AFTERNOON we walk to Atargatis's Fish Pond, now Abraham's Pool, where hundreds and hundreds of carp swim in great rectangular pools. The fish are now fed by the many Muslim pilgrims who visit the mosques which surround the pools. The carp rise to the surface in great boiling numbers as pilgrims feed them special fish food. Once these ponds and fish were sacred to Atargatis the Syrian Fish Goddess and Mermaid – part woman, part fish. She is the life-giving divinity associated with rivers and springs, motherly protector of humans and animals, Goddess of Sexuality and Love. Atargatis was often depicted riding or accompanied by a lion, like the Lion Mother of Çatal Höyük, She sat on a throne flanked by two sphinxes or two lions. Her headdress was usually topped by a crescent moon and draped with a veil. In Her hands She carried various objects: a plate or cup, a sceptre or staff, and ears of grain, but most often She held a spindle and a mirror. Sometimes doves or fish were near or actually on Her. In some places Atargatis was associated with dolphins. At others, the eight-pointed star emphasized Her association with the planet Venus. Written evidence of

Her worship dates from the 5th century BCE, although Her origins are probably much earlier.

IN THE EVENING we fly to Ankara taking one of Turkey's cheap internal flights. We arrive in the dark at an odd Fawlty Towers city hotel and exhausted, retire to bed. I've had no proper sleep for several nights now, as night is the time when my fears about cancer arise in the darkness. I wake from a bad dream in which a consultant is telling me that I have skin cancer, not breast cancer. I am very scared and I wake in tears and cry in Mike's arms. This is my meltdown day, I feel very afraid. My mind is talking overtime with what I will have to do if the lump is cancer. By now I think it is and I really don't like what that might mean. As I lie awake I play through all the worst scenarios, up to and including my slow and painful death.

Mike and I decide to have an easy day and miss out a visit to the Atatürk Museum, the founder of the modern Turkish State. Mike is so great. He really supports me in these hard places. He is the rock on which my fears can crash and tumble. He disguises his own fears that I might face mine. I love him so much.

We go to visit the Ankara Museum of Anatolian Civilisations, which we have wanted to visit for so long because it holds the treasures from Çatal Höyük. It has reconstructed rooms of the great Goddess settlement mound, which until recently was one of the earliest known sites of the Goddess, dating from 7,500 BCE. Unfortunately half the museum is closed for refurbishment – the half that includes the finds from Çatal Höyük. It is disappointing. We will just have to come to Ankara again when the rooms are open. It's important to see and feel ancestral Goddess sculptures and places. Seeing them, feeling them, opens places of memory, for the retrieval of mystery and knowledge, so that it can rise consciously into the world again.

We do see statues of the Sun Goddess Kubaba, who holds a pomegranate in Her right hand and a mirror in Her left. She derives from Hepat, the Mother of all, who sits on a throne or stands on the back of lion. She in turn must derive from the wonderful Lion Mother of Çatal Höyük, who sits on a throne with a feline on either side of Her, giving birth to a baby from between Her legs. We do see a beautiful original image of Her in the museum, which warms my heart.

WE GO FOR LUNCH in the best restaurant yet, in an old building high on Castle Hill. There is a nice atmosphere here and good food. In the afternoon we make our way back to our odd hotel. In the evening Anna and Koko offer me healing. They are sharing a room and as I walk in I begin to sob and cry my fears. I feel held and cared for by them as they help release and remove my fear. I go into a deep memory of seeing an arrow going into my breast, perhaps somewhere at Gobekli Tepe. I can feel the arrow in my body. I feel the pain.

"*Take it out! Take it out!*" I cry.

The arrow is pulled out and I see myself being taken out onto the hillside, where I die underneath the stars. I feel a bit better after the healing and we go to sleep early. In the morning I wake again at 5.00am and lie there thinking, fearful again, but a little less so.

MURAT, our minibus driver, comes early to drive us overland to modern day Bogazkale in north central Turkey, which is the site of ancient Hattusa, a major centre for the Hatti and later the Hittite Empire. On the way we visit Alaca Hoyuk, which is the site of another Neolithic, Hatti (Bronze Age) and later Hittite settlement mound. It lies in a green and winding valley, which is very different from the wide flat plains where we have seen other settlement mounds. Alaca Hoyuk has been continuously settled from the Chalcolithic Age, when the earliest gold ornaments and copper tools appeared alongside the use of stone tools, to the small present day village. The remains of thirteen shaft grave Royal Tombs, dated 2350-2150 BCE, were found containing single burials of the dead, women and men, lying in foetal positions facing south. The women's bodies were originally decorated with gold Twin Goddess images, mirrors, gold chalices, fibulae, diadems, belt buckles and sun discs. The men's burials are plain. The women were obviously highly venerated and the Sun Goddess was worshipped here.

Today the tombs are open so we can see the skeletons lying inside and copies of grave goods. Again we are the only visitors and have the place to ourselves. Skulls of bulls, cows and deer line the tops of the tomb walls, reminiscent of Çatal Höyük, and in the tombs lie replica skeletons and grave goods. It is here that several Goddess figurines were found, including the gold Twin Goddess, who I now understand from the work of Marguerite Rigoglioso, may symbolise the parthenogenic Mother Goddess who gives birth to an identical Daughter without the aid of a male consort. A familiar twinning in the Greek pantheon is Demeter and Persephone. If Kubaba or Kybebe is the Mother in Anatolia, Her Daughter may be Matar Kubileya/ Kubeleya, Mountain Mother, who is Kybele or Cybele, Magna Mater – Great Mother.

WE DRIVE ON to the small town of Bogazkale. It's small, neat and clean, quite different to anywhere we've been before, lying at the foot of high hills. We drive up first of all to Yazilikaya, the mountain shrine of the Hittite king Tudhaliya IV. The Sanctuary was in use from the late sixteenth century BCE and its carvings demonstrate that in this society women and men were regarded as equals. Chamber A contains a rock-cut relief of 64 deities in procession. The left wall shows a procession of male deities, wearing traditional kilts, pointed shoes and horned hats. Mountain gods are also shown with scaled skirts to symbolise the rocky mountains. The right wall shows a procession of female deities wearing crowns and long skirts. The only exception to this divide is the Goddess of love and war, Shaushka (Mesopotamian Goddess Ishtar or Inanna) who is shown in the male procession with two female attendants. The processions lead to a central scene of the supreme couple of the pantheon: the sun goddess Hebat or Kubaba, who stands on a panther, and the storm god Teshub, standing on two mountain gods. Behind Hebat are shown their daughter Alanzu, son Sharruma, and Alanza's grand-daughter. Carvings at this site and the rest of Hattusa seem to depict the time of the takeover from Goddess times to the advance of the incoming patriarchal warriors.

We go to our hotel in the small town. Our room is small, modern and clean with its own bathroom. It feels lovely after the dust and dirt in other places. After a meal made specially for us we drive up to Hattusa, a huge temple/palace complex which spreads up the sides of mountains and across a valley. The earliest traces of settlement are from the 6th millennium BCE, and then the indigenous Hatti of central Anatolia established their settlements, calling the site Hattush, around 2,300 BCE. It became a huge and impressive capital of the Hittite Empire between 1400-1200 BCE. Today the remains of large impressive buildings cover a wide area, once all surrounded by a high and wide enclosing stone wall. This is where patriarchy truly entered in.

The remains of up to 30 Temples have been found at the site, and several of them were large Goddess Temples. We walk in among the low ruined walls of a Temple and there in the centre is a truly beautiful large green stone. It is a five-sided cube of polished nephrite jade, about a metre in length on all sides. It is so soft, smooth and warm in the winter sun. It was too heavy to move as the walls of the Temple were tumbled down when the Hittite Empire was destroyed around 1200 BCE. The green jade has a beautiful energy as if many, many hundreds/thousands of people have prayed here before us. We put our hands on the stone and feel its magnetic pulse. We hold hands around the stone and speak to Goddess here in this ancient Temple. We sit on the stone and the veils shift and the Otherworld opens out.

From the information we later read in the museum it seems that these stones were believed to be sacred. Each Temple, large and small, is described as having an Oracle stone in the centre surrounded by four statues. There were many Oracles in Hattusa, their messages are inscribed on some of the 10,000 cuneiform tablets which were found here.

Hattusa is a huge end of valley site climbing up steep hillsides on three sides, the fourth opening out to the south. It feels like an ancient Creation Site like Llyn y Fan Fach in south central Wales, where Nelferch, the Lady of the Lake, emerged from the waters bringing Her cattle, goats and sheep pouring out from the high mountain lake down into valleys of the world. There are important Creation Sites in many places in the world celebrated by the indigenous people who live there as the places where life begins. Many are lakes or water holes and others are sacred caves or mountains and the valleys that flow from them.

Koko, Mike and I climb up to the Lion Gate and then to the extraordinary North Gate with its wide-based pyramid-like staircase, which faces outwards from the city to a forest and a huge piece of rock in a hillside. What did these people believe? These are the Hittite remains, signs of a powerful Empire. Patriarchy has entered in, the times of Goddess have gone. As the sun sinks in the sky we meander through small temple ruins and find two more large jadeite cubes within rectangular enclosures. One is off centre and we try to roll it back into place, but it's too heavy to move. The Hittities said that all that is needed to create a Temple for the Goddess is a walled garden enclosure, a central stone and two statues of the Goddess.

BACK TO THE clean room with the good toilet – how important the small blessings become for a pilgrim. Mike and I go to sleep early. I wake at 5.00am and worry, dozing on and off. The contrast of exhilarating days, visiting amazing places, connecting in profound ways to ancient landscapes and the people of the Goddess who dwelled in them, and my rampant night-time fears. There feels to be some connection between this land and what may be happening in my body.

AFTER ANOTHER 7.30am breakfast we visit Bogazkale museum, but there are no Goddess images here. We drive up the hillside to say our farewell prayers at the jade stone and then into the minibus for a long drive to Konya via Ankara. Eight hours later we arrive in Konya and find our hotel. Our accommodation is gradually improving as we travel through Turkey. This is clean, attractive, although we share washing and toilet facilities, but at least there is a European toilet. We are in the centre of Konya, a busy town where the men are out on the streets and in the cafes and the women dress in floor-length black and grey coats. There are some shops full of really ugly women's clothing and other shops full of garishly coloured bouffant bridal gowns, for that one special wedding day when girls are brightly coloured in public, before they are hidden away for life.

Konya is famous as the hometown of the 13th century Sufi poet Rumi and there are many grand impressive buildings and mosques. Sufism is the inner mystical tradition of Islam, although there are claims that Sufism predates the rise of both Islam and Christianity. The Mevlevi Order of the Whirling Dervishes was founded by followers of Rumi after his death and tonight we are to see a performance of the Sama or Whirling Ceremony. The Mevlevi Order was banned in Turkey for being political in 1925 when Atatürk and the new Turkish Republic came to power, and it is still banned today, but public Whirling performances are now held, especially in Konya, for tourists and pilgrims on the anniversary of Rumi's death. And there is much wealth in this town, which comes from Arab supporters of the Sufi tradition.

We enter a large modern circular auditorium with high-banked seating on all sides. The performance begins with interminably long speeches by important Turkish men. This is the first night of several days of celebration. The speeches are followed by a man singing with an orchestra which also goes on for nearly an hour. It's all very dull. The orchestra leaves and new musicians arrive. Then at last the dervishes enter, walking slowly. Some are old men, some younger and there are two very young boys. Dressed in long black coats (symbol of the grave), over white skirts (symbol of death) and wearing tall brown hats (symbol of the tombstone), they slowly encircle the floor in step. The Sheikh is a little old man, who is followed by a younger man. He sits in an honoured place on a red sheepskin, while the other dervishes sit on white sheepskins.

The Sama begins with the Naat, a beautiful solo prayer-song in praise of Mohammed, followed by an improvisation on the ney, or reed flute. This is a wonderful haunting melody that evokes the longing of the heart to return to the divine. The older men rise and say their prayers and then circle and bow in acknowledgement of the divine breath that has been breathed into us to give us life. They turn three times in a widdershins (anti-sunwise) direction. I notice that all the movements so far are widdershins, why? I am always looking for Goddess threads hidden in old traditions. The dervishes in their movements represent the moon, while the sheikh who stands in the centre represents the sun. This is a pagan tradition after all.

The bigger group of about 30 men stand, slowly bowing and moving in single file before returning to their places, kneeling and removing their black cloaks. Each dervish moves forward in turn, with their arms crossed over the heart and holding onto their shoulders, self-hugging, and kisses the sheikh upon the wrist. He kisses them on the neck and each one begins to spin widdershins on the left foot. Their arms slowly unfold and rise upwards, right palm facing upwards, left palm facing down to the earth. As they spin their white skirts flare outwards as they move out into the space. The group spin for about fifteen minutes to haunting music, their bodies becoming progressively more surrendered, necks relaxed, heads bent looking up to the heavens, turning, turning, turning. As the music changes the whirling comes to an end and the dervishes glide to the sides of the central circle in small groups, bumping into each other, to support themselves as they come out of the whirling trance, their arms fold across their hearts again.

This Salam is repeated four times to lovely music, which changes for each section. They represent the spiritual journey of the seeker. The first is recognition of the divine, the second represents one's existence within the unity of the divine, the third expresses the ecstasy of surrender to the divine and the fourth, when the Sheikh joins them in the dance, is symbolic of the peace in the heart that comes from union with the divine. The movements are very tranquil and beautiful to watch. There is a final piece of music and a concluding prayer, before the dervishes don their black robes and file out of the auditorium.

This Whirling Practice is believed to have been developed by Rumi from an ancient pagan practice. I feel inspired by its beauty and simplicity. We must create a physical, devotional, ceremonial practice for priestesses to perform together.

WHEN WE GET BACK to our hotel I go for some more healing with Koko and Anna. As soon as I walk in my body is shaking with fear again, tears running down my cheeks. I sob as I speak my fears of cancer. Together they give me some healing which begins to shift the terror that is coursing through my body. I know that this extreme fear is the transforming fire that melts ancient blockages, and sloughs off old and fixed crud, like the blacksmith's forge fire, but it feels so awful. Cancer is one of those diseases which brings the liquid terror, that comes with other life-threatening diseases and threats of, and actual, violence. I calm as the healing energy flows from their hands. They hold me in such love and care.

After the healing Koko takes me on a soul retrieval journey. We lie next to each on the bed and she begins to shake her rattle. She tells me to lie there and receive the journey. As she takes off into the inner worlds with the rattle, my desire to travel with her is strong and it takes all my focus not to journey as well. When she returns she describes what she saw. Her feeling is that when my mother Eileen died in April 2011, a part of me had gone with her into the Otherworld and had not returned from that journey. I think about what Koko is saying. It was a strong experience of death when Eileen died. I wanted to go with her to help her cross over easily, so she might find my father, the man-soul that she loved, that she might retrieve her mind which she had lost, that she might feel safe and unafraid, and free from the burden of dementia in the last years of her life. I did send out energetic feelers and for several weeks my question was, *"Where are you now, Eileen?"* This question went around and around in my head as I try to understand what death is, what life is, from my experience. I do not have experience of close deaths. My father died 28 years ago and his departure, apart from the deaths of animals, is the only close one that I have known.

Koko takes a second soul journey for me which is connected to the pilgrimage Mike and I made in 2007 to Mount Kailash in Tibet. High on the Kora of Mount Kailash I had come close to death a couple of times, once as we were walking in the thin air. I had a vision of my Tibetan brothers welcoming me back home and I entered a rapturous state of being as I walked home into the arms of my soul brothers. I could not stop sobbing for hours. I was so happy and filled with bliss, and everyone, including the Tibetan tea tent owners, thought I was dying.

A second time that I thought we might be dying came when we had to return along the Kora, walking for several hours through a white-out blizzard. It was very tough and I sent out prayers of blessing for everyone I had ever known in my life.

I thought we were going then, but we didn't and managed to come through in the end. Koko said that she felt that in these experiences I had left part of myself there in the sacred place of my Tibetan ancestors and it had not returned with me back to life. It was these two soul losses that she thought were the cause of my cancer.

As she journeys for me to Tibet the call to journey with her is very strong. She tells me not to travel with her, but I go anyway. I see us moving through snow and ice, but in a different time and place. Then she is a shaman and she is carrying me on her back through a blizzard. She has done this before for me and I know that she has saved my life before. She brings the parts of me that were left on Kailash back. I understand then that we are soul sisters, always and forever. Whatever resistances there have been between us before, and there have been some on both sides, they are now gone. We both know we are soul sisters.

IN THE NIGHT Mike dreams about spinning all night. I wake again about five but manage to fall asleep again. The room is very hot at night, even though it's freezing outside. We wake early and have a plain breakfast in our room. Then soon we are driving along rattling roads out onto the endless flat plain, away from the mountain range we can now see rising behind Konya. We travel in the rain along many small roads trying to find our way to Çatal Höyük. Then we see it – a low settlement with buildings covering the excavations. Çatal Höyük dates from 7,500 BCE. It is wonderful to be here on this sacred ground where Goddess imagery once abounded. It was here that the British archaeologist James Mellart began the excavations in 1961, which brought to light new and exciting ideas about Neolithic peoples and their beliefs.

He found more than 150 rooms and buildings closely placed together, entered through holes and stepladders in the ceilings. The walls were decorated with painted murals, plaster reliefs, sculptures, and the skulls and horns of cows, bulls and aurochs. The bones of the ancestors were buried beneath the floors of individual dwellings. In one house more than seventy bodies were found buried beneath the floor, in another two bodies. Here statues of the ancient Mother Goddess have been found, the most famous of which is the Great Mother sitting on Her throne with a feline on each side and giving birth to a baby from between Her legs. Each living space was also a Temple and an ancestral burial ground.

Mellart excavated only part of the city where 5-8,000 people lived. Many of the forms and decorations of the buildings were envisioned and drawn by his Turkish wife Arlette, whose drawings evoked an ancient Goddess way of living, that has since inspired many Goddess-loving people. Later archaeologists have disputed these interpretations and Mellart was disgraced and forced to leave Turkey in 1965 after claims of theft of ancient artefacts. The site lay dormant for 30 years until Ian Hodder began to excavate in the 1990s. His interpretations of finds are different to those of Mellart and are ongoing.

Once again as it's winter after going into the site we can wander where we like, no-one else is here. Looking down into the latest of the excavated ruins we can still see the traces of colour on the low mud walls where digging is still taking place. We see auroch horns protruding from a wall, and we watch as mud crumbles suddenly from a wall in the cold winter air. These ancient walls are fragile as they are uncovered 8,000 years after they were built, but out in the surrounding villages houses are still built using the same sorts of mud-bricks, although entrance is now through doorways at ground level rather than in through the roof.

It feels really good to be here. Standing on the top of the low mound, knowing that beneath lie the homes and bones of hundreds of Goddess-loving people. Underneath this earth there are walls with paintings of the birth-giving Mother Goddess, of animals and vultures, undisturbed, waiting to reveal the beauty of the ancestral way of life.

In the small information centre we see a board, gifted by Lydia Ruyle and the Friends of Çatal Höyük, which describes the Goddess beliefs of Neolithic peoples. This group has worked hard to have the images and ideas promoted by Mellart and since dismissed by later archaeologists, recognised on one board. *Goddess* is such a difficult word for people to speak, to think of, in this Islamic culture, as it is in almost any culture in the world these days.

* * *

"Goddess! Goddess! Goddess!
I shout your name from the rooftops. May you be praised!
May your names be sung once again in every corner of the world!"

AS WE DRIVE BACK across the plain the clouds begin to lift and we can see the edge of the mountains on the other side of Konya. On one of the walls of the houses at Çatal Höyük there was a painting of those same mountains, two breast points, two Paps, Horns of the Moon, the remains of the caldera of an ancient volcano, where the Great Earth Mother flung molten rocks and glass into the air. It cooled into obsidian, which was highly valued by these ancestors. In 2012 two polished obsidian mirrors were unearthed in excavations at Çatal Höyük.

I know that there on that mountain is a Temple as yet undiscovered, unlooked for, where the ancient ones honoured the Mother, to which they travelled to bring back sacred obsidian treasures of the Earth Mother. I served in that Temple in another life. Konya, home of the poet and mystic Rumi, of Mevlana, which was the cultural flowering of the Sufi Tradition, is cradled in the arms of the Great Mountain Mother.

We visit the mosque and Rumi's tomb with its two large dervish hats on top, arranged in such a way that we notice they look like the representations of the yoni/lingam in eastern cultures. The hat is the lingam surrounded by many folds of labial materials. In deference to the tradition Koko and I put on headscarves and Mike takes another photo to blackmail us with – where are the Goddess women now? All covered up so as not to disturb the patriarchs!

THE NEXT MORNING we fly from Konya to Istanbul, arriving at our hotel in the Old Town about lunchtime. The hotel is grubby, Mike and I have a small cramped double. We had been hoping for a gradual upgrade, but this isn't it. We go for lunch to a restaurant overlooking the Blue Mosque and then it's to the Grand Bazaar, where I haggle with an old man for some gold material for the 2012 Mother Goddess Conference. We visit the Cistern, where faces of the

Medusa lie upside down or sideways at the bottom of tall columns holding up the roof of the huge water tank, which once stored water for the whole city. Mike and I go back to our room for a lovely rest – just him and me. He is being so great. I love him and am so grateful for his love. So grateful that he is in my life.

ON SATURDAY 10th Mike, Koko, Gary, Rosa and I go to visit the Sultan's Palace. Stepping over the threshold Mike re-members an incarnation as Sultan Murat III in the late 16th century. The buildings are completely familiar to him and he walks around with a knowing swagger. Koko and I indulge him with a couple of hours of Sultan rule as we follow in his footsteps around the Palace. We lose Rosa and Gary in the many avenues, and then it's just the three of us – Koko, Mike and I. We visit the Harem, which Mike seems to know well (!) and walk through spacious grounds with trees and views of the Bosphorous. It all looks beautiful, but built at a time when very young girls were taken from their families and imprisoned within palace walls in the care of castrated eunuchs, all for the Sultan's pleasure. The excuse was that it was a better life than the one they would endure outside the palace walls. Through our travels in Turkey we have moved from the ancient Goddess times when women were honoured and had power, to this palace and its ruler's power and control over women and their imprisonment for the pleasure of men.

We sit on the banks of the Golden Horn looking out over the sparkling Bosphorus, Mike sipping sherbet and ruminating/remembering, and Koko and I drinking coffee and eating cake in the sunshine, having a lovely time. Then we walk through all the palace rooms and to the Treasury with its bejewelled Sultan headdresses, casks of enormous emeralds, beautiful phials and boxes, and the Prophet's beard. Then on to the large archaeological museum where we see many ancient treasures from Turkey, Iran, Iraq, Syria and Lebanon. I am fascinated by the mummies of women from Sidon in Lebanon. One of the first pieces of writing I ever made, at the age of 10, was about Tyre and Sidon. Here are images of Goddesses and extraordinarily beautiful sphinxes.

Legs aching after five hours of walking we have lunch at a good restaurant in the Palace grounds and Mike's Sultan rule is over now(!). We walk to the nearby Hagia Sofia which was originally a Christian church, but is now a museum. It has extraordinarily heavy stone upper floors – how do they stay up? Candles in jars hang suspended from the ceiling, and high up is an image of the Madonna and child. A Black Madonna painting was stolen from here hundreds of years ago and taken to Poland to become the Black Madonna of Czestochowa. She is the one with the two slashes on her cheek from a warrior's sword.

We try to get into the Blue Mosque but it is closing for sunset prayers – men pouring in through the doors. We watch the birds flying to roost and go to the hotel for a rest. We haven't seen the others all day and it is only late in the evening that we all meet up to say our goodbyes on this last evening. It's an odd ending to our pilgrimage. Tomorrow we fly home to cancer results.

We visit the Blue Mosque in the morning before we leave the city. It is enormous, but nearly all the space is for men. The women's area is really small and hidden away behind a grill in the farthest corner. Spatially as well as in many other ways Islam is a very unequal religion.

Chapter Three

BREAST CANCER

TWO DAYS LATER on December 12th we are at Musgrove Park Hospital in Taunton. I am feeling very afraid. We sit in the waiting room feeling the fear. Fear is an emotion that really expands in space, communicating directly solar plexus to solar plexus between people. How does it affect those who work here, to be in this atmosphere of fear every day? How do they deal with it personally? Perhaps they are just de-sensitised, but it can't make them feel very good.

I ask the radiologist why I am having another mammogram. She says it's because there is an area that they want to look at again. She does another mammogram on the upper part of the right breast at the place where it's begun to feel odd again. Mammograms are just one of the most painful experiences as the breast is squashed and held flat between plates. If it was happening to men's penises they would have invented another diagnostic method by now.

I sit for a while in the waiting room and then go in to see a young woman doctor who shows me that there is a small difference between a mammogram from three years ago and now. I cannot see what she sees. It seems that cancer shows up as a black hole! A black smudge – a smudge of the Dark Goddess. Did I take your name in vain? I called you in, Black Nolava, and you have come. I called you with passion at Samhain and you have come to take me into the next place of surrender. I don't know where I am going.

As the doctor takes me through the process I become calmer. She shows me the dark hole and I realise this is not good. She wants more detail and then says she needs to do a biopsy. She cannot be sure until the cells have been taken, but it does look like cancer. Sixteen and a half years after the first one! It's in another place in the same breast. Why? How? Is it a faulty gene that just gets triggered by something? What? What was it? Travelling in airplanes for hours to Australia? Anxiety? Pressure?

She numbs the skin of my breast and takes several samples. The click machine doesn't work the first two times and then she takes 3 more samples. I am calm. I see the dark hole on the screen. It's smallish, 13mm x 1 cm, I think she said. She says that there is no evidence that taking cells from a tumour leads to cancer cells escaping into the rest of the body via the lymph, but it seems quite likely to me.

I will have the results on Friday, but it seems that it is cancer, unless miraculously it isn't. If it is she recommends a mastectomy – no radiotherapy because I've had it already and the skin could just disintegrate. And no chemotherapy, because I have had that before too – hurrah! They will give me a treatment plan on Friday, with an operation in 4-5 weeks, just after Xmas.

When we get home the atmosphere is sombre. My daughter Iona is very upset when she arrives to hear the news. She listens to me and gives me healing crystals to put in my bra and under my pillow at night. The first time I had cancer she was only fourteen years old and found the whole experience unbearably frightening. She hid from it as much as she could and then felt guilty for being unable to cope. She was just young and the thought of her Mum dying from cancer was too much to bear.

I wake at 5.30am, which is 7.30am on Turkish time. I feel calm, but I may just be numb. It is hard to get to grips with it all. I still can't believe that it's happening, again, although I do have a bandage and puncture holes on the side of my breast to prove it is.

You will take care of me, Lady. I know.

I must write a will. I do not know if this is my journey out. I thought I would be living until I was 90, like Eileen, but who knows now? It is all in your hands, Lady, in your hands.

IT IS CONFIRMED by the breast care nurse Miranda, that I have an intraductal tumour in my right breast, growing between the milk ducts. Last time it was inside the milk ducts, so it is a different kind of cancer. It is Stage 2, not so aggressive as last time, although this later changes to Stage 3. She says it is fully treatable. I will need to have a mastectomy, the complete removal of my breast. They will also do an MRI on the left breast to make sure there is nothing there. She says it is a speckled tumour, rather than being one cancerous lump.

We talk with Miranda for an hour and she is helpful and reassuring. We talk about the possibility of reconstruction after the mastectomy. When I had cancer the first time round I was in my late 40s and could not bear the thought of losing one of my beautiful breasts. I loved their luscious shapely curves, the expression of my sexuality and powers of attraction. But now at 64, to lose a breast doesn't have the same meaning. I can do this. At my age no-one apart from Mike and me, is looking at my breasts in that way. And Mike says, with his wonderful acceptance, hiding any negative feelings from me, that he doesn't mind. It's my left breast that he likes best any way.

I am in shock really at the news, a bit displaced from actuality. I am not feeling ill, apart from a cold. I have a small lump in my breast and the rest of me is fine. Life is such a challenging thing. Tomorrow I am teaching my Priestess Enchantress course. Like actors on a stage, the 'play must go on', life continues despite all adversity.

THIS EVENING I am writing these words because I may not have much time ahead of me. I have nothing to lose, everything to gain. Now is the time to write it all down. My fears and the possibilities of cancer, with its suffering and early death capitulate me into writing down what have so far been thoughts and words spoken with passion, rants against the patriarchy, now become articulate.

I can no longer watch the world go by and be silent. This is my manifesto for a new world where Goddess is loved and adored once again, where peace prevails, where conflict is faced and wounds are healed, where voices are listened to and compassion pours into the world. 2012 is coming and I have cancer again. I am

64 years old. I am lucky. I have a wonderful life. I am a Priestess of Avalon. I do what I love, and I love and am loved by many people. I have so much to be grateful for and I am grateful. My Lady gives me everything and She gives me this trial. I am to become an Amazon in body as well as in heart and mind. Is it one to stimulate the other?

Lady I will stand for you and your planet. I will stand up for your wonderful world.

THE NEXT DAY – Saturday, the Enchantress group are at Dowsborough on top of the Quantock Hills. It is cold, and getting colder as we climb up through the trees and onto the high moorland into the cold wind. We walk up and up past the yew and holly onto the top of the hill with the stunted oak trees and birch wood. We are connecting at Yule with the Great Mother of Air, who blows across these high windswept hills, and with the Ancestors of the land, of Britain, of our families, of our incarnations and of the stars.

In the small wood on top of the hill within the boundaries of Dowsborough camp, an ancient iron-age enclosure, we separate to sit beneath the wind-bent trees to connect deeply to the Old Ones. I drift off into a reverie sitting in a five-fingered tree hand, which moves with the wind. Above, the bare branches of the trees are all touching – connected to each other, communicating secrets we strain to catch. Beneath us the roots of the close trees are also all connected to each other in the earth, either directly or via the fungi in the earth that allow messages of communication to pass between the roots of all plants over long distances. Here we humans sit separately, encircled by the Standing Beings, all connected if we can but notice, connected to each other.

ON THE SUNDAY morning we are at Stoney Littleton Long Barrow near Bath for sunrise to watch the amazing vision that appears around each Winter Solstice sunrise. The ancestors knew so much that we have forgotten and built this hillside barrow to honour their dead and illuminate their ancestors' bones with light, renewing all life. As the sun rises today it fills the long tunnel leading into the barrow with glorious golden liquid light, which illuminates every nook and cranny, every side chamber, reaching to the back wall. It is truly magical. 5000 years ago the ancestors saw this same golden vision as light lifts the colour of the stones. They built this stone chamber to celebrate the Old Woman of Winter, the Old Woman of the Golden Light, to honour their Ancestors.

ON SOLSTICE EVE we go to see the surgeon, Ms Thorne. I wonder where these surgeons get their names from. Last time I recall, there was Dr Pain – a surgeon I saw first at Yeovil Hospital who had such a cold un-empathic manner that I asked to have a second opinion, and Dr Whipp, my oncologist at Bristol. Having come round to the idea of having an implant I then realise in our conversation that she is saying that it is not that simple. Because of my previous surgery and having radiotherapy, my breast skin is very thin and has few blood vessels. If I had an implant and the skin was stretched, it could die and that could get messy.

Amanda the nurse shows me a peachy skin-coloured prosthetic breast, which is soft and squidgy and feels like a real breast. It even has a nipple that has a real shape to it. She gives me a catalogue of underwear and the best thing is that all the women pictured in it, who have missing breasts and are wearing the bras, are smiling. I am shocked all over again, but mastectomy feels like the only choice for me.

My soul sister Apela from Maui called yesterday as she too has had two bouts of cancer and is now having an implant, slowly inflating her damaged breast over time. I hadn't realised what it means to have an implant. The implant is put under the muscles of the chest wall and is slowly filled with saline so that the muscles stretch until it reaches the right size. The saline bag is then replaced with a silicone implant. The other breast may also need surgery to adjust to the new breast's shape and size. This means many visits to hospital, which for me would all be leading up to the next Goddess Conference, distracting me from my Goddess work.

The other possible kinds of reconstruction also require lots of hospital visits and prolonged recovery times. I don't want that. I don't like physical pain and I need to get on with my life. It seems that I will just have a mastectomy. I feel into what that will be like in my body. I don't like that idea either. It's a complexity of bad consequences.

AT THE Goddess Temple Winter Solstice Ceremony we are led on an inner journey up a mountain to the top, where we jump off into space. I let myself be completely in the journey. I jump and feel myself falling through space, letting go, letting go of resistance and falling into the unknown. It is very healing for me. I let go and allow healing to flow into every part of my body.

It takes me a week or two to come to terms with it, all through Xmas, which was a lovely holiday with my beautiful family, Iona and Torquil and Mike. It takes me time to face everything. I avoid thinking about it, hoping it will go away miraculously, even when I know that this does not happen with cancer, no matter how much I wish, or will it. It's so hard to face.

Iona gives me a lovely relaxing healing. It moves me so deeply that my daughter the healer has her hot hands on my wounded breast. Every day I envision the cancer shrinking, or at least not growing. I have lost track of the days, but my surgery is to be on January 6th. At first they said December 30th, but that felt too fast. I need time to face this thing that is happening. Now we joke about the breast harvester coming to Morrisons car park, picking off the women whose breasts it will eat. That is a bad joke. Yesterday a friend brought me a soft pink breast she has knitted. Her thoughtfulness makes me feel better.

I talk to my sister Ann, who had a mastectomy about 6 years ago. Where was I when that happened? So wrapped up in my own life I didn't really care about my own sister? We are distanced, leading very different lives. She loves Jesus. I love Goddess. Both dedicated to our spiritual paths, both with love in the centre but such different practices and beliefs. What is my resistance to love, which can creep up on me unnoticed?

I hope this dis-ease brings more love into my life, less resistance to loving, more love, more forgiveness, for those who have wronged me, for slights received, for failures, for those I have wronged. Open my heart to Love, Lady!

WE GO VISIT Mike's Dad and family and enter that strange stultified family atmosphere, where nothing is acknowledged or faced directly. I knew it would be like this but decided to go and face it anyway, the suppressed family emotions. There is a brief *"How are you?"* and then no further acknowledgment that in a few days' time my breast will be cut off! The familiar disinterest along with the wine and the rich food keeps me awake all night, and allows my primary horror and repulsion to arise. These people didn't create it, but they have the capacity to trigger my childhood reactions.

I lie awake at night full of heat. I don't want to die in 2012. I don't want to be one of the ones leaving the planet. I don't want to be a sacrifice for Goddess, like feminist artist Monica Sjoo, who died not long ago from breast cancer. I don't want that. I want to be Her living Priestess.

AN OLD FRIEND comes round and presses my emotional buttons. She tells me that if I am really going to deal with my wounds I will not have surgery. I must deal with the emotional wounding that lies beneath the cancer directly. She accuses me of not facing my fear and tells me I should do this… that… and the other.…. She confronts me without listening to me at all, and tells me what I should do, while I am feeling my way through this maze of uncertainty. It is shocking. She tells me she can feel my fear. Well yes, I can too, moment by moment. Anyone can, who cares to take a look at me. I do want to heal this fear. Where is the cause of my cancer? What is its cause?

Lynne gives me a really helpful craniosacral treatment, evening out the energy in my channels. It feels good. The difference between her loving care and my other friend with her challenges, is striking. Cancer has a strange effect on people. Some come closer in, full of loving, some become aggressive, some know what should be done without experience of the dis-ease themselves, some move away. It brings us to our own mortality and our own places of fear.

IT IS New Year's Day 2012. What will this year bring for me? Will it be death or renewed life? I do not know. I shake some of the fear out of my body. I am afraid of the cancer in my body. I am afraid that now I am riddled with cancer. I am afraid that it will kill me. I don't want it to. I am immobilised with fear.

I am actually much stronger than last time I had cancer. I have a depth, a strength that was not there before – which came with the experience of cancer or through the cancer. I read of others and know their struggles and fears too. I am empathic with suffering. I am on an equal level with all who suffer, in the knowledge which the Dark Goddess gives to those of us who suffer. And this time I know absolutely that She is with me every step of the way and especially in my fear.

Mike reads my Tarot for the year ahead. It has many major arcana and court cards, including the Magus, Art, the Queen of Pentacles, the Queen of Cups, the Ace of Cups. Love is pouring in, as well as Oppression, Wrong and another negative card. One day at a time. Iona and I go looking for a new bathroom and find floor tiles and a good towel radiator. I am feeling better today. In a few days I will lose my lovely breast.

ONE EVENING we hold a Healing Ceremony in Sophie's yurt at Sally's house. I want to have a Healing Ceremony where in the company of my women friends, I can make a plaster cast of my two intact breasts, before the dis-eased one is removed. Annabel has called the women together for me. It is to be a ceremony to honour my breasts, which have been a luscious part of my body for fifty years, since I was 14. My breasts that I love, that have expressed my sexuality, that have given out my body's sexual signals, that have brought me so much pleasure, that fed my children, and now one of them is leaving my body, taking its death-dealing wound with it.

The yurt is round and red, a real womb space with a small stove to keep us toasty warm. Sister priestesses have gathered for this ceremony – Tegwyn, Annabel, Lynne, Michelle, Heloise, Sophie, Sally, Georgina, Vanda, Erin and Koko. There is a beautiful central altar created by Tegwyn, a mound of sand, decorated with seashells. I place a lighted candle in the sand. It's very warm, and in honour of my breast ceremony I take off the clothes that cover the top half of my body and everyone joins in. We are a circle of bare-breasted women and we are awesomely beautiful, all different shapes and sizes. All gorgeous.

Tegwyn begins with a prayer and then introduces the Pipe. With the smoke, she speaks a long and beautiful prayer calling in Goddess, all the beings of Avalon, all the animals and the elements. It is wonderful and I begin to journey.

Tegwyn offers the pipe to me first. I wasn't going to smoke, but then I took the pipe. It's a long time since I last smoked in a Medicine Ceremony. Then the tobacco was raucous and harsh, leaving a horrible taste in the mouth. But here the smoke is sweet, gentle and soft. I could almost think of taking up smoking again and it's been 30 years since I last smoked a cigarette!

Everyone offers prayers of gratitude and the pipe goes around the circle. It is amazing to hear each person speak their gratitude to me for being there for them in their lives in the past – Annabel, Lynne, Michelle – all say amazing things. I feel held in a wonderful circle of sisterhood and love. When it gets round to Heloise, she says something amazing that spins me out. I see a very old part of a house. It is upstairs, dusty, wood walls, dark, shuttered, unopened, with cobwebs and dry old wood, with a closed door. No-one has gone in there for a long time. I begin to cry, tears falling down my face as I lie on the floor. I scream and scream and let go. The door begins to open. It is fortified with metal. Inside I can see shadow people moving behind the walls. Then I see myself, my little girl, little Katy, the one that was never recognised, never seen by my family.

"You never knew me!
You never wanted to know me!
To know who I am!"

I LIVED IN A FAMILY where they didn't want to know who I was, they didn't know how to know me, and where they never knew me, never in the whole of our lives. I was the odd one, the one who was different, who was over-sensitive, who didn't fit in with their way of living. I feel the pain of that. I cry and scream it out. I wriggle my body and shake, and move and thump the floor. Everyone joins in and helps me release, with their own cries and feelings.

It feels very good to let these feelings out. My little girl has been locked up in that dead part of my house. I didn't know that she was there. But things begin to explain themselves to me, clicking into place like pieces of a jigsaw puzzle. I have the feeling that we, most but not all, of this group of women, have been in such a circle before, when others needed healing. Bare-breasted women sitting in the warmth, in flickering candle flames and firelight. Beautiful!

I think about my relationships with women – how in the past I was always looking for a woman friend and finding her for a while and then she always leaves/withdraws/finds a new friend. I am too much, I want too much. And then I am really hurt when it ends. I realise that these days I no longer put myself in the way of being friends, in case they go away, as they always have in the past. I am lucky that I have Mike who really knows me, who sees me. Over recent times I have developed teaching relationships with women, where I know many people and their lives intimately, but they hardly know me at all. Perhaps this can change now as I bare my wounded breast in the circle.

Now to make the breast cast. Tegwyn smears both my breasts and the front of my upper body with vaseline to stop the gypsum bandaging from sticking to the skin. The bandaging is cut into strips and dipped in warm water and then placed in layers by the women on my breasts and chest. Soon I am covered up in the quickly hardening layers of bandaging. The cast gets very hot as the chemical changes take place between the gypsum and the water and in no time the hardened cast is lifted off my body, and there they are, my breasts immortalised.

It feels wonderful and the idea comes that this is something that all women should experience. Perhaps we can create some Breasts and Bellies workshops for everyone. Women of all ages can make the casts of their breasts and bellies and then paint and decorate them as they want to. Women have such individual relationships to their own breasts and bellies, and to those of other women. The power and beauty of women's breasts, which have such different shapes and sizes. In our society there are a few idealised breast shapes and yet we are nearly all different from these ideal, man-made forms. Our unique breasts should be celebrated. In the coming year's Conference we will celebrate the Mother Goddess and we can have an exhibition of decorated Breasts and Bellies.

We take a break at 10.30 pm after four hours. In the break as Koko and I sit together I suddenly have a strong feeling that Koko was once my sister in a previous life. She tells me that when we first met, years ago now, she knew we had been sisters before. She's always been a psychic woman with her gypsy heritage.

We come back into the circle and there is a ripple in the energy, but Tegwyn takes charge again, leading a drum journey. My concern is that it is getting late and people may want to leave, but I realise that they will leave if they want to. I lie down on the wolf skin and journey with the drum, with Sally, Heloise and Koko, in the wolf pack, the others being outriders of the pack. I journey on the back of wolf. I want to see/find the source of my negative behaviour. What did I do? I know that lots of times I have been done to, I have been a victim, but what did I do that is so wrong?

> *Running through the forest on the back of the wolf we come to a stone circle. I am looking into the circle watching a group of people in dark cloaks performing a ceremony. From the outside I see myself inside the circle. To become part of this group I have to kill the person who is lying on the centre stone slab, to show that I really want to join this group, so that I can learn more, so that I can rise in the hierarchy and not be left outside. I see myself choose to kill and I see myself do it, raising a flashing curving knife and slicing into chest and heart. I feel completely dreadful.*

MY NEED to gain power at that time was absolutely not worth the pain, the guilt and the shame of doing it. I hear phrases like, *"Power is not worth it"*, repeating in my head. The strength of this feeling echoes my long term resistance to taking power, to owning my own power, and being seen to have power.

It also explains my complete lack of interest in this life in becoming part of any cloaked coven.

Each person in the circle tells her experience on the journey. Heloise saw me in lots of different times when I had to flee Goddess Temples or groups of women, for various reasons. Sally saw me in Tibet before Buddhism has arrived when there is lots of conflict going on. Mike recently gave me a book about the native Bon religion, which was there before Buddhism arrived. And I have such strong past life memories of living for several incarnations in Tibet.

Sally leads the Tonglen practice, breathing in my dis-ease as black tar smoke, transforming into light. Breathing in the love, breathing in light. It's a beautiful and effective Tibetan healing practice. There are more prayers and a final pipe from Teg. It's 1.15am and I feel fabulous. I am spaced out, tired and very happy. Lots has been revealed to me that will expand in the coming days. My little girl is out from behind the closed doors. She's coming out to play. Open the windows. Let light in. Dust away the cobwebs. Be seen!!

I am so grateful to Annabel for organising this ceremony, to Tegwyn for leading it, to Sophie and Sally for their hospitality and to everyone for being there. Thank you all for helping me.

A COUPLE OF DAYS LATER I am having an MRI. I am being assaulted by strong magnetic energy and a horrendous thudding sound. I come home shocked and rather blown out by the physical force.

I sit on the earth of Avalon and She inspires me.

Beloved, beloved, beloved Lady
You are my beloved Lady of Avalon
You are my beloved, beloved, beloved Goddess.

Earth beneath my feet, green grass, soil,
Mud, substance, matter, Mother, Lady.
You are earth beneath my feet, Lady
Beloved Earth, Beloved soil, Beloved Earth of Avalon.

Water flowing in the land, in streams and rivers
Fluid, emotions, dissolving, solving, solutions, Lady
You are Water, flowing in the land, Lady
Beloved Water, Beloved emotion, Beloved Water of Avalon.

Fire of the Sun warming my body, Lady
You are Fire in my belly, in my heart, in my womb,
The Fire of Creation, fire of mind, Ring of Fire on the Tor, Lady
Beloved Fire, Beloved creation, Beloved Fire of Avalon.

Breath, Air, all around and within everything
Air moving through the trees, over the land, across the oceans,
Carrying scents, water, soil, bringing rain, replenishment, nourishment.
Beloved Air, you are the Air of Avalon, Lady

How I love you, Lady
How I love you
You take me deep into my soul
To the Place of No Escape
Into my healing, into my wounds
To the core of my karma
To my resistance to change
You take me, Lady
To the breathless places
Where my body shakes in terror
Where I lose control
Where my mind no longer rules
You take me to the falling apart places
Where I am defenceless
You take me to the bare, naked soul places
Where armour no longer works
Where the iron-clad machine can no longer
Crush the tiny spirit of hope
You take me there to my vulnerable heart, Lady
And open me with your love.

Chapter Four

SURGERY AND BEYOND

IT'S FRIDAY 6th January 2012. The day has arrived and I am sitting in surgical admissions at 8 o'clock in the morning feeling wobbly. We drove here in the dark across the flat Somerset levels, the faint light of dawn just beginning to show. Iona got up early with us and gave me healing oils and a crystal she'd put Reiki into, for me to have with me. She is so sweet. I can feel the web of love which holds me today from across the world. My fears are of surgery, of making love with one breast. Will I still be attractive to Mike? How will it feel? He says he will love my Amazon body. It is so weird. And the question is always, why is this happening?

I had a dream about my mum last night. I dream that I am in some kind of building where I can see through some of the floors above and below. Then I think I see Eileen, but that's not possible because she died last year. I see her again later and I am really surprised. She looks good, much better than she did before she died. She's able to go out visiting friends. Apparently she didn't really die. She appeared to die, but in the coffin she came back and banged on the lid and someone let her out. In the dream I am thinking 'What will we do about her money?'. I've given it all away, divided it up. She's still at Southlawns Nursing Home, living there comfortably. I wake up. It's a strange dream for last night.

I sit in the lounge hanging on to Mike's arm, watching the time go by, calming my mind. I get a lovely text from Koko. My phone is hardly ever on but she has managed to get through.

Beloved Lady, I ask for complete healing and good health.

I say goodbye to Mike. He's been in this place himself, with his own cancer operation and knows how horrid this is. I change my clothes to one of those faded hospital gowns. It turns out that the nurse who takes me to the operating theatre has recently taken Reiki 1 and is happy to give me Reiki to help keep me calm. As fear arises I feel waves of love coming towards me and the fear moves on. As the anaesthetic goes into my hand I call in the Morgen sisters – Tyronoe, Thitis, Cliton, Thetis, Gliten, Glitonea, Moronoe, Mazoe, and Morgana and I am gone into the blackness.

I wake to the voice of a nurse asking how I am. Coming to… my breast is gone…. Now I am an Amazon. I do not know what this means. Gradually waking I am taken to another ward to recover. Drinking water I have a sore throat, but no sickness, which is good. Miranda arrives and gives me more instructions, which are hard to take in, about drugs and pain. I am high on morphine and finding everything quite easy and humorous. Give me more of this stuff.

About 6.00pm Mike and Iona arrive to take me home. I have decided that it will be better to be at home in my own bed, being cared for by people who love me. This is day surgery. I am glad to be going, in the next bed a woman is snoring loudly. I wouldn't have been able to sleep next to her. Mike and Iona have both worried about me all day, Mike has been afraid that I would die on the operating table and Iona is in her own pain over a lost love. We are both on a hard journey. I tell her that I am strong like the large oak tree in our garden, which bends in the storm, but does not break. I tell her that she will become strong through these experiences she is having. She says she will never be strong like me, but she is amazing and I see her growing all the time.

The next day I wake in pain as the morphine wears off. Any time I move pure liquid pain shoots around my back. It is excruciating, and why there? I work out that they must have pulled the layers of my skin apart and cut a nerve that is now recovering. The wound itself is not so painful. I take some painkillers and after an hour or so the pain dulls, but I cannot move without pain. If I had stayed in hospital they might have been able to give me something stronger, but now it's just codeine. I feel low and am lower as the day goes on. There are two drains in the righthand side of my chest. I know from last time's experience of surgery that it is the drains that can hurt more than the flesh wounds, as they go in under the skin and irritate every time the layers of the body move. I take some more painkillers but the pain still comes through. My mind becomes frantic with the drugs and I feel afraid. By teatime I feel very low. I lie in Mike's arms and cry for a while. He holds me in his love.

Sunday is a better day. I am managing the pain and the painkillers a bit better. I am reading books. Slow down. Sit still. Don't move or it hurts. I read a book about Tibet which is inspiring as it shows many of the places we went to in 2007 on that magical amazing pilgrimage. It also shows the inner Kora around Mount Kailash, which we didn't see. I wonder if we will ever get back there?

In the night I sleep OK for a while then wake up in pain and take some more codeine. On Monday morning I manage to have a shower. I have to hold the drain in one hand and try not to get the wound and its bandages wet. Laura comes and suggests I take codeine with paracetamol to help with the pain. She is an intensive care nurse, so she should know what she is talking about. No-one from my doctor's surgery, no home visitor or aftercare nurse comes to see how I am, which seems very odd. There is no joined-up thinking in the NHS. Send someone home from hospital on the same day as a major operation and no-one is bothered.

BY WEDNESDAY I am feeling completely poisoned by all the painkillers, sluggish and sick, but I am now managing to keep the pain at bay. I woke at 2.00am and took codeine as I could feel the nerve spot beginning to melt into liquid pain again. Thank goodness there are only a couple more days of this before the drains come out. I am reading lots, spacing out, resting, taking it easy and my mind is no longer speeding. I am receiving so much love from so many people, hundreds it seems – flowers, cards, emails, messages from all over the world. I am so lucky.

I go to hospital on Friday and a nurse removes the drains – quickly, simply.

They don't look at all thick, how come they can hurt so much? It's so good not to have to walk around carrying a bottle of bloody fluid, afraid that any movement can accidentally hurt me. My body was in such resistance to the pain that when the drains came out, so did a huge pile of emotion. I felt done in and cried and cried for a while,

"Why me? Why me, Goddess? Have I not done enough to protect myself from these experiences?"

That's quite a line of statements to investigate later. I remember the slight feeling of boredom that I'd had for a while that nothing was happening for me in the last months before the diagnosis of cancer. I was travelling, giving, wanting to give, taking you, Lady, out into the world, but some part of my personal self-expression was held in. I hadn't done any writing for a long time, which is my personal creative expression and skill. I had not expressed myself much, except when I spoke in Australia at the workshop for 50 plus people. I did enjoy that a lot. It was a large number of people and I knew that I could inspire them and take them to amazing places and I did. I let rip. And I also loved the evening ceremony bringing the elements of Avalon to introduce them to the Australian Ancestors. That was a cool ceremony.

"Lady I love you. Please show me the way through this experience."

WE GO TO THE HOSPITAL to see the surgeon Mr El-Abbar, and a nurse, who look at the wound. Miranda who was so kind before surgery has now disappeared never to be seen again. There is no continuity of care, although it turns out Mr El-Abbar is the same surgeon who did my surgery 16 and a half years ago. He is a skilful surgeon and I trust him. He has now saved my life twice. I have much to be grateful for to this stranger, who has seen more of me unconscious than conscious. Life is so weird sometimes. The first time round he was just beginning as a surgeon in Taunton. How many cancers has he removed in that time? How many women's lives has he saved? How many breasts has he harvested? Ahhhh!

He says that my cancer is a new breast cancer. It is not the return of the last breast cancer from 16 years ago. It is a grade 3 (up from the earlier grade 2) invasive lobular cancer 25mm, node- negative, ER positive tumour. Last time it was a grade 3 invasive ductal carcinoma 32mm node-positive, ER negative. Extraordinary.

Then we have the oddest conversations with me asking questions that are never quite answered. Now for the first time they start talking about what I should do next. Nothing was said of this before my operation. They assume that I will take the anti-oestrogen drug Letrozole, which is given to post-menopausal women to block oestrogen production in the body and so inhibit cancer growth. They start talking about my having radiotherapy and chemotherapy. Alarm bells go off in my mind.

I am sure they said I couldn't have radiotherapy because I had had it before and it could cause the damaging breakdown of my skin. And I seriously don't want chemotherapy, if possible, at all. It was so dreadful the first time around. Panic and anxiety arise in Mike and in me. No-one mentioned anything like that before the surgery. Then they offer me a chance to take part in a trial where a sample of the cancer is sent to the USA to look at markers in the DNA, in my genes, and a score comes back for the chances of recurrence of the cancer. A decision is then made about chemotherapy treatment. They talk about percentages and chances of recurrence, which is mind-boggling. If the score is below 18 they advise no treatment. If it's between 35 and 100 they advise chemotherapy. Between 18 and 35 is a grey area – what does that mean? They think that's where I will be. I decide to have the test as more information is better, but we come home with heavy hearts and the next day I feel low again.

ON THE WEEKEND I am teaching the Third Spiral of the Priestess of Avalon Training with Amanda, Anna Saqqara, Carmen, Laura and Renata. It is so lovely to bathe again so deeply in the Lady's blissful healing energies. This year's group is small but everyone goes deep. I have the thought that if I could teach seven days a week I would feel wonderful. Teaching is my spiritual practice and I love it. I start having ideas for new courses and ways of teaching, but then the thought comes, it all depends if I live or not. Where will Pluto square Mars take me this year?

I swing backwards and forwards from confidence to fear. In the Empowerment of the Practice I talked with the Lady and She said, "*I am not trying to hurt you or kill you. This is about something else.*"

Sally calls me on Monday and really helps me as I tell her about the choices I have to make, she tells me to remember who I am, what I know, that I am who I am and I do know that this is a Soul Journey and the Lady is taking me to new unknown places of my Soul and I must keep this in the forefront of my mind. This is a really helpful, good conversation and only I really know what I need in this situation. In my weak places I hope that someone else will tell me what to do, but I know the answer is in me. I just have to find it.

I speak with Sonja, a priestess and healing therapist from Zurich, who has worked with many cancer patients. She talks about my absorbing negativity from lots of people and I think about how much I might have taken into my body during Embodiments – when I feel completely able to do that at the time, completely protected against absorbing any negative energies into my own body. Have I taken them on?

I am looking at the causes of my dis-ease. There are so many possibilities. It can be too much oestrogen in my body. The world is full now of phyto-oestrogens, in the water, in creams, in perfumes, everywhere. I love perfumes. Have they affected me? Or was it the death of my mother? The lack of grief that I felt at her death. My guilt at not wanting to have her living with us at home, not wanting to look after her in her dementia. But now she feels free and safe, and I am free too. I am thinking of having some therapy for myself. I ask Rachael Clyne for some names of local psychotherapists, which she helpfully provides, but I don't do anything about it straight away. I find it hard to walk towards the acceptance of this dis-ease.

In the next few days I begin to feel better, healing slowly. There is fluid in the damaged breast skin, which is swollen and almost looks like I still have a cleavage, but that can't be right. It feels odd, but the wound itself is just numb. I have a rash on the skin from the plaster used to cover the wound. I look down at myself and see this strange view of one rounded breast on the left and flattened skin on the right. I can feel my ribs now beneath the skin, ribs that have always been covered by breast tissue. It's a strange sensation. I put manuka honey on the wound to help it heal. Then get hydrocortisone from the doctors to put on the rash, which goes in a few days. The fewer chemicals in my system the better.

Evelien Brighid from Holland dies from the effects of breast cancer on January 26th. She lived with the dis-ease for so long. She was a priestess who came many times to Glastonbury and to the Goddess Conference. She was so brave and so out there with her dis-ease, always decorating herself in bright rainbow colours, tall and smiling, even when her ankle broke when the disease went into her bones, even in a wheel chair. She was amazing. Her death is also quite scary. Is this where I am headed?

MIKE AND I travel up to Wrexham to see Damo Mitchell, Mike's Nei Gong teacher, 'little master', for some healing for me. Damo is young, only in his 30s, but has been learning and teaching Qi Gong and Nei Gong since childhood. He has a clean vibration and clear eyes. I like him. He looks at my tongue, feels my pulses at the wrist and puts an acupuncture needle in my arm. His finger is about an inch away from the top end of the needle and he moves the needle without physical contact. I like this a lot. It shows he can focus energy and clear meridians.

He puts in more needles and says that my immune system is good. I have the spleen of a vegetarian, which I am, but my liver meridian is over-active. The pericardium, the protector of the heart, is brittle and needs to crack off. My system is sluggish. He releases a lot of energy through the needles in my feet. Damo says that he thinks the problem is with my father. He also says something happened 3-4 years ago that helped create the cancer.

I can't think of anything. The last few years have been happy and I can't remember anything big happening then. I have done a lot of therapeutic work on my relationship with my father, who died 27 years ago. Then I'm thinking, could it have anything to do with the anger I feel, that has been building, about patriarchy, war, famine, weapons of war, etc., which I have been feeling more and more strongly? Damo says I need to drop the anger – it is harming me. He says I shouldn't express it, just drop it. And I'm thinking, how? Over the last few years I have led lots of workshops for others to help release their anger and emotional wounding. I would do it too but always in a contained way as I was holding the space for others, but were those workshops just my unconscious desire to release my personal anger around patriarchy?

Damo tells me that the cause of my cancer is the same as the last time that I had it. Although this time it is a different kind of breast cancer, the cause is the same. Questions, questions…. What is the cause? Where are the answers? This is a healing journey of accelerated exploration.

When we get back after an overnight stay in a lovely hotel in mid-Wales and then a slow meander back through beautiful Wales, Annabel comes round to visit. She reminds me about my little girl, whom she heard speak and cry during the Healing Ceremony, the one locked away in the upstairs room. I find I have forgotten about her until I am now reminded. She obviously needs to express herself. My father's wounding is not all healed in me. I can still remember and feel the anger, resentment and hatred of my teenage years and perhaps it is hidden there in the underlayers, still causing cancer. Healing childhood wounds seems like a never-ending journey.

I speak on the phone with Anne Napier who runs Cygnus Books. She has had cancer for several years now. A couple of years ago we did a healing ceremony for her in the Goddess Hall. She has been very near to death a couple of times and has cancer fully in her body. She is always trying out new treatments. She says that the alternative route has not worked for her. She has tried the sodium bicarbonate anti-fungus treatment, having it injected into her body, which I have considered, but it didn't work and the cancer spread to the rest of her body. Ann didn't have surgery, which is the majorly successful way to have cancer removed, but she has now tried a specialised form of chemo. She takes Letrozole with no side effects, but I think that she has had so much going on health-wise, that she wouldn't notice. She says she will send me information that might help me. Sadly, couple of years later, Ann dies.

I REMEMBER, as in a dream, the time four years ago when I was 60 years old, feeling that that was it. My life was coming to an end. I had some programming in me that said that life ends at 60 – retirement. And I lost energy. For a year or so I had less energy. I thought that I had got over that, but I notice that as the cancer was growing, my energy was lessened. I felt tired when I was in Australia in the autumn last year. I no longer felt like going to dance 5 Rhythms. Maybe my energy will now return if it's no longer being sucked out by cancer and negative thought forms.

At Imbolc I have a great dream. I am on spaceship flying out into space towards death with someone else. *"I'm not ready to die! I don't want to die!"* I heard myself say. Others are ready, but I'm not. I wake feeling good that this knowledge is deep in my psyche that I don't want to die. It's not my time!

WE GO TO SEE a George Clooney film, *The Descendants*, which tells the story of a family where the mother dies after an accident. It's a bit close to home at the moment. It could be my children trying to come to terms with my death, though not all the other dramas in the movie. After it we drive home in silence in the car. I hear Her speak to me, telling me,

> *"You will not die now. It is over now. You will get better. This is an awakening call. There are new things for you to do. Rest, relax, learn to always be relaxed. Don't get stressed about performances or workshops or challenges, just relax. Driving cars – relax. Find the place of TRUST. All shall be well. There are challenges to come. Don't be stressed about them. I am leading you. You have books to write, things to grow, Temples to build. Relax, relax. No worry, no stress. I am in charge. TRUST ME."*

ON OUR NEXT Enchantress weekend we are in our house for one of the wintry days, cosy in the sitting room with its long views over the fields and the Sacred Isle. I create a flowing inner journey working with a crystal bowl and a rattle. I follow Her energy trusting Her completely, and as we fly with Her swan She takes us deep for a long time. When we return from the journey and open our eyes, snow is falling gently outside in the garden, like soft swan's feather down, covering the earth in the white mantle of Her swan wings. It is incredibly magical and synchronistic.

ON THE SUNDAY we go to the Spring at Doulting where snowdrops grow in the woodland, and then on to Stanton Drew with its Great Circle, which is the second largest known stone circle in Britain, after Avebury, when all its stones were standing. It dates from the late Neolithic from 3-2,000 BCE, but the site has not been properly excavated. The whole complex is thought to be the second largest in Europe, nestling on a large sloping meadow, near the River Chew in the middle of a surrounding circle of low hills. It also has 2 smaller circles and two avenues, as well as outlying marker stones, the Cove and a long barrow, which predates the circles by a thousand years. Geophysical work has shown that there were once nine concentric rings of postholes, that held large wooden posts, inside the Great Circle, creating what must have been an extraordinary structure.

Because there have been no excavations here it's not a well-known site. When we arrive we are luckily the only ones here. After connecting to this ancient stone circle we take some space from each other and I go to lie on a fallen stone, melding into it, becoming one with the stone. I like to lie and just be with the earth, to be one with the stone. There is weak wintry sunshine and I doze/daze and enter the timeless still space.

"You are not going to die now." She says,

"You will not be able to predict your time of dying before it comes. There will be no time to think about it before it comes. There will be no time to think about it for a long time. It's some way away and you have things to do."

We go together into the smaller nine stone circle and call in the Goddesses of the nine directions. In the cold air we run from the stones to the centre, bringing Her in. It is fun and powerful.

* * *

AS I AM ILL I become aware of the suffering of others that I have only partially registered. Jo has recently had a hip replacement and I didn't know. She has had intense pain and has suffered from arthritis for so many years. And she is a lovely person. Susan with her numbness and vertigo, her overweight body and intense physical problems. I think of all those with weight problems, which seem intractable, too much, too little. I pray for each one, holding them in my soul thoughts, sending them healing energy. Praying to the Lady for their healing. There is such a need for healing in our communities.

I take each day as it comes. Relax… put space in my life, and love….

TEGWYN COMES and gives me a wonderful deep tissue massage, pinning me to the table. She is so generous to me, as are many people. I am really grateful and need to show my gratitude. I need to feel, to remember and to give thanks for all that I am being given by so many people.

WE HAVE ONE of our regular planning meetings with the circle of Ceremony Group priestesses for the 2014 Goddess Conference, which is focused on honouring the Great Mother Goddess. We talk about Britannia, one of the original Mother Goddesses of Brigit's Isles. I can feel the deep wounding by patriarchy of our tutelary Mother Goddess. She was taken from Her original essence as a Goddess of Nature, Goddess of the lands and peoples of these islands, and Her image and abilities were altered by the Romans into those of a warrior Goddess with helmet, trident and shield. In Her first images She is depicted as a woman with luscious thighs welcoming invaders to Her bountiful lands, and then She becomes a symbol of resistance to Roman invaders, and a version of Minerva, the Roman Goddess of love and war, who was also transformed from Goddess of love to Goddess of war.

I have a vision of all the Goddesses on Britannia's Wheel being caged in by metal fencing in the centre of the Town Hall. I see us calling each Goddess out from the physical cage in which She has been imprisoned, a cage symbolising the prison of our minds. We want to do some deep healing work bringing the true Britannia out from inside patriarchy's thrall, releasing Her creative and loving Mother energies into the world once again.

In the circle of the ceremony group I have a choice of whether to embody Keridwen, the Goddess of death (!) and rebirth, or Britannia, the Goddess about whom so much antipathy and anger is expressed whenever Her name comes up. Am I able to carry this complex conflict at this time with my dis-ease? Or is it perfect timing? The perfect conjunction of wounding and its healing.

WE HOLD A SECOND Healing Ceremony in Sophie's yurt. This time with Sally, Sophie, Lynne, Michelle, Heloise, Erin, Annabel and Vanda. I want to make a second breast cast with my one breast, but the skin and wound are not yet healed so that will have to wait awhile. We are led by Sally with voice and drum on a deep journey. I am taken to Tibet, one of my soul homes. I find myself weeping and deeply moved. I see several incarnations in that land of the high plateau. I remember. My sadness and grief pour out. Despite all my spiritual work, despite all the meditation in mountain caves and temples, all the spiritual and practical work to balance the suffering in the world, including the taking of the bodhisattva vow several times over to continue to incarnate until the end of all suffering on the earth, my soul people and my world were destroyed. There was the ending of the Bon times and other endings in the Buddhist past and more recently.

> "I love Tibet so much, I love the land. I love the people.
> But when it came to it with all that work, it meant nothing. I could not save my people. I could not save my land."
> I feel absolute despair. I feel distraught, betrayed.
> "What is all that spiritual theory and practice worth if it does not make a difference to how we live, where we live now?"

A FEW DAYS AGO I was writing an article about how I had come to the Goddess path, in my late twenties when I moved to Glastonbury from Wales.

After five years of celibacy I had come to live in Glastonbury and found myself falling in love with an unsuitable man and getting my heart broken. This was something that had happened to me repeatedly in my early 20s. In between times I had changed my life, moving to Wales and spending five years on a Welsh hillside following my newly discovered spiritual path and meditating daily for long lengths of time, like a Tibetan monk up a mountain. It was after having my heart broken again that I came to the realisation that after 18 years of exploring different brands of patriarchal religions, none of them worked for me in the place where I needed them to, in my love relationships, particularly at that time, with men. It was this realisation that changed my life.

THE FEELING of betrayal by male religious paths came now in this memory of a Tibetan past. Inside I could still feel my lack of trust in any of it. Hidden away in my unconscious there were the unhealed words,

"How can I trust any of it if it makes no difference?"

There is the hidden saboteur to faith, to belief, to love.

OTHERS in the group tell me their visions. They see me walking away from places through snow, across flat plains – the Tibetan plateau. I see myself leaving a yurt/tent, to go out through the snow in search of food. It is a bad winter storm and my family are starving. I do not come back. I die in the snow.

I have a brief flash – that in one of the mind-expanding states of consciousness we entered together as monks, as an experiment, I had been sent out into the future on my own, but had been unable to get back into my body. This feeling is somehow related to now. Am I sent out into the future without the communication and connection to my monkish friends – who sit somewhere in time and space waiting for me to come back home and tell them what I have seen/experienced from the future? I have seen them in dreams and in real-time visions at Mount Kailash. And/or am I sent from now into the future to find something to bring back from the future for my people now? Both possibilities seem real in this moment.

As we sit in this yurt on the Crone's Hill in Glastonbury I feel held and nurtured in such a wonderful circle of sisterhood. My feeling is that everyone should have this experience. There are others in this circle who definitely need this experience too. But I must receive this for myself. Later I will help set something up for others to help them heal. Now, I receive this for me. Held in the circle of love by my sisters – my sisters, we are here again. For the first time I feel like I belong in the group, not just as leader, which I know how to be, but as one of the sisters, loved and seen and known.

Someone said a little while ago that they wanted to see me in all my vulnerabilities, and here I am, in this space, nothing hidden. I ask the women if they will look at my scar – my wound that is very visible on my body. I don't mind showing them. My concern is that it might be hard for them to look at the wound. It is not so hard for me.

My scarred (scared, sacred – all such similar words) and wounded body is revealed. They look, they see. I have one left breast and the right side where my right breast used to be, is flattened to the ribs, a diagonal rent with lumpy skin, still healing from the operation. Phew!! It's hard. It's a shocking sight each time I see it myself. No-one flinches visibly. Everyone is kind.

Not wanting the evening to end, but time flies by in this sacred womb space. I want to stay here in this circle of love. I want to live like this. It feels like a very deep healing for my child inside who was not seen or heard.

A FEW DAYS LATER in the dream I am with a group of women on a pilgrimage walking through the countryside. We come to the top of an old brick building which sits above an old mine (mine as in it's mine?) in the woods. We look down over the edge and I can see people walking about on the path far below. I walk/crawl to the edge and look over. It's a long way down and feels scary. Then I feel a foot in my back pushing me towards the edge. I grab hold of another woman's hands, who is hanging onto the grass at the edge of the drop. I turn round to look at the woman whose foot is in my back.

"Take your foot off my back."

She stares back at me implacably.

"I'm getting really scared. Please take your foot away."

I can feel it pushing me over the edge. I feel very afraid.

"Take your foot away!"

I grip the edge of the drop, hard on either side, but I can feel myself being pushed over the edge. In panic I have to do something. I have to twist my body over the edge and away from her foot. I need magic to do this. I move my body in an arc away from her foot, swinging sideways out over the precipice, but not falling over it. I escape from the pressure.

Back from the edge I feel very angry with this woman.

"Why the hell did you do that?"

She looks blank.

"Because I could. You need to feel your fear."

I am so angry with her that I wake up, full of anger. She had no pity for me, for my fear. There is a part of me that is non-empathic – quite cold. The other women are my internal supports, but part of me is potentially destructive to the whole.

In the next few days I have other fear-filled dreams. Mike says that this is a good way to release fear from my body, through the dream. This is all such a Mystery. I meet some old friends on the street, women I was close to when we all had small children and shared the caring together.

One says, *"Sometimes you just can't know why things happen."*

That seems like such an odd statement to me. I don't believe that. Everything has a cause, a reason for being. I know that one day I will understand why all this is happening to me.

Mike goes to his Dad's house for his brother's birthday party. I have no desire to go. I am the one in the family who is/feels excluded. I have been with Mike for 23 years and have never been accepted as I am. They are not my family – such an old familiar thought. I am the child, feeling these things about my own family. I am aware of the projection of my feelings onto Mike's family and they act it all out for me so well. They play their roles beautifully. I remember being a child and a teenager, and wanting to leave my family often. They didn't see me or know me.

It is the Orchard Gathering, the once yearly meeting, when Sisters and Brothers of Avalon, Priestesses and Priests who have studied with us, come to Glastonbury to see each other to share and recognise that we are all part of the Orchard of Avalon, our Goddess Community centred in Avalon. It is lovely to see everyone again.

On the Saturday we hold a Ceremony and journey. We travel across the waters to the Isle of Avalon, where I see hundreds of Priestesses of Avalon. I move slowly across the Sacred Isle until it is my turn to come into the presence of the Lady of Avalon, embodied by Her Priestess Miriam. I feel held and loved by the Lady in my physical form, which is so healing for me. There are three questions:

"What did you receive?" Love.

"What will you create?" A great new Goddess Temple for the Lady.

"What do you desire most for yourself?" That is a good question. Apart from being healed! Lots of things, such as the return of creativity that can lead to many things, new books, grandchildren, a new Temple, new spirals of teaching, renewed and onwards teaching and spirituality, the Keys to Her Mysteries.

Chapter Five

THE HEALING JOURNEY: LIVING IN FEAR OR IN HER CONFIDENCE

I KNOW FROM MY previous experience that cancer is a disease created for our healing on all levels – physical, emotional, mental and spiritual. I know that as well as having the cancer cut out of my body I also need to address all these levels of healing – the food I put in my body, the exercise I take, as well as more psychological and spiritual healing.

I book in to visit weekly Jan Mosja, a psychotherapist I will see for the next few weeks, to explore the hidden emotional issues which underlie my dis-ease. I go to meet Jan who lives in Westbury beneath the White Horse. I get completely lost on the way and so arrive late – resistance is high. Jan lives far enough away from the Glastonbury maelstrom, that she is not engaged in the local gossip, although we have acquaintances in common. She has had breast cancer herself, so knows some of the experiences first hand. She too came out of feminism and Greenham Common, and is now a Buddhist. We have some common reference points and I think I will be able to work with her.

The next day we go to the hospital to meet the oncologist, Dr Cattell, a woman doctor in her 40s. For some reason I don't seem to have understood that oncologists are the ones whose main work is to prescribe chemotherapy drugs to cancer patients. I thought they were there to care for cancer patients in a more whole way, but their area of expertise is actually the administration of toxic drugs. As she talks to me I notice that I am sitting on a low chair and she is sitting right in front of and above me, on the edge of the consulting couch. I note her power-over body language. She wants to impress her point of view upon me, telling me what I need and what I must do. She is giving me no energetic room for thought or to disagree. I am sensitive to these things and I wonder why she is behaving like this. What is she afraid of, that I might disagree with her? Or is it that I am just one amongst so many to be talked to, persuaded, cajoled, put through the system?

She says that my cancer can go to the USA for further investigation, to see how genetically susceptible I am to the cancer's recurrence, that means that I will be a part of someone's clinical trial. I know the euphemisms for these offered opportunities, when you become part of some drug researcher's clinical trial without really understanding that is primarily what is happening, rather than it being necessarily in your best interests.

When the results come back the choices I have will depend on what they find. I remember last time being offered Tamoxifen to take for five years. That was when I first knew that I was taking part in a drugs test without being told that was what was happening. I took Tamoxifen for a few weeks, but it made me feel so bloated and unwell that I stopped taking it. I'm a sensitive soul. When I stopped then the oncologist Dr Whip said that it was okay to stop, and that it would be another drug to have in reserve if there was any recurrence.

Once again all the information they give me involves percentages. They have no way of telling me what is going to happen to me as an individual. After having had surgery to remove the cancer if nothing further is done, then 73 out of 100 women will be alive in ten years' time. If I take Letrozole this would add 5% to my chances of survival. Chemotherapy would add 6%. Taken together they would add 9% to my chances of survival for 10 years, which doesn't seem like too much of a difference for all the pain and anguish that chemo and Letrozole can add to life. As I have already had chemo before they would have to give me a different combination of drugs, as the ones I was given last time may or may not have damaged the muscles of my heart, and twice would not be good. Treatment would last for 4-6 months.

I want to talk to someone who is unbiased and not in the pay of drug companies, which is where it seems to be at in hospitals these days. Doctors and hospitals are all funded and maintained by drug companies who are in it for profit. Why else would there be no room in the NHS for other kinds of healing therapies, for acupuncture, massage, Chinese medicine, many kinds of alternative therapies, that are not based in the manufacture and enormous profits of pharmaceutical drug companies?

There is no joined-up thinking here, no continuity of care. I cannot believe how, for all the fancy new buildings, cancer care here in Taunton Hospital has not improved, and in fact has become worse in the 15 years since I last had it. At least then I did not feel pressured to make such instantaneous decisions. Then I felt that the people treating me cared for me as a human being. Now I feel I am just another person who has cancer, who needs to be fed through the system and dealt with as a number, not as a human being.

AS I THINK ABOUT all this I realise that it comes down to this – shall I live a life of fear? Shall I live a life of adventure? Shall I live a life with complete trust in the Lady? Trust that whichever way we go is the way to go? Not try to manipulate outcomes, but do the best I can, Lady, to live with you?

And to have chemotherapy now would prevent me from being present at the Goddess Conference.

"I can't do that, Lady. You come first.
Lady, Lady, I pray for your help in making these decisions.
Please show me the way. Guide me."

FOR THE NEXT WEEK I have so much confusion in my mind. Each time I go to the hospital I am spun out with the choices I don't know how to make. Before going I am quite calm and then everything they say sends me into turmoil. I have moments of clarity and then they disappear into confusion. I feel the confrontation between my fearful personality and my Dweller on the Threshold and my surrendered Soul, the Angel of Her Presence. I feel the tussle for power. Who shall win? Soul or Personality? Personality or Soul?

My son Torquil and his girlfriend Lahla come down from London to visit for a couple of days. I love him so much. He is such a lovely person and it is just the way he is. He has no qualms about hugging me and holding my hand as we walk down the street and he's always been like that. We have a love relationship that makes me very happy. Lahla is bright and beautiful and a young designer. They warm my heart.

The next week I go to see my own doctor in the local health centre, Dr Montaignon, who shows no interest in my dis-ease. I am just another patient. She does not even know what cancer support services are available in our area. I am astonished. She has been in this surgery for several years. Something like 3 out of 4 people will experience cancer at some time in their lives and this doctor has no clue as to what help is available locally. She advises me to look online to find what is available. Once again there is no joined up thinking between the hospital and the local doctors. What is the NHS doing these days?

This is so unlike my first experience of breast cancer care when I was supported so amazingly well by my then doctor, Phil Jackson. See my book *Breast Cancer: Hanging on by a Red Thread* (Ariadne Publications) for full details. Phil has now retired but comes to see me to see how I am, which is very kind. It turns out that his son, Matthew Jackson, is now an acupuncturist, osteopath and Chinese herbalist. I decide to go and see Matt as acupuncture and Chinese herbs were very helpful last time. I need to take hold of my own healing.

Later that day I go to see Jan the psychotherapist in Westbury and this time I find my way there easily. I talk about my fear and the battle I feel is raging inside me between life and death, between wanting to heal by loving the wounded places better, rather than by fighting the cancer. I have a deep need to face and heal my fear. Jan says that the lymphocytes that clear debris away in the body have heart-shaped nuclei. I like that. This time I want to love my cancer cells, to embrace them, heal them, rather than see them devoured by ravenous dogs, as I did last time.

We follow a line of my experiences from childhood, remembering fears, feelings of isolation, the times I wanted to die. I remember at the age of 8, packing a small suitcase, wanting to leave home, going in the car into the countryside with my family, but being unable to run away, not being able to actually do it. I was too afraid. I remember wanting to die over some boy when I was 19, and then with another at 22, and then at 38 over the father of my children. My death wish is vibrating in my body now. I am being undermined, betrayed by my hidden emotions acting in the body. I have something in my body that betrays me. As I drive home I put my foot down and go fast, something I haven't done for a while. I feel freer.

ON THE WEEKEND we hold a Breast and Bellies day in the Goddess Hall so that women can come and make plaster casts of their own breasts and bellies, which they can then decorate as they wish. We will have an exhibition of the casts in the 2012 Mother Goddess Conference. Everyone divides into groups of four or five women who create the casts for each other, helping and supporting each woman as she reveals her breasts and belly in whatever state they are in, holding each woman as they are nervous, as tears fall, or as they are thrilled and confident. It's a wonderful experience. By the end we have a large group of casts of all shapes and sizes drying out slowly in the Hall.

ON MY NEXT VISIT to Jan we talk about my friendships with women, which often ended through my betrayal of them or their betrayal of me. I remember a teenage friendship with Lesley, whose parents I really liked because they talked to me as a person, something that didn't happen in our house. I really wanted them to be my parents. However in my desperation to get away from home, when I left for university, I left all my childhood girlfriends behind, including Lesley. A couple of years later she tried to reconnect with me. She had married and was living in Bermuda. I had then moved into my 'spiritual life' phase and because I thought her interests were too ordinary I dismissed her without qualms and didn't reconnect. I can still cringe at the thought of my rejection of her.

Later friendships with women often turned to dust as competition entered in. One of the first was Frances whom I met at university. I began my spiritual path in company with her and her then husband William. In the seventies I betrayed her by sleeping with her ex-husband and later she betrayed me many times. Competition entered in for the attentions of men, for moral and spiritual superiority. I continued to search for the woman who would be my *best friend*, just like we women are conditioned to want as children. I loved Diana, but with her family's military background she was always moving on to fresh fields. After a couple of years of close friendship she found a new better friend than me. I felt so hurt, abandoned and lost without her love. This process of looking for and doing anything to try and keep a best friend is wonderfully explored in Phyllis Chesler's ground-breaking book, *Woman's Inhumanity to Woman*.

As we talk Jan suggests that loving Goddess has provided me with a safe archetypal way to relate to the feminine, to women on an expanded level and not on the personal.

Things have changed over the years as my understanding of my own motivations has improved. Now I do have personal women friends, who have come through our connected love of Goddess. I am allowing them into the deep places of my heart as individuals and as a group, a circle of women friends. And then there are the women I love, who live at a distance, some far away. These women are soul sisters, where friendship is always there when we meet again in the liminal in between, travelling worlds, after a time apart – Leona Graham, Apela Colorado, Anique Radiant Heart, Edwene Gaines. Perhaps we would not be such good friends if we lived with each other all the time, but who knows?

A COUPLE OF DAYS LATER in a regression with Annabel I go back to when I was 2-3 years old, living in Derwent Gardens in Low Fell. I can see the front door on the right, leading into the house, and I walk through the entrance going down the hallway into the kitchen. I am sitting in a high chair. My parents are there, arguing. Daddy is angry. Mammy is shouting back. I feel very frightened. They are arguing and I am terrified. My sister on the other side of the table is also frightened and has her head down, looking at the tablecloth. I am so afraid.

I think he will explode with anger and kill us all.

Annabel guides me through the feelings, asking my father's soul to take back the anger, to take back the fear. I find this almost impossible as my adult and my child selves see him as so wounded that he will not be able to cope with taking it all back. It will kill him. Then I remember him killing my puppy Kim, when I was 8-10 years old. The puppy bit the next door neighbour and they thought he was dangerous, rather than just a puppy playing, so they had him put down. I remember coming home and Daddy telling me. I sat on his knee and cried and he hugged me as he said,

"Sometimes you have to be cruel to be kind",

There is a line that I have worked to understand over many years. And this was the only time that I ever remember my father hugging me, when he had killed my beloved dog! I spent a lot of my life trying to persuade him and other remote men to be affectionate and loving towards me, when they were wounded and incapable.

During the session I was eventually able to give the anger back to him and the fear. I asked him to come every day and hold my hand. I asked him to hug me and play with me. My positive child is very strong and playful. My wounded child is a frightened little girl. I cry a lot and release lots of fear.

Later that day I go to see Matt Jackson for acupuncture. He is kind and very like his Dad in many ways, dedicated to healing and helping others. I find it funny that once again I will owe their family a lot for the healing help that they give me. Matt recommends that I take Chinese herbs. He says that there is some good new information coming through about the cancer healing properties of certain kinds of mushrooms and he will find out more about them for me. I am willing to give them a go, as last time herbs were very helpful. I decide to have weekly sessions of acupuncture with Matt to get my physical energy moving.

THE NEXT DAY we priestesses decorate the Goddess Hall for Oestre in green and gold, colours of springtime and fire. In the afternoon I have a metamorphic technique session with Ann James, one of our Second Spiral students. She lightly rubs my feet in circles down the inside edges. It is a deeply relaxing session and I feel that I have released something that I was holding onto. It is great.

ON FRIDAY EVENING I give a talk with slide images to the Second Spiral students about the ancient Goddess. It is a presentation I love to give as we see so many glorious images of Her from the earliest times coming all the way through from Palaeolithic to Neolithic to modern times. It lasts 2 hours, there is so much to impart and only begins to touch on the subject. I could do four hours, but everyone would fall asleep. I feel I want to give more talks and I don't want to teach courses anymore. I am holding directly contradictory feelings. I want to potter along for a time doing the garden, meeting people, hanging out, exploring consciousness. It's what I need to do now.

I meet one of my sister priestesses, Alexandra, and we have a great conversation. I tell her about our pilgrimage to Mount Kailash in Tibet in 2007 and all the amazing adventures that happened there. She says that it sounds like, in my near-death experiences in the snow blizzard on the mountain there, I went through the gateways into the Bardo state of consciousness as I prepared to die. I did return but I left part of myself behind. This is something that Koko also thought.

WE ARE DUE TO GO to the hospital again on Tuesday and fear is rising in me again. It is a fear that comes from having to stand/live in my truth. I don't want their pills or their chemotherapy and the consequence of this is that I might die. I feel my reaction is a reaction to my father, to his authority over me. They are just people. There is something about me living my truth, following my intuition wherever that might take me.

This is one of the deep lessons of this journey and I do find it difficult. I want to be safe. I don't want to die. I want to live. Can I trust myself completely to find the route through all this?

"Help me Lady to find the way through! To really believe in this deep inner knowing."

THERE IS A telephone call from the hospital about having an extra appointment tomorrow afternoon when I go to see the oncologist again for the results of the DNA testing for the likelihood of recurrence of the cancer. When I ask what this extra appointment is for, I am told that it's a chemotherapy appointment!! I am completely shocked. What do they know that I don't? Is this telling me that chemotherapy is what I need, must have? Or is the DNA test they made rigged to produce this outcome? Will they ask me to take chemo because they believe I will need it? Is that true? Can I stay true to myself and my inner feelings? Can I act from an authentic place, not from fear or resistance?

I feel angry that this is the way that they have let me know what they want me to do. And the way they give me no time for consideration or thought. They have made this appointment as standard, even though they know it would make little difference in my case. How can they do that? In the evening I go to Five Rhythms and dance out my fear. It feels very good to release this from my body.

In the night I dream that a stone head of the Goddess speaks to me as an Embodiment. I hold her in my arms and the lips begin to move and the face comes alive. It is all true. You are real! Not just a stone statue. Then I found a tape recorder underneath her that was speaking the words. Did that mean it was all false? But her lips had moved and her eyes had opened even though she was made of stone.

HAPPY EQUINOX! Day of decisions! I love the timing of these things, even down to the date of appointments, then I know that it is meaningful in ways more important than just being there on any day. Help me, Lady, to choose wisely.

At the hospital we once again are sitting in a room, me on a low chair with the doctor on the bed, looking down at me. I move so that we are on a more equal level. We go through my DNA results. My score is 27 – in the grey area. I have an intermediate 16% risk of relapse. Chemo is not so helpful, but they do highly recommend that I take the anti-oestrogen drug Letrozole for five years. I hear the words five years and that is the signal that they are making me part of a drug test. This may not be what I need. After five years the recurrence risk will have lessened by 18%.

Letrozole is offered to post-menopausal women, Tamoxifen is offered to pre-menopausal women. As well as reducing circulating oestrogen in the body Letrozole also leaches calcium from the bones and so is not good if you have low calcium levels. I have found this out for myself, no-one tells me. They reassure me that I can have a DEXA scan for bone density and if it's low then they can support my bones appropriately. What does that mean?

I ask them what my recurrence chances will be if I don't take Letrozole, but they have no data to answer this question. The DNA test assumes that everyone who has taken the test will take Letrozole. No comparisons have been made between those who do and those who don't. Again to me this means it's a trial by a pharmaceutical company to get more people to buy their drug.

I HAVE ANOTHER session with Jan. We get to a place where the pill they want me to take seems huge to me. Jan took it and she sees it as a tiny pill. I move into the place where I feel I am being poisoned by the system. I am taking in bad medicine, bad food, bad milk. I remember at junior school having to drink milk that had been warmed from frozen on the radiator pipes. It was sour and tasted awful. I never drank milk on its own again. I see this now as a good thing – milk is not the best food for humans. Taking in badness with food. Remembering not wanting to eat meat as a child, putting it into my apron pocket. Never really caring too much about food.

WE HAVE A GREAT Enchantress weekend calling in the Green Fire of Springtime, exploring the fires of creativity and life. I encourage everyone to use their voices, move their bodies as we call in Goddess, to work with words, speaking fast and slow, as animals and as birds, singing. On the Sunday we go to Lamyatt Beacon in beautiful sunshine. It is sunny and warm as we walk the ridge of the Beacon.

Later in the morning there is a small moment. I react to a student's repeated negative complaining on this beautiful day, and in exasperation I swear at her, "Fuck off!" It is this, my unthinking, non-compassionate release of my anger, that actually signals the beginning of the healing revolution in me that will continue for the next two and more years. I don't see this at the time, of course, but it is through these small moments when I react without awareness that the Lady leads me to my deeper wounding.

We have a good day connecting into the land, to the trees, sunshine and the green fire rising within the earth and to our renewed creativity. It is wonderful being in Her nature and by the end of the day we feel full of life energy.

CANCER THRIVES in a toxic environment in the body and my body must be toxic. Although I have been vegetarian for 40 years my body must hold some toxicity from hormones and pesticides in food, even though I try to eat mostly organic foods. And the toxicity from having chemotherapy all those years ago may still reside in my liver. So a physical cleanse sounds like a good idea. It's something else that I can do to help myself, rather than just waiting for others to help me.

On Sunday evening I begin a week-long body cleanse with the help of Araura Berkeley, a local health and colonic therapist. The cleanse involves eating no food for a week, just drinking fresh vegetable juices and taking vitamins and supplements, with colonics and a liver cleanse. Mike plans to do the same cleanse the week after me. From Sunday night I eat no solid food. I take a combination of cleansing drinks – flaxseed and bentonite clay, apple juice and juiced vegetables – carrots, beetroot, celery, peppers and herbs. This goes on three times a day for the next 5 days plus flaxseed oil in the mornings and vitamins. On Monday morning I experience a colonic for the first time. Wow! That is something else.

After the colonic I go to see Jan, but I don't have much to say. She talks about my feeling safe to receive. I can relax and feel safe in the world. In my mind I repeat the words, "*I am open to receive.*"

ON TUESDAY I have another regression session with Annabel. In the journey we go to our childhood house in Derwent Gardens again. I climb the stairs to the bedroom. I am very small. I am a happy little girl, but I am worried.

"*I am afraid. He comes in the night. He picks me up. He's very big. When I'm crying he carries me backwards and forwards, rocking me to sleep. Sometimes it's alright. But one time when I don't stop crying he shouts at me. I feel very scared. My mother is asleep. She doesn't care. He's barking at me like a mad dog. I am scared.*

He doesn't know any better. He doesn't look after me. You (my mother) didn't stop him. Nobody knows."

My little girl gets very afraid, late at night when she's on her own.

My mother speaks to me.

"*I am sorry, I didn't know. I was too tired. I didn't know you were afraid. You are too sensitive.*"

"*I just wanted to be held in the night, to be loved, to feel safe. I wasn't safe in the night.*"

When I was older my father continued to bark at me.

"*Kathryn, behave! Be quiet! Shut up!*"

MY CHILDHOOD wasn't all bad. Some of it was good. There were fun times, playing at the seaside, playing in the snow. He loved me in the only way he could.

I hold you, little Katy. You are safe with me. I will protect you and keep you safe. You can relax in my embrace.

WITHIN A DAY OR TWO of beginning the cleanse I really don't like the taste of the vegetable juices at all. They are almost unbearable to drink and by the end of the five days the taste is hideous. I feel that the poison from the chemotherapy last time is being released into my body and I feel poisoned in a similar way to how I felt then. There is an awful metallic taste in my mouth nearly all the time. During the week ages old toxic matter that has been stuck to the walls of my intestines comes out. I had thought that I really wouldn't have much of that as I eat well, but during the colonics loads of strange stuff comes out that may have been there for years, including loads of bile and then white cholesterol as the gall bladder and liver start to cleanse.

Who would have thought a week could take so long to live through? It is awful and I don't yet feel the high that is supposed to arrive with cleansing the body.

I feel like yuck. On the Sunday evening I drink my final drink and during the evening four times take the Epsom salts, olive oil and grapefruit juice, which is to flush out toxins from the liver. After an hour or so I go to the loo and then go almost continuously about 20 times. It's not painful, just continuous. I can't imagine where it's all coming from – my liver I presume.

At last it is almost over! It is hard. So much stuff has come out of my body, so much crap out of my liver and gall bladder. I've never been to the loo so many times in such a short space of time. The final colonic is full of small green stones and white cholesterol coming out of the gall bladder and the liver. Araura is a really great colonic therapist. She is so matter of fact and unfazed by the contents of intestines, whereas me, delicate Taurean who loves beauty, finds this whole thing very distasteful.

DURING THE WEEK I have strong colourful dreams almost every night. The last one ends with me losing my coat, and wearing someone else's old ill-fitting purple boots. I am trying to get to my car which has somehow moved from the road it was on, down to the bottom of a great precipice. A man tells me that the only way to get to my car is to walk from here up to the top of the hill, much higher up, and then go down the other side to the car. He says that it will take me 10 hours to walk there. I will be walking in my ill-fitting boots. I think that I don't need to walk this road alone.

On my next visit to Jan we explore this dream. I understand that the ill-fitting purple boots are the boots for my illness, to help me walk through it all. My car is my body, a healthy body, which has fallen over a precipice and is now in a new place. What does it mean to climb the hill to get back to my car? As a Goddess woman how do I climb the hill?

I go through different thoughts about what this might mean. I think it means that I need a new spiritual practice, but I don't want to do that on my own any more. I had years of meditating alone and don't want to do that any more. I know now that I can get help from others. I can journey with others. I can join someone else's meditation or spiritual development class, but I know no-one who is offering the kinds of experiences that I am interested in.

Or – idea! idea! – I can take others with me on the journey of Self-exploration. I remember a vision I had one day about six months ago, when I was out walking in the fields by the River Brue. I was looking towards Glastonbury Tor from the river. On that day the sun was shining on high banks of clouds beyond the Tor, and beyond and above the clouds I could see high snow-covered mountain peaks – the Mountains of Avalon. I had the realisation then that in the interior of the Isle of Avalon there are Mountains.

To respond to my dream from Her, for that is where I believe that many dreams come from, I decide to create a 10 Hour Meditation/Journey Day Exploring the Mountains of Avalon. I book the Goddess Hall for a 10 Hours day in May and begin to advertise it, not being sure what will happen or what we will do, but knowing this is what She wants for me and for others.

I also come up with the idea of a Four Day Deep Healing Retreat bringing together several different healing techniques to help people who are physically, psychologically and spiritually unwell. To offer some deep healing for the soul, body and mind. I will ask other priestesses and healers to help. I store this idea for the future.

FOR THE NEXT two to three weeks after the cleanse I feel very exhausted and have long vivid dreams on many nights. Some are meaningful and others are just intense. Mike begins his cleanse and also has deep and meaningful experiences. By the end we are both slimmed down, tired and relaxed.

On my father's birthday April 12th, (he died in 1984), I dream that a group of young men are telling me how great the play was which I had produced, that they had come to see the night before. They are obviously very intrigued by all the complex layers. They ask, *"Was the play a Pleiad?"* Yesterday Mike had said that a Pleiad is a collective noun for seven important people, but in the dream a Pleiad is when there are at least three synchronicities happening at the same time. I am laughing in the dream, saying that there are far more than three going on in this play and the more that you are in the flow of the Goddess then the more synchronicities occur. The young men get very excited.

Sunday 14th April is the anniversary of my mother Eileen's death one year ago. I pray for the peace of her soul. She did her best fighting for me with my father, arguing with him, but for me it wasn't enough.

IN MY NEXT therapy session with Jan I remember when I was a very small baby, when I felt completely safe in my body, before life piled in and I had to armour myself. When I was first born I was so happy to be alive on the earth. I have experienced this several times in regressions. I love being here. The Earth is one of my favourite places in the Universe to be. I remember and feel this safe, defenceless place once again and then move forward in my life. I can feel my armouring, my alertness for danger, for the sound of him (my father) coming up the stairs. I feel my defensive body postures in my body now, the tension in my muscles. Jan leads me skilfully back to the place of defencelessness, because at 65 years of age I seriously don't need the armouring.

The thought also comes again that I don't want to teach at the moment, to be responsible for others. I want to do nothing for a while, but relax and hang out in the garden. Of course, then as soon as that thought is expressed, I start thinking of new courses that I would like to teach.

I LISTEN TO Gabrielle Roth, the creator of Five Rhythms talking about having lung cancer. It makes me think that if she, who has danced her whole life, can get cancer, then anyone can. She said that there was a part of her soul that she'd forgotten to take care of and she had had to make a soul retrieval to find it. I think that there is a message there for me too about retrieving a part of my soul that I don't know about or haven't taken care, in caring for everyone else.

ON SATURDAY 21st April it is my 65th birthday. Mike has bought me nine standing stones, which we choose from a stone yard near Willesden. Peter Wood and two young men dig the holes and erect the stones for me. I choose the positions of each under the oak tree. Eight in mostly the eight directions with the ninth wandering stone – nine for the Nine Morgens. The circle is beautiful and the stones are a gorgeous pinky grey colour with waving lines of shining lights inside them. Already energy is being drawn into the circle from all directions and is spiralling around in a sunwise direction. I love it. Thank you, my beloved Mike, for such a great present.

I HAVE A GOOD healing week. On Wednesday I go to see Jan and we talk about my sister Ann. She recently sent me a copy of her diary from 1960 when I was 13 years old. It is amazing to read. Her concerns were all about school and what we did as a family that I have forgotten. We did acrobatics together and played card and board games, and games with the parents. There were lots of car trips on the weekends and family holidays. Our parents seemed to be out a lot, playing golf or just out, and we were left to look after ourselves. I mostly remember Ann being critical and controlling of me. She sent the diary with a note, saying, *"To my long lost sister."* How poignant! I never knew she felt like that. I realise that although she felt she lost her sister, I too lost my sister – I had rejected her and her criticism when she left home to go to university. We lost each other. It is all interesting to recognise.

In the evening Lorraine and Michelle give me a lovely healing, which is deeply relaxing. Mike is staying at his dad's tonight. I have no sleep anxiety, being on my own. Perhaps that fear is now all healed. On Thursday I go to see a Mexican healer Maestro Constantino, who is visiting Healing Waters, down the road. The healing is held in a very hot room full of people in need of healing, some desperately so. He comes into the room all muffled up in layers of clothing although its boiling hot – he's used to the heat in Mexico after all. He walks slowly around the circle, looks people in the eye and then pokes them in different places in the body. I get one poke in the ribs, but I can't feel much from it. Others cry or collapse back onto their chairs.

I feel more when I ask about the cause of my dis-ease. He says that I already know the cause. It is to do with my necklace. I am wearing a Goddess pendant made by Sue Quatermass. I feel a bit disappointed by this – I don't want to hear that it has to do with Goddess, but perhaps he means that it is She who has taken me there, not Her as a cause. I didn't get too much out of this experience, whereas others obviously got a lot. I also didn't like the way that he was surrounded by adoring women, all looking after his every need, too guru/devotee for me.

On Friday I go with Michelle and Heloise to the Spa at Shepton Mallet, which is wonderful. It's a birthday present from Torky with a good massage and a flotation wrap. We have a creative Ceremony group meeting planning the Heart of the Mysteries day for the Goddess Conference. It's so delightful having these days with this circle of women. Matt brings me more Chinese herbs to take. He is so good. I am feeling well, feeling good.

I can feel anxiety in my solar plexus too – the pressure to be good, to do, to succeed.

"I hold you in my arms, little girl. I love you as you are. You are safe with me."

WE PICK IONA up from the airport. She is home from India. It's so lovely to have her back again and she is in a much better place in herself than before. She brings back lots of Indian goodies to sell and make herself some money. Her heart seems much happier. We miss the Goddess Temple Beltane Eve Ceremony as we are driving back from the airport, but on May Day Mike and I jump the Beltane fire together in the middle of our stone circle, making our commitment to each other to travel together once again around the Wheel of the Year for a year and a day. Our love grows stronger each year.

I go to see Jan for my regular session, and unhook from another colleague, who hurt me so badly. I open my heart more. Its feels like a section of my heart which has been closed down since my childhood experiences is unfolding, relaxing, unfurling, opening for the first time since babyhood. I have the feeling of having been unborn, or being born so full of potential and then being shut down by hard experiences. Gradually in my life I have clawed my way (that's an expression) out of my wounding to show my true nature, but that part has remained hidden away. It is now relaxing and opening and I can feel this as a physical sensation in my chest, around my heart chakra.

I drive home full of feelings of love. I feel wonderful. As I come in the door

Mike asks me to help move the carpet where Sasha, our aged cat, has begun to pee in her old age. He hustles me to do it now, before I have barely got my foot in the door. I get angry and tell him to, *"Back off!"* All my open heart and open emotions, and anger arises so quickly unprompted. It is funny, not in the moment, but in the way my anger flared so readily.

Chapter Six

THE SACRED LANDSCAPE TEMPLE OF RHANDIRMWYN

❦

WE ARE OFF to Rhandirmwyn for our Beltane Enchantress weekend – four days in one of the most beautiful valleys in Britain, with my students Tina, Mary, John, Fran, Rosie and Louise. Mike and I have been here often. It is a harmonious and sacred landscape that we first visited many years ago. Through the length of the valley there are several prominent hills, rocks and the winding River Towy (Tywi), which mark a series of chakra points within this Sacred Landscape Temple, described by Peter Dawkins of the Gatekeeper Trust. At these chakra points the energy in the land is really strong and wild, in this more remote part of the world. The devic and mineral realms are pronounced here and it's a perfect place to learn how to open awareness to the Otherworld, in a wild and sacred landscape.

Mike and I almost bought a second house in Rhandirmywn 25 years ago, when the Goddess of this Sacred Landscape Temple, the Lady of this Welsh Afallon, called us so strongly, and an old Welsh Methodist chapel came up for sale for £20,000. It needed a lot of work doing to it and would have taken many weekends away from Glastonbury to make it habitable. At that price it was very tempting, but the call to fully serve the Lady of Avalon in Glastonbury was just that bit stronger. It became clear that we couldn't serve two Mystresses at the same time, so we didn't buy the house. In recent years it has been put up for sale for £300,000, and is still unfinished.

We arrive on Friday and I take everyone up to Junction Pool where the white splurging waters of Afon Towy, flowing down from the Llyn Brianne Reservoir, meet the dark peaty waters of Afon Pysgotwr (fisherman), which flow down from the high hills. They meet and mix in a wide pool and flow on together through the valley as the River Towy. It's been raining a lot and the rivers are deep and fast-flowing, so it's not possible to cross over the river to the great red Ajna rock which sits between the two rivers. Many times I have sat and lain on this rock in sunshine, wind and rain and opened my Third Eye to journey through the veils into the interior worlds, but not today. And I don't want to lose anyone to the river, and not on the first day!

We are staying at Ty Rogof, a stone house almost opposite the village shop. A few years ago it was dilapidated and uncared for, but the owners have done it up and now it's a lovely place where we can stay all together, with Fran in her van.

On Saturday we have a good sharing about how we are all feeling and then go higher up the valley to Dinas Hill where there is an RSPB Nature Reserve. This is one of the most beautiful parts of the landscape, with a high conical hill covered in trees, and the river Tywi curving around the bottom of the hill. This hill is known as the hideout of Twm Sion Cati, (c1530-1609), the Welsh Robin Hood, who was said to rob the rich to give to the poor, although sometimes the poor didn't receive any of the things he is said to have stolen. Twm Siôn Cati was of noble blood, a poet and a heraldic bard of renown. Many of the escapades attributed to him were a confluence of local legends. He was the illegitimate son of Catherine (Cati) and the squire of Porth y Ffynnon (Fountain Gate), near Tregaron. He is named as the son of his mother, indicating a matrilineal family. According to recent research, it is possible that he hid in the famous cave on Dinas Hill to escape religious persecution, rather than to avoid the wrath of people who had been tricked by him.

The grass and the trees of Dinas Hill are bright green, coming into the greening of springtime a bit later than in Somerset. The waters of the river are completely clear, the small pebbles and rocks on the bottom of the river bed sparkling with clarity. We walk on the wooden trackway over the marshy ground and onto a small area of open ground beside the river. Here beneath the trees we call in the Goddesses on Britannia's Wheel, welcoming them to be with us on this beautiful day, running back and forth across the grass to the centre. We are laughing and shrieking with Her greenfire energies.

We continue walking on along the small path through the trees beside the river as it narrows and becomes fast-flowing, as it descends between big rocks which have fallen from steep hillsides. White waters churn around rocks, birds hop in and out of the edges of the river, catching the spray. Water bubbles catch the sunlight and fill with bright colours, creating amazing shapes. Everything glistens with light. My heart opens more and more to Her nature and the Wildness of Her Spirit.

Halfway along this length of the river we climb up to Twm Siôn Cati's cave, which is away from the river, high up the hill. It is a very steep ascent to the cave, which is surrounded by trees and boulders. We crawl into the back of the cave through a narrow gap between fallen rocks. Part of the cave roof has collapsed, and it is now open to the elements. The cave itself has obviously been visited over many years, as evidenced by the many carvings – one reads 1832. We stay there for a while imagining what it might have been like to live there.

We climb back down to follow the path that winds around the hill, rising away from and then dipping closer to the river, as it descends into a deeper gulley. Tina, Louise, John and I climb down the steep slopes of the river gorge to be right next to Her spuming river. We shout strong joyful prayers into the thundering river. I pray to Her wildness for a larger Goddess Temple in Glastonbury. I pray for courage, energy, strength. Excitement fills my soul. I feel amazing, wonderful. We are all invigorated by the energy of the river.

We stand beside Junction Pool for a while on the opposite bank from where we were yesterday evening and feel the bliss of Her wild nature. Then we climb up and away from the river and continue our circumambulation of Dinas Hill, through the groves of trees just coming into bud. From the exit to the Nature Reserve we drive up to Llyn Brianne Reservoir, higher up the river. Because of the winter rains the reservoir is full and the overflowing waters are sliding down over the edge of run off from the Dam. They create beautiful patterns as they slide down the long slope.

We return to our holiday home for an early supper and then in the evening go for a walk along the lower River Tywi. We sit on the river bank and I introduce the students to a wonderful natural, wilderness phenomenon, a way of easily entering the Otherworld. We gaze at the river waters flowing by in front of us, eyes open, focussing on the flow of the waters. Then look beyond to the other side of the river with its still trees and fields. As our eyes adjust to the contrast between the flowing water and the still bank, the opposite bank itself begins to move and opens like a gateway into the Otherworld. Continued gazing and moving our open eyes back and forth creates a bit of dizziness at first and then consciousness opens out. We can look into other times and spaces with our open eyes. We tell each other what we see.

We walk further on to the deep gorge between Penryn and the Solar Plexus chakra hill. This is one of my favourite places in the valley, which we found accidentally one day while out walking by the river, on another visit. The river has been flowing calmly for a couple of miles from Junction Pool, through the broadening valley. Then it turns a corner to skirt the foot of the steep Solar Plexus Hill and flows into a deep dark gulley, the sides of which are perpendicular and never see sunlight. The only way to follow the river here is in a canoe. It's like an entrance into a dark cave, a great place to give away all that's no longer needed into the darkness of Her Underworld places, to emerge beyond into the light of healing and grace. Once again standing upon a high piece of ground above the river between the trees we call in the Goddesses of the Wheel.

THE NEXT DAY we drive south through Llandovery and over the rolling Welsh Hills into the Black Mountains of South Wales and the beautiful lake of Llyn y Fan Fach, which lies high up in a hollow in the mountains. We drive along the single-track road, over cattle grids and as far as the parking place at the foot of the hills. We take our time walking up the track towards the lake with no stress. The river that flows out from the lake falls between rocks down the hillside. The sun is shining. Dippers and grey wagtails hop from rock to rock, splashing in the spray. All is well with the world. We walk past the small trout fishery which is fed by the waters of the lake and then on upwards to the lake high above. There are spaces on this hillside where the silence is almost deafening in its stillness. I love this place. My heart opens out again and again.

The lake nestles at the foot of great high grassy and rocky cliffs that rise up on three sides around the lake. They are green and red and black. A low dam wall has been built across the fourth side, creating the reservoir, with the tumbling river opening out to the lower valleys. The clean waters that once flowed to the households below are now used for the small trout farm. Today the sun is shining on the small wavelets that ripple in the breeze across the surface of the lake, creating wild swirling patterns

I show the students once again how to allow the opening of the Otherworld to sight and vision, by gazing wide-eyed at the moving surface of the lake, then looking at the surrounding high cliffs. As we hold our gaze the cliffs themselves begin to revolve, moving rapidly to the left. A gateway opens and we can enter the Otherworldly realms. For this is the Creation site where Nelferch, the Lady of the Lake, emerged from beneath the waters, bringing domesticated animals with Her into the world.

Here is Her story told on the Sacred Texts website **www.sacred-texts.com/**:

IN A FARM not far from this lake lived in the olden times a widow, with an only son whose name was Gwyn. When this son grew up, he was often sent by his mother to look after the cattle grazing. The place where the sweetest food was to be found was near the lake of Llyn y Fan Fach, and it was there that the mild-eyed beasts wandered whenever they had their will. One day when Gwyn was walking along the banks of the mere, watching the kine cropping the short grass, he was astonished to see a Lady standing in the clear smooth water, some distance from the land. She was the most beautiful creature that he had ever set eyes upon, and she was combing her long hair with a golden comb, the unruffled surface of the lake serving her as a mirror.

He stood on the brink, gazing fixedly at the Maiden, and straightway knew that he loved Her. As he gazed, he unconsciously held out to her the

barley-bread and cheese which his mother had given him before he left home. The Lady gradually glided towards him, but shook Her head as he continued to hold out his hand, and saying:

> Cras dy fara,   O thou of the crimped bread,
> Nid hawdd fy nala,   It is not easy to catch me,

She dived under the water, and disappeared from his sight.

He went home, full of sorrow, and told his mother of the beautiful vision which he had seen. As they pondered over the strange words used by the mysterious Lady before she plunged out of sight, they came to the conclusion that there must have been some spell connected with the hard-baked bread, and the mother advised her son to take with him some toes or unbaked dough, when next he went to the lake.

Next morning, long before the sun appeared above the crest of the mountain, Gwyn was by the lake with the dough in his hand, anxiously waiting for the Lady of the Lake to appear above the surface. The sun rose, scattering with her powerful beams the mists which veiled the high ridges around, and mounted high in the heavens. Hour after hour the youth watched the waters, but hour after hour there was nothing to be seen except the ripples raised by the breeze and the sunbeams dancing upon them. By the late afternoon despair had crept over the watcher, and he was on the point of turning his footsteps homeward when to his intense delight the Lady again appeared above the sunlit ripples. She seemed even more beautiful than before, and Gwyn, forgetting in admiration of her fairness all that he had carefully prepared to say, could only hold out his hand, offering to her the dough. She refused the gift with a shake of the head as before, adding the words:

> Llaith dy fara,   O thou of the moist bread,
> Ti ni fynna.   I will not have thee.

THEN SHE *vanished under the water, but before she sank out of sight, she smiled upon the youth so sweetly and so graciously that his heart became fuller than ever of love. As he walked home slowly and sadly, the remembrance of her smile consoled him and awakened the hope that when next she appeared she would not refuse his gift. He told his mother what had happened, and she advised him, inasmuch as the lady had refused both hard-baked and unbaked bread, to take with him next time bread that was half-baked.*

That night he did not sleep a wink, and long before the first twilight he was walking the margin of the lake with half-baked bread in his hand, watching its smooth surface even more impatiently than the day before. The sun rose and the rain came, but the youth heeded nothing as he eagerly strained his gaze over the water. Morning wore to afternoon, and afternoon to evening, but nothing met the eyes of the anxious watcher but the waves and the myriad dimples made in them by the rain.

The shades of night began to fall, and Gwyn was about to depart in sore disappointment, when, casting a last farewell look over the lake, he beheld some cows walking on its surface. The sight of these beasts made him hope that they would be followed by the Lady of the Lake, and, sure enough, before long the maiden emerged from the water. She seemed lovelier than ever, and Gwyn was almost beside himself with joy at her appearance. His rapture increased when he saw that she was gradually approaching the land, and he rushed into the water to meet her, holding out the half-baked bread in his hand. She, smiling, took his gift, and allowed him to lead her to dry land. Her beauty dazzled him, and for some time he could do nothing but gaze upon her. And as he gazed upon her he saw that the sandal on her right foot was tied in a peculiar manner. She smiled so graciously upon him that he at last recovered his speech and said,

"Lady, I love you more than all the world besides and want you to be my wife."

She would not consent at first. He pleaded, however, so earnestly that she at last promised to be his bride, but only on the following condition.

"I will wed you," she said, "and I will live with you until I receive from you three blows without a cause – tri ergyd diachos. When you strike me the third

causeless blow I will leave you for ever."

He was protesting that he would rather cut off his hand than employ it in such a way, when she suddenly darted from him and dived into the lake. His grief and disappointment was so sore that he determined to put an end to his life by casting himself headlong into the deepest water of the lake. He rushed to the top of a great rock overhanging the water, and was on the point of jumping in when he heard a loud voice saying,

"Forbear, rash youth, and come hither."

He turned and beheld on the shore of the lake some distance from the rock a hoary-headed old man of majestic mien, accompanied by two maidens. He descended from the rock in fear and trembling, and the old man addressed him in comforting accents.

"Mortal, thou wishest to wed one of these my daughters. I will consent to the union if thou wilt point out to me the one thou lovest."

Gwyn gazed upon the two maidens, but they were so exactly similar in stature, apparel and beauty that he could not see the slightest difference between them. They were such perfect counterparts of each other that it seemed quite impossible to say which of them had promised to be his bride, and the thought that if perchance he fixed upon the wrong one all would be for ever lost nearly drove him to distraction. He was almost giving up the task in despair when one of the two maidens very quietly thrust her foot slightly forward. The motion, simple as it was, did not escape the attention of the youth, and looking down he saw the peculiar shoe-tie, which he had observed on the sandal of the maiden who had accepted his half-baked bread. He went forward and boldly took hold of her hand.

"Thou hast chosen rightly," said the old man, "Be to her a kind and loving husband, and I will give her as a dowry as many sheep, cattle; goats, swine and horses as she can count of each without drawing in her breath. But remember, if thou strikest her three causeless blows, she shall return to me."

Gwyn was overjoyed, and again protested that he would rather lop off all his limbs than do such a thing. The old man smiled, and turning to his daughter desired her to count the number of sheep she wished to have. She began to count by fives – one, two, three, four, five – one, two, three, four, five – one, two, three, four, five – as many times as she could until her breath was exhausted. In an instant as many sheep as she had counted emerged from the water. Then the father asked her to count the cattle she desired. One, two, three, four, five – one, two, three, four, five – one, two, three, four, five – she went on counting until she had to draw in her breath again. Without delay, black cattle to the number she had been able to reach came, lowing out of the mere. In the same way she counted the goats, swine and horses she wanted, and the full tale of each kind ranged themselves alongside the sheep and cattle. Then the old man and his other daughter vanished.

LADY NELFERCH and Gwyn were married amid great rejoicing, and took up their home at a farm named Esgair Llaethdy, near the village of Myddfai, where they lived for many years. They were as happy as happy can be, everything prospered with them, and three sons were born to them.

When the eldest boy was seven years old, there was a wedding some distance away, to which Nelferch and her husband were specially invited. When the day came, the two started and were walking through a field in which some of their horses were grazing, when Nelferch said that the distance was too great for her to walk and she would rather not go.

"We must go," said her husband, "and if you do not like to walk, you can ride one of these horses. Do you catch one of them while I go back to the house for the saddle and bridle."

"I will," she said, "At the same time bring me my gloves. I have forgotten them. They are on the table."

He went back to the house, and when he returned with the saddle and bridle and gloves, he found to his surprise that she had not stirred from the spot where he had left her. Pointing to the horses, he playfully flicked her with the gloves and said,

"Go, go (dos, dos)."

"This is the first causeless blow," she said with a sigh, and reminded him of the condition upon which she had married him, a condition which he had almost forgotten.

MANY YEARS after, they were both at a christening. When all the guests were full of mirth and hilarity, Nelferch suddenly burst into tears and sobbed piteously. Gwyn tapped her on the shoulder and asked her why she wept.

"I weep," she said, "because this poor innocent babe is so weak and frail that it will have no joy in this world. Pain and suffering will fill all the days of its brief stay on earth, and in the agony of torture will it depart this life. And, husband, thou hast struck me the second causeless blow."

AFTER THIS, Gwyn was on his guard day and night not to do anything which could be regarded as a breach of their marriage covenant. He was so happy in the love of Nelferch and his children that he knew his heart would break if through some accident he gave the last and only blow which would take his dear wife from him. Some time after the babe whose christening they had attended, after a short life of pain and suffering, died in agony, as Nelferch had foretold. Gwyn and the Lady of the Lake went to the funeral, and in the midst of the mourning and grief, Nelferch laughed merrily, causing all to stare at her in astonishment. Her husband was so shocked at her high spirits on so sad an occasion, that he touched her, saying,

"Hush, wife, why dost thou laugh?"

"I laugh," she replied, "because the poor babe is at last happy and free from pain and suffering."

Then rising she said, "The last blow has been struck. Farewell."

SHE STARTED off immediately towards Esgair Llaethdy, and when she arrived home, she called her cattle and other stock together, each by name. The cattle she called thus:

Mu wlfrech, moelfrech,   Brindled cow, bold freckled,

Mu olfrech, gwynfrech,	Spotted cow, white speckled;
Pedair cae tonn-frech,	Ye four field sward mottled.
Yr hen wynebwen,	The old white-faced,
A'r las Geigen,	And the grey Geigen
Gyda'r tarw gwyn	With the white bull
O lys y Brenin,	From the court of the King,
A'r llo du bach,	And thou little black calf,
Sydd ar y bach,	Suspended on the hook,
Dere dithe, yn iach adre!	Come thou also, whole again, home.

THEY ALL immediately obeyed the summons of their mistress. The little black calf, although it had been killed, came to life again, and descending from the hook, walked off with the rest of the cattle, sheep, goats, swine and horses at the command of the Lady of the Lake.

It was the spring of the year, and there were four oxen ploughing in one of the fields. To these she cried:

Y pedwar eidion glas,	Ye four grey oxen,
Sydd ar y ma's,	That are on the field,
Deuweh chwithe	Come you also
Yn iach adre!	Whole and well home!

AWAY WENT the whole of the livestock with the Lady across the mountain to the lake from whence they had come, and disappeared beneath its waters. The only trace they left was the furrow made by the plough, which the oxen drew after them into the lake. This remains to this day.

GWYN'S HEART was broken. He followed his wife to the lake crushed with woe and put an end to his misery by plunging into the depths of the cold water. The three sons distracted with grief, almost followed their father's example, and spent most of their days wandering about the lake in the hope of seeing their lost mother once more. Their love was at last rewarded, for one day Nelferch *appeared suddenly to them.*

She told them that their mission on earth was to relieve the pain and misery of humankind. She took them to a place, which is still called the Physician's Dingle (Pant y Meddygon), where she showed them the virtues of the plants and herbs which grew there and taught them the art of herbalism and healing.

Profiting by their mother's instruction, they became the most skilful physicians in the land. Rhys Grug, Lord of Llandovery and Dynevor Castles gave them rank, lands and privileges at Myddfai for their maintenance in the practice of their art and for the healing and benefit of those who should seek their help. The fame of the Physicians of Myddfai was established over the whole of Wales and continued for centuries among their descendants.

A FEW YEARS AGO Mike and I went with Mike's Dad to Pant y Meddygon, which is actually a high boggy moorland place up on the Black Mountain. It was September and the whole area was covered in magic mushrooms. The idea of Nelferch revealing the secrets of the herbs in this meadow took new shape as the plants themselves revealed their secrets through the mushrooms.

WE, the budding Enchanters, each go to find our own space on the hillsides surrounding the lake, to sit in the energy of the place, to feel our roots in Her earth, to receive Her visions, to enter the magical realm. We call to Nelferch, asking Her to come out of the depths of the lake and show Herself to us. We sit for a long time on the hillside receiving Her wisdom.

> *Nelferch, Lady of the Lake*
> *Creator, Creation, Lady of the calm waters,*
> *Reflection of Sky, Peaceful Presence*
> *I honour you today*
>
> *You lay upon me a green mantle*
> *You awaken the Sun and warm my body*

You give me rest
You forgive me for unknown faults
Unrecorded, unremembered
You forgive me and I am grateful for your mercy

Great Cauldron of the Mountains
Cauldron of Creation
I receive your love and inspiration

In the great scheme, we are so small
Here only for a moment in time
Make the most of it
Tomorrow we will be gone.

I HAVE VISITED Llyn y Fan Fach many times with Mike but have never walked up to the very top of the cliffs. It has always seemed like a long way and too much after the long walk up to the lake. Tina, who has been losing weight and getting herself fit and healthy for the Enchantress year, suggests that we walk up the steep slope to the top of the cliffs. How can I refuse?

Leaving our bags with the others Tina, Louise and I set off up the grassy track to the rim of Nelferch's Cauldron. It's easier than I thought. It is so beautiful up here high in the air. The cliffs fall steeply away to the lake and on the southern sides slope down in a great wide curve of moorland and rock. As we approach the edge of the Cauldron the desire to jump off the cliff is very strong in myself and in Louise. It's scary.

I have felt this overwhelming urge before, on the edge of Pele's Caldera on the Big Island in Hawaii. Then I was filled with such fear that I would not be able to stop myself from jumping, I held on desperately to the high gravelly precipice, which overlooks at a distance the fiery pit from which molten lava sprays skyward and flows constantly. Mr Makua, our Hawaiian Elder, made offerings to Pele of Her favourite ohelo berries and brandy. Through my fear a great vision came to me of Pele, Goddess of the Volcano, She who creates new Earth with every heartbeat from Her fiery body. She was an enormous shining being, whose presence sent shock waves through my body and sent me into convulsions of sobbing. Pele broke me open.

As we crawl closer to the edge Tina, who fortunately is undisturbed by this closeness to the edge, holds our hands and grounds us as we lie down upon the earth. Louise and I close our eyes and in vision we fly in our bird bodies off the edge of the cliff, soaring high above the lake, above the hillsides. Together we swoop down towards the surface of the lake and, changing direction, rise high again, flying upwards on the thermals that rise up the steep escarpment. The feeling of flying is glorious.

I am a Red Kite. I fly out over the lake and then dive down beneath its surface into Nelferch's watery realm, down into Her underwater palace. I enter Her palace and see a treasure chest. I open it and retrieve jewels for Tina and Louise. Then up through the waters out again into the air. I fly. I turn my head to left and right, my eyes pinning down my fish prey rising to the surface of the lake. Talons down I dive and catch the fish swimming unawares beneath me. Swooping back up the cliff face I land for some moments on a high rock and pull the fish to pieces with my beak. I eat the delicious flesh. Then I take off again and fly free for I am Red Kite.

I fly down to Mary's shoulder as she sits far below on the grass, and remove a great lump of worry that she carries. I crack a shell on John's back. I say prayers of love for Rosie and for Fran.

Tina's voice interrupts my journey.

"*Open your eyes!*" she is saying in a loud whisper, "*Open your eyes!*"

I come to with a start and open my eyes. There in front of us flying just a few feet away over the edge of Nelferch's Cauldron, on the same level as us, are two Red Kites. I can see the beautiful colours of their wing feathers, first from above and then below as they fly up above us. They hover for a long time just in front of us so that we can really see them. They are really beautiful birds. Then in a moment they fly off and away over the hillside. It is a completely awesome and blessed moment. It is really unusual to come so close to these wild and rare birds, which were once almost extinct, and now are breeding in central Wales. Goddess responds to our human longing to see Her by appearing in the forms of Her epiphanies as bird or animal. We three feel incredibly blessed by this experience.

WE WALK ALONG the top of the Cauldron across the high bare earth with a long view to the Bristol Channel in the south and the Atlantic Ocean out to the west. To the north is the great green and cultivated landscape, which Nelferch created, flowing out from Her high Creation Lake, stretching forth in beauty. It is wonderful that we managed to get up here and see the swoop of the high cliffs and the rippling waves moving across the surface of Her cauldron. They fan out as the wind touches the water, rippling over the rocks. I am so grateful to Tina for her determination, which inspired me to climb Nelferch's Cauldron walls.

I REALISE that time has passed and we should get back to the others waiting patiently below. We make our descent down the track back to where the others are waiting. The sun has gone in and a cool wind now blows around the lake. We make the long walk back to the cars and then back to our holiday home. We are all happy.

We entered the Enchanted world of Goddess in these days in the wilds of Wales, which have opened our hearts and minds. I am so fortunate to be able to live in Her presence.

Chapter Seven

SOUL TRAVEL

I AM BUSY during the week, filling up my time. Its feels so good to move about, to feel strong in my body again after going to Wales. I am stronger than I have felt for quite a while. I am excited to be able to do things again. The cancer was there for quite a while, slowing me down, undermining my energy, when I didn't know that was what was happening.

I have my last weekly session with Jan, who has been really great for me. She clearly took me to the heart of my problem, to the wounding and the armour. I open my heart and love myself and no longer need to the armour. The metal is dissolving away. I am deeply grateful to Jan.

THE DAY has arrived. Here we are at the beginning of *10 Hours Exploring the Mountains of Avalon – a day of silence, sound, non-talking, inner journeying.* Yesterday I spent two hours creating a central altar in the shape of the Isle of Avalon with the Mountains of Avalon in the centre. I love creating altars. This day is an experiment. I don't yet quite know what I am doing, but I follow the threads of energy, follow the threads of Her direction, Her flow. My intention is to hold the space for the Lady to come through, to be here. To hold space for everyone to journey to meet Her, to experience Her, to be present to receive Her healing grace.

The day begins with introductions and then we embark together on our individual journeys in consciousness. I call in the Lady and Her powers and presence. I ask permission of the Ancestors of the Isle of Avalon and all those who have gone before us, for us to make this pilgrimage together. We begin our journey with the help of different kinds of sound – bowls, rattles, drums, music, etc., across the waters of the Lake to the sacred Isle of Avalon. On our arrival we make our way by known pathways to the Rainbow Bridge and walk over it.

Continuing along the track we arrive at the local Village, the Base (chakra) Camp where people can leave any items they don't want to take with them into the mountains, and also where we can find any items we need to take with us to help climb the mountains. We go to the Place of Sacred Dreams to anchor our intentions and prepare for the journey. Then we begin to walk into the foothills.

What will you show me, Lady?

That there is much more than I know. I know so little. I am waiting, listening. Lady, show me the way to your loving heart. Show me how I might serve you in more and more ways of wonder. How may I serve you? Help me break through my limitations, any barriers that I have. Help me release my resistances to your love, Lady. For I love you.

We climb up through the trees in the Forest of Memory and begin remembering the memories, good and bad, that rise to the surface. Some we already know and we give ourselves permission to let them go.

I let go of all that no longer serves you, Lady, or me.

I become aware of my wild animal self, roving alongside me through the trees, climbing higher with me, as we make our way upwards through the forest. I move into my animal form and feel the ground beneath my paws, sniffing the scents on the ground and on plants. I love to run quickly through the trees, leaping onto logs and turning swiftly when something catches my eye. I am alert, awake and ready to scent out any prey. I feel free and light, powerful and wild.

After a long time we come out onto the slopes of the Mountain of Inspiration. High above the mountain is a cloud from which the Golden Rain of Inspiration showers our bodies, raining down upon us, cleansing and filling every cell, every pore with your inspiration, Lady.

High in the Mountains we come across the Lake of Deep Knowing and dive into its sparkling waters. Down, down on the bottom of the lake I find a Treasure Chest. I open the lid and see inside the image of a gibbet and that knowledge that once I was hung as a witch. I see its consequences in my lives.

Keep quiet. Do not speak. Do not be seen. Do not show who you are. If you do they will come and get you. They will kill you for who you are.

Under the waters I let it go. I let go of the fear, melting the armour, letting go of the hard metal. This cancer has brought the gift of melting armour consciously.

I am Soul in a body, here to have many different experiences, some good, some bad. I am here to experience many different states, to learn, to absorb, to open my heart more and more to love, to let go of fear. In this moment I feel the tugging as my heart opens more and more. It is held closed by tough threads. I open my heart, Lady.

After a rest we journey to the Cave of the Grandmothers, a circle of Old Women who are sitting in council around a fire beneath the earth. We receive their blessings and then crawl in our child selves through a small narrow tunnel, which is hidden behind them. The tunnel leads to an inner chamber, which is painted with animals of all kinds, like the Palaeolithic caves in France and Spain. In the deepest part of the cave is an image of Goddess, of the Lady in Her earthly form, belly, breasts, thighs, buttocks, vulva.

We return to the innocence of the child, before life came in and did its thing with us. Dipping our hands in red ochre we put our handprints on the walls. We take the child's love into our hearts and feel her/his happiness and innocence. We come back out of the tunnel and through the Cave of Grandmothers, receiving their blessing in our lives. We give thanks and make our way back out onto the side of the mountain. From there we look out at the wondrous view, out across the landscape of the Isle of Avalon.

We climb higher up the mountains until we reach the Peak Sanctuary where the Lady of the High Mountains of Avalon dwells. After due preparation we come to meet Her face to face and receive Her words that She speaks especially for each one of us. We each feel completely blessed by Her presence.

Some time later we make our return journey descending down the mountains, returning back along the known pathways, finding our way back to the Village, where we can recollect or leave behind any of the things we brought but didn't need. Then climbing into the Barge of Avalon we return back across the waters to the mainland, renewed, refreshed, inspired and so grateful for all that we have received on our Sacred Pilgrimage into the Mountains of Avalon.

A COUPLE OF WEEKS later I invite a small group of friends round to our house to make a plaster cast of my upper body, the wound now healed from the surgery. With my one full breast and my wounded right side it's probably more shocking for them than it is for me, to see the devastation wrought to my woman's body. We say a prayer of gratitude for my health and then they carefully and gently apply the modroc bandaging to my breasts and belly. As it undergoes its chemical changes the modroc heats up and dries hard. It shrinks a little and separates from my skin and there is a lasting impression of my scarred body. When it is completely dry I will paint it to match my earlier cast of my complete body.

Tomorrow Uranus conjuncts Mars in my astrology for the first time. It's a challenging conjunction and there are several more hits to go.

AT THE BEGINNING of this experience with cancer my quest was to find the cause of my dis-ease and that quest is still ongoing. What is the cause of this second cancer? And it is slowly unfurling as I vision a dome of expanding awareness – a glass ceiling that was sitting above my head, that is now cracking up. This ceiling now has holes in it. My consciousness is pushing out through the holes. My soul is breaking in and through and down to me in a two way movement, up and in and down and up.

Before the cancer I had felt for a couple of years that I was treading water, doing the same things that I had done before. I had reached a plateau of experience. Having cancer again has catapulted me into change, fear being my companion of resistance. Whenever I people my world with safety, then my face and jaw tighten, my muscles stiffen and it is with fear. Now I breathe deep of the air. I breathe in life and energy and courage to move directly into life. I want to be present with all that is here.

I am reading *"Soulcraft: Crossing into the Mysteries of Nature and Psyche"* by Bill Plotkin, psychologist and wilderness guide. I really like this book, which stimulates my mind. It addresses questions of the soul, plotting the path to initiation, through nature-based experience. It is based in Bill's experiences of taking hundreds of people out into wilderness landscapes on vision quests.

He says some great things in this book:

"The natural world is such an extraordinary teacher, a reflector of truth. The natural world is the world soul and will support our individual soul journeys. When we begin our soul journey the outer world moves towards us to support our soul awakening. A soul-rooted identity is primarily focused on the discovery of and joyous offering of the gift of our soul to the world."

He expands on the notion of the *Loyal Soldier* within the human psyche, who is the protector of our Wounded Child. The idea of the Loyal Soldier is based on George Barnes, who was a First World War soldier, who didn't know that the war was over and hid out for forty more years. When he was found he could not believe that the war was over and had to be told over and over again, with much gratitude towards him, that he could come home and rest.

"Within the psyche… the Loyal Soldier is a courageous, wise, and stubborn sub-personality that forms during our childhood and creates a variety of strategies to help us survive the realities (often dysfunctional) of our families and culture. It keeps us "safe" by making us small or limited, or by further traumatizing us. It is the intra-psychic element that shovels chunks of our wholeness into our Shadow so that we will appear acceptable or invisible to the powers that be."

In our healing journey this sub-personality needs to be acknowledged and thanked many times, *"Thank you for protecting me and keeping me safe as a child, but the war is now over. You did such a good job. I survived, but it's over. You can now retire. You don't need to go on fighting for me. I am strong now. I can take care of myself. I have help from my adult self."*

I really understood this notion and see how my Loyal Soldier has been protecting me all my life, but I don't need him now. I don't need him any more.

I thank you for all you have done to protect me. I love you. You can retire.

I HAVE A DREAM in which I am somewhere where lots of armour is being lifted off my body and I am trying on different kinds of lacy armour.

Self-effacement, shyness and social vigilance have been part of the Loyal Soldier's strategies that kept me safe. Behind that I developed my considerable skills and talents.

I KNOW in this moment that one of my wounds is being shaken to the core by my father as a baby.

I TRAVEL TO Vienna in Austria for the first Austrian Goddess Conference, created by one of our Priestess students, Hildegard Kirchweger, Elaria and friends. It is held in an old Schloss with green lawns and trees. There are wonderful Goddess paintings and glorious extravagant modern day ceramic statues of Goddesses by sculptor Rhea Silvia, which I really love. And there are lots of lovely people wanting to know more about Goddess in their land.

I have come to support Hildegard in this new venture and to offer the Sacred Elements of Avalon, its Earth, Water, Fire, Air and Space, as an initiatory Goddess gift to stimulate this new Goddess event in Austria, the land where the Venus of Willendorf, ancient Mother Goddess, comes from. I also give a talk on Avalon. Outside in the gardens we invoke the presence of the Austrian Goddesses on the Wheel of Noreia –beginning in the southeast with Ambeth, Danu, Willbeth, Rigani, Borbeth, Perchte, Wilbeth, Ostara and centring with

Noreia, all names gleaned from the ancient stories of Austria.

In the afternoon I sleep for a short while and I wake realising clearly that I am on a Soul Journey at the moment, as I am always, but now it is conscious. This is my Soul Journey. I am here in Vienna for my soul. I don't have to socialise or interact unless I feel like it. I don't have to hold up the world. In my moments I need to inspire, encourage and support, but I don't have to provide the energy here anymore. I am only responsible for myself at this moment. This Conference is happening. I can let others take the load.

At this moment in time my journey is with my soul and its expression fully in the world. I am free to be myself. I am entering the third phase of my life. If I live to be a hundred (I am always optimistic even having had cancer twice) then this is the third quarter, and I must face and explore this time of life instead of pretending to myself somewhere that it is not happening.

THERE IS a question in Soulcraft: What is dying?

My physical stamina is not quite what it was. I used to be able go on and on, to press beyond. Now I no longer want to do this. My capacity to remember the names of everything is less now. Giving details of places and names and authors and books is not what it used to be, although really that lessened a while ago when I was flooded with hormones in my pregnancies. My desire to be there for everyone, anyone, at any time, is less. I want to be able to serve but not at the cost of my health – that is cancer. The flexibility in my joints is not what it used to be. My knees feel cramped when I sit for long periods of time.

My right breast has gone. This means that the symmetry of my beautiful luscious body has changed. I am sad about this. I have felt/expressed hardly any grief about this. Perhaps it is hidden away. I justify it with that older woman's words that no-one looks at me in that sexual way any more, only Mike. My body is disfigured, but amazingly I am still woman. My womanliness is not defined by my breasts, which I always assumed it would be, but it isn't.

I want to take the time to let go of the old and see what the new is. I don't yet know what is being born now, but I feel it is deeply connected to my soul and its expression in the world, in a new way, away from action and activity, more into being and contemplation, ideas and energy. I want to be, to sit in my garden and just be, and see what happens. Change is happening. The cancer is forcing/has forced me to shift from doing to being, although the signs were already there on the plateaus of boredom. Cancer brought fear up in me like a volcano, from the depths. My soul journey has exploded through the cover of serenity and ability. I am saving my life, because cancer can kill me.

I can break with the past as teacher, know-it-all, priestess, ceremonialist, holder of the keys, creator of Temples, Conference, trophies. I do not know which of these roles will go and which will remain. They may all go, or none or some. I still follow the promptings of intuition in everything. The Wild is calling me, Wales in particular. I have a strong desire to spend time in Her nature beside rivers and streams and mountains. I want to let go of the fear of the dangers out there, letting go of my self-image of smooth skin and young features. My face is lined and wrinkled by life, by the sun and wind and age. I am no longer the young beauty that I was, that I can see now in Iona's beautiful face and body, although when I was her age I didn't know just how gorgeous I was. Life is funny.

What do I most deeply seek? I seek to find the meaning of life. I seek to find and embrace the cause of my disease, to heal myself, to expand my consciousness, to expand out of the cage and into the new and unknown life. I seek to serve the Lady of Avalon on the inner and the outer spaces of reality.

Who are my people? My family of course, my beloveds – Mike, Iona and Torky, who I love from the depths of my soul. My people are the people who love Goddess, those who are waking up to Goddess. All the priestesses, all those struggling to wake up, to heal their wounds, all who want to grow, all the people who are becoming conscious. These are my people. My people are healers. I love people who want to know more, they are my people. The ones who are happy as they are, yes, I love them too, but I love more those who strive to become aware and whole.

I pray for long life, good health, clear mind, love in my open heart, love in my life. I pray for everyone that I know. I pray that I can serve the Lady always, that

I never forget Her, that I love Her properly, that I let go all the armour, that I heal my loyal soldier, that I expand into the unknown.

On my return home I have a wonderful healing massage with Draupadi Gershewitch. It was a good long deep massage and I released some tears and old holding in my shoulders. She said that she thought I had brought some wounded strand of betrayal from other lives into this life – in fact, many betrayals. The healing of these experiences is the purpose of this journey.

I am lucky. I do feel held and seen by Mike. I am fortunate that I have a partner who really, really knows me and loves me as I am. Lots of the priestesses and students who come to learn with us, lots of ordinary people in the community, have no-one who really knows them, really loves them, someone who holds them. I feel held by the priestess community and in travelling to Austria I know that my work is appreciated by many people. The core of me is held by their love.

In the outer layers I am still not trusted in the local Glastonbury community. Mike and I talk about how one day they might invite me to speak at Chalice Well on Companions' day – why haven't they already? They invite all sorts of people with a similar status or fame, but they don't invite their local well-known Goddess-loving woman. There is still a deep misogyny and fear of Goddess, of the Feminine and I represent that. That is even though over the years different Trustees have been people who know me, have worked with me, been taught by me. I have also held many residential Goddess Retreats at Chalice Well. It's very odd that in 25 years I have never been invited to speak. What do they think I might do? Do they think I have nothing relevant to say? Do they fear I might be offensive and provocative, and upset people? That I might disturb the peace? Do they fear I will speak about Goddess, about the Lady of Avalon?

WE ARE ALWAYS keeping our eyes open for the possibility of buying a larger space for a new Goddess Temple in Glastonbury High Street or nearby. We would like a larger Temple space where bigger groups of people could gather and celebrate Goddess – the Goddess Hall we use now is not big enough in the summer months for everyone who would like to attend our ceremonies. We want larger and smaller meditation spaces, healing rooms, workshop rooms, a cafe, bakery, etc. We would like our Temple to be in the centre of town so that people can find us easily as they walk past, so that we don't become an inward-looking enclave on the edge of town, that is of necessity self-absorbed and cut off from the life of the wider community. We want to be in the heart of the community.

On Wednesday Mike and I go to see an old pub in the High St, which is up for sale. It has a narrow frontage and is very old-fashioned, with lots of rubbish in the corners and the walls covered with ingrained dirt from years of smoke and alcohol. My immediate thought is *"No"*, but in the back it opens into a much wider space with a large barn. The best thing would be to pull it all down and build a new Temple with access from the High Street and from Silver Street. It's a big area and it would take at least £1million to build something that we would want. I'll have to play the lottery.

I remember my 60th birthday party when I asked everyone to buy a lottery ticket for the Temple instead of giving me presents. Out of over 200 tickets only one won anything – Koko won £10, as she would. Ha! Ha!

I GO TO THE HOSPITAL to see a Dr Balfour for the results of my bone scan. She tells me that I have osteoporosis. I have a score of −2.7. Later I read that above −1 is normal, between −1 and −2.5 is osteopenic (low bone density) and below −2.5 is osteoporosis. I can't quite take that in. Osteoporosis? She suggests I take a biophosphonate drug to stop the disease progressing. Is this the Uranus Mars conjunction again or Pluto square Mars? I must check the ephemeris.

I read up about biophosphonates and they don't sound good at all. They help increase bone density by slowing the natural cycle of bone loss and bone renewal which is out of balance because of lower hormone levels. It's quite common after menopause in older women. However these drugs actually end up making bones very hard and brittle and non-living structures. Biophosphonates have significant side effects, too, including back pain, joint pain, stomach pain, nausea, vomiting, heartburn and constipation. The side effects result in 50% of women giving up taking them. Their consumption can lead to atypical femur fractures, oesophageal cancer and some women have suffered osteonecrosis of the jaw – death of bone tissue – a condition that is not treatable. They bring on dementia.

I seriously don't want to take drugs continuously for any reason and especially not these ones. As I trawl the internet for information I also note that as with all these widely prescribed drugs there are other hidden motivations going on. Biophosphonates are a by-product of the manufacture of soap powders, which of course needs to be used for something to make money, and what better than giving them to women?

I decide not to take the drug, but to take calcium and Vitamin D, to exercise, mainly walking and dancing 5 Rhythms, to continue using progesterone cream, and eating well, as I do already. Lady, show me the Way of Life.

IONA'S FRIEND Mark, whom I have just met, gives me some healing. He says that he has removed something which wasn't mine. It is a memory of betrayal by several women in a group, betrayal of me as a witch. He then said something about my uttering a curse and that something happened when I was about fifteen years old. I remember how at that age I hated my parents, particularly my father, but also my mother who didn't stand up for me against him. Daddy refused to let me go to the cinema with one of his friend's sons. He said that boys and men are only after one thing. How I hated him and how that hatred built up in the next couple of years. Perhaps I cursed them both then and anger was held in me from that time, against male authority, against anyone telling me what I could and could not do.

And from other times, me as the witch uttering a curse, which has reverberated through my lives. I take it back, whatever curse I made to whomsoever I cursed for whatever reason, I take it back to myself. I remember that in my imaginative fantasy life I have the thought that if I am ever attacked physically, my imagined response is to curse my attacker, to promise to haunt them to their grave. What revenge would that be, to be tied to chasing someone down for eternity? It sounds awful but it has a ring a truth about it and could be a source of unknown anger in my body.

I release all anger, I release any curses I may have made in this life and all previous lives. I let go of all anger and hatred.

ON MONDAY we hold a Ceremonial Healing Day in the Goddess Hall. How I love these days of healing, offered in the love of the Lady to all who wish to receive Her blessings of air, fire, water and earth and Her healing presence through Her priestess/healers. We set up from 10.30am and I went all the way through until 6.00pm. My energy was good all day! Yippee! Last time in April I could only do a few hours and left the clearing up to others, but this time I feel really good.

In the evening Iona, Mark and I go to the Tor, where it is all lit up with flares to mark the Queen's 60th Jubilee. It looks beautiful, lit with lacy fire. There are lots of people walking in the lanes and fields and sitting on top of the Tor. I like these times when the community is out and about and we all come together and see each other.

I GO TO VISIT a friend whose mother died a few years ago from secondary breast cancer. It was her second cancer and it had spread through her body. She was 72 and died quickly. It is a reality check for me. People can die of this disease. Araura sends me a card suggesting oxygen therapy. It doesn't appeal, but I am thinking about it now.

We buy a new-to-us blue car and at first it started and then died and wouldn't go again. Early in the morning I am lying in an anxiety state – the only explanation I can think of is that I put petrol in the car when it's got a diesel engine. All yesterday I was in denial of my possible mistake, but in the night I felt a really strong guilt, although no-one will kill me for doing the wrong thing here. I lie in bed awake, anxiety circling through my body keeping me awake – as well as the small glass of wine that I drank and the cheese on some pizza. I am in an anxiety state.

I try to talk to my wounded child self,

It's OK, darling, you could have made a mistake. You can admit it.

The loyal soldier is in strong defensive mode,

Do not admit to any mistakes. Do not admit that you could possibly have done anything wrong. Keep quiet all day. They will kill you if they find out.

I shake out the fear from my body and open to my unconscious anxiety state. I reassure both parts that they are each OK. In fact we find out from the garage, which sold us the car, that there is something wrong with part of the diesel pump. They come and take the car away and then fix it and bring it back like new.

THERE ARE TIMES in life when the mythic enters in. The Soul calls and the heart listens and I am sustained for moments or days at a time with clarity and creativity. Then this sense of Her Presence gradually fades back into normality. She speaks, "*Let me take you into the mythic reality, into the heart space of reality, where the soul and its purposes reveal themselves, glimpsed as if through a misty veil that clears and becomes transparent.*"

The world of Avalon, the world of the Soul shines through with greater clarity than before and we know who we are once again.

MIKE comes home after a few days away, which is lovely. He has a strong energy in him which makes me want to look at his face, to look him in the eye.

LADY, OH LADY, I'm concerned this year about numbers at the Goddess Conference. Our bookings in this year of recession are low. Anxiety flows in me again, finding somewhere new to agitate. How can I improve our numbers? How can I make it work better? Is it up to me? What if the Goddess Conference just fizzled out from lack of people wanting to come and participate? That never crossed my mind before – that it could end because no-one wanted to come. Is it over? It seems almost unbelievable, but who knows? Not I.

I go to a lovely day workshop with Stephanie Mathivet, mixing oils and making a Goddess mix for the Lady, creating a roll-on oil and room spray. It is excellent. I must do more of these workshops with our students who are learning how to give workshops.

* * *

WE ARE ON ANOTHER Enchantress weekend and we are celebrating the Mother of Water, travelling south to visit the Lady of Springs and Wells and the great Ocean Mother. I have a strong dream first thing on Saturday morning. We are holding a circle around a hole in the floor in the Glastonbury Assembly Rooms. The hole leads down into a dark cavern below. In reality I have always felt that there is an entrance there to the Underworld of Avalon, a Dark Void from which strange energies emerge, which need to be treated with love and care and consciousness. In the dream three priestesses have gone down into the hole and I am getting upset because the other priestesses who are supposed to be holding space around the edge of the hole are chatting and moving about distractedly. They are sitting on tiers around the hole, but are not focussed on it at all. I am getting more and more pissed off and begin speaking loudly,

"*You have to hold the space while people go down into the Underworld, into the Black Hole! Call yourselves Priestesses?!*"

The entrance to the hole is not big. It has rocky protrusions sticking up from the edges, which mean that I have to squeeze my way through, because I am going down into the hole. It gets dark very quickly. We are not allowed to take any lights down there, so I have no idea what is there. Like the others before me I have to feel my way with my hands and feet, trying not to bump my head on the ceiling. I think it would be much easier if I could flash a light even briefly to get a glimpse of the space and then switch it off. I vision a narrow entrance tunnel leading into a much bigger cavern, then I wake up. It feels like a dream of significance.

WE DRIVE TO THE Cerne Abbas Giant, climbing over the great chalk-carved body that lies on the side of the hill. Then we go down to the Silver Well, which is known as St Augustine's Well or earlier St Catherine's Well, beside the church in the village below. Girls were recommended to go there and pray to St Catherine for a husband, turning around three times as they did so. According to custom, there used to be a chapel dedicated to St Catherine on the hill directly above the well. There is an eight-spoked Catherine Wheel carved on the lefthand stone flanking the well, a Sacred Wheel of the Year. There is a custom of dipping new-born babies into the well when the first rays of sunlight touch the waters. The waters are said to cure eye infections and infertility. Here we offer prayers to the Lady of the Well. Prayers for healing, prayers for our families and friends.

We travel onwards to Upwey and the extraordinary round Well that is there. The waters are deep and clear with rippling textures as the water bubbles up from the bottom of the pool, which is filled with layers and layers of coins. For this is a Wishing Well. We too throw coins into the pool and make our wishes. I wish for good health. The waters flow from the pool into lovely gardens, which I haven't seen before. There are benches to sit on beside the water. I float away to the gentle sounds of running flowing water. It's a very relaxing sound – spacious.

We drive on to supper in Lyme Regis and afterwards to Monkton Wyld, where we are staying for the night. Monkton Wyld is an education centre for sustainable living, managed by a resident community. It hosts a range of courses and conferences and also offers simple B & B accommodation. I gave a course here years ago and have stayed here before. It's an old-fashioned kind of place, tucked into the folds of the Dorset countryside a few miles behind Lyme Regis. I am glad that communities like this one manage to continue through time.

The next day we are beside the sea near Charmouth. The tide is coming in and we find ourselves on a narrow edge between the roaring crashing sea and crumbling rain-soaked cliffs. There is danger in both directions. How long do we dare to stand there? The ocean can sweep us away and the muddy cliffs may slide down the hill. I feel the flickers of fear as I listen to the sound of the waves crashing, to the place inside that does not know what might happen here. Am I safe on this edge, in this liminal place where the forces of your nature, Lady, are pounding?

I do not understand the sea, its gigantic size, its unceasing movement, its ebb and flow, its dangerous nature. Never turn your back on Her.

I do not understand you, Lady. I can feel you, Lady. I can feel my response here on the edge. I can feel you, but I am not comfortable with you, Ocean Mother. There is too much scary stuff. Others are not afraid of you, like me.

They swim in your currents, they float on your surface, they dive happily into your depths – all things that scare me. Could I surrender to your embrace? Happily? Ever?

As I look out at the ocean I see a large purple eye, the Lady's eye looking at me.

Chapter Eight

MEETING THE WOUNDING

I AM ANGRY with the dog. Our black Labrador Poppy is young and she chews everything – chairs, cushions, shoes, socks. Ahhh! I am feeling frustrated and annoyed with her. I am annoyed at the clutter in the house. I allow myself to feel my anger and frustration, directed at the muddle in our house. I am not able to take the time to become clear and the muddle builds up around me. It makes me shrink and grow smaller, when I want to expand.

I am angry, full of rage. There is no obvious reason for it, but if I bottle it up within me, I will bite. Snap, snap, bite, bite! I need to express my rage, put it out there in a creative form. It is time to paint my breast cast. I find some paints and put my rage into the cast we made in the first healing ceremony, the one I made when I still had two breasts. I paint it gold and then write black and red words and draw symbols on it – *Remove, Release the Armour, Be Free, Anger, Rage, Damage, Fear, Terror, Cancer, Karma, Heal the Wound, Toxic Emotions, Break Thru', She's a Wounded Healer, Just a Breast, It happens for a Reason so more Love comes Through,* and *Transform or Die*. I feel much better afterwards.

WITHIN THE Goddess Temple a situation has arisen where an ex-student has become abusive and threatening towards her ex-tutor. As I support the tutor, the student becomes abusive to me too. It is difficult to know what is best to do as she has become mentally unwell. She is abusive towards us online, on the phone, on the street and when she comes into the Goddess Temple. I feel very strongly that no priestess or Temple visitor should suffer any kind of abuse inside our Goddess Temple. If we cannot create safety for ourselves inside our Temple, then where in this patriarchal world can we be safe? We are a Goddess-loving space open to the public, but that does not mean open for abuse.

APELA COLORADO, my soul friend from Maui, is coming to stay. I feel apprehensive before she comes for no good reason. When we meet once or twice a year we are nearly always on similar learning paths. She talks about a current re-enactment by two friends of the childhood trauma of her abusive and colluding parents. She doesn't know what to do. She is feeling lost and afraid. I hear her story and try to help. I tell her that it is OK to be lost and not to know where to go next. I need to hear these words too.

Another old friend, Alene from California, telephones. She is currently dealing with panic attacks. My friends around the world are, like me, dealing with difficult current, childhood and past life patterns. We are being called to heal our primal karmic wounding. My connections to these world friendships always give me a wider perspective on what is happening in my little life and what we are doing here in Glastonbury in our Goddess community. It is so easy to be parochial and to see everything as centred in our small world, but actually many things are happening on a worldwide scale. Healing is being called for everywhere, and my international friends help me to know this.

SEVEN MORE WOMEN dedicate this weekend as Priestesses of Avalon. It is a lovely ceremony. Our numbers grow each year and I am so moved by the words of each person's dedication vow. I know that this day will resonate through their lives with consequences which cannot be foreseen, bringing each person greater and greater healing, life transformations and revelation of the love of the Lady.

During the Priestess Initiation Ceremony I receive several clear messages from the Lady,

* * *

> *You are the Boundary Holder for the Temple. It is your role to hold clear boundaries and to hold a mirror to the behaviour of others. Follow these instructions. Place a clear boundary for behaviour so that healing can occur. Healing will not be in a direct way and it may not happen for a long time, but it will happen one day. Trust in me.*

I TAKE ON the role of Boundary Holder seriously. I feel a strong urge to protect the Temple and all our activities and Trainings from any kind of attack no matter what. It feels really necessary at this time, and there are also echoes from the past. I have no idea really what it means to hold a clear boundary for behaviour and no idea what the consequences for myself and for the Temple will be.

As a community we are not yet able to deal with psychiatric illness. Many women who are called by Goddess to Her path, are often called through their psychological wounding, and we don't always know how to successfully help them. We have lots of skilful people amongst us – priestess counsellors, psychotherapists, healers, but we still need extra professional help when dealing with people who are mentally unwell. Our community is not yet strong enough or big enough to meet all these situations on its own.

It is a conundrum. How do we help people who are psychologically unstable, when the Lady calls them to Her for healing? They are often damaged by the consequences of living in a patriarchal world, which attacks and destroys women, children and men. They may be so damaged that they are unable because of their illness to receive the healing and help that they need. We have to develop new skills and techniques to help those who are most seriously damaged, but this is a life work for someone or some group of people to create and develop, and we are not there yet.

I can remember the early days of the Priestess Training when I thought that perhaps 30% of our students had psychological problems, which had brought them to the Goddess path. I know now that this percentage is in fact much higher and that it is our wounding at the hands of patriarchy that often initiates our quest for Goddess and a different way of living. We nearly all carry emotional, psychological and spiritual wounds from this life and previous lives, which have often been priestess lives that ended many hundreds of years ago in damaging and dangerous situations. We carry the scars of these experiences in our souls. It is in this life at this time that we are being called to re-member and heal these wounds if we can. It is not easy.

IT IS A REALLY intense day, an expression of my own Uranus/Pluto square, and Pluto square Mars/Mercury. Several tutors including myself begin to receive a torrent of negative emails and phone calls now accusing us of unrelated failings. These messages begin to leak out into the wider community involving people who do not know what is actually going on, as we hold a boundary of confidentiality. My solar plexus vibrates painfully and I feel attacked emotionally on the astral level. It feels like some old pattern of abuse and defence is being activated in me and within the Goddess Temple. Acting under my authority as Creative Director of the Temple and now Boundary Keeper, I take the decision, after talking with others, that we must exclude from the Temple anyone who is aggressive or abusive towards priestesses, melissas or visitors. It is not okay for anyone to be abused in our Goddess Temple.

In its organisation the Goddess Temple is a not for profit company limited by guarantee, with elected directors. It turns out that several Temple directors do not support my decision and are upset that they were not consulted by me. Having known *clearly* what I should do, I suddenly feel very uncertain about what I have done, and feel very upset by their lack of support. My body begins to shake and I feel very afraid. I have done something transgressive by acting on my own authority, by not consulting everyone. I feel guilty. I have done something wrong. They are telling me that I have done something wrong, so it must be true.

At the same time I feel that I should be supported in my actions. I remember other times, other Goddess lives, when our actions as priestesses would always be cohesive and supportive, when I could naturally assume that my sisters would always stand with me, no matter what, as I would with them. They would know that I acted from the best of intentions for the good of the whole. But now in patriarchal times it is not like that, and as women we are often set at odds with each other. We do not support each other in situations of conflict.

I call Sally, one of the Temple Directors, and she is very helpful to me in my distress. I feel supported by her in my reasons for holding a boundary. I am really trying to understand my own reactivity, trying to work out what this all means. My current astrology is affecting me strongly. I try to understand what is being healed in me as I feel very vulnerable to attack. A small crack opens in my defensive wall, and I remember to hold a calm clear space no matter what goes on around me, and then the crack closes again as pressure mounts.

The 2012 Goddess Conference celebrating the Great Mother is coming in a couple of weeks and I am feeling really wobbled out. I worry. I worry about numbers, about whether it will work properly this year. I worry about what might happen at the Conference if all the people who are sending abusive and misinformed emails turn up. I feel very pressured.

The circle of abuse rapidly widens and appalling emails are now sent to us from sister priestesses, people we have trained and worked with over the years. They know nothing about the details of the situation only what they hear as rumour and gossip, as dis-ease speaking. Sisters feel free to let rip in online forums, projecting their anger against the weaknesses of the mental health care system, laying all its faults at our door. Unbelievable bile comes our way, pouring towards us in a completely unrestricted way. How and why is this suddenly happening? I seem to have become everyone's 'bad' mother.

Abusive emails are sent to our online Orchard of Avalon and Temple Melissa Yahoo groups. The Orchard group is for all those who have completed the First Spiral of the Priestess of Avalon Training. The Melissa group is for those who serve in the Goddess Temple. No-one asks about facts. It is all opinions. Others in the circle who know nothing about what is actually going on begin to get very confused about the situation. They start to take sides based on the last negative thing that is written.

How do we correct misinformation in a public forum, while trying to maintain some protection for those involved? We do not want to engage in public slanging matches of any kind and as the boundary holders for the Temple and the Trainings we need to maintain confidentiality. It is heart-breaking to be so attacked by sisters who we have taught and known and worked with for several years. It is as if all the unspoken unexpressed resentments of past years are rising up as fuel in this situation. A few vociferous individuals now feel that they must speak up on behalf of others, whom they perceive as being harmed by tutors, who once were their favourite teachers. It's a very strange situation. At the same time we are also being supported personally by priestesses who know and love us. That circle begins to grow and strengthen too.

Now it seems that some Temple Directors are afraid that the Temple will be sued, as a result of my decision to exclude abusive people. I feel my jaw drop open in astonishment. What? They are scared that they as directors of the Goddess Temple will be sued, and that they will lose their livelihoods and their homes, all as a consequence of my holding a boundary. A primal place of fear has been touched within each of them.

I have been trying to give those of us under attack a feeling of support from all Temple directors in this difficult situation. Things are moving quickly from day to day and not everyone is available to speak to about every detail. I assumed and said wrongly that the directors were involved in making the decision, although some of them weren't. I thought they would naturally support me and that was a mistake. They don't support me and now in response I feel betrayed by these women.

I have a dream where I am shouting at one of these directors telling her exactly what I think about her lack of commitment and lack of support.

> *"It is not you whose reputation is being damaged around town behind your back. It's me! All that I have done is to support another tutor, and I am blasted for that and for holding a clear boundary for non-violent behaviour against anyone. What is so wrong with that?"*

Wobble, wobble!! Shit has hit the fan and is flying out in all directions.

THANKFULLY within a couple of days one of the directors comes round to our house. She says that her betrayal of us is something that she has done to her mother, to her sister, to all the women she loves and now to us, who are the ones she really cares about. She has got it, understood it, a pattern of fear, of loss, of poverty, of losing everything if she is caught out. She apologises completely and I accept her apology, for I love her. I am so glad that she has seen and owned her wounding.

MY HEART is really hurting. I feel the pain of my own wound, which is betrayal by women. That is where it has erupted for me. I have gone deep into that cracked broken place of pain and I have lost it. I feel the fronds of a dis-ease entity feeling its way in through the cracks in the wounds in my psyche and lodging in my solar plexus, pulling and eating away at my emotional centre, as it has also travelled into the weak places in others.

I remember other times when I felt betrayed by women. My oldest acquaintance, or rather a woman who used to be my friend, that I have known for nearly fifty years, is such a one. Just a few years ago she felt it was OK to trash our Priestess trainings in a local guidebook to Glastonbury that she has written, which will be in circulation for many years. Why would anyone do this? There was love between us once. Our paths diverged long ago, but to publicly attack me like that, to undermine my work. I don't understand her motivation.

Or there was a work colleague who turned upon me for no reason that I understood. Friends said that she was jealous of my status, influence and perceived power. She wanted it for herself. We worked together for several years making many kinds of spiritual courses available to the public, and then I began to notice that people stopped talking when I walked into the office, or would turn aside, hands in front of their mouths. I felt excluded, ostracised, bullied by her behaviour and that of those who colluded with her to keep their jobs. I never really understood what that was all about, why one day we were friends and the next she really wanted to undermine me. We even had mediation together, but it didn't work. She didn't hear me. Did I hear her? I ended up leaving that work because I felt so hurt by her actions.

LATE ONE NIGHT the words of a poem pour out onto the pages of my journal – *It Was the Women Who Betrayed Me*. It is an expression of my strong feelings of being betrayed by sister priestesses, who I felt should support me in difficult situations, but they didn't. This experience of betrayal reminds me of other times in my life when I have felt betrayed by women, and of memories of being betrayed in other priestess lives by sister priestesses, who I had thought would always support me, and one day didn't. It seemed like a repeating loop through time, culminating now.

It Was the Women Who Betrayed Me

It was the women who betrayed me
I couldn't believe it
But it was the women who betrayed me.

Women who earlier had said, "You changed my life for the better
Thank you so much for everything you have given me."
They were the ones who betrayed me.
They pointed the finger of blame and hate, claiming they were speaking
the truth
Projecting their 'bad mother' onto me without pause for breath.

They were the ones who unlocked the side gates of the castle
Through which the attackers entered in.
They were the ones who lifted the latch for the invaders
To slide silently into the Temple of Goddess,
To maim and rape, to slice off the breast of a Priestess.
Ending Her reign all those years ago,
A tragedy in Her Motherworld.

They were the ones who like Thomas later, denied your existence, Lady,
Who denied knowledge of you when it mattered.
They were the ones who bloodied the bed and claimed to the king,
That I, Rhiannon, had killed my beautiful first-born son.
For seven long years they rode on my back, whip in hand,
Laughing at my distress.

They were the ones who lied to save their own skins
They were the ones who fawned at the feet of princes
Who played like children to satisfy their Mother the Queen.

They are the ones who collude in their own oppression
Afraid to stand up and be seen, afraid to be visible.
The ones who take the knife and circumcise their daughters
Who give away young girls to middle-aged men for money,
Claiming it is duty and like Hades, that love grows out of rape.

They are the ones who fan the flames of conflict in sugar-coated words,
Who say, "We are all equal",
As they beat down other women climbing,
So they can stay ahead.
Who deny they were there in the moment of action,
Who say, "No, not me, I didn't do it.
It was she, that one over there,
She did it. It is her fault".
Who smile grimly, jaw set, teeth tight,
As somewhere inside they know they are betraying their sisters,
But still they continue on.

* * *

Why do they do this?
For fear of standing out in the crowd, head lonely above the parapet,
For fear of loss of face, of income, of reputation,
For jealousy of a sister's beauty, her confidence, her style.
Desperate to be our mother's favourite,
Willing to do anything to bring a rival down.

"Ahhh! At last she falls from the pedestal on which I placed her,
See how the proud are brought low by my righteous indignation.
It is not betrayal, but justice!
She deserved it. She was too full of herself.
On her high horse. too proud, too holier than thou.
She is too big for her boots, too big. She is too big."

How are the mighty fallen?
Felled by the blows of oppression
Or brought down by the small hands of women
Tugging at her spirit, undermining her every movement.

"Let's pull her down, let's take her down.
We never really knew her
We were mistaken
We are better off without her
Back before we came here."

It is the women who betray me
Women that I love.

This poem says how I feel in this moment.

*　*　*　**

WHEN WE ARE YOUNG we all make mistakes and hopefully we learn from them and change the way we behave. Living in a patriarchal world which does not encourage us to really be there for each other as sisters and brothers, we have to learn from the beginning again how to truly support each other in our lives and especially as we come to meet our wounding. We may never have experienced this before. In our priestess teachings and our Goddess community we spend a lot of time emphasising the importance of giving and receiving loving care and support, but when emotional buttons are pressed and wounds are triggered, this loving support often goes out of the window. We fight, defend, control and attack from the place of our wounded child.

THE BOUNDARIES of the Temple are violated again and there is another huge emotional chain reaction in emails, phone calls, texts, both private and public. We ask priestesses to act from their own empowerment, to stand strong for our Temple, but when they too are emotionally damaged, and many are, that is challenging. I took on the role of Boundary Holder but I obviously have not thought this through enough. Holding boundaries is not easy when a person pushes against a boundary and looks for the places where it bends, e.g. the door of the Temple. I have acted and reacted in confusion myself. We have not dealt with anything like this before. It is all very messy.

WE HAVE the Goddess Temple AGM, which the Directors and others attend. Here we try to discuss what has been happening, but the conversation quickly becomes very polarised and hostile as distressed priestesses speak from their own experiences. It is an awful meeting which we don't know how to hold clearly. We don't know what to do when accusations and conflict break out.

Afterwards people tell us that now the Temple is bigger and more people are involved we have to have more organisation, more rules. Hippies at heart, the Glastonbury Temple has grown organically from nothing but inspiration under the guiding hand of Goddess, with hardly any rules at all, just mutual respect and support. Now those who have come out of more conventional backgrounds into our Glastonbury world, who do not know other ways of living, want to bring us into line with normal patriarchal organisations and to introduce some rules. My heart sighs at the thought.

The way forward that they propose is to become authoritarian, to bring in rules to constrain behaviour, as a way of controlling the wayward. By placing a boundary for behaviour, does it then become a command, a rule, which must then be policed and enforced? What is the difference between a boundary and a rule? Can a boundary be enforced? How is it enforced? I don't know. I only know that I must uphold a clear boundary of no abusive and aggressive behaviour in our Temple or our community.

JUST BEFORE the Goddess Conference it is our Lammas circle on the Enchantress course and we are at Avebury for the weekend. It is a relief to be out of the Glastonbury emotional maelstrom. Avebury is a place that I love so much, further up the Mary/Michael Line, so full of ancient knowing and the presence of the ancestors. It is one of few other places in Brigit's Isles where I could live in this life. Saturday is full, driving across the countryside from Glastonbury, following the Dragon Line, then walking the land from the Sanctuary, along the Avenue, touching the stones with our hands, feeling into them, singing to them, sounding them into life. I see these ancient stones like telephone boxes. When we talk into them the ancestors come into and inhabit the stones and communicate with us. We can have conversations.

One of the stones in the Avenue says strongly,

"Avoid the temptation to bring in rules. Don't do it."

I really hear these words. Instead of bringing in rules we are each being called to deepen our priestess practice, to be better priestesses.

After all the controversy it is wonderful to be out walking through the fields where the golden grain is ripening in the sunshine. There is lots of conversation as we walk and now we sit in silence in the Moon Circle, drinking in the quiet ending of the day, resting on Her earth in this Sacred Place. Avebury is such an amazing example of the way in which successive ancestors, over several thousand years, placed their ritual mounds and stones within an existing landscape, emphasising and enhancing different aspects of that natural landscape, making the whole place sacred for many miles in all directions.

Here there is a causewayed camp – one of the earliest kinds of sacred enclosures, ancient burial mounds, long barrows, conception sites, ritual mounds, sacred springs and rivers, large wooden circles, standing stones, a large stone circle, small circles, the great Womb mound; all beautifully placed within the landscape and in relationship to each other. Our ancestors knew so much more than we do about creating harmony between humans and the earth.

Tina and I stay in a local B & B in Avebury and have a good time meeting our hostess and other visitors. The next day we all walk through the flowing waters of the River Kennet, or Kunnet, or Kunt or Cunti, such a glorious name. Often it is completely dry at Lammas, but with all the rain that's fallen recently, today it's deep and flowing beautifully. The water bubbles up through the earth at Swallowhead Spring, which is decorated with small offerings. The Spring has flowed continuously up through the chalk since ancient times and was a water source for the small Roman town which now lies buried under the earth next to Silbury Hill. Sometimes the Spring dries up because of over-use and the lowering of the surrounding water table, but it flows today. We sit in the sunshine on the rocks and dabble our feet in the water. We make offerings and say our prayers to the abundant Mother and the Lady of the Waters.

We walk up Herepath, a track leading out of Avebury high up onto Fyfield Down, where there are many amazing stone formations. It was Terence Meaden, who has been reclaiming Goddess in the academic archaeological worlds, who first took me up there many years ago to decorate and photograph one of the stones, which is shaped like a head with a strong face, with a beautiful flower garland. Most investigators just see this Down landscape as a source of random stones, but as we sit here and move through the high grass, it's possible to distinguish alignments of stones, stones with human and divine faces and shapes, a lion's head, a sheep and many other animals. It is another undiscovered sacred landscape.

We make our way across rough ground, up the hillside to a large irregular mound of stones with three or four gnarled and wind-beaten trees, their roots digging into the crevices between the stones. Many of the stones are large and shaped, placed with purpose yet to be revealed. It's a wonderful high place with views in nearly all directions out over the rolling downs. I find a spray of owl feathers and then a complete hawk's wing, left on a rock for me, its body taken by a fox or a larger feathered predator. I feel completely blissed out as I stand in the gentle wind with the lowering sun's rays falling upon me. It is a place so familiar to me, wild and windswept and the view. A poem arises that I write as we travel homewards.

On Fyfield Down, July 2012

I have stood in this place before
With ancestor eyes I have looked upon this view
Of hills and valleys, dips and notches, barrows and stones.
I have watched the stars rising and falling
The arc of the heavens wheeling overhead
I have read the stories of my ancestors in the patterns of their movement
I have known this place to be home.

Now a pile of rocks, hidden, jumbled in thistles and nettles
A scattering of huge boulders She dropped from Her apron.
Later they were ordered in circles, rows and mounds
A Sacred Landscape to rival the Avebury neighbour,
Where ceremonies of the seasons were celebrated annually,
Holding all in balance
And there was love for Goddess held in every heart.

* * *

We climb to the mound where now grow oak and hawthorn
Stunted by the wind, rooted into rocky crevices
Excitement rises in this ancient place of power
As the horizon opens out to nearly a full circle
A great vista of Her beauty laid out in the land.

There are feathers in the rocks, first a fluttering of owl
Then down between two sarsens, the wing of a hawk
She has left me a blessing, a reminder of Her powers
To take us through into enchanted worlds

The past, the present, the future
In all these I choose love
I choose eyes that can see,
A heart that is open even though it may be battered
I choose this life
A life of ecstasy!

Chapter Nine

RE-MEMBERING MOTHERWORLD

F COURSE, the 2012 Goddess Conference in which we celebrate our creative and life-giving Great Mother Goddess is a wonderful event. I don't know how I can doubt that it will be amazing, as each time it is. Our numbers are lower than usual because of the financial recession and people's fears about money, but it works out fine. Usually we have lots of people who come to the Conference from abroad, but not this year as airfares are expensive and people stop spending and conserve their finances. We have a great Goddess-loving time.

There are wonderful presentations and performances from, amongst many others, Australian Priestess and singer/songwriter Anique Radiant Heart; Priestess Ava from the Orange County Goddess Temple in California, USA; American Italian feminist and Gift Economy writer Genevieve Vaughan; our favourite international singing star Julie Felix; Priestess Letecia Layson from the USA; writer, artist and pre-historian Michael Dames; the inimitable Lady Olivia Durdin-Robertson, Founder of the Fellowship of Isis; Australian songstress Wendy Rule and so many wonderful women, men, priestesses, priests and participants, who all help create an amazing celebration of our Mother Goddess.

There is a great *In Her Image* Exhibition in the Assembly Rooms curated by sculptor Sue Quatermass and centred on the *Breasts and Bellies*, which were created and adorned by lots of local women. Annabel Du Boulay offers a *Healing Womb* Exhibition in the Glastonbury Experience, which is strong and moving.

Plus there is Coventina's Day Spa where we can be pampered with healing massages, therapies and other delights.

When we come together in this Sacred Pilgrimage through the eight or nine days of the Goddess Conference so many awesome things happen that it is almost impossible to describe to anyone who has not been there. I am so grateful to so many women, and men, who help make the whole experience possible and especially to the wonderful women in the Conference Ceremony Group, to Priestesses Amanda Baker, Annabel du Boulay, Erin McCauliff, Heloise Pilkington, Katinka Soetens, Michelle Patten, Sally Pullinger and Tegwyn Hyndman. We have worked together throughout the year to create the ceremonies that now reveal more of our gratitude to our abundant Great Mother for all that She gives to us. I am also deeply grateful to Koko Newport, my soul sister who organises all the Melissas (our worker bees), to Roz Bound, who comes from Canada each year to be in charge of Registration, and to Geraldine Charles who creates our beautiful Conference website, as well as the websites for the Goddess Temple and my own personal website, all portals to Goddess for the people of the world to find.

For the Goddess Conference we create a performance evening called *Mother Matters*. It is done in the style of Eve Ensler's *Vagina Monologues*, where women tell moving stories about their experiences with their vaginas. As a word *Mother* has a similar strong though different resonance to *Vagina* for many women, for good and ill. Katie Player, the director, weaves together a collage of *Mother-centred* stories, looking at lots of different experiences of mothering and performed by our Goddess women at the Conference.

I offer my poem "It was the Women who betrayed me" to be part of *Mother Matters*. It comes out of my recent experiences of being attacked by my sisters for being their *bad mother*. When the evening comes I listen to the other women speaking and am very moved by their stories about their mothers. Then I speak my poem and deep inside my Shadow reacts and more of my personal wounding is strongly stirred.

As I finish speaking my poem to the audience of mostly women I don't feel good about it at all. I feel that my words and my feelings are mean, exposing, unlike all the other contributions, which are generous of spirit. I can feel people moving energetically away from me. I know that women friends/sisters are wondering if I am talking about them in particular. It is too direct, too public, too confronting.

It is healing for me to express my truth to a large group of women, but now I feel very embarrassed to have said such things out loud, so that they are heard by so many. I feel I shouldn't have done it. I am ashamed that I have spoken my truth. I want to creep away and hide, but I can't. I feel very bad. A hidden and repressed Shadow place in me that is rooted in experiences of betrayal in many lives is rising up through the layers of my consciousness.

TEN DAYS AFTER the end of the Conference Mike and I are in Bristol Airport on the way to our summer holiday in Kalkan in Turkey. We are sitting talking over a coffee as we wait for our departure. Mike says that women lack confidence and that we are afraid of the consequences of our actions. We think our way out of acting by going through in our minds and emotions all the possible outcomes of our actions, so that we don't even begin. Men on the other hand are trained to have confidence in their decisions, but don't think about the consequences of their actions at all. They act and laugh and don't worry about what will happen next. They don't think beyond the end of the next step – in business, politics and war. Women are immobilised by the fear of consequences and need to develop confidence. Men need to learn that their actions have consequences.

Our conversation develops and I continue thinking as we fly through the skies. When we women work together in groups we grow and become empowered with the help and support of each other. This is one reason that consciousness-raising circles have such powerful effects in the lives of individual women. In the Goddess Conference, in the Ceremony group and in our priestess training circles we become empowered as we listen to and support each other, although it is an on-going learning process and not everyone who engages in these groups becomes fully empowered.

The challenges over the last months have revealed the cracks in our groups. There are women and men who only take the first steps into self-awareness, who take self-empowerment to mean that teenage rebellious voice shouting,

"Don't you tell me what to think or say or do!"

They don't get much further than the act of saying, "No!" to things they don't like. They are yet to move into their *"Yes!"*

And there are those women and men who back away when confrontation arises, through fear of consequences that lie hidden in unconsciousness, from childhood and past lives.

To become strong as individual women in a patriarchal world we have to support each other in the groups of which we are part. There is a natural bond between women within families, and within soul circles, whether it is as groups of mothers or sisters or friends or priestesses. Living in patriarchal societies this natural bonding is often undermined, when wounds of jealousy, envy, undermining and scapegoating enter in. The group becomes divided and we disempower each other. We women struggle as individuals to hold our own within all kinds of groups, whether it is in the family, where we work, or where we place our spiritual aspirations. We can easily become isolated within a group, if the group is not held consciously. We can feel alone. We can have a hard time. Within patriarchy we are under attack by misogynistic men and misogynistic cultures, and often by women who should be our first support. We all need conscious women-loving groups to support us.

This woman-hurting pattern is demonstrated in what has happened in the Goddess Temple community in the last few months. Instead of being automatically supported by the group, we have instead been aggressively questioned about our actions and motivations. As soon as there is pressure we are attacked not by men, but by our sisters, who seem to sit waiting for the cracks in the group to appear, through which they can express their own wounded realities. They have stored up accusations and allegations and now feel able to vent these feelings from the safety of an attacking group.

Some priestesses who completed their training with us some years ago and were invigorated by all they learned for a time, were not able, because of their own wounding, to truly take on the necessity for self-awareness and self-responsibility. Although students are repeatedly encouraged within the priestess training to become responsible for the healing of their own emotional wounding, they can't necessarily do it. They revert to unconscious blaming and backbiting, colluding with the psychological weaknesses in others.

We have been attacked by sister priestesses who live near and also far away. Many do not know any facts about recent events, as we have kept them private, but rumour and gossip are their sources of information. Instead of talking to us face to face like the sisters we are, speaking directly to us from their own experience, these women send messages on behalf of others. They prefer to write harmful and hurtful words by email and on Facebook on behalf of those they perceive as having been wounded by us. These people are often victims in their own lives. They see themselves as being done to, by organisations and individuals, by Social Services, by the NHS, by the government, by their teachers, and now by priestesses.

But I too have a victim script. It is visible in my *'Betrayal'* poem, clear as day – I feel betrayed by women that I love. This is a victim place in me.

AND IN MY inquiring mind the questions arise. What happened to priestesses at the endings of the Goddess Temples so long ago? What happened to those of us who were killed, raped, maimed, beaten? What happened to those of us who ran away and found ourselves alone outside of our Temple communities? Were we hunted down and killed or did we hide out in far flung villages and countryside unable to trust those we met for fear of further betrayals? How lonely that was. No wonder we have a lack of confidence in the world. No wonder we are disempowered and fearful. No wonder we don't trust each other.

Confidence comes to women when we live within Her natural order of life, in societies where women have our babies within the supportive care and nurture of groups of women and men, sisters and brothers, and children. It comes when our women's groups are supported and held by fathers, brothers and sons.

The centre of these groups is the bond between women, which is essential for our health, well-being and happiness. When groups of women, of mothers and children, are in the centre of society then the world is a happier place for all to live.

HOW DO WE, how do I, address and heal my own victim script?

WE DO THIS through the creation of strong supportive women's groups, here in Glastonbury beginning with the Goddess Conference, the Goddess Temple and the Temple Trainings and all that we create together, which also includes the men who wish to be part of this loving and caring network of people.

I see that this is the way to heal my own wounds, the shadows of cancer in my life, which are expressed through the wounding of my nurturing breast. The first time I had a cancer, I saw in chemotherapy-induced vision, that I was there on the top of Burrowbridge Mump, looking out across the watery Summerland meadows, when invading warriors came to attack a small Goddess Temple, a few miles further southwest along the Dragon Line from Avalon. It was a sister who betrayed us. She opened the side-door to the warriors and let them in. The first attacker entering thrust a spear into the side of my breast, creating a wound that slowly killed me. The echoes of that wound were carried as a seed in my soul, emerging as a growing spot of cancer at the age of forty-eight in this life. It was a dangerous cancer that almost killed me on its healing journey, rising through my memories into consciousness.

And all the other betrayals by sisters in other Goddess Temples, at other times, in other places, what of them? Because this was not the only time betrayal happened in my previous lives, if it was to become a repeating pattern in this life. I think of the places in the world that feel like home places – the Goddess Temples of Avalon, Greece and Malta, Anatolia and Krete. What happened to me in these places? What happened to us?

WE/I HAVE FORGOTTEN how important it is that we women group together, and surround ourselves with our lovers, partners, parents and children, our tribes. We have let this knowledge go from our lives. We have forgotten how important it is that we love and support each other as women, not just along family lines, but along our soul lines and especially along the Motherline. It is important that we support each other always, even when we are wrong, or rather especially when we are wrong.

Over the last months I/we have been jolted emotionally by several Shadow-revealing catalysts – the words and actions of wounded women whose personal wounds reveal the Shadow in the collective, the deeper wounds. Unable because of dis-ease to face their/our Shadows, they are projected onto others. That projection irritates each woman's personal Shadow material – irritates my Shadow wounding, which is my betrayals by women and men. Perhaps even my own betrayals of other women and men – now there is a thought! I see myself as pristine, but I know I have betrayed women and men in this life when I was younger.

I want to heal my wounds. I don't want to repeat them over and over. I want to leave this betrayal script behind. I want to change my line

"It was the women who betrayed me"

to

"It is the women who support me, the women that I love".

Neolithic Goddess-loving cultures first developed and began to settle on the land with the cultivation and harvesting of simple strains of wheat, which were first discovered by women, who were the main gatherers of seeds. It became possible for groupings of people to harvest and store grain, to stay in one place, rather than following the seasons and animals in search of food as nomadic people. The first communal wooden and stone ritual monuments were built in the early Neolithic, as well as settlements where people could live together in larger groupings. The plough was invented to help cultivate the earth and over time is believed to have become the property of individual men, who could then accumulate grain, property, wealth and status, within a community. Perhaps it was then that women began to vie with each other to compete for the attention of powerful and wealthy men and so began to betray their core women's groups.

Now it is definitely time for a return to the Old Ways, where women work together, loving and supporting each other. This connects into the Matriarchy Studies work of Heide Goettner-Abendroth and Genevieve Vaughan, although I don't call for a return to Matriarchy, but to a new re-visioned woman-centred, mother-centred vision for society, for the male-centred world does not work.

NOW WE ARE enjoying two relaxing weeks in Kalkan mostly lying horizontal in the sunshine and warm shade, looking out to a blue Mediterranean Sea and sky, and every so often cooling down in our very own private and modestly-sized infinity (is that possible?) swimming pool. It is becoming less easy to remember which day is which as we leave other people and problems behind and relax. The sun is beating down on the patio beside the blue pool, overlooking the bay. It's a long time since we have been in such heat. Sleeping at night is difficult to start with, as we wake drenched in sweat, until we work out how to use the air conditioning. From the clarity of my thinking a couple of days ago I am now unable to think at all. I am relaxing, gradually letting go, wondering what has happened in the mediation process that is going on in the Temple, and then letting go of thoughts.

Each day as the sun rises I sit on the small upper balcony of our villa and watch the boats leaving the harbour of Kalkan and going out to sea as Mike does his Nei Gong practice. As I relax over the holy-days I begin to have deep and complicated dreams, releasing the challenges of the previous weeks and dreaming the future alive.

I have brought several books with me for light reading. One is the novel *Amazon* by Barbara Walker, who also compiled the inspirational 1983 *Women's Encyclopaedia of Myths and Secrets*. *Amazon* tells the story of an Amazon woman living in a matriarchal *Motherworld* society in the Black Sea area of Turkey. In ceremony the Amazon enters an ancient Goddess Temple on a vision quest. She journeys forwards through time and finds herself coming to life in modern-day America. The book details her perceptions as a woman from a matrilineal, female honouring society, arriving in modern day patriarchal America. The book is an entertaining read, but what really catches me in my heart is the word *Motherworld*. It is a word that resonates deeply inside me.

I fall asleep in the afternoon and wake thinking that I am at home in our bedroom. I wonder if Iona has felt my presence there, just for a moment as she looks after our house. I fall asleep and wake up here. After reading *"Amazon"* I am aware of other lives, other movements back and forth between lives, different possible layers of reality, of which I am conscious.

As I lie on a sun lounger in a warm reverie, visions begin to come to me of a different kind of society that we can create together in the present time – a MotherWorld, where Mother Earth, mothers and the values of mothering, of love, care, empathy and support for each other are placed in the centre of our lives, rather than being put out there on the periphery of society. In the patriarchal world in which we now live, money, greed, war and destruction, and all that proceeds from these values, are placed in the centre of society, rather than the love and care we all long for as human beings. It is so time this changed!

I begin to think deeply about what the values of such a MotherWorld society might be and over the next few days I discuss the whole idea with Mike. I also contemplate again what could have happened to the ancient matrilineal and matrifocal societies of the Goddess-loving Palaeolithic and Neolithic worlds. Why had they ended after thousands of years of successful living? What had happened? Yes, marauders had entered in and harmed us, but had we done anything to allow that to happen? How had we contributed to those changing times? Something is there, evidenced by the ways in which we behave towards each other now.

I dream that a Temple, which is much bigger than ours now, has been trashed. It is uncared for. The altars are not functional. No candles have been lit and the Lammas flower candleholder is broken. The large floor coverings are sodden with water. A woman friend is there wafting about, saying it doesn't matter. I can't get anyone to help clear up the mess. There are piles of unsorted materials. I notice a girl I knew long ago from one of our plays is sitting in the mess, smoking a cigarette. I am furious and shout at her, *"How dare you smoke in the Temple!"* She looks at me as if I am mad, but she leaves. I also shout, *"Don't you know it's illegal to smoke indoors in a public place?"* (Government laws even infiltrate the subconscious.)

I am getting more and more wound up, angry and frustrated that no-one cares. Erin comes in and whispers, *"Why hasn't anyone tidied up?"* I feel guilty that I haven't been able to keep the place clean and clear. I go with a man who is emptying a large bin full of rubbish into a pool of water. I know that it's going to splash over as he pours it into the pool, and it does. Rubbish rains down on me. I put my coat over my head as fish heads cover me, sticking to my hair and my coat.

Later I am about to give birth. A girl I once knew vaguely is going to be my midwife. I don't really know or like her. I can physically feel the baby's head coming down into the birth canal. I can feel the top of the baby's head coming through my vulva. I am about to give birth.

I wake up thinking about writing this book and that I will include something on the endings of the ancient Goddess culture, the endings of the Goddess Temples.

WE GO BY BOAT from a landing place below our rental villa, across the bay to the town of Kalkan, which is centred on the harbour area with bars and restaurants and small shops. We wind our way through the narrow streets and up the hillside to the market area to buy fresh vegetables, fruit, drinking water and wine. We pass a shop owned by a local man, who sells his own self-published books alongside tourist items. I think about having a small shop in Glastonbury, where I could sell my books as I sit and write new books – there is more than this book in my mind now.

Then I move on to thinking of having a larger Temple shop which would also sell Goddess art and craftwork. We sell a small number of Goddess goods in the Temple, but we could really do with having a bigger space. I think about trying to get hold of the Venus shop in the Courtyard of the Glastonbury Experience, which is currently owned by Lui Kreig. I have heard that he would like to give it up. Perhaps he will be open to negotiation. I have money saved that I could invest to make it happen, if the price is right. It could help priestesses earn money from their creativity.

Would priestess Sue Quatermass like to manage and run the shop? We have talked before about the possibility of having a Goddess Temple shop and I know she is interested in possibilities. We both want to encourage Goddess artists and priestesses to earn money from their creative talents. A shop could also employ local priestesses to look after the shop and there is a small room upstairs, which could be used for Goddess-based readings. There are many possibilities and I can see how it might work for us.

BACK BESIDE the pool at our villa I am now reading *"Nature and the Human Soul"* by Bill Plotkin. It's not quite so good for me as his first book I read, but it describes different stages of life and the unfolding of the soul. I leap forward to reading the 'Artisan in the Wild Orchard' chapter. I realise that I have been in transition from the place of successful and happy embodiment of my soul in the world, which happened throughout my late 40s, 50s and early 60s. I had had a feeling of mild dissatisfaction for a couple of years. I knew that I was doing what I already knew how to do. The questions came: *Was this it? Would there be no more inspiration in my life? Nothing more that was new? Was I just repeating what I already knew how to do?*

I didn't recognise that was what was happening, but I had stopped questing for a vision. Cancer came again to waken me up.

I HAVE TRULY absorbed the energies of the creative Great Mother from our Conference: more ideas, small and large, keep pouring through. As well as having Goddess books in the Temple we can have a bookcase of Goddess books in the Goddess Hall, which students can borrow. I will create this when I get home. I also begin to plan the next Orchard Day in February 2013, when all those who have taken the First Spiral of the Priestess of Avalon Training are invited to gather and spend time together. I think about possible priestesses who might be able to give talks and presentations and also a discussion amongst people of what they believe it really means to be a Priestess of Avalon now, in the world today, speaking from their experience.

Ideas arrive for the shape and content of our next 2013 Goddess Conference in a year's time, when following our Wheel of the Year, we will next be celebrating Ertha, the Mother of Earth. I see in my mind's eye the form of a ceremony or perhaps it is a sacred drama, in which Mother Ertha moulds red, white, black and yellow clay with honey and water into the images of the First Four Mothers of the Four Races. The First Mothers are embodied by four dancers, who dance themselves alive in the world, and give birth to the traditional four races of human beings, who go onto multiply into all the tribes of humans who now live on earth.

I have not written a sacred drama play for many years, as the impetus for producing individual sacred drama plays moved in the 1990s into creating the Goddess Conference. Instead of a three or four hour play, I wanted to create a much longer transformational experience – a four, then five and six day sacred drama, so that transformation could really happen for people through the means of the Conference. I can feel the seeds of an idea for writing a new play forming in my mind and I give it an evening slot in the Conference programme, which I plan now in my mind for the following year. Sometimes this is how it happens. In the time of release and recovery from the current Conference, the seeds for the future Conference are clearly laid down. The first inklings for the following year often come in the weeks just before or after the current Conference, I just have to be open to receive Her visions for the future whenever they come. The detail we work out together in the Ceremony group.

Now I plan the 2013 Conference programme with the speakers and presenters that I would like to invite and the broad themes – Celebrating Ertha, Mother of Earth; asking participants to bring earth from all over the world from all sorts of places, to mix together in ceremony, and then send out into the world as a blessing; Pilgrimage and Preparation Ceremonies on the Sacred Land; Honouring our bodies as the Temple of the Soul, Her Temple on earth; Sacred Drama performance; the Grounding of the Vision of Motherworld, because this too is now anchoring and forming in my awareness. We can suggest to people that they make a commitment to take care of a piece of the earth, whether it be a window box, or a garden or a meadow, a mountain, riverside or beach.

NEARLY EVERY NIGHT and also during naps in the day I have long intense and colourful dreams, some happy, some deeply emotional. Time expands and it feels like we are here for a good long break. On Friday I wake to another beautiful day in Paradise with the sun shining again. Paradise is the landscape Garden of the Mother. The Isle of Avalon is also known as the Paradise Isle, the Isle of the Hesperides, where the Golden Apples of Immortality grow. I am lucky to live there.

I wake from another dream thinking about all that has happened. I send love and healing to all who have attacked us, from my heart to each of theirs. I send their friends love and healing too. I realise that something in me has changed in all this. It is not what I expected. It never is, but an old script is healing/is healed? And a healing poem is waiting to be birthed, which is the opposite to my earlier poem of betrayal.

IT IS THE WOMEN WHO SUPPORT ME *August 2012*
(This is my poem. This is the healing of my wound.)

It is the women who support me
I believe it now
It is the women who support me.

After eons of forgetting our Motherworld ways
Lost with the ending of the Temples of the Goddess
Priestesses attacked, raped, maimed and killed,
Cast out from the Holy Ground, alone and bereft,
Betraying each other as fear entered in.
Priestesses of Kubaba, Cybele and Isis,
Of Artemis and Hecate, Athena and Demeter,

Of Danu and Rhiannon, of Keridwen and Ker,
Of Brighde and Artha, Bhanbha and Domnu.
Priestesses of ancient lands and sacred places,
We betrayed each other again and again.

Through the ages of the Patriarchs
We have undermined each other,
We have fought for love of mother, of sister and of man.
We have whispered in dark corners, behind each other's backs,
Betraying foes and friends alike, we have stood in defensive anger,
Pointing the finger, mouthing the curse that brings our sisters down.

But now, in this time of healing
I support all of my sisters.
I offer you my love, my respect, my holding,
In a place of safety, in a new Sisterhood.
I support you in your healing, in your life's unfolding,
As you uncover your soul's destiny
To be free from oppression and power-over patriarchy.
For this we incarnate now and I support you absolutely
In becoming who you truly are.
I support you always, in all your endeavours,
In your struggles and disappointments in illuminating shadows.
I support you when you step out in the alien, normal world
Bringing Goddess into the centre of our lives.
I support you when you succeed and I support you in your mistakes
This is no competition, I support you,
And your children, your sisters, mothers, fathers, brothers.

I hold the treasure of your heart, of your yearning to be whole
To create a better world of women, a new Motherworld

As I hold the treasures in my heart,
As I heal my ancient wound of betrayal.
A wound that's brought me Cancer
Death-threatening illness twice in my breast.
The first time I learned to receive love from unexpected people,
From the blessed Lady and from Her world.
This time I transform my pattern of betrayal
Learning to receive love from women that I love.

I am Priestess of Avalon, the Mother Land of Goddess
Now emerging from the mists as a beacon in Her world
Together we co-create a new Sisterhood
Of love and support, encouragement and power.

You are the women who support me
Yes, now I believe it
You are the women who support me
The women that I love.

IN THE LONGING of my heart for the transformation of my wounding I hopefully believe that it can happen easily, through the simple recognition of my desire and the writing of a poem. Unfortunately it is never quite so simple and the course of my healing is to continue unabated through the coming year. The stars are aligning, the squares are forming, the oppositions are becoming fixed, the conjunction of conflicting planets, inner and outer, are coming and the heavens conspire to bring me further down into the depths of my wounding in order that I might truly heal.

I make a commitment to the Lady today that I will further develop the Vision of Her Motherworld and what that might mean in the present day. The words are already beginning to form, but it needs to be really clear, so that it speaks to many people.

Chapter Ten

WHERE ARE YOU NOW, EILEEN?

 HERE IN THE Land of the Mothers I think deeply about my mother, Eileen Mary Jones, for the first time since she died last year on 14th April 2011.

Where are you now, Eileen?

She is the first person who I knew intimately who died when I had some awareness about the processes of death. The only other people in my life who I have known well who have died, are my grandmother and my father, a long time ago. I am a novice in the initiations of death and I find it fascinating. Where do we go when we die? What happens to the Soul? Where is it? For I do believe that the life of the Soul continues after death, but what does that actually mean? I have studied the Death texts of different patriarchal religions, the Tibetan Book of the Dead, the Egyptian Book of the Dead, but what does death mean in our Goddess world?

Eileen was 96 years old when she died. My father Jimmy's birthday had been on the 12th April. They got married on 13th April and Eileen died on 14th April. Although she was unconscious for several days before she passed away I do not think that the coincidence of these dates is insignificant. I think somewhere in her consciousness she waited for these special days to go by as she left the world.

Eileen had had a good long life by her beliefs and standards. For the last ten years of her life she suffered from increasing dementia, steadily losing her grip on the past and the future, living more and more in the immediate present.

She looked at the flowers and loved their colours. She liked her food and her cups of tea. She forgot who her grandchildren were. She remembered only my sister and me. When I first brought her to Glastonbury she lived for a few years in sheltered accommodation, until she began to forget how many glasses of gin she drank in the evening, and would fall over and hurt herself. I watered down the gin but she knew and would often be seen walking slowly back from the supermarket carrying another fresh bottle. She put the pans on the top of the oven and left them to burn dry. It was time for her to move into full time care. Although I loved her, I knew that I could not look after her in our home. I was out of the house too often teaching, and she would have driven me mad.

For the last few years of her life she lived happily at Southlawns, a good care home nearby, in Street. I visited her several times a week, at first to take her out for walks and to play cards or dominoes with her, which she still managed to win although other parts of her mind had stopped working, until near the end. There was no conversation to be had and I would gently massage the dry skin on her hands, legs and feet with cream and paint her nails pink, which she liked.

In the last few weeks of her life she stopped eating and lost interest in anything outside of herself. She began to close down. She lay still in bed. When she stopped eating I asked the care staff if she was dying, but no-one would give me a straight answer. She had stopped eating a couple of times before, once for two weeks, when she had an infection. Then suddenly one day she recovered, saying, *"Take me to the dining room! I'm hungry."* Was it going to be like this again? Then her personal carer said to me one day, *"This is a good way to go, peacefully, in her own room in her home."* And I understood this time that she was dying.

In the last week I sat with her, holding her hand, soft and wrinkled with age. We listened to Andrea Bocelli singing. Tears rose swiftly, filling my eyes and I sobbed for a few moments with grief. She had been lying with her eyes closed, still apart from her breathing, her chest rising and falling gently. As she heard my sob she turned her head towards me once. As I looked at her, she opened her eyes and caught my eye. Then she closed her eyes again and turned away from me. I felt rejected as she closed down. My mother was no longer there to comfort me, but in fact she hadn't been there for many years, since her illness began. She had disappeared as my mother many years before. She became the child as I became her mother.

She died early in the morning at about 5.30am. The care home telephoned about 5.00am to let me know that her breathing had altered and they thought she was dying, but I didn't hear the telephone ringing. I heard the next phone call at 7.00am when she had already left her body. Mike and I raced to Southlawns in ten minutes. Eileen lay peacefully in her bed, her skin still warm to the touch. I held her hand. The numinous gateway stood open. She was free of her old body and mind, which had contained her spirit. We sat with her and prayed for her soul and performed Phowa, the Tibetan practice for the dying, seeing her Soul merging with Goddess, Great Spirit, the Mystery, whatever my mother believed in for herself. She didn't have a spiritual belief to sustain her in life. She was an atheist all the time I knew her. For her, life ended at death and that was it. We sat with her body for a while.

Where are you now Eileen?

Later as Mike and I drove home we stopped down by the River Brue and walked along its banks. It felt like Eileen was rushing backwards and forwards across the meadows, so happy to be free of her old body. A beautiful heron flew along the river. Herons open the gateways to the ancestral worlds and it was as if Eileen was with us in the form of the heron.

It was only in the next few days that I felt Eileen's confusion,

"Where am I? What has happened?"

The question went round my head,

"Where are you now, Eileen?"

I journeyed in consciousness with Eileen into the Otherworld, trying to be there for her to help her cross over, reassuring her, trying to help her feel safe as she moved further out into the Great Beyond. I went with her. I hoped and visioned that my Dad, her Jimmy, was there in some familiar form to meet her. He had been her lover, her husband, for many years although she had forgotten him too in the last years of her life. I had made him a promise the year that he died, that I would take care of her later in life. I had fulfilled my promise as best I could. He was the only man that I knew that she ever loved.

When my father died in 1984, to the great astonishment of my sister Ann and me, my mother declared that Jimmy had been the most perfect loving husband in the world. Ann and I could not believe what she was saying. As their children we had never even glimpsed this love affair between them. We had only experienced him as a severe controlling Victorian father, and her as an often critical, though affectionate mother. I never saw them kiss, and only once saw them touch, her arm in his, several years after I had left home. The rest had been for us an experience of listening to acrimonious argument.

Eileen was such a mixture – an ordinary stay at home housewife, in the days when that meant the woman looked after the house, the husband and the children, while the man went out to work long hours. Her interests were varied. She liked old stones, Roman ruins, archaeology. She took us to many ancient and sacred sites, places that bored me as a child, but which I now also love. She liked drives in the countryside and gardening. She went to evening classes in practical things like woodwork, car maintenance and cake icing. Her main interests were playing golf and bridge, the source of endless arguments with Jimmy.

She never liked to talk about anything of depth, of meaning. If something difficult came up her voice would become a quiet whisper in case the neighbours might hear. In my early 30s when I was pregnant and unmarried she told me that if I went home no-one would know about my baby. To be single and pregnant was the biggest disgrace I could bring to our family. In my world it wasn't, but in their world it was a heinous crime. Once her granddaughter was born everything did change with the living presence of my beautiful baby girl Iona, and again when Torquil was born three years later, also out of wedlock. My father had always longed for a boy in his family of girls.

When they were young I took my children every Xmas to visit my parents and after my father died, to see Eileen on her own. She was kind to them and they loved her, and they loved to go and visit her. She was also very generous to me. In the years when I had little money she would always give me some that would help tide me over a bad patch. She'd fill my car with petrol and we'd go to the supermarket and she would buy us a trolley full of groceries. It really helped. She didn't have to do that, but she was a kind and generous woman too. I did the same for Iona when she struggled.

What I did not realise until later on in my life when I was in therapy and remembering my childhood, was that all through the years we lived at home, Eileen had competed with my sister and me for Jimmy's attention, acting like a jealous lover. She attacked, criticised and undermined her daughters out of fear that he might not love her alone.

I did not grieve for Eileen when she died. It felt like she had left a long time before and my grieving had already taken place over several years of caring for her and mothering her as our roles reversed, she becoming more childlike in her needs and wants. My sister lived several hours away in Bedfordshire and could only visit every three months or so. I became Eileen's main family carer.

My sister and I are such different people too, with such different lives. We are similarly devoted to the divine, but in very different forms – my sister to Jesus and me to Goddess. But beyond that how did we come to have the same parents? They provided the perfect launch pad into life for what we became – me the wild priestess, and my sister following a controlled and conventional life as a teacher of chemistry. We were both damaged in different ways by the severities of our karma and upbringing.

A couple of days before Eileen's funeral I felt her lift off from the earth. Lorraine Pickles was our funeral celebrant, who helped Ann and me design a non-religious celebration of Eileen's life. Eileen had believed in neither god nor goddess, so there was no need to let her go in that way. My sister strove to give Eileen a Christian farewell to which I objected as she claimed my mother for Jesus, and Lorraine helped us find the middle ground.

Where are you now Eileen?

Eileen's ashes came in a cardboard cylinder with a pretty bluebell wood photograph on the outside. My sister wanted nothing to do with her ashes as

Eileen was no longer in them. They were irrelevant to her. I scattered small amounts on the rose bushes in our garden. Eileen had often bought me roses and other shrubs, so that *"You can remember me when I am gone."* And I do. She lives on in our garden in the pink, yellow and red roses. A small amount of her ashes are in a special pot in the ancestor tower by the main altar in our house. It feels good to have her there.

Where are you now Eileen?

A few months after her cremation Mike and I took the bulk of her remains to the top of Glastonbury Tor to release her to the winds and wilds of Avalon. We stood on the top facing north, the place of the ancestors, with the wind and rain blowing from the south. I thought the ashes would fly away from me out over the slopes of the Tor. As I upturned the urn the wind changed suddenly and a gust of air came from the north. I was covered in my mother's ashes mixed with the rain – my face, hair, arms, coat, my legs, everything. I could hear Eileen, "Got you!" she said with a wicked laugh.

Where are you now Eileen?

Criticism, attack, undermining, disempowerment and collusion were all part of our dysfunctional family patterns. Two or three members of the family, which included mother, father, two daughters and my grandmother, would collude unconsciously against one person, often me as the youngest daughter. I was a naturally happy, exuberant and emotionally sensitive child, who gradually over the years lost self-confidence. They called me a 'show off', as I expressed my natural love of life. When they criticised me and I walked or ran away from them, I was 'too sensitive'. They would say often, *"There she goes, off in a huff again."* I was easily hurt by them. To avoid pain I hid myself away from my family and from life.

In the years when Eileen came to live near me, first of all in her sheltered home, she would try the same old unconscious disempowering tactics, as if I was still seven years old. By then I had grown enough that I was able to stop the behaviour in its tracks, by seeing it, naming it and refusing to play the game. Each time Eileen would give me a knowing look and would say,

"*Sorry, dear. Don't take it seriously. I don't mean it.*"

"*Then why do it?*"

She would continue on as if she had done nothing. When my sister came to visit the two of them played the game of attacking and undermining each other with gusto. They tried to include me, but I didn't join the game that just ends with people feeling hurt. My sister did not like my mother. She felt unloved by her and visited Eileen out of a sense of duty as a daughter.

WE COME INTO LIFE with our foundation characters already formed from a mix of our soul qualities, the seeds of our karmic wounding and our genetic inheritance. You can see that character already there in the face, eyes and body of each baby that comes into the world. Our personalities are formed through the experiences that our characters have in life, interweaving together, creating a reality, which we identify as 'I', who we think we are. This 'I' develops likes and dislikes, fixed attitudes, prejudices, beliefs about life and experience – '*This is who I am, this is what I believe, this is what I want*'. However our true identity as a Soul is none of these and through life we must unpick and disentangle the threads of character and personality to first glimpse, and then gradually come to know and express the Soul who we truly are, the one who is the originator, who inhabits our physical, emotional and mental bodies.

This disentangling of personality, character and soul, is particularly so for those who follow any kind of spiritual path, and especially for those who would be priestesses and priests of Goddess, emerging out of a patriarchal world. We have all been conditioned by the beliefs and thoughtforms of the patriarchal cultures in which we all live and we have to make conscious the unconscious threads that we have absorbed as children from within our families and cultures. As we seek Goddess within and without, we can uncover our true Selves and emerge, like butterflies from within a transforming cocoon. It is this healing path that is a principle work of transformation within our Priestess/Priest of Avalon Training.

Over the years of my life as my Soul has expressed its longing to come more and more into expression, I have been healing the wounds to my inner child, my sweet little Katie, who got terribly hurt by her family. I have healed much of my family drama and the karmic seeds that are carried in the folds of my soul.

> Oh, Eileen,
> As I write down these memories
> Here in Lycia, in Anatolia
> Ancient Land of the Mothers
> I thank you for being my mother
> For loving me in your way
> For caring for me as a child and as an adult
> For doing the best that you could do
> I hope you are rested and healed
> Unafraid and becoming ready for your return
> On the Great Wheel of Life
> To this beautiful wonderful Earth.

I THINK with fondness about how Eileen was before the last ten years of her life, before she became demented. I feel the love I had for my mother.

And my question is still,

Eileen, where are you now?

As I feel her considering coming back into incarnation again. I believe that my father, who died years ago is now someone's child, growing up, in his 20s, finding his or her way in the world.

Chapter Eleven

The Shock of Sudden Death

WE HAVE BEEN HOME from holiday for a week or so. The negative emails and telephone calls resume. I feel harassed. I am thinking about how my Shadow projects itself outwards from me to appear as an unstable woman with the potential to be attacking, dangerous even. She might come and get me, try to harm me. What is the Shadow part of me that is still there, afraid of the attacker, the fear that I am projecting outwards, and which is appearing in the world for me to feel. I tell myself to embrace the Shadow, unpack the Shadow, but how to do that.

A DAY OR TWO AGO I was walking along with Poppy, feeling happy, then we came upon another dog and Poppy stole its ball and wouldn't let go of it. Anger arose in me and I felt I could almost have killed Poppy because she wouldn't obey me and drop the ball. I don't want my anger to be seen by the other dog's deaf owner, who can't understand what I am saying. I so nearly hit Poppy hard, although thankfully something stopped me, stopped my rage at the dog. My anger which was once hidden from me emerges again through Poppy. How do we express the Shadow, hear what the Shadow has to say and hold clear boundaries for those who embody the Shadow?

ON MONDAY 17th September Koko emails and says she'd like to come over and see me, which is lovely. We haven't seen each other since the Conference.

For many years Koko was the *hostess with the mostest* in the Priestess House and Pilgrims B & B in Glastonbury, where she looked after so many people, students on Temple courses, priestesses, visitors from abroad, all sorts of people. A couple of years ago she moved to Weston-super-Mare to the area where she had been brought up. She wanted to return to her youthful stomping grounds and to spend more time with her family and grandchildren. I had wanted her to stay in Glastonbury. She felt a strong call to go back to her roots and be with her family.

Koko arrives at the house at tea-time with her little dog, Charlie, who likes to sit on her lap. We talk and laugh a lot as usual and discuss all our future travel plans. She is about to go to China in ten days time with a friend. Mike and I are going to Mexico in October for the first Mexican Goddess Conference, organised by our lovely Mexican Priestess Aline Castell. We all love travelling to new and ancient home places.

Koko tells us that yesterday, Sunday, she took part in a Charity Fun Raft Race on the river near Weston-super-Mare, where she lives. She and the same friend she is about to go traveling with, were dressed as the Owl and the Pussy Cat on their raft. As is the way with these things in the water the raft soon fell apart and Koko was pitched into the river. She banged her head on something under the water and had had a slight head-ache ever since, but it is fine.

We laugh and joke together about what happened at this year's Conference and it is lovely to see her. I feel close to her after our deep connection in Turkey and the realisation of our soul sisterhood. Then I get ready to go out dancing 5 Rhythms. She will pick up Freddie's Lammas Mother sculpture from the Temple on Friday and we will meet again next week.

WEDNESDAY 19th September is my mother's birthday. I have a day teaching a couple of Correspondence students who are beginning the Third Spiral of the Priestess of Avalon Training. Then we have a meeting to work out the Goddess Temple Ceremony for Mabon (Autumn Equinox). As Mike and I are sitting down after supper there is a telephone call from Rosie, who sounds very tearful. I wonder what is happening. She puts John on the phone, who also sounds very upset.

The Shock of Sudden Death

What is it?

John tells me that Koko died this morning.

The shock is overwhelming. I can't believe it. She was only here two days ago. How does that happen? We laughed and talked together.

Koko, you cannot be dead!

One moment she is vibrant and alive and the next day dead. It is unbelievable. Lovely Koko who sat in our sitting room right here just two days before, is now dead?

I listen to the details. On Wednesday morning Koko was supposed to be seeing her daughter, Leiza, for a treatment for her headache and didn't arrive. Leiza phoned Andy, an old friend, who lived nearby, asking him to go and check on Koko. He found the key by the back door and went into the house. He found Koko in the bathroom, dead on the floor. What a terrible shock that must have been for him. She had been dead by then for a few hours. It looked like she had had her breakfast and then she had gone to have a shower, and she collapsed and died, just like that. Andy held Koko in his arms for three hours, telling her how much he loved her, how beautiful she was. He had known her for 20 years and they had been in a relationship for the first ten years of that time. Koko was very fond of him, but didn't want to be with him. Andy called John, who is a friend of his and John has called me.

I am in shock. I tell Mike and Iona who are listening to my end of telephone call, what has happened. We sit quietly together and pray for Koko's Soul. We perform Phowa for Koko, visualising her extremely bright soul energy merging into the great love and light of the Lady of Avalon, to whom Koko is dedicated as Her Priestess. In a while I call a couple of Koko's close Priestess friends, who I know will pray for her soul too and tell them that she has died. We are all in shock. My tears do not fall yet. I feel calm and still, in awe of it all.

I let everyone know that we will hold a vigil in the Goddess Temple on the following afternoon. The awful news travels fast. Koko is a popular member of our community, loved by many people. We need to gather to express our feelings. I find a beautiful photograph of Koko from the Conference and print it out with others. I make a collage of photos of my lovely friend and put them in a frame. We will need a focus for our grief. In my mind I can hear Koko's voice. I reflect on the fact that that she has died on my mother's birthday. How strange.

MANY PEOPLE come into our Vigil for Koko in the Goddess Temple, and it is soon full. We create a lovely shrine for her, next to the main altar, with photos, flowers and candles, that will remain until her funeral has taken place. We cry together and hold each other in our shared grief for a long time. We pray together for Koko's soul and tell stories about her, our experiences of her. It soon becomes clear that many people saw her as their best friend, someone they loved, who loved them in return. It is truly beautiful as we come together in our sadness. Sometimes we have no idea how people feel about someone until they are gone. Our Vigil continues into the evening as people who work in the daytime find their way to this Sanctuary of Sorrow.

On the following morning I wake early thinking about Koko and what she wants for her funeral, feeling the weight of what she needs and wants for all those she has left behind. She will be our first close Priestess Ancestor and how we honour her lays down a template for the passing of future priestesses. She touched so many people's lives – as the mother of Leiza, Sally, Zoe and Wills, as a loved grandmother to her grandchildren; as Priestess she was also for many years the Keeper of the Priestess House, where she was the welcoming arms and ears for so many students and priestesses who stayed with her.

She was the Keeper of the Camino and another circle of people in the Glastonbury community. She knew many craftspeople and artisans as she designed and redesigned every space she ever owned. As she travelled the world to different Goddess communities and conferences, she touched the lives of many. She made a difference in Spain, South Africa and Ireland. She loved to travel, her gypsy heritage made travelling a breeze for her. She had had quite a few lovers and husbands in her time, who still love her. She loved exploring different spiritual and therapeutic teachings and was a therapist and healer for many years. She had taken so many courses and was always adding to the sum of her knowledge. She had so much knowledge that I continually encouraged her to develop her own teaching and she was about to offer her first year-long training through the Goddess Temple this autumn. It will not happen now.

One of Koko's greatest gifts was manifestation, which she offered as a fine art for the Goddess Conference. For the last seven years Koko has been my partner in creation, bringing together diverse people and uniting them within the Conference beehive, as her Melissas, (bee priestesses) those who work in the Conference in exchange for a ticket. She was the Queen Bee and could produce almost anything out of her magic cauldron.

"Koko, I forgot, we need a couple of high stools."

"When?"

"In half an hour."

And they appeared in five minutes. She went over the road and borrowed them from the pub. People willingly gave things to her that were needed. She manifested things out of the back of her van – plates, tablecloths, plants. One time we needed 14 china dolls to re-dress as Wild Maiden Dolls and she found them on sale in a charity shop in Weston, for almost no money.

On the first Priestess Enchantress training I spent so many enjoyable hours with Koko sitting with her in the front of her people carrier, as we made our pilgrimages across the countryside. On our Morgen Sister year we were based at the Camino, meeting together every few weeks to be creative and to work with the Nine Morgens of Avalon on transforming our Shadow emotions. We travelled together on Goddess Pilgrimages in Spain and Turkey. Last winter in Turkey when I was just finding out that I had breast cancer and was filled with fear, she really helped me to release that fear from my body. Through her soul retrievals for me we realised that we are in truth friends and soul sisters.

And now my soul sister is dead.

There are also all her friends from all the different communities of which she was a part in her life, from earlier before she came to Glastonbury, when she wasn't very happy in her life. She found her happiness when she moved here and became the Priestess she is. She has friends in Weston-super-Mare where she grew up and where she was living now, and in Bristol. All the neighbours she brought into her home to create community, which she did wherever she lived. The friends she went running with. She touched the lives of so many different kinds of people. She touched my life deeply and I love her.

She is a unique and amazing being and we are so lucky to have known her.

HER DAUGHTERS come to see Koko's shrine in the Temple and we all cry together. Just like Koko they think of others in their own time of need, and bring scones and jam that Koko had made, to share with others. I speak with them and offer my deepest sympathy. I offer my services as Priestess for whatever they need or want. I don't know of their individual beliefs or faith or whether they have any, if it is the same for all of them or are they all different? I can only offer my service to them as Priestess of the Lady of Avalon. I step forward in this moment to be available for this completely real ceremony for my friend. Although it makes me feel very nervous, if I can't offer to do this for my friend, what is the point of any of it? This is what it means to priestess for each other as we pass through one of the greatest Rites of Passage that there is.

A FEW DAYS LATER on Saturday it is the outdoor Dedication Ceremony for the students completing their First Spiral in the Priestess of Avalon Training, and we all need to be very present for them in that ceremony too. They did not know Koko, or only briefly, perhaps in the Conference, and Erin, their tutor, who was also Koko's friend, and I, have to hold the energy of the ceremony and the space of embodiment. I am glad that we have done this ceremony many times before and know what we are doing. With our many years of ceremonial experiences in the Goddess Conference we do know how to hold energy through challenging circumstances.

On Sunday it is the Goddess Temple Mabon Ceremony, celebrating the Mother of Earth. She is the Goddess we will celebrate at the following year's Goddess Conference and we lay down the seeds for that future event in this ceremony. Mary and Trevor build a beautiful mound of earth in the centre of the floor, decorated with flowers and plants, around which we invoke the Mother of Earth and all Her earthly blessings. As part of the ceremony I speak my new poem, *"It is the Women Who Support me"*. All those who heard the first *'Betrayal'* version in the Goddess Conference know what it means to hear this second version. It feels very healing to speak this poem of support aloud, especially at this time of Koko's passing, when we all need each other's love and support so much.

IN THE coming days many people come to the Temple bringing photos of Koko, bringing flowers and candles, leaving words of love for her. We learn after the post mortem that she died from a haemorrhage on the brain. When she banged her head underwater she broke some blood vessels, which explain her headache, but she didn't think anything of it. The bleeding gradually got worse and then killed her. The message is clear – always get checked out if you bang your head.

KOKO'S DAUGHTER Zoe and her family ask if I would like to conduct the funeral and of course, I say *"Yes."* I feel very honoured to be able to hold this ceremonial place for Koko. What greater honour can there be than to be present for the passing of my beloved sister priestess. We meet to discuss how the family would like Koko's funeral to be. They want it to be a celebration of all parts of her life. I have been thinking about how we can create something meaningful for everyone and about the ways in which we might honour Koko as a Priestess of Avalon. It seems important that we get this really right for her and her family and friends.

I can see us sitting in vigil with her open coffin, so that people can come and say goodbye to her body personally. Mike and I sat like this for a day with the body of Helene Koppejan, who was the original owner of the Glastonbury Experience complex of shops and function rooms. It was her generosity which allowed many of our spiritual educational ventures to begin, by letting us hire rooms at low rents for our activities. Sitting with Helene's body had been an amazing experience as those who had known her came to say goodbye. Although I had not known Helene personally that well, it somehow fell to Mike and I to take care of her funeral and her body, as Mike was in charge of the Glastonbury Experience at the time. I know how moving a vigil will be for people who love Koko.

I want to help the family to have what they need in the funeral. I also want to honour Koko as the first Priestess of Avalon to die here in Glastonbury, in the present time. I know that we have to do something really strong that creates an energetic template for how modern day Priestesses pass over into Avalon at death. I feel very nervous about asking for this, but it is as if Koko is there by my side, prompting me to ask for these things for her.

The family are very open and want to give everyone everything they need. They tell me that Koko's life had often been difficult when they were all younger and that she only really became happy when she moved to Glastonbury, so they are grateful to us. They tell me new things about Koko's life from before I knew her, that I didn't know. There is time to work everything out as we wait for Koko's body to be released from the post mortem.

IT IS TUESDAY in the week of Koko's funeral and I am in the Temple waiting for Koko's son, Wills, to arrive to see the altar we have made for Koko. He is coming back from South America. A woman who has been asked not to come into the Temple because of abusive behaviour, enters the Temple. I ask her to leave and she refuses. Her voice is raised and she begins to shout at me. In the ensuing argument I find myself retreating backwards into a corner of the Temple – the priestess is cornered in the Temple. I feel frightened. As soon as I notice I am cowering backwards I move forwards out of the corner. Others step forward to help and the woman leaves.

I remember feelings of being aggressed by my angry father and retreating into a corner, protected by my mother. I also remember an ancient place of fear of being attacked in a Goddess Temple.

This is the last thing I need to deal with at the moment and this intrusion feels like the last straw. I am already feeling under a lot of pressure because Koko's Vigil and Funeral are happening in the next two days. I feel open, strong, and vulnerable, and I am holding a lot of people in their grief. It is full moon and everyone is wobbling in the strong energy. I want to do everything so well for my friend, for her family and for the community.

On Wednesday 3rd October about 4.00pm the undertakers bring Koko's body to the Goddess Hall in a lovely violet painted coffin, the priestess colour chosen by her daughters. Priestesses go to the gate to welcome our sister's body and walk with her into the Hall. There are lots of us here to be with her. We do everything in a still and sacred way, for our beloved sister priestess, and it is so sad. We cannot have an open coffin because it has been too long since Koko died and because of the post-mortem wounds to her head. But we can still sit in vigil with her. The Goddess Hall is beautifully decorated and we place Koko's coffin in the centre of the Hall and surround it with flowers and candles at the corners, and fruits and nuts. We smudge the coffin and the whole space.

There is a large circle of chairs around the edges of the Hall and people come to sit with her over the next three hours. Some pray, some weep softly in their sorrow and also as their personal wounding around death is triggered. By seven o'clock there are a lot of people in the Hall. Some of Koko's family also arrive and sit with us. I think its very comforting for them to experience all the love that people have for their Mum. At a certain point I catch a glimpse of Koko standing leaning her elbow on her coffin, with one of her familiar expressions on her face,

"Lighten up, everyone. I'm still here. When is the party going to begin?"

Koko took her name from Kokopelli, the Native American trickster, fun-maker, prankster.

Our ceremonial circle of priestesses are all women who knew Koko well and had strong loving relationships with her. We are Anna Osann who has come from Spain, Annabel Du Boulay, Erin McCauliff, Katinka Soetens, Rose Flint, Roz Bound who has come all the way from Canada, Sally Pullinger and me. We can all hold a strong and grounded energy together. We call in Britannia's Wheel of the nine directions and we call in all the parts of Koko – Koko in her earthly body, Koko as Crone, Koko as Air and Breath, Koko as her Maiden self, Koko as Fire and Creativity, Koko as Lover, Koko as Water and Compassion, Koko as Mother, and Koko as her Soul in the centre with the Lady of Avalon. It is beautiful invocation, bringing together all the parts of who Koko was in her life, to celebrate her whole person.

Then with drum from Tegwyn and Lydia, I lead a deep and slow journey with Koko's Soul Self travelling across the waters to the Sacred Isle of Avalon and Western Isle of the Dead. We all go with her in a large Barge to the Sacred Isle. We journey together with Koko in Her light body from the shoreline up the slopes of the Island to the Temple of the Lady of Avalon. There we see Koko merge and become one with the Lady of Avalon. The energy and feeling is awesome. It is amazing! Everyone experiences this, even those who have never journeyed in this way before. After a while we all come back together leaving Koko behind with the Lady. We travel back across the waters from the Isle and return to our bodies, sitting in the Goddess Hall. We make sound, flowing on the energy, and sing together for a long time sending loving energy out into the world. It is done.

After the end of the journey most people leave the Goddess Hall to go home. Several priestesses – Tegwyn, Katie, Lorraine, Jacqui and others are staying with Koko's body through the night. Tomorrow is the public funeral and I need to be wide awake for that.

The funeral is held the next day in the Town Hall as we know that many people want to come. It is where we all spent so many amazing times together in the Goddess Conference. In the morning Caroline, Sharlea and Michelle create a beautiful altar on the stage of the Town Hall, with a great photograph of Koko, flowers and candles on lovely cloths. Everything is soon prepared with horseshoe circles of chairs encircling a central space where Koko's coffin will be placed. I check to see that all is good. Everyone is so amazing in the ways in which they have stepped forwards to give their energy and talents for Koko. I feel very proud of who we all are and what we can give to each other, especially in these times of deepest need.

I return to the Goddess Hall where people are gathering for the procession of Koko's coffin through the streets to the Town Hall. Everything is prepared and more and more people arrive to pray and spend these moments with her. Koko's family arrive, her children and grandchildren, ex-husbands and lovers, well as old friends who knew her a long time, other people that none of us know. Men from our community come to carry Koko's coffin, Mike, John, Andy, Duncan, Peter and Trevor. As they lift the coffin Terry takes the trestles to the Town Hall, so they will be there for the coffin to rest upon when it arrives. People just think of the things that need doing and do them at the right moment. Everything flows easily into place. It is wonderful.

The coffin is carried out through the door along the pathway in the Hall garden. The sun is shining, there are clouds, and there is a rainbow in the sky, the sign of a great soul departing. Sue and Marianne scatter rose petals along the path before the coffin. In the road Lydia leads the front of the procession, beating a slow beat on her big drum. I come next followed by the pairs of ceremonial priestesses. We are dressed in priestess purple, which I know Koko likes. She always loved to dress up and was a fine role model for us all. Behind the coffin are the family and then all the rest of the mourners. We carry some of Lydia Ruyle's Goddess Icon banners, for this is a colourful life-affirming procession too. As we walk however it feels like a deeply sad occasion.

The traffic and the people stop as we walk slowly up Benedict Street from the Goddess Hall, although not too slow because the coffin is heavy for the men carrying Koko's body. We turn into the Market Place and from there into the Town Hall. As we arrive at the Town Hall we have Melissas to welcome everyone – Helena, Tressy, Daina and Georgina. The Town Hall is full of people, about 350 squeeze in, many standing around the edges. It takes a while to get the coffin into the centre of the Hall and to get everyone in and as many seated as possible.

It is a simple ceremony based around the natural elements of the Goddess's nature – earth, water fire and air, that we hope will speak to all the different kinds of people who knew and loved Koko. I introduce everyone and call in the Lady to be present. We offer blessings for Koko and her family and friends within the circle of the elements. There are wonderful poems and words of remembrance from Zoe, Leiza, Sally and Wills, from Annabel, from Koko's grandson and an old friend. There are wonderful songs that melt the heart from the Avalonian Free State Choir. Julie Felix, who knew Koko in the Goddess Conference, sings a beautiful song that we know Koko loved. Through it all I feel strong and centred. I hold all the emotion, all the grief and the humour, that rolls around the Hall through the ceremony. I hold it until the end when Julie and the Choir sing the Celtic Blessing Song, when tears rise up and overflow from my eyes and roll unstoppably down my face, in grief for the loss of my friend.

> *May the Road rise up to greet you.*
> *May the Sun be always at your back*
> *May the Rain pour soft upon your face*
> *Until we meet again,*
> *May Goddess hold you*
> *In the hollow of Her hand.*

I cannot stop crying for quite a long time.

We have to wait until the hearse arrives. It is a camper-van hearse, that reminds Koko's grown up daughters and son of the times in their childhood, when Koko would pile them all into her camper van and take them off on another exploration, another trip somewhere exciting, often when things were difficult at home. The hearse arrives and we sing for Koko as she leaves the Town Hall and the coffin goes into the van. Only Koko's adult children are going to the crematorium. They want to spend their last moments altogether with her.

The hearse goes off up the High Street followed by her children. It turns out that it's a bit early to get to the crematorium, so the hearse stops and parks higher up the High Street and they all go into a café for a cup of tea, before continuing on to the final destination. Koko would like that, stopping on the way for a cup of tea and a cake.

We go back to the Town Hall where everything is being cleared away, and then back to the Goddess Hall, which has also been completely cleared up. Our priestesses and priests have been so amazing with all that they have given today. I feel really proud of our Goddess community.

THEN WE make our way to the Camino where Di Milstein and Penny Gould and other friends have set up a lovely space for Koko's Wake, with more photos of Koko when she was younger, as well as food and drinks. There are short speeches and toasts and we all get rather drunk, as we share memories of Koko, and all that she meant to us. There are tears and laughter, sadness and dancing. I see Koko several times, sitting on the arm of a chair, standing next to her family, sitting up on the roof beams looking down on us, comforting us from the Other Side, assuring us that life continues after death.

This has been such an amazing time for us all. We have said farewell in a wonderful way to our soul sister Koko, who is now our First Priestess Ancestor in modern times. We have laid down an energetic template for the passing of a Priestess of Avalon and everything feels complete. I know that Koko is there on the Other Side of the Veil, available and willing to share her wisdom with us.

THE LAST FEW DAYS have been so awesome, so intense, so amazing, holding the people. It has been such an incredible time. I thank you, Koko, for this opportunity of creating this template of how we release our priestesses into your world, Lady, into your world of Avalon, with grace and beauty, sadness and joy – the whole mixture of feelings. I have held so much grief for the family, for priestesses, for children, for myself. It is such a privilege to lead our community through this process.

I think I have learned not be so afraid of death, or rather the process of death and the after-death state. I have the feeling that I am being trained in the ways of death and dying through re-membering and through experience. These are skills that I already have, but have not had to use so far in my life. These are skills for the dying, for those who have passed over and for those who remain behind.

You lead me onwards, Lady, always into new territories. The Priestess path unfolds into more and more meaningful ceremonies – real ceremonies/real happenings.

Teach me to be good at this, Lady. Teach me well, that I may learn well.

* * *

Chapter Twelve

Falling Down a Hole

N SATURDAY just a few days later, I am holding another 10 Hours day, this time *Exploring the Inner Landscape of Avalon*. Once again I journey for myself as well as leading others.

As part of the journey we go to visit the Priestess House on the Isle of Avalon. I see Koko living there now. She waves to me. She has already begun to modernise the house. In previous journeys the Priestess House was always a bit old, from an earlier time. Now Koko has been there for a while and she has already begun renovations. She plans to modernise everything, to put in new bedrooms and en-suite bathrooms, just as she would do in life, in any house in which she lived. She is preparing the house for future residents, for the times when we will each cross over, one by one, to join her, although hopefully not for a while yet.

I see you there in Avalon, my friend. And I miss you.

As we journey into the Forest of Memory I am contemplating leadership and what it means to be a leader in the present. I wonder why I have such a resistance and always have had, to being a leader, to being seen as a leader, even when I know that I am one. I have a reticence about leading others. I don't want to be the figurehead, standing alone, up there on some pedestal from which I must inevitably fall. I don't want to be a guru. I don't want acolytes. I don't want chelas. I don't want adoring students – well, only sometimes. I look for equals, even when I know that I do know many things that others do not know.

Then as I journey through the Forest I remember a time when I was a King, who gave orders and was obeyed through fear of pain and death. I have a reluctance to lead, because of my fear of becoming him again, although he can leap out sometimes, as I shout at the dog, until I catch him and squash him back in again.

"*Obey me!*" He shouts, "*You should obey me, no matter what. I don't need to tell you why, you should just obey me!*"

I don't like this Shadow part of myself. I am afraid to admit this Shadow part exists, because then the others will say,

"*Told you so, you patriarch, you! You only want power over us!*"

So I have sat back many times in confusion over who leads in certain community gatherings. I am taking the lead more and more. I have to dare to tread there, dare to do it without making too many mistakes. I have to learn to ask permission, to ask what others think, to take notice of what others think, to allow myself to be persuaded if necessary, and also to have the strength of my convictions and to inspire others with my passion and vision.

As I contemplate all these thoughts a poem arises.

> *How can I lead when I have a ruler inside*
> *The King who demands obedience*
> *To his every whim, right or wrong?*
> *How can I lead the oppressed to freedom*
> *When I have a Tyrant inside me*
> *Who wants to squash all opposition down?*
> *How can I empower the dis-empowered*
> *When my power-hungry Emperor wants to conquer all?*
> *I see you, my interior Lord of the Shadowlands*
> *Light flashing brightly on your raiment*
> *You have revealed yourself to me.*

* * *

I am afraid to lead because of you.
I am afraid to be bigger than I am
To show myself as Queen of my Realm
In case you should come roaring out of the Shadows
Demanding unbridled power over all you survey

Oh, little Prince of the inner lands
You who in previous lives and ages
Took power by force of arms
By birthright of the fatherline
Now you must rule a small domain.

But I was not only a ruler in the times of the patriarchs
Once I was also leader in the Motherworld.
Now I have returned to reveal a new way.
I walk with my fears, with my hope
To create a new world
To lead from within
To empower and support
To love without boundary
To hold all with compassion
The healthy, the sick, the halt and the lame
We are all wounded by the times of the patriarchs
Together we can heal, together we can change.

In the last few weeks I have been doing lots more thinking about the values of MotherWorld and what it would really mean to bring those values back into our patriarchal societies. I am beginning to write down a first statement about the Vision of MotherWorld.

* * *

A COUPLE OF WEEKS later it's Friday 19th October and we are about to decorate the Goddess Hall for Samhain. Sandi has said that she has some rolls of black material that we can use for decorating the Goddess Hall and the Temple. I go around to her house at nine thirty in the morning to pick the material up before decoration begins. I walk into her charming house. Her two dogs are running around the hall floor. They are very sweet.

I follow Sandi into her small sitting room where I can see rolls of black material and lots of artificial black roses piled up on the sofas. They look great for our purposes. Sandi turns round and I step back to give her more room in the small space.

I step backwards into a void. There is nothing beneath my foot!

I fall through space into a hole. The left side of my body crashes down onto the edge of a square hole. There is a crushing searing pain in my left side as my ribs are squashed upwards by the force of the fall. My left leg and the rest of my body hang down through the hole. My right foot has caught the edge of the hole and my right leg is twisted up through the hole. It feels like my knee is going to break. I have stepped backwards unawares into an open trapdoor to a cellar, which I did not know was there. Sandi has not warned me there is an open trapdoor in her sitting room behind the door.

The pain is huge. My body goes into shock. I am scared that my knee is going to break. I hold onto the sides of the hole with my arms, holding myself up to prevent myself from falling further down into the cellar, my sides screaming in agony. I look up. Sandi is just standing there, in shock too, not doing anything to help me. She is terrified that she has killed Kathy Jones – the great archetype.

I scream in pain,

"Help me get up! My knee is breaking! Help me!"

Then she moves. She leans down and helps haul me up as I push up on the sides of the hole with my arms, with the little strength that I have left. Somehow we manage to get me out of the hole. I look down into the dark cavern of the Underworld below, with a small ladder coming up through it. I have been saved by the ladder and the narrow width of the opening. If I had fallen to the bottom I could easily have broken my back or my head, and could even be dead, like Koko.

It all hurts so much that I go into deep shock. I lie next to/over the mouth of the Underworld. Beside me there is the back of a sofa in one direction and another on the other side. There is no room to move, to roll away. I have no strength to move. I am crying with the pain of it all. It is hard to breathe because of the pain and my ribs have been badly crushed on one side.

Sandi does not know what to do. I ask her to call for an ambulance. I know this accident is bad. I ask her to call Mike and Iona to please come. The ambulance arrives first in about 20 minutes. The paramedics check me out for broken bones then give me gas and air so that they can lift me up to sit on the sofa. They are kind and sympathetic. They check me out thoroughly and give me a strong painkiller. I have never had an accident like this before. I feel broken.

Iona arrives and then Mike, and I feel their love and care for me and that is so wonderful. I ask Iona to let the people who are decorating the Goddess Hall know that I won't be there. Iona takes the black material I already have in the back of our car to them so that they can get on with it anyway.

The paramedics advise me to go home and rest. They don't think that the local hospital will do anything more than they have already done for me. I must just watch for any crackling in my breathing, otherwise they don't think I have damaged any internal organs, but I probably have a few cracked ribs. In hospital they wouldn't X-ray me anyway, because they can't do anything for cracked ribs, except leave them to heal. After a while, dosed with painkillers, I manage to climb into our car and Mike takes me home.

TOMORROW, Saturday, I am due to teach the first weekend of the Third Spiral of the Priestess Training. I will still have to do this. It is so important for these students beginning the Third Spiral to receive the right initiatory and energetic experience. Erin is away for her birthday in Wales with Duncan. There is no-one else who can do this at this time. There is no space in the Hall until mid-November, the students need to begin now and some are already travelling here from long distances away. I cannot let them down. I can see no other alternative, I will have to teach this weekend. The show must go on.

Fuelled with codeine and paracetamol and sheer willpower I teach the Third Spiral weekend. I have to sit very upright and still through the weekend. It takes me a day or so to get the dosage of the painkillers right, so that I feel the minimum of pain, but my side and my knee hurt all the time. I know that I look really pale and awful, but I need to be there for the students. They are very kind to me as well, and look after me. All goes well with their First Circle. They are a good group.

On Monday my body begins to collapse into lots of pain. I am in bed and cannot, do not want to move, except to ease myself slowly to the bathroom. I am on codeine and paracetamol for five days until I feel so poisoned by the codeine that I move on to ibuprofen and paracetamol. Sandi comes to see me with some flowers and an apology. She never comes again or enquires how I am. She must feel so afraid and guilty, although it was an accident.

It is a very hard week. The muscles in my side are crushed and twisted. My knee hurts so much. I don't have the energy to move or to think. All I can do is feel the pain, sit and read and watch TV and be bored.

Lady, this is a hard one. I don't deserve this. I really don't. I try to fathom the experience. Mike and I are due to go to Mexico for the first Mexican Goddess Conference next week. Now we cannot go and our air tickets which have already been booked and paid for by Aline, will be forfeit. Perhaps this was the only way to avoid death by an unknown hand in a foreign land, or by hurricane or earth changes. Who knows? The only way to stop us going was to completely immobilise me. If it was less painful than this I would still have tried to go to Mexico. I have a strong sense of duty. Once I have made a commitment to support a priestess I like to keep my promises. She knows me well.

I do not like pain at all. Lady, I pray that it eases soon. The thought comes to me that pain is the price paid when Mother Death passes by, but does not take us. Thank you for not taking me yet, Lady.

The pain-filled days go by slowly. Over the next couple of weeks leading up to Samhain, as I rest and recuperate, I entertain myself by becoming creative.

I begin to write some words about the Vision of MotherWorld.

Samhain comes and goes and I am in too much pain to attend the Temple ceremony, which is unusual for me to miss if I am in Glastonbury. As pain interrupts my sleep I have strong dreams on many nights. In one of them I am walking along Paradise Lane with Koko. It is lovely to see her. Along the path towards us comes an acquaintance, head down listening to her phone. On the right is a garden and a group of young men are looking out through the mist at the view. They say, *"Look at that view."* Looking at the young men I say jokingly to Koko, *"I like the view this way."* The young men come out of the garden and begin to follow us along Paradise Lane. From behind they think we are two young women. Koko and I turn around and the boys realise that we are old. They are only about 16 years old. I apologise to them, laughing.

Then I wake up and I laugh lots more – one dead woman and one old woman.

As I sit and rest I also think and write more about the MotherWorld Vision which I first received in August 2012, refining it from all our discussions which continue over the next months. Here I am including the most recent version. This Vision has been discussed in Priestess and Orchard group sessions in person and on line and tweaked many times. I offer this Vision to the world with love.

The Vision of the MotherWorld

This vision of MotherWorld is inspired by the Lady of Avalon, Great Goddess of love, compassion, healing and transformation on the Sacred Isle of Avalon.

MotherWorld is the society where mothers and the values of mothering – love, care and support for our Mother Earth, for each other and for all Her creatures and nature – are placed in the centre of our lives, rather than being left out on the periphery.

MotherWorld is the society in which creative and life-affirming values, actions, insights and awareness are honoured and encouraged in women, men and children. It is the society that is grounded in the fact that we all live upon our Mother Earth. She is the source and foundation of all that we are and all that we have. We need to take care of Her, of each other and of all life.

The primary values for the new MotherWorld are:

Honouring Mother Earth as a living being. Love for each other, kindness, support, respect, care and compassion. Honouring all forms of mothering, honouring fathers, and the celebration and nurture of children and young people. Protecting and taking care of the earth, water, fire, air and space in Her world.

Suggested values for the new MotherWorld include:

Honesty, personal integrity, authenticity, relationship, diversity, choice, discernment, inclusion, trust, beauty, emotional expression, listening, hearing, clear boundaries, reflection, soul development, empowerment, shadow-healing, the pursuit of wisdom, the encouragement of self-responsibility, self-worth, self-respect, self-confidence, self-discipline and self-reflection; prayer, ceremony, service, connection, partnership, generosity, sharing wealth, gifting, receiving, humour, creativity, education for all, non-violent methods of resolving conflict, honouring and protecting Mother Nature and all living beings, ethical production of goods and services, the protection of the vulnerable, and valuing the Wisdom of the Elders and of the Ancestors.

MOTHERWORLD is the society where the patriarchal structures and values of dominance, power-over control and coercion, greed, excessive profit, destructive competition, violence, rape, war, slavery, suffering, hunger, poverty and the pollution of Mother Earth and Her atmosphere, are recognized as shadow expressions of humanity, which need to be challenged, deconstructed, transformed and healed. In Motherworld healing practices are encouraged and made readily available to all.

IN MOTHERWORLD it is recognized that all human beings, women and men, carry wounds from our patriarchal conditioning – emotional and mental patterns which may be activated as we try to change our world. Within the Goddess community we are particularly aware of our own shadow material, which includes envy, jealousy, judgment, competitiveness, undermining, back-biting, blaming, collusion, resentment, naming and shaming, projection of negative emotions, of anger, rage, fear, loneliness, lack of self-love, lack of self-esteem and lack of self-confidence, all of which are the result of individual cultural and karmic life experiences.

IN MOTHERWORLD one of our first works is to love and support each other in taking responsibility for our repressed and often hostile shadow emotions. These shadows undermine all our best endeavours to change the way we act in our personal and social relationships, in our lives as Goddess-loving people living in a patriarchal world, as Her returning Priestesses and Priests, as Her Melissae, and in our personal commitments to Goddess. They often prevent us from experiencing true empowerment. In our circles we already have developed skills and techniques of emotional expression, such as really listening to each other and offering reflection and support so that we may heal these wounds. This personal healing work needs to, and can accelerate at this time with the help of the MotherWorld community, which helps hold us in compassionate safety as we work to heal our wounds.

ALTHOUGH the name MotherWorld comes from Barbara Walker's novel *'Amazon'*, where it describes an ancient fictional matriarchal society, this is not a return to such a society. It is a forward movement to a new kind of mother-centred community, where all are valued, supported and appreciated, and where we can experiment together with new ideas and forms. MotherWorld evokes a loving world where we recognise that we are all held safely in the Great Mother's embrace.

THE CALL OF MOTHERWORLD

- *We call for the empowerment of women and girls, men and boys.*
- *We call for peace in our world.*
- *We call for an end to all violence – violence against women and girls, boys and men, including assault, rape, genital mutilation, circumcision, slavery, people trafficking, torture, murder and war.*
- *We call for an end to intimidation and power-over aggression in all forms.*
- *We call for an end to the arms trade and the personal and societal ownership of harmful weapons.*
- *We call for an end to hunger and starvation, poverty, homelessness and the ownership of the resources of the earth by the few at the expense of the many.*

- *We call for an end to all human and animal sacrifice for religious, political or social purposes.*
- *We call for an end to all forms of human and animal cruelty.*
- *We call for an end to all inequalities based on gender, race, sexual orientation, disability and age.*

This MotherWorld Vision was first received by Priestess of Avalon, *Kathy Jones* and then added to and refined by the Goddess community of the Glastonbury Goddess Temple, including

Amanda Baker, Amanda Posnett, Amber Skyes, Ann James, Beci Monks, Becky Thomas, Carmen Paz, Cherry-Lee Ward, Chrissy Heaven, Christine Watkins, Christine Watts, Duncan Howell, Elin Hejll-Guest, Elle Hull, Erin McCauliff, Francine van den Berg, Geraldine Charles, Lorye Keats-Hopper, Joanne Foucher, John Reeves, Josie Shaw, Katinka Soetens, Leona Graham, Lieveke Volcke, Lisa Newing, Lorraine Pickles, Louise Tarrier, Luiza Frazao, Luna Silver, Mandie Thorne, Marion van Eupen, Marisa Picardo, Michelle Patten, Mike Jones, Miriam Wallraven, Paul Brady, Peter Huzar, Renata de Quieroz, Ronnie Hudson, Rose Flint, Sandra Roman, Sharlea Sparrow, Shirley-Ann Millar, Stephanie Mathivet, Suzanne Viney, Tina Free, Trevor Nuthall, Vera Faria Leal and Vikki Winstone.

THE VISION is also supported by many others who have signed their commitment to the MotherWorld on line and by post. Everyone who agrees with this vision is invited to make their personal commitment on the Facebook MotherWorld page.

THIS VISION is also being received by others in different communities and places in the world, and in different forms.

The MotherWorld vision is inclusive and without borders. It supports all people – women, children and men everywhere, who are endeavouring to bring feminine values back into our lives and societies, changing our world for the better.

The MotherWorld favours diversity of expression, as a Mother loves all of her children with their different characters and expressions.

MotherWorld communities and networks can be formed by any group of people who agree with its values and principles. We ask that all those who make the commitment to the MotherWorld connect with each other and stay connected, creating a worldwide network of love and support for our creative values and actions.

Commitment to the MotherWorld

The following are suggested commitments to be made by all those who wish to co-create the MotherWorld:

I commit myself to loving and supporting the vision, the people and the values of MotherWorld as described. My intention is to help bring MotherWorld into being in my thoughts, words and actions in the world. I support the Motherworld Vision. I commit to taking responsibility for my own emotional and mental wounding and for its healing.

You can register your own commitment to MotherWorld by sending it to

    Glastonbury Goddess Temple,
    2-4 High Street,
    Glastonbury BA6 9DU,
    United Kingdom

or by signing online at **www.goddesstemple.co.uk**
or the MotherWorld Facebook page.

In mid-november 2012 I share the first MotherWorld Vision with about 30 priestesses in circle at our Orchard Gathering. People are enthusiastic and happy and have good ideas, which we add into the Vision. There is lots of discussion and more alterations are made to it through our email groups and it is further refined. It continues to be discussed over the course of the next nine months, up until the 2013 Goddess Conference, when we plan to ground the Vision ceremonially and launch it into the world.

ON THIS Orchard day what also happens is that as we are talking in circle three priestesses dump their stuff on me, and I don't catch it at the time. While talking about not competing with each other and supporting each other I realise only later that all three have said undermining things to me in the circle. Sometimes I don't quite hear what is said at the time, especially if it is negative. My ears switch off. One of the women is competitive about her work. She is making some point about the value of her own work at the expense of mine. Why do we do this to each other? Why do people have to undermine rather than support each other? It is the weakness of many women to feel less than their sisters and to strive to bring them down.

It is only later, after the meeting, that I hear the words she and others said. I feel that I have MUG written over my face. By putting forward the MotherWorld Vision I also open a gateway that allows people to dump/project more of their crap onto me, not less. DYCH. Dump Your Crap Here. You are my *bad mother*. Somehow the word Motherworld allows people to dive straight for their childhood wounds around their own mothers and play them out. They are expecting to be mothered by someone else rather than honouring mothers. I/we have to be so clear in myself/ourselves, and so vigilant to catch these things as they are happening in the moment and point them out to each other.

IN OUR Ceremony Group meetings for the 2013 Conference where we will celebrate Ertha, the Mother of Earth, we begin to discuss how to ceremonially ground the Motherworld Vision. In our meetings this year we seem to be having lots of miscommunication, which is really unusual. Normally we argue and discuss a lot, but we don't really antagonise each other. Why is this happening? It seems like every time the Motherworld Vision comes up, an antagonistic energy also rises up out of the collective unconscious, not necessarily connected to discussing the Vision, but as an energetic reaction. It is interesting to observe, though rather challenging.

I HAVE DONE something provocative again. Oh dear! How do I stop myself?

I am Vision Holder for the Goddess Temple and for how it looks and feels inside the Temple, with the help of lots of other lovely people. About three months ago prompted by the Lady, I suggested that we change the painting of the Lady on the altar in the Temple that has been there for some time now. Before this painting was placed above the altar, the central images changed with the seasons and we hung different people's paintings of Goddesses from around the Wheel of the Year, as well as earlier versions of the Lady of Avalon. There was always some new face of Goddess to look at. When the current painting arrived it embodied a strong presence of the Lady that almost everyone loves, which is why it has stayed so long. For many people it has become an image completely identified with the Lady, and our Temple is the Lady's Temple.

However it has felt for some time like the energy in the Temple has become a bit stagnant, with things looking the same each day. I know that this painting is loved, but my strong instinct is to shift the visual imagery on again, to allow other artists into the Temple. It is hard for an artist not to see this as rejection, but it isn't. It is about the needs of the Temple rather than the needs of the artist.

I have been talking with other artists about their paintings of the Lady and how I would like to see them on the main altar, when they are ready. As with many troubles challenges often begin with miscommunication. I discuss the change with the painter of the current image but do not know exactly when the next painting will arrive. After a few months and on hearing rumours the painter unceremoniously removes her painting from the altar. She tells everyone that I have done something very bad to her.

Then the negative emails pour in telling me that I am an awful person again, to make this decision on my own. I do always discuss things with others, with Mike, with other directors/ priestesses, but not with everyone. Anyone who wants to have a real say in the running of the Temple needs to take responsibility and put in their time and energy as I do. It is all too easy to have an opinion from the sidelines without actually doing anything to contribute to the whole.

I see that there is confusion about my role within the Goddess Temple these days. I am confused too. Am I still the Temple's Creative Director empowered by the Temple Directors and Members to make decisions for the good of the Temple or not? It feels like there are stirrings of resistance in the community that are being expressed indirectly. Do you want to be a decision-maker? Do you want my job?

It is my inspiration and energy which has created these Goddess ventures – the Goddess Conference, the Priestess Trainings, the Goddess Temple and lots of other Goddess activities here in Glastonbury, with the help of lots of other people. Without my initiatory and continuing energy none of these activities would sustain themselves for long at the moment. What will happen when I am gone? I am the Vision-holder and my visioning will continue as long as I am alive. It is part of my nature to bring the future into the present.

What is unclear to me is, as more people get involved with all our activities and want to contribute, who makes the decisions? Is it those who take day to day responsibility for the running of the Temple? Or those who support us from a distance by making a £2 monthly donation and have strong opinions about what they think we should or should not do? Who decides?

Which beliefs decide? Is it the conservatism of the fearful or the unfolding Vision of the few? From the beginning we have always moved from Vision in the Temple and in everything we have done. It has worked so far to create everything, under Her inspiration, but not everyone has experience of working in this way. I don't want to be limited in my capacity to respond to Her inspiration by other people's fears. I am trying to be honest here.

I am portrayed as some kind of tyrant who now has removed a painting by force, because I don't like it. This is despite the fact that the artist removed the painting herself, and that I have a large copy of it on my own altar wall at home. I do really like the painting. They believe that I just want to control everything. I am forwarded an email from someone's priest friend's private facebook page in which he slanders me and soon has other people joining him. These are people who I don't know, but who obviously don't like the Goddess Temple at all and don't like women. The internet can be a really horrible place and there are some horrible people out there. How could someone who has trained as a priest of the Goddess encourage and support people in writing such dreadful things? It's on his wall and he isn't objecting.

We all have such different values. Just because we train people does not mean that they learn what they are taught. Just because they make a dedication to Goddess does not mean that they all have integrity. The majority do, but some do not. Students are taught to be self-responsible, but they don't always learn what that really means. Once again I find myself thinking that for some people two or three years Priestess Training is simply not long enough.

What actually happens in the Temple after the painting has been moved out is that the energy frees up and the Temple opens out again. New paintings and images of the Lady and of the Goddesses on the Wheel of the Year begin to come into the Temple once again. Several people express how sad they are that the painting has gone, but new life comes into the space. It is not to do with the painting itself, which is and always will be beautiful, it is to do with how we hold a creative energetic living Temple space. We are not a church. We are not a fixed religion. We are an evolving adventurous spirituality. We don't want to become stuck in any one form so quickly in our story. We are a changing, moving, sacred and creative organism, which I hope will continue long after I am gone.

Chapter Thirteen

The Wounded Child

T IS A NEW YEAR – January 2013 – and more negative emails come to me. I begin to doubt that some of those who say they support me are actually doing so. Do they actively stir the pot against me? How supportive are they? I am feeling afraid. I am afraid that someone will go completely mad and attack me physically. I feel real fear in my belly and I ask myself why? I know that people are afraid of me and now I am afraid of them. What is this mutually triggering energy all about for me? It feels like the fear I had of my father. I feel oppressed by the all too frequent emails. I have tried to appease and calm everyone, but that does not work.

'I must have done something wrong, Daddy. Why are you shouting at me, Daddy, saying these things about me that are not true?'

I have tried to protect people and hold them in confidence. Somewhere my fear is about being found out not to have acted well, even when I have.

'Daddy, Daddy, you are angry. I didn't do it.'

Release the fear, let it go....

It doesn't help that my current astrology of Saturn square Pluto from January through March indicates possible violence towards me. I am scared I will be harmed physically. I feel lost in these emotions.

MIKE AND I go to Barcelona for a few days and the pressure is relieved. It is Mike's Xmas present to me. As usual we talk and have interesting conversations.

I realise this morning that my father probably suffered from post-traumatic stress disorder or something similar, after his experiences in the Second World War. He was a Sergeant Major in the Military Police who are amongst the harshest of all military personnel, as they have to control the rogue elements within the army itself. The few times that I dared ask him what he had done in the war, he would never tell me anything. When I asked him if he had ever killed anyone, he said, "*You should never ask that question.*" Now I know that probably means that he did and I must have known that then. I think I internalised the fear that he had killed once or more times and could kill again. He was always so angry and he could kill me. I was afraid of him most of the time. With the current abusers it is the same hostile defensive vibration that sets off my fear.

Saturn the great limiter is working in my life. Mike talks about how this whole year I have been affected by Saturn, starting with the cancer, then the online attacks, then Koko dying, then the accident, all things that have stopped me in my tracks or made me sit down or distracted me. They have also released great creativity at times. First there was Saturn opposition Sun, then Saturn square Saturn, then Saturn opposition Moon and now Saturn square Pluto. The last time this happened was when I was 37/38years old when my children's father, one time after I provoked him, kicked me and broke a rib, and this time too my ribs have been crushed. After those Saturn transits came all the creativity of Ariadne Productions with all the plays that we wrote. This time too I am thinking about writing a play, for the first time in years. The very first time these Saturn transits came round was when I was 7/8/9 years of age and I wrote my first stories and my first plays, which we performed in our family garage.

IN BARCELONA we go to look at many of Gaudi's buildings with all their amazing curving forms, colours and paintings, especially in La Sagrada Familia Cathedral, which I absolutely love. Gaudi's artwork, sculpture and architecture are all based on forms found in nature, in plants, flowers, trees and animals. His work is based in the natural world, so Goddess in every respect. It is truly wonderful and inspiring. I want a Gaudi Goddess Temple in Glastonbury, when we can build our own. I am blissed out by the wonder of the space that he and those who have followed in his footsteps are still creating. In the Cathedral the only jarring form is the image of Jesus hanging on a cross. Why does this religion place such a hideous image of suffering in its centre? If I stand in the right place, glorious coloured light comes through the stained glass windows, falling on a forest of tall tree columns, and the ugly dead man is hidden. I am inspired and restored again.

WHEN WE RETURN from Spain the emails, texts and phone calls continue. I am plagued by my own reactive thoughts which go round and around in my head. I wake each morning trying to work out how best to deal with the situation.

I feel powerless, angry, afraid. I am lost in my wounded child.

"Daddy, Daddy, don't hurt me...."

What to do? Feeling to hold a boundary, afraid that I will be shouted at or hurt when I Melissa in the Temple on Tuesday. This has gone on for so long now. I feel worn down by it. I am afraid that it will affect me cancerously. Then I find my centre again and am calm. I am an adult, no longer the wounded child, but still afraid. I am on a roller coaster of emotional reactions and I own them, these are my reactions.

I think about the energetics of what is happening. A wild and hungry wolf, as Sally described it, is prowling around the perimeter of the island and roaring in every few days. The wolf is hungry and feeds off all the emotions, including mine, as people take sides and the Temple community cracks apart under pressure.

I GO TO THE hospital for a check up and an X-ray of my remaining left breast. It is all clear, there is no visible cancer there. One year on, I am cancer free, as far as we can know. Yippee! I have continued to eat good organic vegetarian, almost vegan food. I have had weekly acupuncture and Chinese herbs for the last year, as well as massages and healing and other alternative therapies. I am taking care of my body. The wounds in my emotions and mind, which are the creative causes for cancer, still need a bit more help.

I TALK WITH my sister Priestess Sue Quatermass about the possibility of us having a Goddess Shop associated with the Goddess Temple and whether she would like to run it. We have talked several times over the last year about possibilities. She is interested. In the Temple we sell Goddess cards, Temple incenses, candles and various small items. This brings in a small income for the Temple, which is very helpful for our funds. It would be great to be able to expand the range of Goddess products we sell to make more money for the Temple, so we can build towards a new and larger Goddess Temple in the future.

We know the kind of shop we would like to see – something that is filled with beautiful Goddess artworks and statues, paintings, jewellery, all the different kinds of things that Goddess women and men like to buy. Sue really wants to support Goddess artists and craftswomen, providing a place where they can sell their creations, which is often difficult in the mainstream world. We can also give priestesses the possibility of working in the shop and so helping them in their journey to become full-time priestesses. We would like our customers to be served by priestesses, who are not just selling them products, but opening their eyes to the meanings of the lovely things we might sell.

I have noticed that Venus, the shop in the Courtyard is hardly ever open this winter. I wonder if Lui would like to give up/sell his lease to the Temple. It is in an ideal location for us, just below the Goddess Temple. I bump into him in the Courtyard one day and say that if he is thinking of letting his lease go we are interested in taking it on. In a few days he comes back and says he is. However at this moment he is asking for a huge amount of money for the remainder of his lease, which isn't very long. We don't want to buy his business, we want an empty shop. We will wait and see.

BY IMBOLC I have traced back to the nub of the problem of my emotional reactions. As I wake one morning in the dream state I see a small red jelly with something like a gold button on the top of it – this is a symbol of my feeling of guilt and fear that comes from childhood. I have such a potent feeling of guilt for having done something wrong. My memory goes back to when I was about

8 years old. One evening after I had been playing with my friend Jennifer and it was time to go home, I needed to return her precious tin full of tiny shells to her. Afraid for some reason to go into her garden and knock on her front door and give them to her, I threw the tin over her wall onto the lawn. What was I afraid of? Her parents? The tiny shells spilled out all over the grass. I ran away in fear and felt awful and didn't tell anyone what I had done. I pretended that I hadn't done it, although of course they must have known when they found the empty tin.

"*I am afraid what the adults will say… Daddy, don't hurt me….*"

There is such a sweet (red jelly) mix of guilt and fear that grew and expanded over time with other experiences. I so wanted to be a good girl and do nothing wrong, to make Daddy happy. All that has happened over the last months has triggered that core wound of having done something wrong and being guilty. I think that at some point I said, "*Sorry*," for dropping the shell tin, but I never recovered from the guilt. It was added to over and over.

In my current confused emotional state I feel that I must have done something wrong. Although all I have done in this whole thing as the Director in charge of Temple Trainings, is to support a tutor completely. I have done nothing other than this. I have done nothing wrong, so why do I feel that I have? I have gone into my wounded child guilt place, which conflates with the places where I am accused and innocent,

"*I must have done something wrong. They are telling me I have done something wrong. I don't know what it is but since they are saying it, it must be true.*"

I try to look into the red jelly with the gold button, what does it mean? Where does the image come from? What is it?

This morning I saw a woodpecker on the oak tree, which is always a good omen from Her nature that something is moving creatively.

ON VALENTINE'S DAY February 14th we join in the V Day One Billion Rising campaign for the End to Violence Against Women and Girls. This is a dance initiative from the wonderful Eve Ensler of Vagina Monologues fame, and is the day when we gather to dance our protest against the continuing misogynistic violence that goes on against women and girls worldwide.

We begin the day dancing in the Goddess Hall, encouraged by different dance teachers. Grael Corsini and Anna-Saqqara are really great in helping organise the day and Stephanie makes food for people. Lots of new people come into the Goddess Hall, who have not been in before. We practice some songs and dances for the demonstration, and then we dance our way up Benedict Street into the Market Place to stage our Flashmob song and dance protest, singing Goddess songs. It feels really good to publicly say *"NO to Violence Against Women and Girls!"* Very good. I feel quite inspired by the idea of public protests again, as we used to do them in the 1970s and 80s.

MY INBOX is battered almost every day. I do not reply to these missives. I am learning my "*No*". I am learning to say "*No*" to aggressive and abusive behaviour from anyone and this is a "*No*" without reaction or any emotional charge. Just "*No.*" I set my boundaries ever more clearly for myself and for others. As I don't accept it for myself, I don't accept it from others and my behaviour towards others also changes.

I HAVE JUST found out that I am No 84 in the Watkins Bookstore 2013 List of the 100 Most Spiritually Influential Living people in the World. Extraordinary! It makes me laugh out loud. I can't get my head round it. How did that happen? How did they even notice me? I haven't done anything to make it happen. I don't think that some of the people who currently abuse me would see me like that.

WE HAVE the first good meeting of the Conference Ceremony group, which this year is Katinka, Sally, Erin, Katie, Marion, Sharlea, Michelle, Amanda and me. Everyone has moved on and through their stuff and good ideas are happening with some singing and laughter. We discuss how we want to honour Ertha, the Great Earth Mother in our ceremonies. We talk about how we already live in Paradise if we have the eyes to see it, if we take the time to experience all the beauty of Her nature. Life is not a journey where we get to Paradise in the end after we die. It is about recognising that we already live in Her Paradise, here on Her Earth. The older I get the more I really experience every day the beauty of flowers and trees and grass and hills and mountains and streams and rivers and seas, as well as all the amazing creatures who live here. We live in such an awesome world and many people don't notice it. They live in cities surrounded by concrete and never really see Her amazing nature.

I want to create a vision of Paradise for everyone to experience in the Conference. How to do it in the Town Hall, which is not very pretty in the first place? We always decorate it with large Goddess wall hangings and banners, which cover the dullness. Now there are new green bug eye lights along the walls of the hall, which are really intrusive into the proportions of the room, and the uncoordinated furnishings take some disguising. In my mind's eye I have a vision of plants and trees, lots of them, filling the Hall. How to do this? I will talk with Peter Freerson, who has worked with plants on large country estates and see if he has some ideas of where we might be able to get hold of trees in pots, that won't cost too much – beg, borrow or hire.

We will ask everyone to bring some soil from their parts of the world and we will mix it all together ceremonially with love. Then it will go back out into the world after the Conference as a blessing for the world. I also want to create a sacred drama which tells of the beginnings of the human race, through ancient MotherWorld times, through the fall of the Temples, and the effects of that fall through time and individual lives, as people incarnate as both women and men. In my mind's eye I briefly see a scene where Ertha moulds the bodies of the First Four Mothers of the First Four Races of humans, the black, white, red and yellow, out of clay. It is the Source Vision from which the sacred drama will spring.

A GROUP OF US take a priestess trip to London to see the Ice Age Sculptures Exhibition at the British Museum. We have such a great day. It is so wonderful to see original ancient Goddess sculptures so close, just through the glass.

Our noses are just a few inches away from these wonderful Goddess images that I have only seen in photographs before. They were carved by our ancestors from bone and stone, antler, wood and clay, and are tens of thousands of years old. They were made by the ancient people who knew as we do, that Goddess lives in Her nature. There are the Swan Maidens and plaques from Mal'ta in Siberia, drawings of which I put in one of my first books, years ago. There is the Venus of Lespugue and several other familiar Neolithic Goddess figurines, some so similar to the Venus of Willendorf, who I saw last year in Austria. All are so much more delicate and beautifully carved in the flesh, than in photographs. They are not free-standing, although they stand in this exhibition. They are the perfect size to be held in the hand or hung on a string or placed in a pouch and hung around the neck in ceremony. Perhaps every woman, man and child had such an image of Goddess, that they made themselves or which was given to them, to be a treasured possession, in a special ceremony of dedication to the Earth Mother of Creation.

What is so amazing are the similarities in their forms, created as they were by peoples living thousands of miles apart and over thousands of years in time. They are similar in their nakedness, in their enlarged breasts, big bellies, buttocks and thighs, in their hair-styles and hair coverings, in the meaningful placing of hands and arms, and in the lack of feet. Although these things are so obvious to anyone who can join the dots, the exhibition catalogue and the wording of information signs does not acknowledge their obvious connectedness across time and space. How did this happen? Why did this happen? Clothing only appears much later in time, after patriarchy has entered into the mix.

The archaeologists do not even ask the right questions – why are all these images so basically similar? This is not the 'bulbous woman art' they claim it to be. They are not idols or images of known women. They have a similar style, a similar recognition of the bounty and beauty of the female body, but these are not human women or dolls, they are images of something numinous and prescient. They are images of belief in Feminine Divinity. Just as today we make images of Goddess so did our ancient forebears, in their quest to find the meaning of this glorious life on earth. 99% of all the ancient figurines so far unearthed, stretching back over hundreds of thousands of years, are female. Why? Archaeologists are unable to ask the right questions of these images, misogyny is so endemic within academia and particularly in this discipline.

In the exhibition there are also beautiful carvings of many different kinds of animals, which demonstrates such a love and respect for animals and the natural world. Again the carvings are on antlers and bones, so delicately carved by skilled craftspeople, who knew what they were doing, carving with flint tools – no metal knives here.

THE MAIN PERSON who has been harassing tutors and Temple decides to leave Glastonbury. We are relieved. I pray to the Lady that healing will happen for us all.

BY THE END OF March, Sue, Mike and I have made the decision to create our new Goddess Temple shop, in the old Venus shop. It will be called Goddess Temple Gifts. Lui has brought the price right down to something reasonable. When my mother died she left me some money which was just sitting in a bank collecting dust so I am going to loan the Temple £20,000 to pay for the lease and to cover start up costs. Sue is in charge of creating the shop. We are all very excited about it. However as soon as we make the decisions to begin and bring in others to help, there is resistance in the energy field, and two people who come in to help with administration and accounts have meltdowns. They don't want to take on the pressure and commitment of setting up the venture and withdraw rapidly. We have to think fast on our feet. I encourage Sue to take her power, not to give it away, as she really doesn't want to give it away. She has a clear vision of how the shop should be. I want to empower her and help her to do this well.

We set up a new Goddess Temple trading company for which Mike and I are the directors. I am the investor and random suggester of good things to have in the shop, although Sue is in charge. We have fun thinking of great things to sell in the shop. With some reticence Mike will keep an eye on the money stuff.

At first he really doesn't want to be involved but gradually over time as others show they can't do the job he takes on more of this role. He does this in so many areas in the Goddess Temple as well. It is so important in all our work to have someone who has the good of the Temple in their heart and who knows how to set up companies, organise accounts and do all that legal stuff. We plan to open the shop at Beltane. This seems like a good time to begin as celebration will be in the air with the Goddess of Love.

I am feeling much calmer, creative and more centred, not so much on the back foot and in reaction, at the effect of astrology and events. Katie Player and I begin to talk about the sacred drama for the Conference. We have discussions sitting at the kitchen table, my favourite place for this kind of creativity. I invite Katie to write the sacred drama with me. Over the next couple of weeks we have very helpful discussions about the themes of the drama, but I notice that nothing is actually getting written down as script. It turns out that Katie's skill is more in improvisational drama, rather than in writing scripted plays. I realise that I am writing the sacred drama and Katie will direct it for the Conference as I will not have time with everything else I need to organise. I begin to write the scenes as they appear.

DURING THIS springtime I lead two Emotional Healing weekends, in which people are helped to release and express their emotional wounding. These are powerful healing and transformative weekends for many. I also lead another 10 Hours: Exploring the Underworld of Avalon. I sit in the flow of your energy, Lady, in your Grace. I listen for the movements of your energy and respond to them, so that everyone can receive what they need for their healing and their soul's nourishment.

TOWARDS THE END of April I travel to Venice where I have been invited to offer a couple of Goddess workshops by two of our priestesses, Anna Bordin and Laura Oselladore. Sarah Perini, another great Italian Priestess, has translated my book *The Ancient British Goddess* into Italian, with Anna's help. The workshops will help launch the book. I lead a weekend Goddess workshop near Venice, which is very enjoyable.

The city of Venice is an eye-opener. I didn't realise it would look as it does. It feels familiar. There is a view along a side canal that I feel like I know. I don't know if it comes from watching movies, whether it is the strong energy field of the place or whether it is a memory. Mike comes over half way through and we all drive to Turin to take part in a Conference called *'Indigenous Peace Cultures. Re-Educate ourselves in partnership!'*

The promotional material says that the goal of the Conference is

> *"to propose instruments for a re-assessment of education and the transmission of knowledge in gylanic terms, analysing the stories that foster patriarchal culture. We will organize workshops held by scholars working in such different fields as history, archeao-mythology, pedagogy, psychology, economy, art, spirituality and the body. How can we approach history in non-sexist, non-violent and inter-religious ways? How can we recover an egalitarian symbolic order within language? How can we bring across the understanding that life does not necessarily imply domination, possession and exploitation, but can mean caring, sharing and nurturing? What tales and what myths are we to tell our children in order to abandon the domination model once and for all? How to build a love relationship with partnership values?"*

Mike and I are invited to speak amongst Goddess luminaries such as Genevieve Vaughan, Starhawk and Luciana Percovitch. I have met some of these amazing women before at our Goddess Conference and also on the Goddess circuit. We are all staying in the same hotel by the station in Turin and are ferried by car and bus to the Conference venue. It is good to spend time with these sisters again, just talking at meal-times, hearing their words of wisdom when they speak to the Conference. Mike and I are to demonstrate how a couple devoted to Goddess work together and support each other in a partnership model.

We arrive in the afternoon and that evening with the Italian Priestesses we are creating the Conference Opening ceremony. It's a bit impromptu. The first room we are shown for the ceremony is a huge gym hall full of equipment, with children and young people running, bouncing around on trampolines, jumping over vaulting horses. It's a completely unsuitable venue for a Conference ceremony as most of the equipment cannot be moved and the children are not leaving until a few minutes before we are due to begin the ceremony. We are taken to another room in the building, which is also bare and utilitarian, but it will have to do. I don't know what the building is normally used for, something educational, but I cannot understand why these modern buildings have to be so ugly and bare of decoration, with harsh utilitarian lighting. How are children supposed to thrive in such grim settings?

We create a circular altar in the centre of the room and lots of people come in and encircle the altar. The Italian Priestesses call in some of their new-found Italian Goddesses of the directions in Italian. The Goddess research group in Italy are slightly inhibited in their recovery of the names of early pre-Roman Goddesses, as they so want to get it right. They want to find ancient Goddesses who were here before Roman culture expanded throughout Italy celebrating Goddesses whose names are familiar to many – Diana, Hecate, Minerva, etc. There are many ancient and new-found Goddesses whose names and qualities are being collected and collated from all over Italy, all expressions of Diana, Di-Ana or as I feel to name Her, Dea Anna – Goddess Ana, the same root Goddess as the Ana in Brigit-Ana or Britannia.

After the Italian Goddesses are called in Mike and I ceremonially bring in the natural physical elements of Avalon – Earth from Glastonbury Tor, Water from Chalice Well and the White Spring, Fire in the Flame of Avalon and Air from Avalon, mixing them with the natural physical elements of Italy – their earth, sacred water, fire and air. I invoke the spacious, numinous and initiatory energy of the Lady of Avalon to connect with and honour the Ancestors of the land where the Conference is taking place, to connect with the Italian Goddesses, sparking the exploration and development of the Italian Wheel of the Year.

It's part of my spiritual practice as a travelling Priestess of Avalon to take the natural elements of Avalon out into the world and to mix them all together with the natural elements of the land I am visiting. I believe that the Lady of Avalon wants me to do this. We have recognised and helped expand awareness of the ancient and present-day Goddesses in Brigit's Isles, and many people love Her and respond to Her instinctively. Taking Her physical and energetic elements to other lands and peoples has an initiatory and stimulating effect within those lands and peoples. I have experienced this several times across the world in different places, including the Netherlands, Hungary, Argentina, Sweden, Australia, the USA and now Italy. It is such a privilege to be able to do this work for Her. Goddess, and the Lady of Avalon in particular, wants to be recognised widely in the world and the work of the travelling Priestesses of Avalon is to offer this service.

Once the elements are mixed all together into a bowl – the earth, water, fire and air – I anoint myself with the mud mixture, smearing it onto my face, arms and hands. It's a great feeling of immersion in the land we are visiting, and has a magical and invigorating effect upon participants. I invite everyone who wants to, to anoint themselves in the same way. After this part of the ceremony with our mud-splattered faces and limbs we all sing and dance Goddess songs in Italian and English.

The next day we listen to interesting talks from various speakers, translated from or into Italian. Mike and I talk about the Goddess Temple and our way of teaching Goddess Spirituality to women and men in Glastonbury. We talk about our experiences in bringing Goddess back into the world and offer the Vision of Motherworld to the Conference.

When the Conference is over we go back to Sarah and Mirco's lovely apartment, high above the streets of Turin, where lots of young friends have been staying on sofas and floors. Sarah and Mirco are a lovely young couple, both devoted to Goddess. Everyone is very tired from all the work that it has taken to create such a successful event. Small arguments break out between all the couples and friends involved. They are all young and this is the way of young people's relationships, to project outwards. But I love the energy of these young Goddess people that we find in many countries, where it is younger women and men who are drawn equally to Goddess. It is very exciting to see this happening across the world, not just within our older pioneering generation of women. I love these young people and especially our Italian priestesses Sarah, Anna, Laura and Claudia, and their partners. Our connections feel old and strong, returning relationships from ancient priestess times.

Chapter Fourteen

LONG LIVE THE WITCH!

ON OUR RETURN from Italy we quickly enter the luscious and creative Beltane season. Our new shop Goddess Temple Gifts is opening to the public on Beltane Eve. Sue Quatermass is doing such a great job, painting and decorating the shop and then displaying everything in a feast of Goddess art and sculpture. The shop looks beautiful and there are all sorts of lovely Goddess goodies for everyone to buy. Lots of people come for the Opening when I cut the purple ribbon across the threshold and we invite everyone into our new enterprise to support the Temple and Her priestesses. We offer everyone champagne and encourage people to spend their money.

That evening we have a great Beltane ceremony in the Goddess Hall with lots of visitors from other lands coming to join in, Mexicans, Spanish, Dutch and other Europeans, who come regularly to participate in our Beltane ceremonies. Because of the many non-English speaking people we create a ceremony that has lots of movement, singing and dancing around the Maypole, and then leaping the Beltane fire in the cauldron, with lovers and friends. The sacred agreement on Beltane Eve is to journey in love for a year and a day with the person with whom you jump the fire, before releasing or renewing this sacred vow.

THE FOLLOWING weekend I have organised for Starhawk, the well known American Goddess and earth-based feminist activist, to come and give a weekend workshop at the Goddess Hall. The workshop is based on ideas put forward in her latest book *The Empowerment Manual: A Guide for Collaborative Groups*. This is a very good book for anyone trying to work in a group such as our Temple community. It contains masses of great ideas, and is sometimes overwhelming in the amount of detail of all that needs to be considered. The book is based in Starhawk's many years of working in all kinds of groups and the wisdom she has gleaned from that work. Starhawk is a really inspiring teacher for many, from her earliest writings, such as *"The Spiral Dance"*, and her setting up, with others, of the Reclaiming Movement, which organises teaching camps and large group rituals all over the world. You can find out lots about her on her website – **http://www.starhawk.org/**

Starhawk is teaching two workshops for us with a Saturday evening concert from Starsong, who are our own Sally Pullinger, Heloise Pilkington & Jerome O'Connell. On Saturday we have *"Times of Hope and Chaos"* and on Sunday *"Power, Magic and Co-Creation"*. The workshops are really helpful in looking at the ways in which our own Goddess Temple community is developing and growing. We have been looking at the conflicts that have occurred just in the last year with all the difficulties, seeing how our community is as vulnerable as any to gossip and miscommunication, to undermining and lack of support when it is most needed.

Starhawk describes three parts of the Self that are understood within the Reclaiming teachings – the Talking Self who is the checklist self, who likes to keep track of everything; the Young Self who likes music, dancing and play; and the Deep Self, which is the Soul, beyond just this life, and which is the connection to Goddess. The way to the Deep Self is through the Young Self. All successful teaching must address all three selves. I like that simple analysis.

At some moment during the weekend I am looking at a painting on the wall of the Hall by the unique Goddess and feminist artist and writer Monica Sjöö. I suddenly have a deep and emotional remembrance of the title words of another painting by Monica, *"Are there great Female Beings out there waiting for us to be free?"* The words arise unexpectedly into my mind and tears well up in my eyes.

Monica wrote,

"*Ever since the late 60s when I started to do women and Goddess centred paintings, I have had a sense that ancient women were communicating with me in visions and dreams. It felt as if I was being used as a medium and that my paintings came from another… archaic time. In 1973 in London during our Womanpower exhibition when 'God Giving Birth'(the painting) was nearly taken to Court, a zen-type, light-flooded dramatic moment occurred in which I 'knew' that past, present and future coincide and therefore this ancient sisterhood is with us now and in the future. We are each other's ancestors and descendents…. During a visualisation-meditation with Bob Stewart I suddenly and equally dramatically 'knew' that I am one of this sisterhood but had chosen to come back here. I felt great grief, sadness and loss at this. It also explained a lot. Are my paintings 'portals' for them into this realm? If this sounds crazy…so may it be.*"

FOR MORE about Monica Sjöö, who passed away after a long journey with cancer on 8th August 2005, and the inspiring force that she was and still is see http://monicasjoo.com

In this workshop I too had one of these epiphanies and felt tears coursing down my face. I am not sure even what triggered the moment, but I knew again that I am one of the priestesses who has chosen to return to the earth at this time to bring Goddess back to our human awareness, to bring Her Temples, Her Priestesses and knowledge of Her back into being.

AT HOME I hear someone talking on the radio, who has been told that he has a bad cancer that is likely to end in his dying. He said that he has decided to live fully and be creative for however long his time might be. If I have ten years left of energy and life I want to fill them with you, Lady, with you.

UNFORTUNATELY online abuse continues against us from disaffected priestesses and others, expanding to include many areas of our priestess and teaching work. We are accused of many bad things. Now I feel like I am being hunted down as if I am a witch of old. As I am writing the script for the sacred drama which will be performed in the Conference a deep disturbing memory arises, precipitated by all the negativity that has been sent our way many times now. This memory forms the foundation of a scene in the play and continues to develop after the play is performed in the Conference.

"I SEE MYSELF in a square-checked dress with a white flounced edging, dirty around the hem from dust and mud, a bit tattered, wooden clogs upon my cold feet. I am standing in front of a church tower looking at a paper stuck to the wall. On it I see a crude drawing of my face and myself named as the 'witch', Amy Smallhouse. I am chief amongst the accused, who are my sisters – Molly Spidgeon, Sarah Applegate, Miranda Greenwood, Lily Martin and Emily Partridge. We are accused of making spells, of black magic, of giving harm to others. I am particularly accused of enticing poor souls by spells, to leave their hearths and homes, to give up husbands, wives, families, everything known and familiar to come and dwell by my side, to become part of my coven. And then that I did abandon them to their own devices, that I let them starve, did not give them work or pay them for their company. (All a mirror to the accusations made about us in the present time.)

That they were put under a magic spell from the first moment that drove them mad. So distressed that they must leave their child or children and that in their grief they fell in love with another poor mad soul and were led into years of madness and self-destruction, all by our actions – for by now it was not only I, but I and my cronies, other witches who wait about me, ready to harvest the weak and the vulnerable, to subject them to foul acts and mean incantations.

Suddenly it seems there are many ready to testify to the wrongs this coterie of women have committed. An open trial is called for against this coven, but all accusers have the right to remain anonymous for fear of retribution by the infernal witches of the night. They, the accusers, will have every right of free speech, to speak with each other and with the magistrate, although hidden from the public gaze, protected by their secret society.

"We are the good people afraid to be seen, to speak out, in case she or they cast their spells against us and all manner of pestilence and abomination will be cast upon us by them."

My feet clatter upon the cobblestones as I run. I am afraid. Where shall I go? They know where I live. They will come to find me. They will break down my door and carry me to gaol to rot in the darkness, like many before me in other places. They will take me before their magistrate and line up against me to list my misdeeds, for who can claim never to have made a mistake in the whole of their lives? Who was it said, "Do not look for the mote in her eye, but rather look to the plank in your own." and "Who will cast the first stone?"

For that is my other fear: that they will come to my door with clubs and ropes, and will attack me, hurt me, stone me to death. I have no spells that can repel an angry horde, whipped into a frenzy by the righteous. I have herbs for healing to help the sick and tired. I have prayers to the Mother that soothe a troubled heart. I can help mothers in their birthing and the aged to die peacefully, but I cannot ward off an angry mob.

I must go home and grab my herb bag quickly. I run, run across the cobbles to my small home on the edge of the village. I duck in through my door and fill my cloth bag with herbs and bread, a small bottle of healing draughts. I kiss my cat farewell, who I must leave to fend for herself. A last glance around this small sanctuary of mine and then out through the door into the woods, around the edge of the village, running, running for my life.

Running first to my sister, Molly Spidgeon. I must warn her, tell her to be wary, to spread the news to all in the coven. Be Ware, my sisters! The buzzard calls her greeting in the high branches. Be Ware!

"Molly, we are called witches, demons, whores. I flee and fear that you too must run from the gathering clouds. They will come for you too, for all of us. Let our sisters know we are named by those who take no cause for their own lives, who say that we have damaged them and it is our fault that they are sick, unwell, poor and needy. Nothing to their own laziness, lack of self care, and fear to speak out against the rule of the fathers, against husbands, fathers, mothers, sons and daughters, judges, rulers and masters. Now the Lord will save them. They have given themselves away to a safer cause perceived, than serving Life and Nature, our Lady of the Forests, Streams and Mountains."

Molly sends her serving girl to run to tell the others,

"Fly like the silent owl to my sisters and warn them that trouble comes and we must hold together in our innocence! Accusations are made, will be made, by all who hold a grievance, a bitter tongue, by all whose journey is difficult in these strange times of change. Be Ware, my sisters, Be Ware!"

Where shall I go? Where is safe for me? To the Green Grove of Healing I shall flee to find my shelter among the greenwood this night. I run swiftly along the leaf-strewn pathways, my dress catching on bramble thorns, tearing as I run in terror.

"Oh my Goddess, what shall I do? Where shall I go? Beloved Mother, hold me in my fear in this my hour of need. Hold me always!"

MY TEETH chatter in the cooling air, the breeze rising and leaves rustling upon the trees. The hairs rise upon the back of my neck, a twig is broken. There are running footsteps and suddenly I am on the ground, felled by a blow to the back of my head. I see stars and lose consciousness for a few moments. When I come to, my nose and mouth are full of dirt — beloved earth, my love, my love. I cannot breathe and turn my head to the side, spluttering, pain wracking the back of my skull.

"Turn her over", a rough voice calls, "Let's see the witch!"

SIGHT BLURRED, a slap to my face, startled, my eyes open and close. I see them standing above me, two men and two women, whom I know well. One woman I had given herbs to one time to help her gouty limbs, but it had not helped for she was too far gone from daily stout and fatty meats, and would not keep to the commended foods.

"That is her, the witch who harmed me! Don't look in her eyes. Don't let her entrance you with her gaze. Don't let her escape! "

"Bind her eyes and take that bag of wickedness away from her."

"See 'tis full of her poisons!"

THEY TAKE *my healing bag of herbs and bread and trample it upon the ground, stamping on it and breaking the contents. A dirty cloth is tied around my now streaming eyes, filled with tears of pain and shock. Then they take hold of my feet and drag me across the woodland floor. Pain shoots through my body, through every joint, as stones and tree roots cut through my thin clothes, flesh scraping earth, soon bleeding, raw. As they drag me along my clothes become tattered and soon I am faint with the pain.*

I wake upon a wooden cart and everything in my body screams with pain. Dirt and dust fill my mouth, nose and eyes, although the covering has slipped and I see under. I can hear others moan beside me as the cart bounces along a broken road. There we lie my sisters and I, all caught together, we soul-sisters lying there in grave distress, hands now bound and piled upon one another. I feel another's limbs beneath me and try to lift myself off her, but all strength is gone from my aching body.

Miranda lies beneath me scarce breathing and I can feel how shallow the life in her has become, "Hold on, my sister, hold on. This must end soon."

Muscles stiffening I raise myself as much as I can to relieve my weight upon her, but it is a poor thing that I can do.

The cart rolls on across the countryside for what seems like hours. Where are they taking us? It must be to Middlefield, the nearest town, our village is too small a place for a witch's trial. They must make example of us to a wider gathering. It has been foretold that this would happen, but we had not believed it. We had not believed that as the witch craze moved across the countryside they would come to our small village, so unimportant in the grand schemes of things. We harm none. We are not important enough to be noticed. But we are betrayed by mean-eyed, envious women, slighted men and children bought for the promise of a hot meal, a new plaything, a new dress.

Our kindness forgotten, our love, our holding in childbirth, our care through the lean times, the hard times, all forgotten in the fear of being named by others.

"Accuse them before they accuse you! But do it behind their backs in anonymous letters, in silent revealing glances, in whispers behind closed doors, in the hidden Collective."

NOW they have come out into the open, overstepping the boundaries of sisterhood and charity, picking, picking with moon sickles at the hearts of the free, righteous in their indignation.

"No, she is no friend of mine! She did these terrible things to me, to my family, to my friends. We will hold her in the House of the Lord and He will bring her to justice for all her many crimes. For we do love these poor begotten souls. They are our sisters in Christ and must be justly tried, then shriven, forgiven for their misdeeds, before they are hung from the gibbet."

WE ARE THROWN from the cart into a dark hole in the round stone gaol in the centre of the town. Down in the darkness on the muddy cobbles with the rats and other worn souls. Miranda is in a really bad way, her breath now scarce moving in her body. She is dying without aid. As best we can we untie the bonds that hold our wrists and eyes and adjust to what little light there is coming in beneath the door. We who are less wounded sing soft songs for her soul as she prepares to cross over from this vale of pain to the Summerlands.

Each of us retreats into our own places of pain, fear and sorrow, but still we touch, hold hands, rest arm upon arm, comfort coming in this shared moment. Sobs rise and fall as music and the others held in the darkness join us in these mournful times. The night is long and sleep is fitful. There is no balm for bloodied backs and torn skin, which stings as it dries and pulls. Drifting into deathless sleep, waking startled to a pain-filled moment. Why this? What have we done? What red-eyed wolfish monster stalks the land, picking off the vulnerable, as it homes in on its prize. Find their leader! Take her down!

Then they will all be gone and no more shall the devil, full of pride, walk these lands. We will be safe under the Rule of the Master's Hand.

Through the dark cold hours wild thoughts enter my mind. What is real? What a memory? What a trick of the light in the darkness? Ghosts of the ancestors and spirit beings appear and disappear in the high rafters, ever moaning, whispering, chattering, cawing like ravenous crows over a decaying body. Are we dead already and these are the In-Between lands?

"Lady, Lady, lead us gently to your Summer Isles."

The tiny light beneath the door grows slowly brighter. We shift our bodies and see for the first time where we lie. Miranda is gone, gone to the Summerland. We lay her body out on the cobbles and sing the soft songs of blessings for her soul, scattering over her the few leaves of sweet herbs still remaining in the bottom of a pocket.

A crack, a shout and the door opens. Light floods in, blinding the eyes for a few moments. "Come out, you witches, come out here!"

"Our sister has died in the night. She did not survive your rough treatment."

IN COME *two burly men, pushing us aside, to carelessly lift her body from the floor and haul it away without ceremony, off to an outcast's grave. It is the last we see of her body. Our tears flow for she who is gone, for our sister Miranda and all that is lost.*

We are harried, hurried out of the gaol to a dirty washroom and forced to undress, to remove all our torn clothing in front of ogling men. Standing naked we are soaped down by slatterns, who care nought for our wounds, with pails of ice-cold water thrown over our bodies. They dry us with rough cloth. Stinging, hurting, such cruel pain, such lack of compassion.

We are given sack-cloth to cover our bodies, all that is deemed appropriate for a witch to wear. Then a piece of dry bread and a cup of ale. We are now five scared and sorry women. We look into each other's eyes and feel the pain and fear, but no-one else knows or cares for the depth of our suffering. We are condemned before the trial has begun, before a shred of evidence is offered, before any defence is raised or considered.

We are led towards the Courthouse, through a waiting crowd who are primed and ready to shout and jeer. Looking into these people's eyes, they cast aside, unable to take in what they must do, unconscious, terrified for their own fates if they should disobey their rulers. They bay as hounds on the scent of fox women.

We are hurried in through the back gate and taken into a crowded Court Room. Cries rise at our entrance. The atmosphere is wild and volatile, ready for the accusations. Undercurrents of fear ripple across the thresholds, masks of anger, tightness of jaw, raw hatred are all on display. We five must stand together in the dock, each now chained to her sisters and to the floor. We must be weighted to the ground lest we fly up on broomsticks. At least in this way our flesh can touch flesh, however cold and damp with terror. We are here together.

The magistrate enters and all rise to flatter. A hush moves across the court and then as a signal is given the shouting begins again, brought quickly to an end by a wave of his hand. There is no mistake as to who is in control in this place of power.

We are named, each one of us, as witch, as devil's whore and tormenting demon. Where does this naming and this hatred come from? Until a few days, just a week or so ago, we were loved by many, known as healers, midwives, comforters and friends. But now some hidden tide has turned within the land. And we have become an enemy of the people.

Hidden from us behind a wooden screen, one by one our accusers come forward. We are not allowed to know by sight who they are for fear we will fix them with our powerful spells. So little they know of what we are truly capable. We can call Goddess and the love and blessings of Her presence. We can calm the winds, bring rains to make the land fertile, but we have no interest in horror and the magic which maims. But this does not hold their interest. It is devils and darkness, black magic and the rule of demons, false order, discipline and constraint, that move their hearts. Not truth, not consciousness of self, and the soul's path to healing.

We hear their voices ringing out in condemnation, telling tales of victims destroyed by our teaching. Untruths, lies, distortions, all fall from the lips of women who were our sisters, from brothers we once kissed beneath the Beltane bowers. Some voices we recognise and we exchange a look of knowing as we catch a familiar tone, an accent of betrayal. We know most of them, but there are also those unknown, or known and forgotten from some distant time.

They tell tales of money stolen, offences of ignorance,

"She walked by me and didn't speak to me."

Offences told by one to another over garden walls,

"She did nothing to me, but I speak on behalf of others who have told me what she did to them. I speak for those who cannot speak for themselves. I speak on behalf of the weak who have been harmed by her, by them."

"Each one speaks blasphemy against the Lord, together they are a coven of devils!"

"Let us take them, my Lord Magistrate. Let us force them to recant. We can do this for you."

And on and on with accusations which pour forth from hidden chasms. Eventually the time comes for our pleas and our defence.

"What is your plea to these charges, Amy Smallhouse?"

"Not guilty, my Lord." My weak voice trembles and shouts rise from the Courtroom.

"And you, Sarah Applegate?"

"Absolutely not guilty, my Lord!" Her voice strong, I glance at my sister, soft love in my eyes as the voices rise all around, baying for blood.

"You, Molly Spidgeon?"

"Not guilty, my Lord!"

"Lily Martin?"

"Not guilty, my Lord!"

The sisters are strong, thank Goddess.

"And you finally, Emily Partridge?"

Emily breathes in. We wait for her answer, smiling, encouraging. She looks *away and then speaks in a whisper.*

"Guilty, my Lord."

"Speak up, what did you say?"

"Guilty, my Lord."

And the Court erupts.

As one we look in horror at our sister and she looks away, tears streaming down her face. We know our sister is just so frightened, so afraid.

Through the raging crowd in the Courtroom, Emily's voice rises, piercing the crowd, who hush at her voice.

"I did it, my Lord. I slept with the devil. I cursed the weak and harmed the strong. I made images in wax and brought pains to stomach and heart. I delivered poisonous letters to those she wanted to harm. I am guilty, my Lord, with these, my sisters!"

"Emily, it is untrue. You lie!" I cry.

We four are truly shocked, horrified at Emily's lies, her fearful nature revealed in these sudden words.

"I do not lie, Amy Smallhouse. You made me do it. I was just a go-between. I spoke for you. I only did your bidding. I did it for you!"

There are shouts and silences in the Courtroom as the horror unfolds. We are betrayed by our sister, who is over-ruled by her own terror. I had thought that she loved me. We are undone, undone!

SOON IT IS OVER. The sentences are given. Four of us will die by the gibbet and one will be saved, although her life will be one of penury and isolation. The choice that she makes has still placed her fate in the accuser's hands. Who will trust her now, neither friend nor foe? I cannot blame her. I understand the dilemma she faced as each one of us does. To stand in the truth of the heart or through fear to turn against. Some fears are too great to face.

The day has passed quickly and we four – Molly, Sarah, Lily and I, are taken outside and placed in the stocks to await our final fate. Locked in at neck and wrists, everything hurts, tearing already torn skin. At first the crowd shouts at us, throwing abusive words on our sorry heads. Then a cabbage is thrown, rotten to the core, it splatters on head and nose, smelling foul, but what is one more horror added to the pile. Then a small pebble, sharp and painful, biting into soft cheeks. Eyes close, heads down, as a rain of small sharp stones comes towards us. We all cry out as we are hurt and then I hear Molly scream and blood pours from her eye.

"I cannot see. Oh merciful Mother, take me, take me now!"

A bitter rain, a rain of hate. What did we ever do to these people, but love them and hold them, help them and heal them as best we could? We taught them the little knowledge they could learn from us, now all forgotten. Blame heaped upon blame for wrongs unknown.

As darkness falls the crowd slowly disperses. My sister Molly now hangs silent. Has she gone too?

"Molly, Molly, are you still here?"

Out of this place of pain Molly lifts into the starlight groves. Only Sarah, Lily and I remain alive. Under the breath we say prayers for the safe passage of our sister across the waters to the Summerland.

In the dark night a young girl comes silently running towards us. She gently wipes our faces with a cloth. She lifts a cup to our lips, a cup of pure, clean water to ease our aching throats.

"Thank you, gentle sister, but be safe. Go quickly lest the guards who pass by each quarter see you too and take you under."

But she is quick, a light step and a gentle touch and she is gone before the guards' next round. Then she returns,

"Sister, do you choose the death draft to outwit the hangman's noose?"

It is a choice to make, to stay with some wild hope of being saved at the last moment's mercy or take the sweet Crone nectar now. I wish to be alive until the very last moment I can be. I love this beautiful world in which I have lived and still live. I refuse the gift. And Lily too, while our sister Sarah accepts the draught. She looks sideways into my eyes,

"We will meet on the Other Side, sweet Amy, my friend, my teacher," she whispers. "Fear not for we will meet again in another time and place and we will remember the love we have shared in this life. We will remember who we truly are and our love for the Lady. We will build Her world once again."

And then in a moment the girl pours the death-dealing liquid into Sarah's mouth. Sarah gulps it down. I know the taste is bitter. Her breath falters, soon becoming harsh and rasping. Her eyes begin to glaze over and in a few moments that stretch long, she is gone, her spirit rising like the mist, sparkling in the starlight. She is gone and there is only Lily and me. We are alone, so alone, in this moment of mystery. This time is so hard, so impossibly hard to live through and to fathom.

The dawn light rises slowly. The dogs come to lift their legs upon the wooden stocks, upon the bodies, two dead, two alive. They lick at faces and dried blood, a meal awaiting. I shout at the dogs to be gone, but I cannot stop them. As the dog mob gathers to see if we can provide them with meat, a guard arrives shouting, scattering their barking bodies.

He unlocks the heavy stocks, releasing my sisters whose bodies hang lifeless on the wooden gates. He unlocks Lily and me, and I can scarce lift myself and roll out of the wooden prison. Every part of my body screams in agony as it moves again. I should have drunk the poisonous draught. Human bodies are so fragile – skin, sinews, bones, no fur to limit the pain. I have entered another state of being, rising and falling in and out of consciousness, and the blessed relief of passing through the gateway.

In fevered reveries I see my long life flowing before my eyes, memories of my mother who taught me with her sisters, the ways of MotherWorld. They taught me love and compassion for all beings, the wisdom of the sun's seasons and the mysteries of the moon, the gifts of healing, herbs and medicines, of journeying and song, of oracling and embodiment. They showed me the secrets of our blood, the blessings of sexuality, birth-giving in its right timing, the lighting of the central hearth and its nurturing fires for all women, children and the guardian, questing men. They taught me loving and giving, sharing and tending, ceremony and ritual in due season, of the miracle of life and its sacred return to the Mother at death. Oh, they showed me so much, how to live in peace upon our Mother Earth.

My father was one that I knew, for not everyone did know, in this time when domination and ownership were also all around. He was a kind man, just and caring, holding the welfare of his people as his first concern. I had been fortunate in my choice of parents in these times, before they became uncertain. We were a hidden community far away from the thronging crowds in towns, now found and brought into the harsh reality of the ruler's times.

I wake suddenly, my body lurching in the cart as it bounces on the stony road. I lie there next to my sister, ice-cold, our calves touching, but now it seems I am less frightened. I can feel the love of my sisters, there now on the Other Side, just beyond the Veil. They are there supporting us from the Beyond. I can feel them. We lived such lives together, shared so much joy, so many amazing experiences in the name of our Lady, graced by Her love.

On a high hill the two-faced gibbet stands. The wind blows and the scudding clouds are full of rain. Our hands are tied behind our backs and we are forced to stand at the back of the cart as a noose is placed around each of our necks. The noose pulls tighter as we say our prayers.

"Lady, bless me and bless all my sisters, all who have gone before me and all who remain. Bless my family, my beloved, my child, my friends. Bless all those who I have ever known in my life, the good and the bad. Bless them and heal them. I pray that my life be a blessing for others and this, my death will send a blessing out into the world, that each might sense and feel in some way that will be a boon for their souls."

I PRAY *to my beloved Lady for my sister here beside me. Neck turning I can just see Lily. I turn back and gaze with love at the land of beauty all around me, this wonderful earth on which we live. My fear has subsided, now the moment is here and death is approaching. Bless all. Bless the Earth.*

"Take me, beloved Lady, to the Isle of the Dead. Lead me into the Paradise of Avalon, so that I might meet with you in truth and reality, and meet once again my sisters, my family and my friends."

The cart moves beneath us, there is a pull, a sharp tug, breath is removed from my body. I hear/feel the snap of my neck as my body swings. Pain shoots through and then is gone. I rise out of my body, a blur of light and colour, sparks and darkness. I depart my earthly home, moving swiftly like a phantom in the dawn light.

THEY SAID, *the few people who were gathered on the high hill at sunrise, that in that moment of death the sun broke through the clouds and a rainbow appeared in the sky. There was not one, but two, then three, radiating rainbows, filling the sky with colour and light. The people watching gasped and gazed in wonder at the beauty revealed in this bleak place of suffering.*

The witch is dead! Long live the witch!"

Chapter Fifteen

CREATING PARADISE

BY LATE MAY I finish the script for the sacred drama that will be performed at the Goddess Conference. I have given myself a life-line to finish by, so there would be enough time to bring the actors together and then rehearse in time for the Conference. For an Ariadne Production it used to be six weeks to write a play, and six weeks to rehearse before the performance. I have managed to allow a bit more time than that. It is the first full-length sacred drama I have written on my own for many years.

The Mythos of Ertha: The Stones of Wonder is a reclaiming of the energetic Motherlines which connect us back to the First Mothers from whom all human beings descend, and to the ancient Motherworld in which Goddess was once universally honoured and adored as the centre of all life. The play follows the soul lives of a group of people as they incarnate through different lives in different times, including part of the witch life I had re-membered in vision. It demonstrates how the destruction and loss of the ancient Goddess Temples and communities, and the loss of Motherworld values, has repercussions that resound through the lives of past and present day people and societies. It hopefully gives a glimmer of hope as to how we might change our world once again.

Katie Player and I begin to call together the actors, several of whom have acted before in earlier Ariadne Productions in the 1980s and 90s, and have a sense of what is needed. There is Sue Real (Newcombe), Gareth Mills, Paul Perry and Dreow Bennett, who will play some of the soul characters who move through the play in different incarnations.

The play is set within and around an ancient Goddess Temple and circle of standing stones, which was erected long ago by a Motherworld community, which was then attacked and destroyed. The stone circle is broken and neglected through time and now in the present day is calling to be restored. The challenge is how to make on stage a circle of standing stones that look real. I talk to Sue about how we might do this and to Freddie (Foosiya) Miller, the wonderful sculptor who makes the withy Goddess statues for the Conference each year. Freddie comes up with a plan to create nine large standing stones using chicken wire and mesh and coating them with fabric and plaster, then painting them to look like stones. It's not a small job.

Beloved Lady, you who are the Wind, the Sun shining,
The Breath, Air, Earth, Green Plants, Animals
How I adore you.
You are the blessing of the rain
And the Gift of warmth on a cold day
You are the healing of the heart
And the simple wounds of the child.
Heart opening, I surrender to your love.
Lady, let me love you and serve you
Without fear or hardship
Let me give everything to you
Without resistance, without reaction.
I do my best for you, always
And for your people,
Trying always to be clear and fair
Yet sometimes failing
Triggering reactions where none were meant
Feeling the sorrow of others
I call to you, Lady

To bless me with your love
To show me the way always to follow you
With love in my heart
To be more compassionate
To have greater clarity and wisdom
With clear speech and insight
Hold me always in your loving embrace
Lady, always.

Planning for the Goddess Conference is well under way. I write in the programme, which seems each year like writing a whole new book,

'In 2013 we honour Ertha, our Great Earth Mother, on whose body we all live and move and have our being. In our Conference we will be walking upon Her Earth body, making pilgrimage through the Sacred Landscape of Avalon, experiencing Her Paradise which is all around us. We will be grounding the Vision of Motherworld, a renewed society in which mothers and the values of mothering – love, care and support for each other, are placed in the centre of our societies, rather than being left out on the margins.'

For this is the year when we will ceremonially ground the Vision of Motherworld, which has been honed into a clear statement over the last year, through many conversations and communications within the Goddess community.

ON JUNE 15TH a small group of priestesses including Sally Pullinger, her grand-daughter Gabi, Georgina and I, plus members of the Avalonian Free State Choir which Sally conducts, travel up to the Leicester Square Theatre in London, for Julie Felix's 75th Birthday Concert. Julie is one of the Goddess Conference's favourite singers, coming each year to sing for us. She is such an amazing star and has the capacity to melt hearts and reduce us all to tears with her wonderful Goddess songs. It's all very exciting for those of us who live in the country to be priestessing and performing in the centre of the capital! The choir are going to sing with Julie and we priestesses are going to do a ceremony on stage to honour Julie in front of her normal world fans. Here we are, priestesses abroad, in the heart of London. This is playtime.

Early evening the theatre fills with people and we sit at the side of the auditorium. The first half of the programme begins with a filmed birthday message for Julie from David Frost. It was on the Frost Report that Julie became a household name in Britain for her political folk songs. During the evening Julie is joined on stage by some famous names – Madeleine Bell, Rosalie Deighton, John Cameron and John Paul Jones. The music is really great.

The second half of the evening begins with Sally, Gabi, Georgina and me, priestess-dressed, walking up onto the stage and placing Julie in the centre of our circle. I tell the audience how we are priestesses come from the West, from the Sacred Isle of Avalon, specially to honour Julie on her birthday. I invoke the presence of Goddess Britannia and I can feel Her awesome energy enter the theatre, so that She can be felt by the people. This is an amazing thing to do, here in the heart of London, to call in our ancient tutelary British Goddess once again, with power and meaning, to be present. She comes upon me in the moment. I feel very honoured.

Then Gabi speaks as the Maiden expressing gratitude for Julie's maiden qualities. Georgina speaks to her as the Lover, thanking her for all the love she has given. Sal speaks to Julie as the Mother, thanking her for her personal mothering and also for mothering many people in the world. I speak to her Crone self, thanking her for the wisdom that she shares from her long life. It is very moving for people to hear. At the end we crown Julie on her birthday with a crown of flowers. It is simple, beautiful and powerful. The audience are very attentive and respectful. Most have never seen anything like it before. Then the Avalonian Free State choir comes on stage to sing with Julie in some of her best Goddess songs. It is a blast. A priestess life can be such fun.

* * *

MID JULY, two weeks to Conference – Katinka has come round to our house and as we are going to sit down I am walking too quickly and not looking where I am going. My right foot slams into the metal leg of the sofa. Ow!! My foot and toe really hurt. It feels like it is sprained or even broken. At first I ignore the pain hoping it will pass, but the pain gets worse. Another mad accident!

On the weekend I have to walk the land doing ceremonies with the Third Spiralers on their final weekend. Oh, my foot hurts! They are good ceremonies. Walking all day and into the evening in pain. I trust in the loving energy of all the priestesses helping hold the Initiation Ceremony for the new Priestesses of Avalon.

Waking on Sunday I cannot walk without strong pain. The Conference is in only two weeks and I can't walk, dance or move easily. If it doesn't rapidly improve I will have to step out of the Ceremony Group. How do I feel about that? I can see that I have over-committed myself this year to many things and I can't do it all if I can't move easily.

I think deeply about this moment, for the day will come in time that I can no longer be in the Ceremony group of the Conference. Is this the beginning of the end of my participation? I find that I actually feel OK about it. It feels like change and I can always welcome change. It feels emotional and sad and OK. I don't have to be the One to be seen any longer. This year's Third Spiral journey began the day after I fell down into the cellar opening and ends with damaging my foot. It is Mars/Uranus conjunct.

On Thursday I wake from a dream with feelings of anxiety about there being enough income from the Conference as our numbers are down again with the recession. When she came to visit I had been wanting to talk with Katinka about my worries. I wasn't trusting the Lady to provide as She always does. She always makes sure that it works out. Moving too fast in worry creates accidents. It's a hard lesson, Lady, a hard painful lesson.

FOR THE Opening Ceremony of the 2013 Goddess Conference we create Ertha's Paradise. Earlier in the year I had a vision of a wooded glade with a circle of ancient standing stones nestling between the trees, and the naked painted bodies of ancestral earth beings melding into the stones. Peter Freerson helps me find lots of trees and shrubs we can hire in for the week of the Conference. Freddie, Sue and I create nine beautiful standing stones, and by some magic we bring it all together to create a magical Paradise, while everyone else in the Conference is out on the land for the Preparation Ceremonies. I can't go out on the land because I still can't walk easily, but I can direct others to place the trees in the best positions to take people into magical visions. I so love doing this kind of arranging, creating altars to Goddess on a grand scale, which people can enter physically and psychically.

Throughout the Conference we ground the Motherworld Vision ceremonially in several beautiful powerful ceremonies, anchoring in the values of love, care and support for each other, for all beings. We perform *'The Mythos of Ertha: The Stones of Wonder, A Sacred Drama and Ariadne Production'.*

The play is a reclaiming of the energetic Motherlines which connect us back to the First Mothers from whom all human beings descend, and to the ancient Motherworld in which Goddess was universally honoured and adored as the centre of all life. Our Sacred Drama begins long, long ago in a time beyond memory, when Ertha, Great Goddess of the Earth, first created the four original races of human beings – the black, white, red and yellow races, from Her earthly substance. As human societies and cultures grew, Ertha was honoured as the Source of all life on Earth, and mothers and our children – the future of the human race, were safely held in the centre of life by all. The four races gradually expanded across the world, meeting and mingling to become the nine. Then comes the Fall, the loss of Grace, as patriarchal ideologies and values entered in and became dominant. We forgot who gave us life. We forgot to honour Ertha, and all Her bounty and generosity to us.

Our play follows the lives of a group of souls through their incarnations in different eras and societies up to the present day, and our hopeful Return to honouring Ertha and Her nature once again. On the night the Town Hall Temple is full to overflowing and our performance of *'The Stones of Wonder'* is powerful. The cast create an amazing and deeply moving spectacle. We are all very happy.

Late August Mike, Katinka and I travel to Söderhamn in Sweden to take part in Priestess of Avalon Gittan Wigren's first Swedish Goddess Conference. We have a wonderful time staying on Gittan's land, in her small B & B, which is on the ground floor beneath her beautiful Goddess Temple. All around there are extensive forests with trees and rocks, moss and lichen, smooth water, lakes and sea inlets, and pale blue, wide skies, with many different kinds of clouds – they are different to the kinds of clouds we have in Somerset. There is a beautiful stillness in the forest with thick layers of pine needles underfoot, green layers with blueberries, bilberries, red berries. Huge rocks cover the forest floor and rise up from it, homes for trolls and elementals, visible in the corner of one's eyes. Just out of sight are foxes, moose, bears and wolves. It's very magical and it would be wonderful to spend more time here in the woods.

Gittan's Temple carries the energy of the forest, the energy of Hel, Great Goddess of these northern lands. Goddess Hel comes from Norway and the ancient people who survived on the margins of the last Ice Age, it is said, on a small area of coastal land warmed by the Gulf Stream. In Norway and Sweden, the Scandinavian lands, She is Hel. In Germany, Belgium and the Netherlands She is Frau Holle, Hulda, Holda and Holla, Goddess who brings the snow. Soderham is in the region of Helsingland – Hel's land.

Other Swedish Priestesses of Avalon who have trained with us in Glastonbury, Elin Hejll Guest, Ann Forsberg and Lola Ravenstar, are here too for the Conference. I feel so proud of them all, proud of what we can create, especially when we work together. We offer great opportunities to connect deeply with Goddess and take steps on the journey of personal transformation. I bring the natural elements from Avalon – the earth, water, fire and air, as an offering to the Goddess of this land. I mix them ceremonially and alchemically with the natural elements of Helsingland. I give a talk about the Motherworld Vision and the healing work we must do together, particularly as women.

One day I suddenly get really angry with Mike when he interferes when I am having a direct exchange with one of the men helping with the Conference. I have spotted a chink in the man's armour, and am making my way towards it, but Mike comes and stands between me and the man, and wags his finger at me, blocking direct communication between us. I am furious and feel really angry. *"Fuck off!"* I say.

Later Katinka points out to me that this anger is coming from a 'child' place, not from an adult place and she helps me to follow the thread to the wound in me. At first I can't understand what she is saying, but I know that confusion is a sign that there is something there, something Shadow, something hidden. I track it to the feeling that Mike was colluding with the man, protecting him against me, the sensitive child. I realise that I have been tracking that experience of collusion between adults against me, over the last couple of years, since I have had cancer. I can feel the little girl place in me that is small, wounded, overwhelmed and fearful. I feel how I have turned that scared place inwards against myself.

In the last year I have been getting angry when I feel collusion or that my feelings are being dismissed as unimportant, rather than feeling defeated, which was a pattern through my life. It's a big change to let myself be angry and I have actually quite enjoyed being angry – being able to say, *'Fuck off!'* to someone who is attacking or dismissive of me. I have said this a few times now, to Mike, Iona, to a student, to a friend who was competitive and undermining. But, perhaps I've said it enough now.

Katinka points out that there are other creative ways to react, not either curling into a ball or shouting. She asks me if I trust Mike and our relationship. She wants me to say *"Yes"*, and I do say *"Yes"*, but I realise that this is not really my true feeling. Of course, I trust him in many, many ways, but on a particular layer, in a particular wounded child place, I don't trust him at all. I am defended against him and I don't know it until that moment.

Later in the weekend after teaching my own workshop, I participate in Katinka's workshop. She leads us/me to another wounded place and as I stalk it some more I find the place of the wound in my body. I find myself curling into a ball and feel the pain in my belly. It hurts. I remember something – a family weekend a year and a half ago, when I felt completely excluded by Mike's family. Their sibling behaviour triggered me into a really horrible feeling of being rejected as a child, a childhood grief space. Feelings arose that weekend which I hadn't felt since my childhood, memories of collusion between my parents and my sister against me, the youngest child, the littlest one. *"No, you can't help, you are too small".*

At the time I knew my feelings were childhood feelings, but I couldn't step away from them and I reacted emotionally as a wounded child. I didn't ever want to spend time with these people again. I felt that Mike had colluded with his family against me, so how could I ever trust him? Since then I have been defended against him all the time.

Through the workshop process unfolding I feel very vulnerable. I tell Mike how I am feeling and my heart opens to him again. My eyes open to his. I see the pattern really clearly and its results – sadness, anger, a lack of forgiveness, coming from the place in me that is defended against them all, against Mike, my lover, my best friend.

Now I can see it I have a choice in how I react, how I behave in similar situations. I did not have a choice before, the wound was deep and hidden, now it is softening and begins to heal. I feel lots of gratitude towards Katinka for helping me to track and find this wound, the wound which began to reveal itself before the second bout of breast cancer.

Damo, Mike's Nei Gong teacher and acupuncturist, had said to me that this cancer was about the liver and anger. I didn't know what he was talking about as I didn't feel angry at the time and couldn't remember feeling angry. It has taken two years and many Uranus/Mars/Mercury squares and conjunctions to find the raging anger hidden deep in my psyche, the anger that makes me defend against all collusion, repression, inhibition of my sensitive soul. The Loyal Soldier has defended me well and kept me safe from my enemies. Now we shall use the fiery energies released, not for defence, but to pursue the cause of peace and Motherworld values, being able to listen and hold true meaning and argument.

* * *

AT THE BEGINNING of this before I had cancer a second time I did not know where I was going next. Now life is changed. I want to fill my remaining years with life, using as much of my energy as I can to change the world for the better, before I die. This has been a time of transformation for me, from the healing of wounds that were inflicted at the endings of the Goddess Temples, reaching through to the wounding in this life – the blocking and controlling of my sensitive soul – to my disempowerment and imprisonment in an alien world – listen to those words. It feels like I was once caught and imprisoned for some time and then escaped and ran. Then it took a long time to find any like-minded people and when I did they were still battling and fighting amongst themselves and with me. Until now?

Change comes.

This is my prayer,

"I ask for your blessings, beloved Lady, on our Temple community. I ask for your help in healing the wounds in all of our relationships."

The Lady hears my prayer, and brings Her transforming love to heal our wounds.

WE RETURN HOME for a couple of days and then we fly out to California to take part in Goddess Spirit Rising, an international Goddess gathering created by priestesses Anique Radiant Heart from Australia, and from the US Delphine DeMore and Laura Krajewski. Many of the luminaries of the American Goddess world are there – Amalya Peck, Jennifer Berezan, Joan Marler, Judy Piazza, Letecia Layson, Lydia Ruyle, Max Dashu, Ruth Barrett, Susun Weed, Vicki Noble and Zsuzsanna Budapest. It's good to spend time with them, to experience their workshops, and just to hang out all together. We have a great time but later find that here too there are all sorts of competitive undercurrents going on between the women that will take months to work out. These too are the consequences of the wounds suffered at the endings of the Temples.

Chapter Sixteen

A Small Miscommunication

WE RETURN HOME and after a couple of weeks' grace another descent begins, another turn of the downward spiral into the wounds that we all carry. It begins so easily – a miscommunication, a misunderstanding, a confusion, a word said out of place, then fear of the consequences of owning mistakes, of being found out, which triggers denial of wrongdoing. The wounds of childhood and other lives vibrate again and the pain of these wounds is expressed inappropriately and has repercussions that last far into the future.

Once more I find myself in my 'victim' place. Now I am accused of disappointing others, of betraying others, of bringing disillusionment. The attacks on Facebook on me personally and on the Temple enter a new phase. I have never experienced anything quite like this. I feel assaulted, not so much by contents, but by the fact of it being so public, so out there for anyone to read. I feel publicly shamed. I feel exposed. I must have done something terrible to warrant such an attack. How has this happened? A few days ago all was well, but now suddenly everything has changed.

I have forgotten that just a few days ago I asked the Lady to heal the wounds in our Temple community, in all our relationships. She heard me and is responding.

IN THESE NEW missives I am written about not as Kathy, a sister priestess, but, repeatedly, as 'Kathy Jones', the archetype, the authority figure, the parent who has betrayed us. It is hard for people to separate me, the woman, from the archetype to which they relate when they write of me, both positively and negatively. Still I am unable to distance myself from the accusations. Some of those writing are people I have cared for as students, held through difficult times, supported and encouraged to become more and more themselves and now my care is a crime. I feel betrayed by women again.

I react emotionally to undermining facebook messages and to all the support that they are receiving, as people 'like' what is being said, which I can also read on the internet. Now I am criticised by new voices, in public messages from people that I know, but who again have never spoken to me personally about their complaints. They feel freed now to attack me publicly. How far has this gone? Where is the support for me? In only a few days venom builds in the language. I am being attacked from many sides. I am suddenly everyone's bad parent and I don't like it. I am over-reacting. I am in my stuff. My victim wounds are triggered. I feel very afraid.

THERE ARE 18 people at our next Temple meeting. Everyone is confused by what is suddenly happening within our community as they read on facebook and talk worriedly behind backs, about all that is written in and outside of our Temple groups. I am in tears. I cannot cope at all with all the aggression. I feel like a very small child being attacked by adults.

In the four hour meeting the group makes several decisions. These include placing the Temple Melissa and Orchard Facebook groups on moderation. This is where many of the attacks are appearing, and the purpose of these groups is actually to give support and care to each other, not to be places of abuse. Marion, who has Mediation skills, will set up a Temple Complaints Procedure and invite those who have expressed grievances against the Temple Management Group to come to talk about their complaints. Lisa will meet with Mike to discuss Health and Safety Policies and Procedures, and Lorraine will draft a Child Protection Policy. Suddenly we need all these new procedures.

We have been in a process of change over the last six months in our management of the Temple and we are endeavouring to make the decision-making process more collective, unless formally delegated. We are trying to create clarity and transparency in all our procedures, because we have reached a certain size and more people are now involved. In the beginning we were just a few people trying to create a Goddess Temple together for the first time. Many complaints and accusations are now being made against the management of the Temple, because we don't act like a large institution or business corporation. We are committed to working through a process to address these issues without joining the patriarchal world. It is all a challenge to create new ways of doing things. I feel very wobbly.

A WOMAN FRIEND tells me that it's a *normal* part of women's culture to undermine and gossip about each other behind one another's backs. It is what women do. But actually it is not a normal part of behaviour. It is the result of damage, and is certainly not part of what we are trying to create for the future in our Vision of Motherworld. I didn't know that friends did this to each other. On the whole I don't *bitch*. Sometimes I will offload my feelings about someone, but that's really to get clear in myself about some issue, and I know I'm doing it. I have a great compassion for people and our wounding.

It is all very shocking to me. I consider what this friend has told me and I think: did you challenge people when they bitched? Did you join them in the bitching? Where do you stand? Did you agree with them? Did you speak up or join in? And what about others? There seems to be little positive support out there. There is lots of negativity, but no positive words on these public forums. Where is everyone? Do you all agree with what is being said? It is too awful!

OVER THE DAYS I continue to feel devastated – shot in the heart, peppered by gunshot. (*Is this an actual memory, an ancient wounding?*) The pain in my heart is so strong. I get to the place of thinking I should just walk away from everything. If they really don't like me that much I can just leave. I don't have to take this abuse. Mike and I talk. We can leave and go to Wales, our other heart home. We can set up our Goddess Retreat centre – Afallon in Wales. It's another alternate life dream for us that has been there for many years, on the back burner, waiting for the right moment. Is that moment now? It seems like a very attractive idea especially to the child part of me, little Katy, who wants to run away and hide from all these horrid people.

I hear my thoughts with my dispassionate mind. I feel a tug between she who holds the Vision of Motherworld and the little girl who wants to run away – between strength and vision, and deep fear of hostile forces and people. I consider leaving and letting go of all the things we do – the Priestess Trainings, the Temple, the Conference. I am tied into Glastonbury in so many ways, but I can just walk away. Is this the time to plan my exit strategy? I will not live forever and this must all be handed on one day. Maybe my departure is coming earlier than I thought.

I like to be in charge of my own life. I want to do what I want to do. I want to be free to follow my vision and creativity – no matter what. I do not want to be stopped by the small-mindedness of others, by their limitations, worries and fear.

MISTAKES have been made and I know how hard it can be to publicly own a mistake. Mike is my greatest teacher in this regard. In our first years together he demonstrated to me repeatedly that it was okay to admit when I make a mistake – that I will not die. This was my great fear, the wound held in my soul from previous lifetimes, a wound that has healed over the years as I have practiced saying, *"I am sorry, I made a mistake".*

I FEEL SICK when I read Facebook messages and the justifications for actions now made public receive more sympathy. I am again written about as the bad person. Little Katy is very hurt right now and wants to die. She's so unhappy. I touch into a deep old wound in myself. Driving back from walking the dog the thought enters my head, that I could just drive the car into that wall straight ahead. I look at the wall ahead of me with intent. It would just be a push on the accelerator pedal and it would all be over, all this pain, all this hostility and aggression. Then I'd be dead or badly injured, and then, *"They'll all be sorry!"* Perhaps then they might feel something empathic, they might feel some guilt. I hear myself thinking these thoughts and the wounded place in me that they come from.

Wow! I haven't had that kind of self-harming thought for thirty years.

I don't drive into the wall, and the pain is great….

OVER THE NEXT days and weeks the barrage of abusive flaming emails from priestesses, from my supposed sisters increases. These are people I have known and cared for, loved and supported over many years. Others join in, people who are or have been Temple Melissas, local people in Glastonbury who have a competitive opinion to share about me, people I know only by sight and strangers I have never met. Many people have something negative to say about me. I am being *trolled* on the internet. Until now I do not know what *trolling* is.

> *Black poison rains down on me*
> *Dark mist hides the gold of the Summerland*
> *The Fox is in the henhouse destroying without reason*
> *The Trolls have come out from beneath the bridges*
> *And are stalking the meadows of cyberspace*
> *The ravenous Wolf with red hollow eyes*
> *Has come in over the perimeter fence*
> *And is now amongst us*
> *Seeking out the weak who are vulnerable.*
> *We saw you there some time ago*
> *Watched you pace the edges of the lake*
> *Looking for a way in*
> *And now you have succeeded*
> *Admitted by those who are not vigilant*
> *Who care more for their own righteousness*
> *Than the continuation of the Temple*

They would pull it all down brick by brick
Rather than face their own fragility
The smallness of their egos
Filled with the bile of unmet wounding
And the falsehood of projection

You, you did this terrible thing to me
You, you, it is all your fault.
I am innocent, I did nothing.
You, you have taken everything from me
You made me silent
You stopped up my mouth with your power
You told me to, "Fuck Off!"
You don't let me make my hateful suggestions
Now we have you in our sights.

AN ANONYMOUS GROUP calling themselves 'The Collective' forms, to express grievances against me, against the Goddess Temple, the Temple Management group, Temple Tutors, the Trainings and the Goddess Conference. A pit of poison opens up beneath us. The Collective is a group of individuals who wish to remain hidden. Each one has a complaint to make, but they are afraid to speak to us individually and personally. The Collective spokesperson claims to speak on behalf of those who are silenced by our bullying management style. Their accusations are vague, unsubstantiated and anonymous. In one of the main ones which we can only read on facebook posts, we are accused of being a 'cult' in its most negative meaning, taking people's money, controlling them, blacklisting them, separating them from their families, preventing them from leaving – who, when, how?

This is all such complete rubbish. The Goddess Temple is not a cult in that pejorative sense – we do not take your money and run, no-one is getting rich here, no matter what people surmise – they say that I own half of Glastonbury

High Street – if I did we would have a much bigger Goddess Temple by now. We do not isolate anyone from their families. We do encourage you to try to work things out with partners, to get help or to leave abusive relationships. We do not brainwash anyone, we encourage you to follow your own heart, to find your true path, to find yourself. We do not hold onto you at any cost. If you want to leave please go in peace with love in your heart and gratitude for all you have given and been given.

I am said to be suffering from Founder's Syndrome, that it is time I left the Goddess Temple and let other people run it. Who might that be? Yes, I am tempted to go but I cannot leave the Temple in your untrustworthy hands and hearts.

Facebook pages become fora for dissent and accusations. Those who support on Facebook, add to the abuse either by direct collusion or by their laughing empathy, posting onwards in public abandon on their own pages. They did not learn these malicious skills in their priestess trainings. These are wounds arising from lives of unconsciousness. And so much more. It is all so truly extraordinary. Where does all this abuse come from?

THE LADY calls to us,
"Wake up, wake up, to your unnatural ways of relating, especially as women. These are wounds of the past which need healing, wounds that come from the endings of my ancient Temples. Become conscious of what is being done. Whom do these attacks serve?"

AFTER WEEKS of public abuse I cannot hold myself back any longer and I send out my own reactive message, expressing my feelings of being hunted as a witch, of being stabbed in the back by so-called sisters. Like everyone else I become emotionally caught up in this mess of miscommunication and my memory of the Witch-burning times vibrates strongly.

We offer the services of the Goddess Temple Resolution Procedures to anyone who has a complaint. All attempts inviting people to come and talk to us are repulsed. It seems that no-one actually wants to resolve anything. Their interest is only in continuing to express their anger and unhappiness with us. Their accusations creep beneath my skin, poking at the places in me which feel guilty for unknown crimes,

"*I must have done something wrong or they wouldn't be so angry with me. Daddy, Mammy, why are you so cross with me? I'm sorry. I must have done something really bad. I don't know what, but you are so angry it must be true.*"

Little Katy is afraid of these angry people. She thinks that they must be right, although she knows she hasn't done anything really wrong at all, or if she did she didn't know it was wrong, or if she did do something wrong and did know, it doesn't warrant all this anger towards her. I'm only little, only a child.

"*I am very sorry. Please forgive me. I didn't mean to make you angry. I love you and I thank you.*"

This is my wound of believing that just because people say I have done something wrong, means that I have. When it is completely healed in me, then the hook will not be there, but until then….

WE RECEIVE an email from Georgina resigning as Melissa Mother, who is the person who organizes our volunteers and makes sure that there are always Melissas holding the Temple open to the public. She has given so much to the Temple over the last years. I will always be grateful for all that she has given to help the Temple grow and develop. For a while there was really only myself, Mike and Georgina holding the centre ground of the Temple, taking responsibility, being present, keeping everything going. I am grateful for all she has done to help us. We invite Dawn Kinsella to become our new Melissa Mother.

IT IS FOUR in the morning. I am awake and my heart is pounding with fear. Next to me, Mike lies softly sleeping, breathing, dreaming. I cannot get out of the bed because it is too cold outside the bed cover and I already feel frozen. I must lie still in the bed, unmoving so as not to wake him. I must lie here and feel my fear. My heart pounds with terror. I can feel its strong beat, blood coursing through arteries and veins, breath coming in short shallow gasps.

RUN! RUN! *They are coming to find me! They are coming to kill me!*

I slip through dimensions and am there again in the place of terror. I hear the footsteps on the stairs, the cries, the shrieks of horror, the crash of falling statues, the tear of material, as they rush onwards towards this Sanctuary, this Holy Ground of Goddess. I am so afraid!

I am cold like ice, shivering, awaiting the inevitable. They will not spare me. They have easily overstepped the outer boundaries of the Temple grounds, the boundaries of honour and respect for Priestess Sisters and Elders. They have breached the inner circles of care and compassion for other human beings. They have wounded by word and deed and already killed so many. Nothing will stop them from killing me, here and now, I who am the Lady's loyal servant, Her Heart Priestess, Her devoted one.

There is nothing I can do. There is no other entrance or way out from this Sacred Chamber of my heart.

Lady, where are you in my hour of need? Where is your cloak of protection? Your cloak of invisibility? Hide me so they cannot see me? Where is your embrace, your radiance, your compassion? Where are you when I need you most?

She does not speak. Her image is still, Her lovely face impassive. Silence greets the throb of my fearful heart. Breathe, be calm. Breathe, open the heart. Hands pulling to prise open closed doors, pushing against the forces of terror.

Open, my Heart! Open! Radiate Soul love, radiate!

The pounding slows, my fear subsides a little.

You enter the Sanctuary, the Holy Ground where burns Her Flame, Her perpetual Violet Flame of Her love for us all. You pause on the Threshold for a moment, even you are stopped in your tracks by the sheer power and beauty of Her Holy Place. Stillness hangs in the air.

Then you plunge in, coarse stone knife ripping, stripping cloth. Club, feet, legs, arms kicking over jug and bowl. Holy Water of the Springs of Life splashing on the stone floor. Sounds roaring, man voices shouting, flame catching cloths rising up the walls. Silence broken into pieces. Nothing to stop the force of such hatred for women's place, for women's natural life power, for the Lady and Her sacred Temple of love.

I feel your sharp knife enter my body between my ribs, beside my heart. The pain is sharp but not too strong. A breath, a relaxation. This moment I have feared since I heard that you were coming, is here now. My end is close. I look into your warrior eyes, your pupils contracting, expanding, changing fast. There is a moment of recognition, a flash of puzzlement in your pale eyes. You will know that you have done this, that you have killed me, warrior soul. I shall not be a nameless body on your battleground. You will know that you have snuffed out my life and you will feel regret for the loss of the unknowable Mystery of my life.

Breath slowing, voice weakening, I speak the names of my Motherline, my birthright, my place in Her Motherworld.

"Hear my names, Warrior of Death. I am Moon Woman, Priestess of Avalon, Priestess of the Lady, Priestess of Nolava of the Sacred Lands. I am Vivienne, daughter of Madron, daughter of Avalon."

I feel the soft warmth of blood flowing as you pull out the bony blade. I see hate/fear in your face as you plunge in again. How does this weak woman hold so much power over you? This frail, flesh and blood woman, this small, soft-skinned woman, this priestess?

I feel the powers of death coming towards me – heat, cold, sight retreating, breath surrendering, rasping as the knife cuts open the covering of my lung and air escapes with a hiss. Knife cutting into my heart, emptying for the last time. Life is dying. Her beloved Temple that I have cared for my whole life, fading from view. The strong sour smell of your harsh breath. Sounds grow louder, boots on stones, the roaring of men, the screaming death throes of sisters as they too face the same end. And you and I, we will meet again in future worlds as we have met before, dying to face this repeating karma.

Who got away? Who ran for their lives? Strange thoughts arising. There will be flowers soon in the meadows, in the fields grain will grow again and ripen, red poppies will blossom with meadow sweet and columbine. The sun will shine upon the Lake of Glass.

And you, my poor sister, you who opened the outer gates for love of a man who was not worthy, your karma and depression will be endless until satisfied.

For it was you who led the band of renegades by the secret pathways across the marshes beside the lake. It was you and your sisters, who welcomed them into the defenceless Mother Temple. This day will haunt your incarnations. I wish I could make it easy for you to know the truths of love. I wish I could save you, but know that I am unable. All is in Her gift, Her compassion, Her saving Grace. I pray for your soul, for my soul, for all souls on this tragic day.

All sight has gone, now only sound remains, the grunts and whispers as blood lust fades, then the whispering, too faint to catch, too faint....

AHEAD OF ME there is light – a shining lantern hangs in the prow of the Barge. My brother the Faeryman holds out his hand to me and I step aboard the ancient craft. My soul sister who went to Avalon before us, Jane of the Radiant Brow, leads me to soft pillows,

Lie down, my darling one. Rest now as we journey home to Avalon.

The Barge moves off across the waters, leaving behind burning buildings on the shoreline, the screaming and the mayhem. On the cushions beside me lie my sisters, Elen of the Isles and Fair Katina. We smile and hold each other's hands. We are not alone on this our final journey to the Enchanted Otherworld. The shining Priestess Ancestor sings softly as the Barge moves away from the shoreline. Above there are ten million, million stars, each a Soul shining in the firmament of heaven, sparkling in the black velvet sky.

The Priestess sings songs of Peace for the Soul. In the Secret Language she calls the Mist to come forth and pale violet white mist arises from the surface of the lake, quickly obscuring our view of the night-time sky. The cradling Barge moves gently upon the waters, rocking us like babes in Her loving embrace. We glide through the mist, feeling dampness on skin, hearing water lapping against the sides of the Barge, sounds receding echoing far away.

Then comes the Calling, the Parting of the Mists again in the Secret Language. The Priestess parts the mist with Her wand and ahead we can see the sun shining upon the wilder shores of Avalon. Beautiful green swards and forests, bubbling springs, streams flowing, rocky clefts, high interior mountains to climb, deep valleys to explore. Here birds and animals freely roam in safety. There are voices singing, and people waiting to greet us, some cheering, welcoming us home once again.

I WAKE trembling from this early morning dream. I decide to write a long email to our private email groups, which tells my side of the whole sorry story. I have waited until I feel clear enough in myself, that I am not just defending myself against the slings and arrows of outrageous fortune. I write the story from my own perspective, telling my truth about the events, about the Temple and all that we are trying to do. At the end I ask those who have complaints to come and talk face to face with those of us who hold the Goddess Temple open. I ask them to hold us all in their hearts with love as we try to do our best always.

No-one comes forward to talk.

Chapter Seventeen

FAILURE

AM BEGINNING to feel that the emotional remembrance of wounds that come from the endings of the Temples and the consequences of those wounds in later life-times, is in itself healing. Somehow by bringing the past into the present the wounds that have been rooted in my soul begin to heal themselves, without me having to do anything but let myself remember them.

I AM TEACHING a workshop on Avalon and Oracling in Turin, Italy, organised for me by our wonderful Italian Priestess Sarah Perini, helped by her lovely husband Mirco Havath. It's a good weekend. I have Sara Ramadero on my right hand side, translating for me. I have the strongest feeling that she has been my assistant before, that I have been her teacher/mentor and she has been my helper, apprentice and even translator in previous lives. I feel completely confident in her translation and she quickly matches her voice to mine in tempo/strength and softness. I love it that I am currently meeting these younger women as they are stepping into their priestess memories and life. They give me great hope for the future.

The following weekend we are in Poggibonsi in Tuscany and I am teaching about *The Path of a Priestess*. It is the end of a successful two days. We thank the Goddesses of the nine directions for all we have received through these amazing days. As the intense energy begins to release from the room tears rise in my eyes.

I sit quietly and pray to the Lady, as I often do at the end of an event, of a teaching circle, of an oracling or embodiment, etc. The words come again,

"*I wish I were a better priestess, Lady. I wish I could do this better. I wish I had perfect concentration, and that I could serve you better, be better that I am.*"

MIRCO CHANGES the CD track I am listening to in the background, one which he knows I like, to another that I do not like, and fury rises in me.

"*Don't do that!*" I snap at him.

He tries to find another track, to make me feel OK, but for me it's too late. I completely disconnect from him, now suddenly after 10 days of great shared friendship and love. I cut him off – for failing to obey me? I feel like he has insulted me in some way, which is odd. I watch my erupting feelings.

Then I register what I said in my prayer to the Lady and realise that I have had these thoughts of failure as a priestess and as a healer before, many times. Where do they come from? Who is criticising me? I am the only person criticising me in my mind in this moment. Everyone on the workshop has had an amazing and powerful Goddess experience and is deeply grateful. It is only me criticising me. It is an internalised, repetitious voice – whose voice? Where does it come from? It is a voice which as I let it run on, says,

"*You are not a good priestess. You have failed in your duty to Goddess! You have failed Goddess, you have failed your people!*"

I realise that in these meanderings the voice is male. Whose voice is it?

Mirco, in another time and place?

In the present I have cut Mirco off emotionally, he's no longer my friend. It's ridiculous and I really don't want to go on feeling this hostility towards him. Later I speak with him about what has happened. I feel like he is a brother who has turned on me, and is talking to me in a patriarchal voice, telling me off.

Luckily Mirco and Sarah and I have a strong past-life bond and we can talk about these things together. They share a past life in Tuscany when they had a familial relationship. It was in a time of change in the Etruscan civilization, which was one of the last remaining Goddess cultures in the European world, in the centuries BCE, before Rome became powerful and its empire grew. The Etruscan Mysteries were taken over and used by Roman patriarchs to massively expand their empire in a relatively short space of time.

Was I there too? With Sarah and Mirco in Tuscany? I am the young daughter who fails. In the inner space I can hear myself being told that I have failed in an important ceremony, by a brother who does not want to be a priest, who criticises me for failing my people, for not being good enough.... The story begins to unfold in visions and dreams.

The next day Mirco, Sarah and I drive south and west to the Etruscan necropolis of Sovana. We walk through trees along the banks of the Calesine river coming to the remains of high stone altars, small rounded caves, steep banked gorges and underground tombs of this ancient Goddess civilization, all carved out of tufa, hardened volcanic ash that once erupted out of the earth. Here on the vertical banks of a gorge there are larger altars and carvings of Melusine with Her twin serpent tails with lion guardians and other creatures hidden in the woods. Several long and increasingly deep trackways with high vertical walls carved from the tufa lead down from upper fields to the tombs of the necropolis and the river.

Mirco and I are ahead of the others and climb up a small rise on the side of the gorge. I walk into a small dark oval-shaped cave carved out of the tufa. As I enter the cave I suddenly slide to the earth. The floor of the cave is covered in a layer of soft mud from the recent rains, which I don't see because of the darkness. I lift my head so that it doesn't strike the floor. My back, my clothing, is covered in mud. Mirco follows me in and helps me to stand and then we sit on the earth bench which encircles the edge of the small cave. This is where the dead were laid before burial in the deeper earth. I am shaking with memory.

> "The air is warm, the stars shimmer in the night sky. I am young, maybe sixteen years old, but still old enough to be Her priestess. I am shaking with the energy of the earth. Here the underground waters bubble and boil and the land of Cel shakes. We are in Tuscana, ancient land of Goddess. We know that we

are the last of the few who still practice Her Mysteries, surviving in the greater land where sons and brothers fight each other for power, wealth and the spoils of war. Our sacred land lies hidden in the wooded clefts and caves of hills and mountains. Our secrets still held in Priestess groves, though now the brothers have joined us and the rise of their powers has begun.

My brother (Mirco) is Maru Cathsc, Priest of Ati Catha, the Sun Mother. He is older and more experienced than I, and he only helps me when he feels like it. He does not really want to be a priest. He prefers to be a Prince. It is only out of duty to our mother (Sarah) that he follows this path. She has left us for the protection of a strong man of Rome. In these difficult times priestesses of Goddess who are outspoken, can find themselves mysteriously disappeared, and she does not want to die in that way. She believes us to be safe here. I cannot blame her, although I miss her terribly. Why did she leave me behind?

I am still learning the art of priestessing and tonight I carry the Ram's Head Rhyton down the Hallow Way to the Underworld. We are praying for a new planting and harvest after inauspicious rains damaged nearly all the ripening grain in the fields. I will carry Melusine's sacred waters mixed with wine, to be poured onto Mother Cel's Earth body to fertilise and bless the grains. We will honour Losna, Goddess of the Bright Moon, which shines full this night as we plant the grains again and ask for Ati Catha's Sunrays to shine on the plants, so that the second harvest may restore the grain to carry us through the winter months. If She decides our offering is not enough, our people may starve this winter.

We walk slowly in procession down the sacred Hallow Way, lined with the high caves of the Ancestors. The drums beat ancient rhythms that open the heart and awaken the soul. It is my priestess duty to carry the Sacred Rhyton and let no drop fall to earth before its time. I, the Melusine Maiden, bring myself as an offering to Cel, that Her fertility flows through me into the sacred vessel. Our journey takes us down the Hallow Way to the Underworld, where the sacred grains are to be planted in ceremony so that they will be deeply nourished and come again in beauty and strength. Each Goddess must be duly honoured in Her turn if all is to succeed.

The path of the Hallow Way is uneven and still slick with the mud that pours down the roads in the flooding rains. As we begin to walk downhill my feet slide a little on the earth. Although the moon is rising in the sky, deep in the Hallow Way it is dark. Torches flicker on the high edges but it is hard to see the pathway. I feel the sharp quills of a startled porcupine brush my ankle. I am reminded of sweet Giovanni, who offered me a gift of quills for my hair. My mind wanders to the quick touch of our lips and my heart beats faster as I remember the soft dream of my love.

Suddenly without warning I feel my feet slide from beneath me. Time slows as I slip to the ground and find myself lying in the mud upon my back. I lift my head so that it does not crash on the road. The Rhyton meets the vertical wall of the Way and is pushed out of my hand. It falls to the ground. The sacred waters flow out onto the Way, and into the small stream that flows by the muddy edge.

I am shocked, first of all by the suddenness of my fall, and then fear enters my body. I have dropped the Sacred Rhyton. I, Priestess Maiden of Melusine, have spilled the sacred liquid, the offering of my community to Cel. Accident or no, it is my fault. I have failed in my duty to Her, and to my people. I have failed myself.

My brother comes up behind me, his voice shaking with anger,

"What have you done? You stupid girl!"

His hand grabs my arm and hauls me up off the ground.

"You have dropped the Rhyton!"

Yes, my dear brother, I know.

"You have dishonoured our Goddess. You dishonour our family, our mother!"

In the darkness, I feel the edge of his hand as he strikes me hard across the head. My teeth shake in my head. I bite my tongue and feel the flow of blood in my mouth. When we were younger he would often play-fight with me, but his slaps were always a little harder than they needed to be as he took out on me his resentments of my mother and anger at our father who he never really knew, but wanted to impress with his strength and power. I learned to be quick, to step out of the way to avoid his approach. He did not often show his hand in front of others, just in the private moments of his frustrations.

Now in the darkness the full force of his anger is meted out upon my head. I duck my head and move to the side to avoid the rain of blows. Others come towards us in the darkness – a torch, a flare and others see, with dismay writ upon their faces, the misfortune that has occurred. Melusine will be angry. Losna and Ati Catha will turn their shining faces from us. Cel will not now bring us a second harvest. We will starve. The people will starve. And it is all my fault.

Tears begin to flow down my face. I am mortified and ashamed. My soul is scarred by the knowledge of my failure. No thought that I am barely more than a child myself, given a task too onerous for my age. Great Mother can turn Her face from us in any moment She chooses and mend our ways by flood or fire, by disease or pestilence, and now by my hand.

One of the older priestesses comes to my side and helps me pick up the Rhyton from the ground. She holds my shaking hand and murmurs in my ear.

"It is the waters of Melusine that made the Hallow Way slick. It was She who threw the cup."

I do not believe her words. It is all my fault. How shall I ever be able to make this right?

The scattered procession continues down the Hallow Way. There is nothing else to be done. I hold the empty Rhyton in my hands and as we arrive in the Sacred Place I see the looks of dismay on the faces of the gathered priests of the Mother. All I had to do was to carry the Rhyton safely down the road and I have failed to do that. I am no priestess. I thought of my lover instead of my Goddess. This is my secret – no slick mud road, except the slippery road of my own mind. I shall have to give him up now.

Although his blows have ceased my brother is still there hissing in my ear.

"You are no priestess, girl! I knew you were no good – you are too young and too stupid. I am much better than you. You are a failure as priestess and because of you our people will die."

As soon as I can I run and hide myself away.

The spilling of the Sacred Waters disheartens the people in their superstitions. That year the second harvest fails too, perhaps for lack of trying, for mischief or for power, and people go hungry in the winter months. From this unhappy time onwards as in many other places patriarchal powers rise and the powers of priestesses shrink. I am very afraid in case I make a mistake again. My punishment is to be shunned by my community. I am allowed to be free as an example to all, of the failings of a once powerful priestesshood.

I become Priestess of the Underworld, meeting and sitting with the dead who are brought down the Hallow Way at death. I am veiled and hidden so that no-one knows that it is me, the priestess who failed her community. This is my penance to hide from the light in the darkness of the Underworld, and I am still so young."

SUCH A SMALL accident with such great consequences and repercussions, life to life. These feelings I have carried, one moment repeating into centuries of fear of failure as Her priestess.

In the cave with my brother Mirco, together we release the memory of the ancient times into the darkness of the cave, into the earth. I let go of my sense of failure from this ancient time. In the present I always do my best, as I can with who I am. Perhaps now I will be able to be fully present as I want to be, without that old wound arising because it wants to be recognised, re-membered, brought to consciousness, released and healed. I forgive myself for my mistake in that and any other life. I send out my blessings from this cave. May all be forgiven and as we forgive ourselves, we forgive all others.

Goddess bless my brother Mirco, with his youthful sensitivity. Bless his beautiful soul as he grows into his selfhood. Bless beautiful Sarah, amazing wonderful priestess! I love her so much. Bless Barbara who has hosted us, as she re-members her priestess path and also her partner as she begins the healing of her Catholic-borne fear. Blessed be to all our Italian sisters and brothers in Goddess!

* * *

Soul and Shadow: Birthing MotherWorld

Chapter Eighteen

The Orchard of Avalon

NOTHER MORNING I lie still, in the place between dreaming and waking, and think about what is really going on within our Orchard community, because the conflict that has broken out seems symptomatic of something other, something older, something deeper, something that comes from other times. I believe that it comes from the endings of the Goddess Temples two to seven thousand years ago. Repeated endings at different times in different cultures in different lands, which began early on in Old Europe in perhaps 5-6,000 BCE and spread in a slow wave across Europe and the world from that time over 4,000 years, reaching Britain in the middle of the third millennium BCE.

It is now time for us to re-member the wounding of those ancient times. In order to bring an end to patriarchy and its powers, to bring the full Vision of Motherworld into being, we have to meet and face the memories we are carrying deep in our souls of the wounding that we received or inflicted on others, from those times. These wounds are surfacing within us all and being enacted in small and great emotional and physical diseases and dramas between us.

THE ORCHARD OF AVALON came into being in 1999 with my realisation at the end of the first year of the Priestess of Avalon training that those who had trained together would want to stay in touch with each other after the course ended. I had begun teaching the Priestess Training because I had something to teach which I felt was important, but I had not thought about what might happen to the people when training was over. So the Orchard of Avalon came into being haphazardly, without structure or form. Everyone who self-initiated at the end of the training became part of the Orchard, with the aim of staying in touch and loving and supporting each other. Since Avalon means 'the place of apples' each priestess or priest is an apple tree within Her Orchard, and there are many varieties of apples.

After five years as a one year training, the Priestess of Avalon training expanded to become first two years and then three years in length, as I came to understand the depth of learning that people needed in order to truly become Her Priestesses and Priests. Of course people's expectations after one year or three years of training are different. In fact everyone within the Orchard is different – they have different personalities, different soul journeys to follow, different experiences of life.

Some people have journeyed with Goddess for 20 years and more when they begin the training, while others have met Her just a few times in their lives or have no other spiritual experiences, just a response in the heart to the sound of Her name. In the early days some people who self-initiated after one year as Priestess or Priest of Avalon became the most dedicated, while others left this path and we have never seen them again. Some people have trained for three, four, five years and their dedication to the Lady is their life, and others train with us and leave Her behind to return to or to follow other spiritual paths. We are not all the same.

Many begin to become conscious, more self-aware human beings, healing the wounds of lifetimes. Others fail to take responsibility for themselves, despite repeated encouragement. A few blame the training for their own failings. Yet in the Orchard we say that we are all equal, but equal in what kind of a way?

During the training we learn to sit in circle each weekend and really listen to and hear each other's truths. After training has ended there are fewer opportunities to sit in circle face to face with sisters and brothers on the same path. In the last few years as technology has taken over communication, our main forums for discussion within the Orchard were first Yahoo groups and now Facebook groups, neither of which works as a circle. These online groups work when we are in agreement, but now that there is discord, on these faceless groups only the most vocal, the loudest and often most angry voices are heard. The majority remain silent not wanting to enter the fray, to be seen and attacked themselves.

It now seems that, 14 years on from the beginning, the simple structure of the Orchard no longer works. As a Goddess community we are unable to talk safely about our conflicts now in the online Orchard forums which are available to us.

I put forward a suggestion asking those who wish to, to come together to create an Orchard Development Group, which will explore ways to create a workable structure for the Orchard. My questions are:

How does everyone have an equal voice within the Orchard?

Should a person who did one year of training 15 years ago, who we haven't seen or heard from since, have the same rights in the Orchard as someone who does 5 years of training and is a practicing public Priestess of Avalon?

How do we discuss issues when people live in very different situations, often in other countries with different kinds of challenges in life?

How do we encourage and help people to lead priest/ess lives when they have left the training and don't have that regular on-going support?

How do we help and support each other to continue to face our wounding and our fears after the end of our training?

What do we do about people who bring the Temple, the Tutors, the Training into public disrepute, eg by flaming and trolling on Facebook?

How do we ask people to leave the Orchard? Under what circumstances?

ALTHOUGH we have the agreed Developing Rites and Responsibilities of a Priest/ess of the Goddess and of Avalon, which have been discussed in many circles of students, do we want to have any way of enforcing these Rites and Responsibilities?

How do we make these decisions?

I SUGGEST that within the Orchard there can be smaller groupings of Priestesses who work together for different purposes – to support each other in local areas after they have left the training; to create and maintain a Goddess Temple, such as the Temple in Glastonbury, or other Temples in Sweden, London, Holland; to help the homeless, to work with animals, to support political or environmental aims, etc.

The result of this call is that we decide to set up the Orchard Development Group, which evolves to become a group of about 10 people, who agree to communicate privately and regularly via email and in person, to discuss all these things and to present them at the Orchard Gathering, which is held each year in February.

The Conference Ceremony Group goes to a nearby Spa for an evening of relaxation. As we play and splash around in the lovely warm water we discuss possible names for small local groups of priestesses living in the ordinary world, who gather together for support. The name comes to me – Priestesses In Real Life circles or PIRL circles. We will propose the setting up of PIRL circles, which anyone can create for themselves, wherever they live in the world.

I TAKE Poppy for a walk in the field beneath the Tor and hear the cry of the buzzard, long before I see it sitting on the branch of a tree.

> *I hear your call on the edge of the green field*
> *Before I see you sitting there by the rhyne*
> *On the bare winter branch of the tree.*
> *As I come closer you watch me*
> *We look at each other, eye to eye*
> *Then you spread your great buzzard wings*
> *And lift off, flying low and mewing*
> *All the way to Brighde's River Brue.*

> *Now I know that your call is a warning*
> *You have called to me many times*
> *In these last strange weeks*
> *A wave of trouble is coming*
> *Flying in on the cyberwaves*
> *Dropping poison and anger*
> *Venom and abuse*
> *Into the electronic gateway.*

And still more abuse pours in from known and unknown sources. These people are not interested in resolving matters, in healing wounds. They just want to speak from their wounding, out into the anonymous void of the interweb. One day I find the button that defriends people on Facebook and this is very good for my health and peace of mind.

Now I have opened to them, memories of wounding from other lives come flooding into my experience, nearly one a week. Each begins as a feeling of compression and an aching in my chest above my heart, in what I understand to be the place of Da-ath, the mystical void on the Tree of Life, that carries the ancient knowledge. I place my hands on this spot and let the heat pulse through, loosening my resistance to remembering. I do not claim to yet know if each of these is from my own past or whether these are strands of memory from a past that is collective.

I AM HERE AGAIN in another time, at another ending.

> *I AM RUNNING, running so hard. My lungs are bursting. My heart is pounding. Fear-filled adrenalin courses through my veins. I can barely breathe but I keep going. I am running for my life. Away, away from the Temple of Artemis, away from that Sacred Place which has been my home since I was a child. I have to get away. Are they coming after me? I dare not pause to look, to see if I am being chased. I only know I must run and hide. I must merge with the crowd, become invisible.*

I have learned the practices of invisibility, but my fear overwhelms the centre ground and I know that I can be seen, as a whirl of colour and energy rushing by. Heads turn to watch the frantic woman pass, veils streaming. I glance backwards and there on the far hill the stone Temple gleams in the sunlight. I see the spiral of smoke reaching upwards to the sky, a tiny tendril of flame curling out through a window. By the gate there are men in strange garb, looking towards the town.

I duck down to hide. Voices around me have also noticed the smoke,

"Look, look! Is our Temple on fire?"

"Mystress, can we help you?"

As my veil falls open a man with pale grey eyes looks into mine, glancing upwards to the pale moon tattoo upon my brow. I draw my hand across my face, disguising myself again.

"Forget that you have seen me. Tell no-one."

Pulling my veil across my face I run on, away through the town and the now burning Temple where the warriors have entered in, to destroy the Mother's holy ground.

As a child I was brought often to Her Bear Temple by my mother, who loved to sit and listen to the Thetae chanting in praise of Artemis Callisto, the Great Bear Mother. She loved to come and take part in the seasonal ceremonies, to help with the healings, to see the bears at play, and on special occasions to listen to the Oracle of Artemis. The Temple soon became my favourite place to be even though I was just a little girl. The Melissae – the Bee Priestesses who serve the Hive of the Goddess – were kind to me. They let me sit near them or walk with them, as they held the Sacred Space of the Temple open to the pilgrims, sometimes hundreds daily, who came to honour Artemis. Sometimes they let me help them, bringing drinks of cool water, lighting a candle safely, gathering up the dying petals of the flowers, sweeping the floor, small things that made me feel special and needed. I entered the circle of the Arktoi, the younger girls and boys who were educated in the ways of the Bear Goddess within the Temple walls.

It was only natural that when I became old enough I celebrated my menarche, my first moonblood in Her Temple with the Lunaeae, my moon sisters, rather than in the home of my mother. The ceremony was so wonderful, so sacred and filled with love. It was scary to be the centre of attention in the Red Womb Sanctuary, but I think we all felt the same – excited, nervous, over-awed, especially when the Red Goddess Herself appeared and gave us Her blessing. What a time that was. Afterwards everything changed. I felt stronger, more self-confident, although I didn't know those words at the time.

As time went on I spent more and more of my free time in the Temple and then when I was old enough I entered the Silvae Training, which is for those young women who know they want to become Priestesses, but don't yet have enough life lived. I felt so strongly the Call of the Lady. When I passed my twentieth birthday I began my formal training to become a Melissa, part of Her Hive, a Guardian of Her Temple. And then later I began my studies to become a Priestess of Artemis.

The Priestess Training is long and can be arduous. Some feel that if they repeat the right words and do the right practice that means they can with pride then call themselves priestesses, but it is so much more than this. To truly dedicate is to offer one's whole life, one's thoughts and actions, all one's person, into the lap of the Lady, that She might transform us as She wills. This process of deepening goes on for many years, perhaps a whole lifetime, long after formal training has ended, and even then some do not make it to become a Moon Priestess of the Deep. I completed formal training some years ago and now I am a Guardian of Her Moonstone, and Holder of Her Mysteries, but there is so much more to learn.

BUT NOW, *now I am running away, away from my beloved Temple in fear and terror. How is my training so easily lost?*

Artemis, are you with me as I run? Have I left you behind?

No, that is a falsehood, I can never leave you behind.

Breathe, calm, centre, even while running.

I have to pause for breath, my lungs hurt so much, air forcing in and out.

The path I follow rises up the rounded Hill of the Calyx into the trees where Artemis of the Woodland dwells. I stop beneath a small stand of trees to catch my breath. Sunlight falls in dappled rays through the leaves and it seems like a lovely summer's day, but it is not. It is a sad and dangerous day for my people, for Her Moon Priestesses and Melissae, for Her Guardians and Gatherers, for us all.

How has this happened? Where did these warriors come from? It seems only an hour or so ago that we first heard that they were coming, men in skins and leather armour with drawn swords. The Temple Mother had seen this day in visions and the portents had appeared – the buzzard's warning cries, the river running backwards as the tide came in, glittering – the glint of light upon the horizon, as sunlight shone on metal, although we did not know it to be such. Today She bade me run and save myself.

I had left the people behind as they ran towards the fire burning in the Temple, drawn to help put out the fires, to rescue, to take care, not knowing that these mercenaries are heartless. That many lives would be cut short today or turned into those of servitude.

I cannot stay. I must run. I must be gone, before I am found. As I run my body trembles, shakes with fear, shakes with fatigue. I must run on and on until the Temple of my beloved Artemis of the Moon and the town which has served Her are a mere mirage on the horizon. Something once held so dear is now so far away.

My heart is breaking! Who will comfort me as night draws on? Who will lie by my side and speak with me of love? Who will love me, love my Lady Artemis? I feel so alone.

Chapter Nineteen

SISTERS, SISTERS

AS A CONSEQUENCE of all the attacks against the Goddess Temple Management group, we are now discussing everything that happens in great detail. Our group is becoming much stronger, more cohesive as everyone understands the pressures we are under collectively as well as individually, in upholding the boundaries of our Temple. I am no longer alone as Boundary-Keeper. We are brought together by adversity and our decision-making becomes much more consensus-based. It feels very good. We decide to change our name to the Goddess Temple Weavers. As a legal entity the Goddess Temple has to have directors and members, but we decide that all our regular decision-making will now go through the Temple Weavers. Our group of 12–16 Weavers meets every fortnight and we all experience the love, care and support that we have for each other in these difficult times. I am especially grateful as my sisters and brothers now feel able to speak out against the hostility of the outer world, as they too experience the onslaught of aggression.

A COUPLE of months ago Mike and I spoke with artist Jonathan Minshull, who painted the mural on the entrance to the Glastonbury Experience and the wonderful mural at St Benedict's School which celebrates the bounty of the Earth. We ask him if he would like to paint a mural on the front of the Goddess Hall. I speak to Jonathon about the painting being of the Isle of Avalon as the Barge comes towards it from across the lake. The landscape of the Isle in the painting is to reflect the position of the actual landscape surrounding the Hall. It will be a painting of an ancient time before present day buildings, before the arrival of the Tower on the Tor.

Jonathon comes up with a beautiful image of the Isle of Avalon, that includes an ancient Goddess Temple from the times of the Ancestors, created from the tusks of Ice Age mammoths. It's a wonderful picture. He begins painting the front of the Goddess Hall and in such a really short time, just a couple of weeks, an inspiring image unfolds. He is an amazing artist, especially of these larger murals. We are all blown away by the beauty of the painting that covers the whole front wall. I am very happy.

Within a few days of this image being shown to the world, complaints arrive that we, the Goddess Temple, are in favour of the killing of elephants as we are encouraging the use of elephant tusks in our painting. They do not ask what the tusks are, or the reason for them being there. They jump to the most negative conclusions. Nothing could be farther from the truth. We are all animal lovers and would see no animals harmed. But it is just another excuse to attack and undermine all our efforts to create beauty and harmony in the world. Patriarchy so rules the minds of many.

I HAVE BEGUN working on next year's 2014 Goddess Conference, when we will celebrate the Crone Goddess, She who holds the Cauldron of Mystery and Transformation. Carolyn Hillyer will have a major exhibition with us of her *"House of the Ancient Weavers"* with 9 of her extraordinary, life-filled paintings of the Ancestral Mothers of the land. This will be the seventh in our nine year cycle, journeying around the Wheel of the Year, when we will honour the ancient Wise Crone, who holds us in Her love and wisdom throughout life, asking us always to surrender, to release and let go of all that no longer serves us, or Her. She shows us how to allow change and transformation to happen easily in our lives, for our greatest good. She walks with us as we descend into Her Underworld. She leads us into the great gateway of death, holding us in our fear and joy, in our grieving and gratitude. She shows the promise of all that lies beyond. We will celebrate Her Cauldron and Loom.

Presenters have already sent in their offerings for the programme and I begin collating them, weaving them into a comprehensive whole. I have decided to ask many of our older Conference regulars to speak this year, sharing the wisdom they have gleaned through long lives of being pioneers in bringing Goddess back into the world, with the rest of us. This includes wonderful Lydia Ruyle and Starhawk from the US, Ann Cook our Conference photographer, regular Conference Melissa Helen Anthony, singing star Julie Felix, poet Rose Flint and lovely Roz Bound. We will also have great musicians coming – Anique Radiant Heart and Wendy Rule from Australia, and Kellianna from the USA. It's going to be a bumper year (isn't it always?), all held in the arms of the Crone. I love weaving the Conference with Her magic, but the contrast to the daily abuse coming my way is extreme at the moment.

IT IS another night, another early morning. The pain is there again above my heart in the Void of Da-ath, in the place of memory surfacing. A more recent consequence of ancient wounding is remembering itself.

> *"The days when sisterhood was easy are over it seems. Here we sit, black coarse cloth covering soft skin, around the rough wooden refectory tables. Backs are straight for those who can, we sit like silent crows on washing lines. The Sister's voice drones on, reading the Holy Scripture, as we begin to eat our repast on this Feast Day of the Saint. Eyes down, unfocussed, we taste the palatable meal.*
>
> *I feel the uncomfortable prickling of new growth on my recently shaven head. Once a year my now-greying locks are cut off, an outward shriving for the sins of my soul. I long to scratch my itching scalp, but I must suffer and set the good example. Mother Superior, I must demonstrate the correct behaviour to these younger, less able souls. I try to be kind, but sometimes harshness is the only way, as the Devil makes work for idle minds and hands, and the whip is mine to crack. I know that some must really hate me, although they know the need for Holy Rule in this nunnery, this Sanctuary for women in a hostile world.*

We have all sorts here — those who truly love the Lord, who came here by vocation as young girls, some from poor families, one or two out of a family of ten/fifteen children, who will be cared for by us. Some come from the local gentry, the ugly, mad and lame, those who cannot be married off to fortune and title. There are those who have run here from rape, assault and cruelty, exiled from their own lands, by mean lords and invading soldiers. And sometimes we are the jailors for the unruly wives of husbands whose only choice given is – "Hie thee to a nunnery", or face penury and certain death. It is these masters that give us the money to continue our holy work, as well as those who pay for their place in heaven with our daily prayers.

A fluttering of energy moves through the refectory like a soft breeze across the floor. I am sensitive to the weaving of energy in all our spaces. Hours of silence broken only by prayers, sacred hymns, Holy Word, tears and whispered words. I listen with an open ear to the ground. We are Holy Women of the Cloth – black scratchy cloth. I try to catch the meanings in the ebb and flow of unspoken emotions. Something is going on here today. I see the sideways glances, not obvious, but there, then eyes down again. All but the most stupid must feel it. What is going on?

The different courses of our meal are brought in to us from the kitchens and then the final sip of mead, sunshine in a cup for each of us to bless our Feast Day meal. I stand and take the shining chalice in my hand to make the final blessing. Light radiates from within, so pure, so full of honeygold. The familiar words of scripture come to my mind and lips and I look around with love for my sisters. I am practised. I can move easily from the places of criticism to deep compassion.

I drink it down in one draught. I look around; with eyes opening I notice that all present are looking at me, cups raised, but none drinking. Some eyes hold fear, some sorrow, some horror and others incomprehension. I feel a pull in my stomach, a tightening and then a pain that starts in my belly and grows stronger. My breath catches, my heart pounds in my breast. Oh, poisoned chalice! I did not see you coming.

Knees buckling, the cold stone floor comes sliding up towards me. Oh my earth, my heaven, my rest in you, Lord. Pain fills every corner of my body gripping my entrails like a vice, a rack of torture. Faintly I can hear the screams of Sisters as they realise what is happening. Chairs scraping, bowls overturning, feet running. You have betrayed me! My sisters have betrayed me! After everything I have done for you, you have betrayed me. Why? Oh, Why? Did you all know? Were you all in this together? Not you, sweet Sister Paul, not you, my friend. Oh please, not you too. I feel your hand upon my brow, your words faint now. Oh cruel fate! Darkness comes as pain overwhelms. This ending is so strong, so quick. I feel my heart jump in my breast as the poison stops its beat.

The pain flows away and I rise up to the Refectory ceiling. Looking down I see my body on the floor and black crow nuns flapping their wings in distress. I turn my head and move through the walls into the countryside and my life is laid there before me. No judgements, only truths. A small girl child running down a path of flowers, skipping. Happy memories in sun-filled meadows, by streams and rivers. The joys of family days, playing tag with my sisters and brothers. I hear the sounds of shouting, of war and wounding, my mother raped and tortured, my father killed in battle. I am so lonely that only the grey walls of the nunnery are thick enough to hold my fear. I have lived here long, working my way through the horrors of memory as a frightened novice, finding solace in Holy Scripture. Clever girl, I quickly saw how things worked here and learned the practice well.

Slowly as I grew I made friends with the powerful. My whispers learned to undermine, to compete and gossip behind the backs of my sisters, using words and silence as weapons of deceit. Over this long life I climbed the poles of power, sharp words to the weak and smiles to the holders of treasure. I became educated and loved the learning, limited as it was by the texts which were available. I loved it when the pedlars came bringing books from foreign places, stories of places that lay beyond my small horizons, of lives and truths that I would never know. My vice – the secret books beneath my mattress.

I tried nearly all the major occupations in the convent, their daily tasks sharpening my mind, honing my skills. I became Almoner – I liked to give alms to the poor, both from love and from being seen to do good in the world, those receiving curried my favours and I built the core of my standing. I was Sacrist for a time with the safekeeping of the books, vestments and vessels, the care of our buildings and their preservation. I learned where money came from and where it was spent. After years I became the indispensable Cellarer – I knew all the convent's needs. I learned to store and save, to provision for high days and holy days, to give my betters their superior cuts, so they would look upon me well.

I did have friends, sisters that I loved, and touching love could be hard to find within the holy walls. Particular friendships were frowned upon, all our love must be in service to the Lord. But there were hands to hold, soft skin upon skin, sometimes a kiss, a hurried declaration behind a covered hand. There were those sisters I loved, my friend, my love, Sister Mary-Jesus, I loved her so. But she was taken from me by the infectious pox, which spread throughout the neighbouring lands. The Lord saw fit to take my beloved from me, to take her back to himself. I think it was then that my faith died. How could he be so cruel? How could he take the woman that I loved from me? My heart went cold. I grieved for a long time.

When Sister Paul died I became Prioress. I was the obvious choice to become Assistant to the Abbess. I knew so much about how everything worked in our convent. I liked the power of my position. I knew how to serve the Abbess and the Nunnery, how to keep everything running smoothly, day by day. I knew how to serve myself. When the Abbess died after slipping on some wet stones and falling down the Sacristy stairs – She broke her leg, which didn't mend properly and became infected – it was natural that I would take over her position.

I had risen to my natural place of power and I felt satisfied. I became Mother Superior. I knew that I had probably hurt others in my rise, but some are born to rule and others to be ruled. And my rule was clear and humane. The Divine Offices were celebrated daily and we tried to help all those who came seeking refuge. They often had to be coaxed and cautioned for their behaviour. I have been Abbess for nearly ten years and thought I was doing well, my wisdom appreciated by the sisters, but it seems not.

I had felt undercurrents of competition but nothing that seemed serious, just the usual jostling for position that goes on in any community of women, between those who wanted to be my best friend and those who would bend my ears to their grumblings about their sisters. This is the usual way amongst groups of women, between those who have, and those who have not and cannot see a way to better themselves. Women have such fragile wounded hearts, such a pale sense of themselves, locked away safely behind these dark walls of religion. Yes, we pray daily to the Lord for his love and mercy to be with us, but our own lives can be bleak and lonely, without family or loved ones to hold us in the night and comfort us.

Black night has come and the bright light of life is fading from me. Could I have done better given the life I had? Could I have been a better sister to many, more loving, kinder perhaps, wiser? But my starting point was so low. I have done well to get so far. Ahead I see a speck of light growing brighter and the voices of the angels begin to sing in my ears. In the gateway ahead I see a precious outline. Who is it?

My mother! My mother! You are here waiting for me by the gateway. My beloved mother, lost so long ago. My soul heart sings with joy. Who stands there behind you? Is it you, my father, so tall and handsome, holding out your hand to me, your little daughter? You wait to welcome me home and I am so blessed. There is mercy for me at last after all the pain. Mercy and love for me alone."

Chapter Twenty

Re-Membering the Queen

A WEEK LATER as I lie again in my bed once again the icy tendrils of fear clutch my heart. I read a long email, couched in the language of rationality and counsellor-speak, hemmed around with protestations of Christian love. There are so many mirrors in the accusations that were made in the past and are now made in the present.

TODAY in December Mike, Katinka and I fly to Iceland for a short minibreak. I begin writing the full version of the witch life memory in the airport and on the plane. We arrive in Iceland just as a snowstorm begins. I don't know what we thought we were doing. The clue is in the name of this Ice Land. We find our way to the car hire place, as the light begins to disappear in flurries of snow. Daylight hours in December are short here. Mike is driving as we set off into the unknown, and the flurries soon become a blizzard. The roads become less and less clear and signs disappear beneath layers of drifting snow. We are booked into a spa hotel beside a hot spring about an hour away in normal weather to the east of Reykjavik. Snow falls in blankets, which blow across the roads. Soon we are lost.

I pray to the Goddess of this land of fire and ice to show us where to go. We ask the way in a petrol station and they say,

"You're not going over the mountain, are you?"

And yes, it turns out we are, our destination is over the snowy mountain, but luckily She has brought us somehow near to the right road. We set off up a long hill climb, driving slowly with little visibility. We were told that if our car breaks down,

"Do not get out and leave it. Stay in the car as you can easily die outside in the cold. Wait until you are found."

We accidentally drive off the main road down a side road and have to turn around in snowdrifts which blank out all roads. We somehow (by Her grace) get back onto the main road again. There seems to be no other traffic on these roads. We are alone in the snowstorm. It is scary. However when we ask the snow to stop falling, it does stop and we can see a little way ahead. On either side we glimpse dark shapes in the night, but cannot see where we are going. We eventually reach a high plateau and the road descends down the other side of the mountain. There are lights ahead as we near our destination. That makes us happy.

Eventually we get to our hotel and it has been an initiatory test in this dark cold land. The hotel is single storey and we have rooms next to each other, surrounded by snow-covered paths. We can see steam rising from holes in the ground and below is a dark flowing river. During the first night Mike and I can't work out the heating system and the room is cold. We have the curtains open in the hope of catching a glimpse of the Aurora Borealis, the Northern Lights, between the clouds, but they only usually appear on cloudless nights. There are small illuminations in the sky, but no Lights.

The first morning we go to a Health Spa in the nearby small town and swim in warm pools heated by geothermal energy. We go into the steam rooms and saunas, into the hot tub, and then into a mud bath, where we lie deep in bathtubs of hot thick mud for fifteen minutes. Then we are hosed down by a man and swaddled in towels like babies, lying on couches for another half hour. We all begin to relax.

We go back to our hotel and in daylight can see small hot tubs steaming in the snow and the river which flows below. The water in the river is not icy although there is snow on both banks. It comes boiling hot out of the ground some distance upstream and gradually cools as it flows towards the sea. On the other side of the river is a geothermal area of land, from which pipes take water and steam to large greenhouses, where vegetables and fruit grow even in winter. A keen cold wind blows all the time.

We return to our hotel and I climb into bed although it is only afternoon. I am tired. My heart is breaking. I feel such sadness as I let myself feel all the hatred and destruction that is going on around us. This sadness must be what others feel, being left out of the Temple now, as they have excluded themselves. They want a say in running the Goddess Temple, but their say is one of continual criticism, rather than construction.

In my life with Goddess I have only ever heard Her voice and followed it, creating, experimenting with ever more challenging ceremonies and spiritual practices for myself and others – with no thought for safety, only the protection of the heart. Was that wrong? I don't think so, but all the destruction breaks my heart. All I ever want is for us all to be able to experience Goddess more and more deeply, in ways that are more and more real, and for us all to become more loving. But now I can see no way out or forward for our community.

I offer it to you, Lady. I do not know the way. I offer you everything and ask that you show me the way.

I wake next morning with the idea to invite everyone individually who has a problem, to come and talk to me. They can have a witness. I can have a witness and there is a mediator to hold the centre. But I slip into a sad reflective depressed space at the thought of meeting those demons face to face as they speak their horrible truths. I feel so weak. How can I protect myself from their projections?

It is still freezing today and we go for a walk across the river into the geothermal fields and get frozen faces and noses. It's $-13°C$, very cold. Back in our room I lie on the bed and fall asleep, feeling very low in energy. This is the first time for a long time that I have done nothing all day – no computer, no dog walking, resting. And then my feelings emerge. I feel completely awful, depressed/compressed by what is going on in our community. I have come all the way to Iceland, the northern Land of the Crone, to feel this and am overwhelmed by it all. I cannot cope today.

When I wake Katinka is in the dining room with a glass of wine, cheerfully writing her book on the Teachings of Rhiannon. In the evening Katinka, the bravest of us all, runs from her room clad only in a towel, through an ice cold wind, to the Hot Tub. As she sits in the hot water, icicles form as the steam rises and cools on the back of her head. She is such a warrior woman. I can barely get outside the door fully clothed, never mind with just a towel around my body. We laugh and giggle.

We drive to the airport the following morning to fly home. It is no longer snowing and it is daylight. The landscape we could not see on the way here, is extraordinary. It is a vast and wild landscape of mountains and glaciers, steam vents and warm rivers flowing. It must look amazing in summer. We shall come here again.

On the way to the airport we go to visit an Icelandic shaman, Reynir Katrinar, who lives nearby. He came with Unnur Arndisardottir and her mum to sing at the Goddess Conference a few years ago. They were really unusual and different performers. Uni has now taken the First Spiral of our Priestess Training and is a lovely, creative and magical young woman. Reynir is an artist and sculptor, as well as shaman, making beautiful stone scrying objects, carving them from volcanic stones. We spend our money with him – Iceland is an expensive place to visit since the banks all collapsed and the government did not bail them out. Everything had to begin again from a less corrupt foundation.

We are all aware that in Iceland we have been visiting the Crone of Winter. She has shown us the dangerous edge that is near to death, the place that is not safe. Here if you do not have the right equipment, physically or mentally, you can die quite easily. We feel honoured by our short, but deep encounter with Her powers.

ON THE NEXT weekend I go to Katinka's workshop in Glastonbury on the archetype of the Queen, who is in the west on our Goddess Wheel. A couple of years ago, Ava from the Orange County Temple and Yeshe Rabbit, both Priestesses from the USA, gave a wonderful presentation and workshop on the

Queen archetype at the Goddess Conference. Katinka has assimilated all their wisdom, combined it with her own knowledge and practices and has created a great workshop. We explore various faces of the Queen, from Britain's Queen Elizabeth, to Queens in other countries, as well as the Shadow of the Queen, with the fear of being killed as a Queen, which happened several times to British Queens in earlier centuries.

The archetype of the Queen is often of an older experienced woman who is in her power, who has a Realm that belongs to her, for which she takes responsibility and which she governs. This Realm has strong and clear boundaries. Younger women have not usually matured into holding their own Realms clearly, but the Queen is an archetype to which we can all aspire, no matter what our ages are. The Realms of different Queens can overlap and women can move in and out of each other's Realms in confidence, lending support to each other. The clarity of holding of your Realm gives strength to others.

During the workshop I realise that I have a definite problem with thinking about my Realm, about owning my Realm, about being a Queen. I have a resistance to the whole idea. I wonder why that is. I glimpse myself as a Queen, perhaps five or six hundred years ago somewhere in a European land, perhaps France. This vision later expands in my dreams and in conscious visioning as I sit Melissaing in the Goddess Temple on a quiet day just before winter solstice.

"The carriage bounces along mud-rutted roads. Inside the panelling is trimmed with velvet and pale coloured furs, which soften, but do nothing to prevent the continuous rolling gait of the carriage. Outside the French countryside passes by, with its woods and heathlands, the expanses of water and rivers, the small hamlets where the peasants live. I am wearing silk taffeta and lynx. It is cold outside and not much warmer within – the charcoal warmer now losing its heat. I am alone but for my maid, who sits head bowed on the other banquette. Mistress and servant, we are separated by class, by heritage and destiny. We are returning home to the King's Chateau from a visit to my aunt. As we

approach our family home the roads become smoother, the countryside a little more manicured, more care taken. Our lands are spread for many miles around.

We arrive at the Chateau gates, now opened to receive me. The guards stand straight as we sweep through, the horn blowing to signal our approach as we enter the long driveway. Here is the Lodge by the gate, and to one side the lake, glistening in the winter sunlight. At the far end of the avenue of trees which line the drive is the Chateau, standing tall on the rise of the hill. The horses pick up speed and carriage rattling, we blaze our trail towards the Grand Entrance.

There are sounds of greeting, dogs barking, servants standing straight-backed, as we come to a halt at the Grand Entrance. For I am Queen in this land and this is my home with my King, my Sovereign Lord. We rule in this land of beauty and bounty. I married the King when I was just fourteen years of age, the gift of my father, the alliance of our lands. Now I am nearly twenty and two. I have learned what it is to be Queen, to be primped and preened, decorated and adorned, presented to the world as a trophy.

At first I was just the King's plaything, but over these years I have accumulated some powers for myself – powers over servants and courtiers, who though they are older than I, do not have the King's direct favour, unless I whisper their desires or complaints in his ear when we lie abed. I hold this power in my hands. I have learned discretion in these things, who to raise and who to hold lower, who will bring favours and who needs to learn patience.

Our children are, of course, beautiful and cared for – Amelie, Ricard & Eugenie. At least I am an abundant wife and mother, though I do not see so much of them – at meals and for an evening kiss. The King wants me for himself, ready for him at any time he chooses, looking perfect. Nothing must get in the way of my availability to him.

There is one large thorn in the side of my happiness – his mistress La Marquise Virginie. I cannot abide her and her bastard children. If she is here now while I have been away, I will explode. I am not supposed to be, but I am jealous. As I place my foot upon the wide stone steps of the Chateau's entrance my suspicions overwhelm me yet again. She is here. I can feel her presence.

How dare she be with him, while I am gone? How dare she try to take him away from me?

I sweep up the staircases to the Royal apartments. Just the thought of her being here while I have been away, and then when I return, sets me aflame with anger. The servants and courtiers bow low as I race past. I will catch them together. My eyes dart about suspiciously, seeking evidence of their wrongdoing.

The door to the Royal apartments opens, and there she is coming out of MY rooms. Her cheeks are rosy, her hair in gentle disarray. She dips a curtsey to me and rises smiling. Is that a smirk, even? This cannot be, this is unforgiveable.

I enter our bedchamber, his and mine, and there he is, my Lord and King, lounging easily on the chaise. He too with coloured cheeks, looking satisfied. As I enter he stands and adjusts his clothing, as if all has been hurriedly rearranged, a button still undone here, a wrinkle of cloth unwarranted there.

I feel hurt, angry, but know that I must hold my tongue, show nothing on my face. Inside, I burn with anguish. This betrayal is beyond words – in my rooms, in my palace. How could they? How could he betray me like this? I am filled with pent up fury. I can barely bring myself to look at him, as he comes forward to kiss me on the lips, as if he has done nothing, as if he had not been in another's embrace just moments ago. The art of betrayal is well-practiced in this man of power. How often has this happened before and I have not known it?

I will have my revenge. I will be careful, but I will find a way to take revenge upon these wretched people, upon her and upon him. No-one treats me like this and gets away with it.

Some weeks *later I find the way and have my revenge. I plot her downfall with care, some other requiring my favour, revealing the theft of important Documents of State, showing that she is a spy sent from Spain. A large royal ruby also goes missing that is found in her apartments, the theft laid at her door. There is talk in the Court of spells, black magic and foul deeds – the gossip-makers of the Court are expert in creating such scandals. The King has no choice but to dismiss her and her bastard children from his favour, from our Court.*

The King can barely look at me, he knows that I have meddled and makes me pay with vengeful and brutal sex, but when I fall pregnant again and my belly grows, he begins to forgive me and I soften towards him. As she loses favour with King and Court, La Marquise loses her status in the nobility. Gone are the days of comfort and well-being. Her life becomes one of penury, few daring to come to her aid, and she is still young too. One child dies from the pox, another from river sickness, from living too close to the water's edge. Their end is sad.

I move from feeling angry, cold, justified, certain of my actions and their causes – she had taken the love of my King, my man – to uncertainty. I begin to feel guilt. I have abused my power. I have sent those children to their deaths, not by my actual hand, but by sending them away from the King's hearth. I am haunted by what I have done. The guilt grows and becomes so strong that I am never truly happy again."

THE WOUNDS of this life are the consequence of earlier wounds from other lives, built upon the wounds of other lives all the way back to the endings of the Goddess Temples of the world. The karmic response of my Soul to this life of a French Queen is that I became a monk again, so that love relationships would not plague me – no jealousy allowed – lives where physical love was sublimated to the divine – justifiably in pursuit of detachment, perfection and holiness. I became a Christian monk and a Tibetan monk several lives over, and I learned to love the solitude of a disembodied spiritual life.

The purpose of all this is that when I incarnate in this life now, to truly become Queen of my Realm bringing Goddess back into Her world, I will not abuse my power. Rather I will follow the bliss of the Queen, the love of my Goddess, empowering others with Her love. Until these moments I have had a dilemma, which has been unconscious, hidden from my knowing, between claiming my Realm as Queen and the guilt that stems from abusing my power in that life and probably other lives, with the fear that I might do it all again.

The archetype of the Queen must come forth again into the world. The world needs strong, powerful women to help change the world, to bring awareness of

Goddess back into the world, to help dissolve patriarchy and its destructive forces. We need to take responsibility for who we are as Her Priestesses and Priests, true Queens and Kings in our realms, returning again from ancient times with our memories and visions of a different way of living.

As an individual I need to reveal my own wounds, my failings and my fears. I need to write of this journey to bring Motherworld into being from my personal point of view, with my awareness, knowledge and places of wounding. There is no quick panacea for this healing journey, which we each have to take for ourselves.

THE WORDS arise in me:
> *I may be powerful, but I am responsible*
> *I choose to be Queen of my Realm.*
> *I am surrendered to the Lady of Avalon*
> *I am a Queen in Her Realm.*
> *I am a Queen in Her Motherworld.*
> *I am a Queen in Avalon.*

MY REALM is Glastonbury Avalon and the Leading Edge of transformation and love. Within my realm are my family and my soul friends in this and in many other lands all around the world.

My Realm is Glastonbury Goddess Temple, the Priestess of Avalon Trainings and all the Goddess Teachings we offer through the Goddess Temple. My realm is Glastonbury Goddess Hall and all our activities there. My realm includes all Temple Ceremonies, all Temple Healing, everything that is offered through the Goddess Temple, supporting and empowering all who do their work for Her in the world. My realm is Glastonbury Goddess Conference, now in its twentieth year, with all that is offered by so many during that experience. Mine is the Realm of Ceremony and Sacred Drama.

My Realm is international. It includes meeting, supporting and working with Goddess women and men, who are returning Goddess to Her rightful place in the world. I attend national and international Goddess Conferences, Ceremonies, Trainings, supporting Priestesses and Priests of many Goddess traditions as they begin and continue their Goddess work.

My realm is Her Nature, Her world of Beauty. I am Queen in Her world. I uphold the Motherworld values of love, care and support for all beings. I empower others to become who they truly are as I empower myself to be who I truly am. I encourage others to meet and face their personal karmic wounding, as I meet and face my own, bringing love and healing to all beings.

My Realm is the Realm of Wonder, of Mystery and Meaning. My realm is of the Soul and of Goddess. My Realm is a Realm of continuing Surrender to Her, to Her Transforming Power and Love.

DANCING Five Rhythms each Monday helps me to discharge unwanted emotions and also access unknown feelings and inspirations from within my body. I had earlier been thinking about the power of Remembering and Forgiveness, but as I dance in the rhythm of Stillness a new phrase arises, which I dance with passion and power. It comes out of the witch-burning memory, which is now over, the power of the wounding now ended.

"I will never again be silenced by false accusations and lies!"

I dance and I dance and I dance my truth into reality.

AT THE END of the year the Orchard Development group agrees to meet and talk regularly in person and online about the future of the Orchard of Avalon. It feels like times have changed and we need to think about how we want to move forward. When the process is complete we will put proposals forward to the rest of the Orchard, for agreement or not.

* * *

It is New Year 2014 and I have a cold. I am forced to slow down and retreat inwards into stillness. On the Hera's Journey first identified by Joseph Campbell, the American scholar, there are different stages in the adventure of becoming a Hera, reworked by Christopher Vogler, which I am adding to here.

http://www.thewritersjourney.com/hero%27s_journey.htm

The stages of the Hera's Journey are:

1. **The Ordinary World** The Hera, uneasy, uncomfortable or unaware, is introduced sympathetically. The Hera is shown against a background of environment, heredity and personal history. Some kind of polarity in the Hera's life is pulling in different directions and causing stress.

2. **The Call to Adventure** The Herald, a person or event, sounds the Call to Adventure. The Hera is presented with a problem, a challenge. Something shakes up the situation, either from external pressures or from something rising up from deep within, so that the Hera must face the beginnings of change.

3. **Refusal of the Call** The Hera feels her fear of the unknown and tries to turn away from the adventure, but returns or is returned to meet it.

4. **Meeting the Threshold Guardians** The Hera encounters the Threshold Guardians who include jealous and competitive enemies, professional gatekeepers or her own fears and doubts.

5. **Crossing the Threshold** The Hera commits to leaving the Ordinary World and to entering a new region or condition, an Otherworld, with unfamiliar rules and values.

6. **Tests, Allies and Enemies** The Hera is tested and is forced to make allies and enemies in the Otherworld, sorting out her allegiances. The Hera reaches within to an inner source of courage and wisdom, to her guide or guiding principle. She meets Goddess.

7. **Approach** The Hera and newfound allies prepare for the major challenge in the Otherworld. The Hera comes to a dangerous place, often deep underground, (in the Underworld, in the unconscious) where the object of the quest, often unknown, is hidden.

8. **The Ordeal** The Hera enters the Underworld and touches bottom. She confronts death or faces her greatest fear, and is brought to the brink in a fight with an inner mythical beast. Out of this meeting in the moment of death, she experiences Goddess and is reborn to new life.

9. **The Reward** The Hera takes possession of the treasure she has won by facing death. There may be celebration, but there is also danger of losing the treasure again.

10. **The Road Back** About three quarters of the way through thedrama, the Hera is driven to complete the adventure, leaving the Otherworld so that the treasure is brought home. There may be a chase, signalling the urgency and danger of the mission.

11. **The Last Surrender** At the climax the Hera is severely tested once more on the threshold of her Ordinary World home. She is purified by a last surrender, another moment of death and rebirth, but on a deeper and more complete level. By the Hera's action the polarities that were in conflict at the beginning are finally resolved.

I WONDER where I am in this Hera's Journey, how much further I have to travel to emerge back into the Ordinary World.

Chapter Twenty One

THE ISLE OF STONES

AM THINKING about what it means to be a Priestess or Priest of Goddess in modern times and what the relationship is between priestesses and Goddess Temples. In the minds of many, dedication to Goddess as Her priestess is a private affair, something that is just between the individual and Goddess. But this is not actually how it was in the past and is not how we teach priest/essing in our Priestess of Avalon Training. We teach priest/essing as a public role, rather than a private, sometimes hidden fantasy.

In ancient times priestesses were always part of a Goddess Temple which lay at the heart of a community. Priestesses lived in and worked within Temples, within communities of priestesses dedicated to a particular Goddess or series of Goddesses. Unlike witches, shamans, traditional healers and ceremonialists, priest/esses did not usually practice their spirituality alone. They usually worked in circles, in groups of equals within a Temple. I am giving a talk to some students and want to speak clearly about this realisation. I come up with this little ditty.

> *A Priestess without a Temple is like:*
> *An actor without a stage*
> *A surgeon without her operating theatre*
> *A dreamer without the sky*
> *A dog-walker without a dog*
> *A wolf without her pack*

A geek without a computer
A craftswoman without her scissors
A cook without her kitchen
A musician without her instrument
A conductor without an orchestra
A librarian without books
A smith without a forge
A fisherwoman without a boat
A child without a playground
A bleeding woman without a Red Tent
A lover without her boudoir
A mother without her nursery
A queen without her palace
A crone without her arbour
A cailleach without her mountain
A Priest/ess without her Temple
Is missing something vital and important!

S/HE MISSES the support and care of community. S/HE misses the encouragement of like-minded people. S/he misses the sharing of responsibility. S/HE misses the shared empowerment of one another. S/HE misses the sharing of skills and the creation of something greater than the individual. S/HE misses the wonderful experience of working in ceremonial circles of equals, of daring to be greater than her small self.

WE MUST BRING HER TEMPLES BACK INTO BEING.

I DECIDE to name 2014 as the year of new Goddess Temples in Britain and abroad.

I pledge to support all those priestesses who wish to open a new Goddess Temple, whether it begins as we did with a Pop-up Temple open seasonally, or if they open a permanent Temple straight off. I will help with seed finance, advice, publicity, encouragement, experience, listening, holding you in the process if you need it, as you take your courage in your hands and become a Priestess of a Temple in your community.

WE MOVE into the new year and my sister has her birthday. We are both getting much older. She says that now she looks like Grandma Jones, my fama or father's mother, who scared me as a child.

A NEW MEMORY emerges from my heart spaces of a time long, long ago…

> "I lean back against the soft fabric hanging, looking out through the entrance to the Temple of Melite, here on Her Isle of Stones. The light diaphanous cloth in the open doorway floats in the gentle breeze. My heart is singing at the ending of this day and it is a beautiful soft evening as I walk outside into the Courtyard. There before me to the west the orb of Shem-shi the Sun Goddess is making Her slow descent into the watery depths of Night, gold reflected in the waters of the Turquoise Sea. The light sparkles on the wavelets as they move across the ocean's surface. The air is warm with the scents of wild herbs rising, to bring the evening breath to the insects as they collect nectar for the night's harvest. It is time to light the lamps in Her Temples.
>
> I am Guardian Priestess of Her Womb Temples by the ocean and tonight it is my joy to care for Her Sanctuary through the night. Here there are three small Temples grouped around a courtyard. Each is shaped like Her body with the round curves of Her buttocks, belly and breasts. Entrance into Her Temple is through Her Sacred Vulva as we return again and again into Her Womb of Life. The walls are thick limestone, ancient rock hewn out of the Island quarries, and brought on rollers to this special spot. The Vulval entrance to the smallest and oldest Temple, the Temple of our Ancestral Mother, opens to the southwest. It is aligned to the small Isle of Stars out in the Turquoise Sea, where there is a Retreat Temple Cave for those who wish to be filled for a time with the solitude of the ocean and the seabirds. The middle Womb Temple faces southeast and

the newest Healing Temple faces east with its alignments to the equinox sunrises and markers for the summer and winter solstices. They all face the abundant fields where we grow vegetables and grains.

Just a few pilgrims came to the Womb Temples today to sit in the silence, to hear Her Oracle, to receive Her blessings. We and our larger sister Standing Temple, higher up the hillside, are far away from the main thoroughfares of the island, so it is only those who know we are here, that come. Selira, my sister priestess, is gone today to stock up on provisions for the coming week and will spend the night at our Mother Temple in the city. Other priestesses are caring for the Worship Temple with its larger and grander spaces. So I am here alone, but I love the quiet of the evening and the stillness of Her presence in Her Holy shrine. It is such a privilege to be here with Her alone.

For it is in these nights that I can enter into an intensity of ecstasy with Her, as energy and sounds weave around the curving walls of the Temple and She begins to speak to me. Her voice echoing as I sing into the hidden Oracle holes and She replies in ways that I might hear, Her voice arising magically moving in waves between the walls as they are designed. The Oracle holes also allow visitors to ask their questions and to hear Her answers spoken through Her hidden priestesses' mouths.

But it is on these nights of solitude that something strange and wonderful can happen, when the breeze moves in the right direction and the warm air flows between the stones and I sing to Her of my love for Her. Then sounds and words arise from Her spirit communing with mine. These words tell me how I may grow and expand my priestess wisdom for Her, what I must do in the world. I am filled with gratitude. In recent times She has spoken of times of trouble coming, but there are no signs and all is so still here, that I cannot truly believe these words.

I look out across the Temple Courtyard in a reverie to the far-off small Isle of Stars. There is no-one living there at the moment that I know, but then I notice small puff of smoke rising from the rocky edge. What is that? Someone must be out there that I do not know. This happens sometimes, when passing boatpeople pause in their voyages across the Turquoise Sea. Now the smoke is gone. Perhaps it was just a mirage, a false vision in my eye.

I turn to enter the Healing Temple, once inside gathering up the flame-maker and carrying oil to fill the lamps, making sure that the wicks are floating in their vulval holders. The round chambers of Her body begin to glow with the light of the setting sun reflecting on the rocks, as She sinks lower in the sky. I move slowly through the different womb chambers of Her body, lighting the lamps, chanting Her names. The fabrics which cover the inner walls are brightly patterned, and glow in the flickering light. I sing the evening prayers to Her, praying and giving thanks for another day of beauty.

"Melite, Melite, Melite!

Thank you, Great Mother, for this day. Thank you for your great light that rose to illuminate the land and sea and sky. Thank you for the food from your body that I have eaten this day. Thank you for the air that I have breathed. Thank you for the sweet water I have drunk from your springs. Thank you for the gifts that you brought with each person who came here. Thank you for the warmth of Shem-shi at midday and in the evening, which allows the herbs to grow, from which we can make the healing potions to give to those in need. Thank you for the fruits and the delicious berries that we offered at your altar and then shared together. Thank you for my life here, my life as your priestess. Thank you the generosity of your love, for everything that you give to me each day. I am so grateful.

Melete, I offer prayers for the healing of each person who came to see you in your Temple this day, and every day. I offer prayers for your priestesses, for Selira and sweet Rose, for Marietta and Charis. I pray for my sisters in the Standing Temple and in our Mother Temples, and for all those who walk your priestess path."

I AM ENTERING a state of reverie as Shem-shi sinks to the horizon, my personal self expanding, to allow my greater Soulself to enter in and be present. As I begin to enter this light trance and feel Her love and harmony entering my body, I feel a wobble in the periphery of the energy field. I notice an uncertain rhythm. What can that be? I come up to the surface and feel my way across the strands of energy. Shadows are coming into the Courtyard. Who is it at this hour? I had not noticed them as I was busy with my prayers. I hear feet running. As I look to the entrance I can see shapes moving too quickly across the ground. I feel a haste that is not usual. I, who am usually calm and unruffled by the arrival of strangers, feel a strong need to be cautious.

Suddenly the frame of a man is outlined in the doorway, carrying a weapon in his hand. He roughly pulls aside the curtain and shouts in a language that I don't understand. I know that it will take time for his eyes to adjust to the low lights of Her Temple and I slide behind one of the thick curtain tapestries that hides an entrance to the Oracle walls. I move quickly out of sight and peep out through a small eye slit in the curtain. I am not sure if he saw me or not. I think not. Behind him two or three more men come in, charging with force, and pausing to pant with wild breath on the threshold as their eyes adjust and they feel the awesome presence of Melete in Her Temple.

For moments time stands still and I can hear their loud breath and feel my own heart fast-beating in my chest. Their voices are harsh in Her silence. Perhaps they will be so over-awed they will turn and just go away. They smell of the sea, of sweat and salt, of fish and smoke! I remember the small plume I saw rising on the Isle of Stars. Had these men passed through the Isle, setting fire to that Sea Temple? Fear begins to course through my veins, rippling in my belly. I am alone here and I have no defences against marauding raiders, but I can feel aggression and fear of the other, pouring into my belly. It has never been like this before. Our isle has always been a peaceful sanctuary of the Mother, where She is loved and adored, and where it is known that women are created in Her image as the vessels and carriers of life, where men are the guardians of life.

I remember Her words that I did not believe, of danger coming.

This must be it!

AS I HIDE behind the thick coverings that seam invisibly with the other painted materials that cover the walls, I can hear their bodies crashing as they move *from chamber to chamber. They are looking for the one who lit the lamps. They are looking for me. I hear pots falling and the sounds of roughness in the softness of Her Womb. I know that they do not know what to make of this Temple, but destruction is upon them. I hear the plates on the altar fall to the floor as they grab the food left as an offering to the Mother. I hear their shouts and the strange language of these men from the sea.*

Then I can smell smoke. The falling lamps have set fire to the soft fabrics of flax and hemp. Which chamber did it begin in? The inner or the outer? I feel afraid all over again. If it is the inner I may be able to escape through the Oracle exit. If it is the outer then I may not survive. The fire will send the men out soon enough, but do they know that I am here, hidden behind folds that must soon catch fire too? This hiding place is also where we store oil and carpets and some of the many ritual items that we use perhaps once a year. I crouch low on the floor, the air there will stay fresher longer. I cover my nose and mouth with my Temple scarf to stop myself coughing. The curtain that hides the entrance moves a little, but I think they are just slashing at the walls with their weapons. They still do not know that there is a space between the walls.

Do they know that I am here alone? Perhaps they think they can smoke me out. As the fire catches and the smoke increases I hear them stumbling out of the Healing Temple and crashing into the next, into the Womb Temple, searching for the guardian priestess, searching for me. Why do they come here? Why do they attack a Temple? How does it serve them as men to come to a strange land and just destroy what they find? Will they find their way onwards to the Standing Temple? I must escape and warn the others.

The air is thickening with smoke in my Oracle niche. I move further along between the walls, away from the Oracle hole which opens into the Temple. This too is covered with material on the inner walls of the Temple, but the material is burning. My throat tickles and I gag in the effort not to cough. As long as they leave before the material burns through I might be safe. Perhaps they will think that I ran away before they came. But I have to get out of here.

I pull on a dark cloth to cover my priestess robes and push my way through the piles of storage baskets to the exit, which lies at the back, between the two Healing and Womb Temples. Dusk has come quickly and darkness is falling as the Goddess of Love shines in the west with Thrinacia's crescent. The rocky earth glows dimly in the pale nightlight. I must run. I cover my head and carefully look out to either side. The men seem to be busy inside the Temple and I can hear crashing jars and plates, and the smell of smoke and fire.

Oh, my beloved Melete, they are desecrating your holy ground!

A huge sob of grief is arising in me, but fear too fills my heart and I must run. I run for the goat path that heads up across the hillside, away from the main track that they will follow, if they come after. Did they see the Standing Temple higher up the hill as they came into land? It is possible that the stones were masked from the sea, but I do not know what they can see and know. My feet slip on the loose stones and I nearly fall, but then onwards and up across the hillside. No-one follows me yet. I run so fast that my breath is hard rising in my chest. I cough from the smoke in my lungs and wheeze my way up.

I have to pause for breath. I look down and can see flames licking around the edges of the Temple, materials burning, oil catching fire, roofing catching alight. The flickering shapes of men as they stand in the Courtyard. I can hear them laughing. How can they laugh at what they have done?

A shape comes towards me on the goat path from the Temple above. At last I am safe. One of my sisters has seen the fire and is come to rescue me. My heart fills with hope and relief.

"Thank you, Great Mother, for saving me." I whisper.

Then I see an arm rise and the form grows bigger. It is not a woman's shape. It is a man. Terror strikes once again into my heart. Rough hands sweep me to the ground. I feel the stones under my back cutting through to flesh. Words in a strange language are hissed into my ear. Stinking breath and spittle are in my face. My robe is torn from me and strong arms hold me down. Time slows, but in no time, brute force parts my legs and my sacred vulva is torn open by a hard penetrating thrust.

The Sanctuary of the Goddess is violated! I scream and scream as pain fills *my body in this Her sacred intimate place, which has only ever shared Her love and blessings, completely and in full surrender to Her. Fighting back I bite the hand that tries to cover my screaming mouth and he, the violator, strikes my face with force. I hear a crack as bone breaks and pain spears through my head.*

I leave my body to the wretchedness of the wild raging inhuman body that pins me down to the ground. As I rise in the ethers I see myself flattened on the earth by a great weight. I see flames flickering in both Temples. I see priestesses running, stumbling out between the stones, being caught and struck down. The marauders must have divided and come also upon the Standing Temple as well as ours below. Oh, my poor sisters!

Oh, what a sad terrible day this is. Great Mother, Melite, how could you let this happen to us? To your priestesses? To your Temples? Why did you not save us from this horror? Why have you forsaken us? Why have you forsaken me, the one who loves you best?

I return again to my body, wracked with pain, as he finishes his punishment of woman. How can this be a man? Grunting his release, his teeth and eyes glint in the pale moonlight, but I cannot see his face clearly. I may never know who this man is, the one who has violated Her Temple in me.

I feel so afraid. Afraid for my broken body, afraid for my vulva, my womb and the new life that might be born from this attack, afraid for my own life, afraid for my Goddess. Will I now be afraid of all men I meet?"

Chapter Twenty Two

CONSTRUCTIVE DEVELOPMENTS, THE WAR AND ALL THAT

I HAVE AN IDEA for a new Spiral of teaching within the Priestess of Avalon Training – we are gradually getting towards 9 Spirals of learning. When priest/esses make their vow of dedication at the end of the Second or Third Spirals, they are filled with their surrender to Goddess. Through the two or three years of training they have been held within a circle of support by their tutors and from everyone else who is on the same journey and making a similar dedication. The end of each Spiral is a high moment in life.

But there is always so much more to learn and part of that learning is how to translate one's private priestess aspirations into everyday life. For example, how can people earn money by being Her priestesses, when Glastonbury Goddess Temple is so far the only Goddess organisation in Britain offering any kinds of jobs? There are currently no modern day Goddess Temples which priestesses can automatically enter and be employed. We are at the very beginning of a new Goddess movement. We have to build everything from the ground up and hopefully not in patriarchal ways. And we will, of course, make mistakes.

As has become painfully obvious we are all wounded by living in a patriarchal world dominated by violence, for the last four, five, six thousand years. We the returning Goddess people, all carry emotional and spiritual scars from the wounds that we received at the endings of the Temples. These wounds have repeated themselves in different forms through the lives in between, and now we continue to re-enact them in our everyday lives, through our competitive, undermining, slandering, destroying, reactive natures. There is so much healing to be done within every individual, as well as within our Goddess communities as a whole. The place to begin is always with the individual. Change the individual and the communal will then also change.

I write my ideas for an advanced Priestess Weaver Training, which is designed to help deepen the dedication of a priest/ess and empower them to become Her fulltime priestesses, working in new ways.

A Fourth Spiral course can explore:

Healing the wounds of the past, of this life and previous lives, working especially with the memories of the ending of the Goddess Temples and the consequences of those experiences in other lives.

Fulltime Priestessing – no separation, no compartmentalising – all of life as a priestess life. Offering everything we are to Goddess – all gifts, talents, ideas, activities, objects.

Energetics of Ceremonies and creating Goddess Temples.

Temple Priestessing.

How to create a Pop-up Goddess Temple working with others as a group.

How to create a permanent Goddess Temple.

Abundance, money, wealth and the resistance to these.

Developing a daily spiritual practice, developing a public spiritual practice.

Leadership, group development, empowerment, delegation.

Performance skills, entrance, voice, walk, dance, singing, presence.

Self-promotion, Event promotion, Temple promotion – media skills.

Shadow hunting, self-reflection, self-responsibility, commitment and openness to challenge.

Trust, surrender, dedication.

Creation of new Goddess wheels, exploring local sacred landscapes. Invoking ancient Goddesses once again in new places.

Taking Goddess out into the world through art, culture, writing, music, film, media, etc.

* * *

In February 2014 we hold our annual four day Orchard Gathering. It is with some trepidation that I have designed this four-day event as it will mean inviting everyone to gather and we will be discussing all the recent conflicts within the Orchard. The Orchard Development Group (ODG) has been meeting online and in person and we have come up with proposals for discussion by everyone.

On the first day after introductions we hold a lovely ceremony of Return to the Goddess Temple in our Temple, welcoming back the priestesses and priests we haven't seen in Glastonbury for a while. This includes several foreign priestesses who have made the trip especially to be with us. The Ceremony is a simple invocation of the Lady of Avalon and an Elemental Blessing Ceremony, which is very loving and beautiful, priestessed by Dawn, Michelle and myself. In the afternoon there are workshops from priestesses, Lieveke Volcke from Belgium, presenting her *Nine Morgen sprays*, and Luiza Frazao from Portugal with her presentation on the *Garden of the Hesperides and the Sisters of the Sunset*. In the evening Christine Watkins, the fabulous priestess storyteller, tells one of her magical stories *Feathers: A Crow, a Swan, a Peacock, a Jay and Maiden Bridie by the River*.

The next day Katinka presents a *Great Queen, Forgotten Archetype of the Goddess* slide show, which is inspiring as always, reminding us of this powerful archetype. In the afternoon everyone divides into small groups of 4-5 people with a priestess facilitator with the opportunity to share and own feelings and concerns around the events of the last months within and outside of the Orchard. This is good for many. After this sharing Anna Saqqara leads some dance to release any emotional residues out of the body. In the evening Divine Roots, our local Goddess band led by priestess Sally Pullinger, is playing a gig in the pub next door.

On the Saturday lots of people arrive for the day. It's really wonderful to see so many priestesses coming for the Gathering. They have come to support rather than attack us, and that feels really good. My fears recede as several say that they wanted to make the effort to be there to show their support after everything that has gone on, and that feels really great. We begin with a Grand Invocation of the Lady of Avalon, welcoming Her into the Goddess Hall, which is built on Her Sacred Land. Everyone introduces themselves, because not everyone has met everyone else in person, though they may have read their words online. It is so important to put a face to a name, to hear individuals speak. This is followed by *Bringing in the New Stories*, our ODG proposals for the development of the Orchard. Elle Hull introduces and leads this discussion part of the day.

This is the presentation put together by us:

Orchard Gathering ODG Presentation
February 2014

In the Orchard Development Group discussions it has been recognised that:

1. Kathy is the woman who initiated and created all we are talking about & more (PoA Trainings, Orchard of Avalon, Goddess Temple, Goddess Conference, Goddess Hall, plus Library of Avalon, Isle of Avalon Foundation, Bridget Healing Wing) & this needs to be honoured by all. Over time she has opened all of this to include everyone else.

2. Not everybody is well informed about the existing structures, organisations & the corresponding responsibilities of people. More transparency & information is needed on these basic facts and is given in attached documents.

3. The Goddess Temple and the Orchard of Avalon are separate entities, although it is acknowledged that there is a close association between them.

4. The Orchard needs greater structure than what already exists.

5. There needs to be greater support for priestesses on local and regional levels.

* * *

We propose:

1. *The setting up of PIRL (Priestess in Real Life) Circles* within local areas in Britain and in other countries. PIRL circles are local/regional groups of priest/esses, who have completed part or all of their training, who meet up in person to share and support one another in their priestess work and lives. These could be small groups that are akin to the support groups experienced during training. The focus is on sharing, support and creativity. There could be different types of PIRLs. Some might be for support or sharing only, while others might be specifically for creative endeavours as well as sharing, with some creative component that goes on between circles. PIRLs meet physically however many times they wish, e.g., weekly, monthly, etc. In any area any priestess/priest or small group is empowered to take the initiative to start a PIRL in their area. (We also discussed the setting up of Groves, which are groups of priestesses gathered around a particular project or interest, which could also include people who are not members of the Orchard of Avalon. We decided to leave this idea until a later time.)

2. *Creation of an Orchard database* of all who those who have completed the First Spiral of the Training, asking whether they wish to remain in the Orchard, also allowing people to see who else lives in their area, to invite to join a PIRL circle.

3. *Creation of a Code of Conduct* for all members of the Orchard, which is signed on joining the Orchard at the end of the First Spiral, or signed now in agreement to stay within the Orchard. Most professional organisations have such a Code of Conduct and as the Orchard has grown and priestesses have become more recognised in society it is important for us to have a visible Code that we can all say that we agree with.

Our suggestions for the Code of Conduct are:

i. I respect and am supportive of all members of the Orchard of Avalon and I endeavour to work harmoniously with all Orchard members.

ii. I continue to study, learn and develop as a Sister or Brother of Avalon, and as a practising Priestess/Priest of the Goddess and/or Avalon.

iii. I do not do anything that will bring other members of the Orchard, their lives and their work into disrepute – in every case there would be discussion about the question of what disrepute means.

iv. I aspire to live my life according to the Developing Rites and Responsibilities of a Priest/ess of the Goddess and of Avalon.

v. I embrace the values of the Motherworld, of love, care and support for all beings.

vi. When conflict arises between myself and another Orchard member I call on my PIRL Circle sisters/brothers, other priestesses or the Orchard Guardians for help in resolving the conflict (see 5).

4. *The setting up of Cauldron Circles*

    Cauldron Circles are private emotional releasing circles, with or without a fire, where individuals can express and discharge emotions, with support from sisters and brothers in a safe environment, as part of taking responsibility for their personal wounding. These could be requested as part of Conflict Resolution for individual parties.

5. *The setting up of an Orchard Guardians/Spaceholders/ Boundary-Keepers group*

    This is a small group of experienced priestesses whose job it is to uphold the values and boundaries of the Orchard and the Code of Conduct. Guardians need to have a feel for the Orchard as a whole, energetically and practically. These Guardians would include priestesses who have been in the Orchard for many years and have lived through the cycles of change. It could also include newer members who see things with a fresh eye. The Orchard Guardians would have the power to look at any behaviour which breaks the Code of Conduct, and to consider any sanctions, up to and including asking someone to leave the Orchard.

THERE IS GOOD discussion around all these ideas by everyone present, breaking into smaller groups and then feeding back to the larger group. Lots of good ideas and comments are added into the pot. We agree to go ahead with the setting up of PIRL Circles, the creation of the Orchard database and more discussion on the Code of Conduct by the ODG. We all have a resistance to any forms of policing each other – rather let's call it peacing ourselves. For example, who decides who has overstepped the Code, and who enforces the Code, etc. There is much more discussion to be had, but this is a good beginning.

THE NEXT WEEK Erin, Duncan and I fly off to teach in Turin, Italy, for a group of mostly women brought together by priestess Sarah Perini. It is so lovely to see Sarah and her partner Mirco again and I get to see the Italian translation of my *'Priestess of Avalon'* book. Sarah is gradually translating all my books into Italian and publishing them, which I greatly appreciate. She has done a good job as always and we will launch the new book at the workshop.

It's an exciting weekend. On the Saturday we create a Labrynth with Erin holding the entrance and our Italian priestesses Anna Bordin from Venice, Claudia Carta from Rome, and Sarah, holding the boundaries. I sit in the centre and embody Goddess for 42 people. Phew! My small self wonders whether everyone has received what they need from the Lady. I still wish I was a better priestess – able to be more focused than I am – slow steps with this wound. The feeling is not like last time. I am good enough, even though I wish I was better. The feedback next morning is good and then Sarah, Anna and Claudia offer

Goddess Oracles to the group. Erin and I hold the encircling space and bring participants to meet the Oracles. It is a lovely deep dance. Erin and I have different styles of working with people, which complement each other.

After the weekend we go north to the mountains where snow still lies on the ground. We visit an abbey, which is built on a high pinnacle of rock with commanding views into and out of the mountains. It is much better being out here in nature rather than in the wet and rainy city, with its traffic pollution and cigarette smoke, and prostitutes with long red boots loitering on the street corners near where I am staying. While I live this amazing priestess life, I am so aware that life for many people in this world is grim and filled with suffering. The contrast is hard to encompass. Why is my life so good and why are others' so awful? It hurts to think about this horrible conundrum.

WE RETURN home and the following weekend I'm teaching my Soul Healing course. They are a great group of students and it's always good to see them again. Each one is now going deeper, not only in their learning about healing and practicing healing, but also into their personal self-healing journeys. This weekend as well as doing more practice of Magnetic and Radiatory Healing they are learning Psychic Reading. It's so cool to see everyone find out that with a bit of encouragement and learning of a technique, they can read people's auras and speak truth to the hearts of others. I love this work. So many times it is just about giving people the opportunity to practice something they have never tried before and then they find that they can do it. Yippee!

A week or so later I go into the Spiral One training for a couple of hours to show them a wonderful slide presentation I've collated of Goddess Images from Old Europe. It is such a revelatory set of images of Goddess figurines, the first of which comes from Israel, found between layers of earth dated between 233,000 BCE and 800,000 BCE. Goddess was worshipped by people for hundreds of thousands of years before patriarchy intervened.

99% of all figurines and carvings found from the ancient world are female and in this slide show I present the progression and continuity of Goddess imagery through the millennia to the present day. I love showing this presentation as I can see people recognise that although they think our Goddess worship is only now beginning in Europe, it is actually a spirituality that has existed for tens and hundreds of thousands of years. We are not the first in time to honour Goddess, although we may be among the first to honour Her once again in Europe.

THE FOLLOWING WEEK I am about to teach a four day Nine Morgens Retreat in the Goddess Hall. The Nine Morgens are the Nine Sisters of Avalon, who are the essence of the feminine in nature, in the weather and in womankind. In Avalon the Nine Morgens are particularly connected to trees and plants, to animals and birds, and to the play of the weather upon the landscape in the form of clouds, sunshine, wind, rain, ice and snow. They beckon to us through vibration and sound, colour and movement. They are dakinis, sky dancers, space-goers, celestial women, cloud faeries and transforming powers. As we open ourselves to them they show us how to work harmoniously in circle. Each of the Nine Morgens is associated with a particular and different negative emotion, assisting in its transformation and helping us to overcome our resistances on the spiritual path. Elemental in character the Morgens are pristine and peerless. They are the feminine principle of wisdom that manifests in female forms to benefit all human beings. They give us experiences of the ineffable reality and divine grace.

I love teaching this Retreat with the Nine Sisters. There is something about it that really connects us into a deeper layer of the Mystery of everything as we explore their qualities and open ourselves as vessels of their energies. They teach us to listen to and deeply hear each other in circle and to move in the flow of the energy within the circle as it rises and falls, expands and contracts, speeds and slows. It's a blissful way of learning.

However, the evening before the Retreat begins Mike and I watch a film about a couple going to Paris for their anniversary weekend. The film is all about their spikey relationship, which touches a chord in our relationship, which is not so harmonious at the moment. We argue as we lie in bed, but I cut the argument off as I don't want to go into that place of conflict with the Morgen Retreat beginning the next day. I fall asleep, but sleep is disturbed.

I wake several times in the night feeling full of fear, which increases each time I wake. The first time I wake as Mike, also disturbed, leaves the bedroom. I feel fearful, then fall to sleep. I wake a second time hearing Poppy our dog who hardly ever barks, now barking wildly, as if there is someone in the house or someone prowling around outside who should not be there. Waking suddenly from sleep to the barking I feel intense fear. I hear Mike go downstairs to see what is happening. The dog stops barking, but then there is no sound.

What has happened? Mike does not return. Have they both been overwhelmed by an intruder? Has Mike gone mad and killed the dog? Has Mike been killed? Is he going to kill me? Wild, strange and fear-filled thoughts come into my mind. My body lies rigid in the bed. I cannot go downstairs. He is there. They are there. They will kill me.

I am in that place between sleep, memory, dream and actuality, between realities. I think about hiding on the far side of the bed, or behind the door, in the cupboard, somewhere they can't find me, anywhere. I am now really afraid. I lie still trying not to breathe, to make no sound, so that he/they don't know that I am here. My hearing strains to catch every sound, every creak of the central heating pipes, every possible movement of the dog, of Mike, of the air. After a long time of no movement, I fall asleep again.

Sometime later – I have no idea how long I am asleep – I wake suddenly, completely drenched in sweat and terrified. Now I know that he is coming to kill me. My husband, the angry mad man, is coming to get me. I don't think I have ever been so physically afraid in my life. It is a memory arising to the surface, held in my body from babyhood in this life and also from my last incarnation, which ended in 1944. Whether it is a true personal memory or a strand of a collective memory, I cannot say, but it feels very real.

* * *

THE BEDROOM DOOR *crashes open. I lie in the darkness trying to be invisible, flattening my body beneath the bedsheets. I hear him as he strides over to the bed and rips the covers off my body. I lie shivering in my shift – white cotton. He screams,*

"Slut! Traitor! Collaborator! Witch! Bitch!"

He grabs a handful of my hair and pulls me out of the bed and onto the wooden floor. Spittle slips out between his lips as his great hand descends to slap me hard across the face. Slap! Slap! My head rocks from side to side. I feel shock and then pain as hard rough hand meets my soft cheek, pulls against my mouth and eyes. My lip splits with the force, the taste of blood dripping from my mouth under this onslaught of anger. Then his feet join in, kicking my body, into my ribs and soft belly. I feel something crack and gasp with the pain.

"You sleep with Germans! You whore! How many were there? How many times did you open your legs for those evil bastards! Whore! You are no wife of mine!"

THIS RAGING ANIMAL *is Henri, my husband, now returned from hiding, come back at the war's end to reclaim his rights, his home, his wife. He is back after many months away, full of anger and frustration, blood and fear. Early on in the war he left, went to where, to whom? I do not know. He sent no word, for whole long years. I only know he left me. He left our farm in the green fields of France. He went into hiding, away from fighting the Germans and now he takes it all out on me.*

Pain fills my body with every kick of his boot, every tug on my hair that he still holds in his hand. I feel dizzy and full of pain. I see stars as his fist cracks into my jaw and I lose consciousness. When I come to, he is still kicking me. He drags me across the floor by the hair and pulls me down the wooden stairs, my body bouncing in agony on each step. Then across the flagstones, smooth, cold and out into the yard.

There are fiery torches and other figures in the yard, more men. I see their stiff and angry faces illuminated in the flickering light, each a mask of hatred, baying for blood, like a pack of wild dogs. What have I done that is so bad?

I couldn't help myself. You were gone a long time, Henri. I fell in love with a good man. What is wrong with that?

Except that he was on the other side. He was a soldier and German, but he was kind and gentle, so different from my husband. He brought me flowers and sweet tokens of love. He was not like Henri, the great boor, who wouldn't know kindness if it came and hit him in the face. My husband, the man old enough to be my father, that my father gave me to as a young girl, in some agreement about farmland and money. I had little choice in the matter in those days. He was a worker, but he was uncouth, his manners were always poor. I had hoped to soften him, improve him, but he was set in his ways and drink took its toll in his life. We rubbed along.

Gunter treated me like a woman. For the first time in my life I was loved truly by a man. He did not hurt me. He loved me with such gentleness. How could I not love him in return?

He arrived one day on a motorbike and knocked at the farmhouse door, looking for directions to the local town. He was tall and fair and good-looking. There was a connection, an immediate spark between us. It was as if I had known him all my life, yet had never seen his face until that moment, but he was in a German uniform. I was on guard. We all knew that these Germans were dangerous war-mongering animals and could kill us all without a thought.

In a completely unexpected way I found myself inviting him into the house, offering him water to drink and then in a while, a small glass of brandy. We talked about nothing in particular that first time. He was the first man that I ever really talked to like that. We were both careful what we said, not giving too many things away because we were on different sides. He stayed for an hour that first day. I didn't know what to think about myself. It was so unlike me, but war changes many things. I knew it was wrong, but I liked this German.

He was to be stationed in the nearby town. A few days later he came to see me again. Henri had been gone for some months and I had heard nothing from him. As the Germans poured through France he left me to look after everything on my own, the house, the farm, the animals, the fields. Henri left in search of some hero's glory and only the old men stayed behind and they weren't very helpful on the farm. It was hard work keeping everything going.

I was also glad when he went. It meant an end to having to deal with his drunkenness. Nights he would go to meet his friends and drink brandy until he could barely stand. Then he would stagger back in the early hours and climb upon me in the bed, without asking. He'd pump away without care for me. I was just a necessary object for his lust. Often he collapsed like a sack of flour on top of me, squashing me. I would struggle out from beneath him and leave him there for the night. I slept many nights on the kitchen settle.

Luckily I knew the herbs to keep me barren. I wanted no child to come into the world from these harsh couplings. Nothing came of those nightmare rides. Although he would taunt me with my barren womb, "Where is the son I deserve?" I didn't tell him what I was doing. I would pray to Holy Sainte Marie and to the Black Madonna, to please, make sure I did not have his child. I couldn't bring a child into that loveless world. I also prayed to the Holy Mother to bring me love to release me from this sad life. I was a good woman. I did my best but it was never enough for him. I so wanted to be loved.

The Holy Mother has answered my prayers and I am filled with gratitude and love for Her. Now I know love. I have known love. I have breathed love in my body. I have made love, love with a beloved, love in my body. I know passion. I know what love is. Love has been with me and in me. My beloved Gunter, my gift from the Holy Mother. He loves me. He cherishes me. He holds my face so gently in his hands and kisses me so sweetly, as if I am the most wonderful gift to him in the world.

For those few precious months we lived with love. I remember the first kiss, standing there in the kitchen, a trembling delicate soft kiss. He touched my hair, my face. My body turned to fire and everything inside melted. There was no resistance in me. Our kisses became strong and full of passion. They were the first of many. In no time we were climbing the stairs to the bedroom, clothes discarded on the way. Making love.

After that first time Gunter would come to the house under cover of darkness and we would talk and laugh. He would gently take the pins out of my long dark hair, letting it down across my shoulders. I felt so alive sensually and sexually. We would make love and then talk and laugh some more and make love again. Those nights there was little sleep, love was all that we needed. They were such magical times. I picked flowers every day to lay at Our Lady's shrine in gratitude for the love which had entered my life.

Then after a while we became less careful. Gunter began to come in the daytime too when he had time off, or was on his way somewhere. People in the village began to talk as the whispered news travelled that a German soldier had been seen visiting my house on more than one occasion and sometimes at nights. There were always spies about, old men, young children, women. No matter how discreet he was, slipping away across the field or through the woods, Gunter was seen enough for the stories to begin.

When I went to market in the town I could see the women who were our neighbours, in the same position as myself, alone looking after a farm and animals. They turned their heads away, placing their hands across their mouths to conceal their gossip. Their eyes said it all. They knew that I was sleeping with a German. No-one asked. Nobody talked to me. They just stared and tutted.

But I was emboldened by love. I didn't care. I was defiant. I stared them back in the face. I was in love and even though it was dangerous I didn't care who knew it. Gunter was different. He wasn't like the other soldiers. I was feeling loved for the first time in my life. I was full of love and I wanted everyone to feel it too. I knew truth in my soul. I felt so happy.

I wanted his child. I did not think to the consequences. Soon the war would be over and Gunter and I would be together. I thought to stop taking the herbs to prevent conception. We could have a child together, a child of love.

I forgot almost that Henri even existed. Wherever he had gone perhaps he had died. I understood that I must have been a cold and heartless woman before, because I had not known how to love him, and he was incapable of loving me. I even began to feel sorry for my missing husband. He couldn't help who he was, a country man born and bred. If he was still alive he would just let me go on his return. He would give me a divorce and I would go to live with Gunter. We could *move south and begin a new life somewhere different, away from wars, a life of love with our child or children. We could have more than one. We could be a family.*

The war came abruptly to an end. I was so entranced by my lover that I didn't really realise what was happening. One day in 1944 the occupation was over. Gunter came quickly to see me. His company were leaving the local town, packing everything up as quickly as they could. He only had a few moments to come and tell me. He had to go with them. He had no choice, but he would come back for me as soon as he could. We would be together again. That last goodbye was so quick. I haven't seen him since, not yet.

Now I am lying in the yard and the dawn light is rising. I can see the familiar faces of the men around me, men from the town who stayed behind and colluded with the enemy. The ones who took their places in the Vichy government and lined their pockets. My husband is there amongst them, hailed as a resistance hero, something he always wanted, and now kicking his wife. The Germans are retreating across France yet these Frenchmen do not go after them. Instead they harry and attack their womenfolk left behind.

They pick me up roughly. I can barely walk. I am bundled into the back of a car. They are taking me to town. I know that there are other women in the neighbourhood, like me, who found love with a German soldier, and others whose only solution to the austerities of war was to sell their bodies, to buy food for their children, grain for their animals. War is cruel to those who go off to fight, but also to those who are left behind in an invaded land. War does not discriminate between good and bad. War is always the impossible action, wreaking havoc on all generations and into the future.

The car comes to a screeching stop in the middle of the town and I am bundled out into the road, which is lined with the women of the town. Some were once my friends, girls I grew up with. Now they wear masks of fury. These are the ones who have betrayed me as a friend of the enemy, betrayed me out of their own righteousness, their own high and hard-edged morals, or simply to gain advantage over one of their perceived rivals for the love of returning heroes or their standing in the community.

I am stood alone in the place of shame, where I and other whores will be brought to be condemned. Ahead in the street I recognise a woman I know from the market, I think her name is Justine. She also stands alone but she has her head shaven, and her body is bent over weeping. I feel such pity for her at the horror which is unfolding for her, and for myself.

"Holy Mother Mary, forgive us our sins.

Intercede on our behalf with your beloved Son, Jesus Christ, our Lord.

Beneath your compassion, we take refuge."

SOBS RISE WITHIN my own breast as I feel overwhelmed with fear and sadness, as I pray the sacred prayer.

"Remember, O most gracious Virgin Mary,
That never was it known that anyone who fled to your protection,
Implored your help, or sought your intercession, was left unaided.
Inspired with this confidence,
I fly to you, O Virgin of virgins, my Mother.
To you I come, before you I stand, sinful and sorrowful.
O Mother of the Word Incarnate,
Despise not my petitions,
But in your mercy, hear and answer me.
Let this day of judgement pass away."

IN THE MIDDLE of the street the tondeurs begin to hack off my hair with sheep shears. They wrench out my beautiful dark hair in handfuls, the same hair that he held with such tenderness. Then the razor scrapes across my scalp removing all traces of hair, cutting into flesh. I stand in pain and shock amongst these familiar faces, now filled with justification, participating with venom in this public humiliation of their sisters.

The familiar oft-repeated prayers pour from my lips, although nothing saves me now.

> *"Hail Mary, full of grace.*
> *The Lord is with thee.*
> *Blessed art thou amongst women,*
> *and blessed is the fruit of thy womb, Jesus.*
> *Holy Mary, Mother of God,*
> *pray for us sinners,*
> *now and at the hour of our death."*

IS THIS WHAT AWAITS ME NOW?

Justine and I are forced to walk along the street as the good folk, mostly women, of this small town spit upon us, and vent their rage at the German occupation on the poor heads of their own sisters. The women scream at us, the tondues, releasing years of repressed hatred in torrents of abuse.

Further down the street we come upon the tar barrel and are daubed in the hot tar that burns our skin. Feathers are thrown. We are kicked and mauled. There are no words to describe the horrors of this day. Tears fall helplessly down our faces. We cannot comfort each other. We are each alone in our terror.

I feel rough hands pull me down into a side street and here the real fury is enacted, by a small group of men and women. Kicked and cut in my most private holy places, with punch and blade I am left to die on the cold stones. The last of life that I see are feet departing. I am alone...

I HAD REMEMBERED some of this last incarnation before – the first time that I had breast cancer, when I had chemotherapy in 1996 and my hair began to fall out. Then we did an amazing head-shaving ceremony, a death and rebirth ceremony, which helped me face the loss of my hair and the real possibility of my own death. The ceremony was an important part of my healing journey.

Ten years later I watched a television documentary that told the individual stories of a small number of women in France who had their heads shaved for "collaboration horizontale". I was glued to the television the moment the programme began. I knew in my bones the story these women told. I knew how it had happened and what had happened. I knew, because it had happened to me.

An article by Anthony Beevor in 2009 in the Guardian newspaper includes the following information:

"The punishment of shaving a woman's head has biblical origins. In Europe the practice dates back to the dark ages, with the Visigoths. During the middle ages, this mark of shame, denuding a woman of what was supposed to be her most seductive feature, was commonly a punishment for adultery. Shaving women's heads as a mark of retribution and humiliation was reintroduced in the 20th century. After French troops occupied the Rhineland in 1923, German women who had relations with French men later suffered the same fate. During the second world war the Nazi state issued orders that German women accused of sleeping with non-Aryans or foreign prisoners employed on farms should also be publicly punished in this way.

During the Spanish civil war Falangists shaved the heads of women from republican families, treating them as if they were prostitutes. Those on the extreme right had convinced themselves that the left believed in free love. The most famous victim in fiction is Maria, the lover of Robert Jordan in Hemingway's 'For Whom the Bell Tolls'.

Head-shaving became widespread during the leftist liberation euphoria in France in 1944. Many of the tondeurs, the head-shavers, were not members of the resistance. Quite a few had been petty collaborators themselves and sought to divert attention from their own lack of resistance credentials. Yet resistance groups could be merciless towards women. In Brittany it is said that a third of those civilians killed in reprisals were women. Threats of head-shaving had been made in the resistance underground press since 1941.

There was a strong element of vicarious eroticism among the tondeurs and their supporters, even though the punishment they were about to inflict symbolised the desexualisation of their victim. This ugly carnival became the pattern soon after D-day. Once a city, town or village had been liberated by the allies or the resistance, the shearers would get to work. In mid-June, on the market day following the capture of the town of Carentan, a dozen women were shorn publicly. In Cherbourg on 14 July, a truckload of shaven young women, most of them teenagers, were driven through the streets.

A large number of the victims were prostitutes who had simply plied their trade with Germans as well as Frenchmen, although in some areas it was accepted that their conduct was professional rather than political. Others were silly teenagers who had associated with German soldiers out of bravado or boredom. In a number of cases, female schoolteachers who, living alone, had German soldiers billeted on them, were falsely denounced for having been a 'mattress for the boches'. Women accused of having had an abortion were also assumed to have consorted with Germans.

Many victims were young mothers, whose husbands were in German prisoner-of-war camps. During the war they often had no means of support, and their only hope of obtaining food for themselves and their children was to accept a liaison with a German soldier.

Jealousy masqueraded as moral outrage, because people envied the food and entertainment these women had received as a result of their conduct. When Arletty, the great actor and star of the film 'Les Enfants du Paradis', died in 1992, she received admiring obituaries that did not mention the rumour that she had her head shaved at the liberation. These obituaries even passed over her controversial love affair with a Luftwaffe officer. But letters to some newspapers revealed a lingering bitterness nearly 50 years later. It was not the fact that Arletty had slept with the enemy which angered them, but the way she had eaten well in the Hôtel Ritz while the rest of France was hungry.

After the humiliation of a public head-shaving, the tondues – the shorn women – were often paraded through the streets on the back of a lorry, occasionally to the sound of a drum as if it were a tumbril and France was reliving the revolution of 1789. Some were daubed with tar, some stripped half naked, some marked with swastikas in paint or lipstick.

In Bayeux, Churchill's private secretary Jock Colville recorded his reactions to one such scene. 'I watched an open lorry drive past to the accompaniment of boos and catcalls from the French populace, with a dozen miserable women in the back, every hair on their heads shaved off. They were in tears, hanging their heads in shame. While disgusted by this cruelty, I reflected that we British had known no invasion or occupation for some 900 years. So we were not the best judges.' And so a blind eye was turned to this cruelty.

Colonel Harry D McHugh, the commander of an American infantry regiment near Argentan, reported: 'The French were rounding up collaborators, cutting their hair off and burning it in huge piles, which one could smell miles away. Also, women collaborators were forced to run the gauntlet and were really beaten.'

Women almost always were the first targets, because they offered the easiest and most vulnerable scapegoats, particularly for those men who had joined the resistance at the last moment. Altogether, at least 20,000 women are known to have had their heads shaved. But the true figure may well be higher, considering that some estimates put the number of French children fathered by members of the Wehrmacht as high as 80,000."

THESE NUMBERS begin to sound like those of the victims of witch burning.

"*The basically misogynistic reaction of head-shaving during the liberation of France was repeated in Belgium, Italy and Norway and, to a lesser extent, in the Netherlands. In France, another wave of head-shaving took place in the late spring of 1945 when forced labourers, prisoners of war and concentration camp victims returned from Germany. Revenge on women represented a form of expiation for the frustrations and sense of impotence among males humiliated by their country's occupation. One could almost say that it was the equivalent of rape by the victor.*"

NO WONDER that this terrifying recent memory echoes fearfully through my present life.

THE MORGEN RETREAT goes really well despite, or because of, this strong re-membering. I am finding more and more that these eruptions of emotion into my everyday life release the stuck energetic places within me. This seems to have repercussions in my healing of myself, in my teaching, in my interactions with others, in the places of wounding which they too are able to find and heal within themselves. This does not necessarily happen by any direct expression of my own, I don't have to say anything, although I can and do. It happens through an energetic connection, just by my presence, after my own realisation has occurred.

On the Retreat after I give an introduction to who the Morgens are, we invoke them, asking them to come and be present for us. We rotate our own bodies and open up the space which is in the centre of the body, calling them into our bellies, hearts, sacra, circling, moving arms, sounding their names. We journey across the waters of the Lake of Avalon, travelling in the Barge with the faeryman Barinthus, with the Queen of Northgalis, the Queen of the Wasteland and Morgen La Fey, the Faery Queen. On the Sacred Isle we are taken by Morgen La Fey to the Garden of the Morgens, to meet them in their forms as plants, trees, birds, creatures, elementals and energies. We meet them as crows, one of their most familiar forms. We bathe in their complex energies, threads of light, expanded energy, with healing threads weaving through each of us.

In one of the processes I hear/see/know that once there were 9 Morgen Priestesses, a circle of nine women who worked together. You were/I was, one of the nine – now there are many more of us, remembering, some coming back again with fragments of the Nine within our being. They were real women, and are again now, real women and a few men. We are able to work with plants and trees, birds and animals, with the weather, with sound, movement and energy to heal and create the new. This is another part of the jigsaw, another missing fragment that is being brought together in the remembering of our priestess path. It is our heritage to learn to work together in circles, in ceremonies, in community, in ways we are only just beginning to explore.

By the end of the Retreat we are all exhilarated.

* * *

Chapter Twenty Three

IOUA

IFE CONTINUES as it does with teaching and preparing for the 2014 Goddess Conference when we will be celebrating the Crone. Bookings are coming in, all the finer details of creating the Conference have to be taken care of, booking venues, beginning to write the full programme, finding out everyone's requirements and dealing with many small details.

My own emotions rise and fall, reaction and peace. I wake in the night filled with non-specific anxiety and fear. I have a sense of a glowing inner soul being that is caged by a web of woven wicker sticks, although some are stronger like they are made of steel. They are the experiences, attitudes and rigidities of my conditioning. I feel one of my fear strands become so acute and rigid, then just turn to dust, disappearing into nothing as the energy which sustained my fear dissipates. I feel my fear and resistance to dealing with difficult people, but this may be something that I can do when I feel strong enough and clear enough, when I have healed my own part of the experience.

My prayer is that all who come after me will be inspired by all that I have offered and given in life, that they might learn from the mistakes that I have made, although I know that we really only learn from our own mistakes. I pray that the priestesses of now take up the mantle of the ancient priestesses who knew their place in the world, who love and adored Goddess throughout their lives.

"*Rise up, Priestesses and claim Her Holy place in the world. Build Her Temples again. Be courageous! Be strengthened in Her love, always and forever!*"

In May my daughter Iona and I travel to the beautiful isle of Iona off northwest Scotland, where I am going to lead a Goddess Retreat. I have a deep and ancient love connection to this small sacred island and it's the place of my daughter's arrival on the planet. We went again to Iona when she was a child and now it's lovely to be going to Iona with her as an adult. She will be offering massages and reflexology treatments to the retreat participants. We fly early on Friday morning from Bristol to Glasgow, where Helen Anthony kindly meets us and drives us to Oban. The last time we were here three years ago for another Goddess Retreat a huge storm prevented us from travelling from Oban to Mull, and we had to wait it out in Oban until the storm passed. We were almost blown away by the mad winds and watched from the window of our B&B as boats overturned or crashed wildly into the rocky shore.

Today the weather is much calmer and we catch the ferry to Mull. There is a place part way across the sea, to the northeastern end of the Firth of Lorn, just passing Lismore, where the energy changes and it feels like we are moving between dimensions, not only physically but psychically. We reach the port of Craignure on Mull, then drive through rain, across the beautiful moorland landscape, over mist-laden hills and back down to the shoreline, to Fionnphort, the small harbour for Iona. Since Helen has a disabled sticker she can take her car in the ferry across the Sound to Iona. The small ferry rises and falls on the waves, as it turns into the wind, bucking like a horse. We land safely and Helen drives us to the hotel. It takes a long day to get from Glastonbury to Iona, but it's wonderful to be here once again on this Sacred Isle. I breathe in the salty air, the wind blowing as usual over the green sward, that is just awakening to springtime in this northwestern part of Brigit's Isles. I open my heart once again to the Mystery of this Sacred Isle, with its creamy beaches, cold turquoise seas and wide skies.

Iona is a magical island, which lies far, far away at the edge of the world. Getting there feels like travelling to a lunar landscape, where ancient grey rocks carpet the hillsides. I have been here about ten times in this life. I love it so. It is a Place of Ancient Silence and Far Memory. Its original name is Ioua

(I-ou [as in bough]-a), which may derive from Io the Moon Goddess, or from Ivo meaning Yew-Place, although few yews remain there today. I am inspired by Her ancient name of Ioua, Ioua – Goddess of this island. The sound of Her name evokes Her presence.

St Bridget was said to have come from Ireland as a girl in the 5th century to live on Ioua, where she became known as *St Bride of the Kindly Fire, St Bride of the Shores*. Brighde, whose name means Goddess, was already present on Ioua. She was here in the grey rocks and green earth, in the pale sands and the surrounding seas. Her healing flame shone in Her Sun golden rays, Her silver Moonbeams. Her poetry came on the soft breeze and in the roaring winds. She blessed the land with Her sweet rains, and pilgrims drank from Her Sacred Spring of Eternal Youth.

Fiona Macleod, who was the dream self of the 19th century essayist William Sharp, collected and wrote down many legends of the Western Isles, particularly those of Iona – stories of sea and foam, sunshine and rain, rainbows, rocky heathlands and mythical peoples. In 'Iona', published in 1900, she wrote:

> *"There is one Iona, a little island of the west. There is another Iona of which I would speak. I do not say that it lies open to all. It is as we come that we find. If we come, bringing nothing with us, we go away ill-content, having seen and heard nothing of what we had vaguely expected or hoped to see or hear. It is another Iona than the Iona of sacred memories and prophecies: Iona the metropolis of dreams. None can understand it who does not see it through its pagan light, its christian light, its singular blend of paganism, romance and spiritual beauty. There is too an Iona that is more than Gaelic, that is more than a place rainbow-lit with the seven desires of the world, the Iona that if we will it so, is a mirror of your heart and mine."*

ON OUR RETREAT we will be opening ourselves to this *Other* Iona – Ioua, more mysterious and beautiful than we know with our minds – Ioua of the heart. We will open ourselves to Goddess in many forms as we experience Her in legends, in the land, the ocean, the weather and the wildness of Her nature, and in our inner spaces with Her. I am looking forward to this retreat, to spending time holding space for others and also time for myself to go within. I have always found Iona to be a place of deep peace, even though the wind blows almost continuously and the weather can be unfriendly.

Fiona Macleod also wrote of a prophecy she heard which seems very apposite in these days of the returning of Goddess,

> "….he (a young Hebridean priest) told me once how, 'as our forefathers and elders believed and still believe, that Holy Spirit shall come again which once was mortally born among us as the Son of God, but then shall be the Daughter of God. The Divine Spirit shall come again as a Woman. Then for the first time the world will know peace.' And when I asked him if it were not prophesied that the Woman is to be born in Iona, he said that if this prophecy had been made it was doubtless of an Iona that was symbolic, but that this was a matter of no moment, for She would rise suddenly in many hearts, and have Her habitation among dreams and hopes.
>
> The other who spoke to me of this Woman who is to save was an old fisherman of a remote island of the Hebrides, and one to whom I owe more than to any other spiritual influence in my childhood, for it was he who opened to me the three gates of Beauty. Once this old man, Seumas Macleod, took me with him to a lonely haven in the rocks, and held me on his knee as we sat watching the sun sink and the moon climb out of the eastern wave.… (An Angel) had come in answer to the old man's prayer. He had come to say that we could not see the Divine One whom we awaited. 'But you will yet see that Holy Beauty,' said the Angel, and Seumas believed, and I too believed, and believe. He took my hand, and I knelt beside him, and he bade me repeat the words he said. And that was how I first prayed to Her who shall yet be the Balm of the World.
>
> And since then I have learned, and do see, that not only prophecies and hopes, and desires unclothed yet in word or thought, foretell Her coming,

but already a multitude of spirits are in the gardens of the soul, and are sowing seed and calling upon the wind of the south; and that everywhere are watching eyes and uplifted hands, and signs which cannot be mistaken, in many lands, in many peoples, in many minds; and, in the heaven itself that the soul sees, the surpassing signature."

THIS PORTENT described in several ways by Fiona Macleod heralds the return of Goddess years later, into the hearts of many of those of us who feel called by Goddess to pray to Her, to remember Her once again. It is especially so here on Iona on this sacred Isle of Goddess Ioua, which in modern times is now socially and religiously dominated by christianity, by Iona Abbey and the Iona Community. Iona Abbey was first founded as a monastery in the sixth century by St Columba, who came to Iona with 12 companions after being exiled from Ireland because of troubles in his homeland. The monastery rose and fell into ruin after Viking attacks and rose again to become an important Benedictine Abbey in the 13th Century. An Augustinian Nunnery was also founded in the 13th century. Over the centuries the buildings have fallen into disuse and disrepair, but have been revived in modern times under Reverend George Macleod, with the founding of the Iona Community, who began to rebuild the Abbey.

Many early Scottish Kings were crowned on Iona and up to 48 are said to have been buried on Iona, as well as kings from Ireland, Norway and France. Like the Isle of Avalon it is another Western Isle of the Dead, for Scotland rather than England. It is a numinous Otherworldy Isle where it is believed that the souls of the dead can pass freely into Paradise, into the arms of the Beloved.

MOST OF OUR fourteen retreat participants are arriving the following day so we have time to walk and feel where we are. When we gather for our first meeting on the Saturday evening it's a pleasure to meet these women who wish to retreat from the everyday world into a deeper connection with themselves. I already know some of them and some I have not met before. They include priestesses, old friends and new. It feels like we will have an interesting time together.

Everyone spends some time thinking about their intentions for their Retreat. It is my intention to be present to the needs of all the retreatants, to enjoy being on Iona, to relax, to have some deep conversations with everyone, to have some inner time for myself, to be with my daughter and to be moved by the wild hidden places of this island.

On our first full day we go on a great long walk across the wild landscape to the southern end of the island, across bogs and mounds, rocks and streams. We accidentally find our way to the remains of the Iona marble quarry, where green and white marble was quarried and loaded from the rocky shore onto ships bound for Scotland and England. It's a strange place with the echoes of hard-working quarrymen and sailors breaking stone beside and on dangerous seas.

We make our way around the inlets and eventually arrive at St Columba's Bay where the saint was said to have landed from Ireland on his journey into exile. No-one knows where the young Bridget landed in her coracle from Ireland, although it may also have been in this bay which faces Ireland. The bay is covered in richly-coloured beach pebbles, moulded by the sea. A couple of men are also on the beach collecting stones. It turns out that they are staying on retreat at Iona Abbey. On hearing that we are on a Goddess Retreat they offer us some of the small green marble stones, known as Mermaid's Tears, which they have collected. They are said to bring protection against drowning.

The story goes, "One day a mermaid fell in love with one of the monks on Iona. Every day she would pray to God to give her a soul so that the monk could marry her. Each night she would come ashore, all the way up to the monk's window. Realising that again God had not answered her prayer, she would run back to the sea crying. Where her tears touched the ground became the green marble stones that litter Iona's beaches. These are known as Mermaid's Tears."

Such stories of Mermaid's Tears are found all over the world in various forms from Greece to Nova Scotia. Perhaps they tell more of the sorrows of Mermaids, creatures of the Sea Goddess, who are no longer recognised as Her epiphany by the human world.

* * *

WALKING FAR on this first day tires everyone out, which helps us to relax physically, emotionally and mentally. Iona gives treatments to some of our participants, which are greatly appreciated.

Next is a day of silence from early in the morning to the following day. It's a great practice not to talk at all, to be with oneself, to hear one's own thoughts and feelings, to experience oneself, aside from the rest of world. Most people never do this in their busy lives – just take the time to be quiet. It's a simple practice which brings up many emotions for people. Early on we have a difficulty with the hotel staff, who I have spoken with the previous day, telling them that we are having a day of Silence and that participants will not be speaking to them. Unfortunately it seems that some staff do not want to understand or respond to sign or written messages, and become quite agitated by the whole idea. Last time we were here there was no problem, but this time with different staff it's a problem, so people have to speak simply about what they want to eat. From then on we are all in Silence together.

We gather at the hotel entrance to walk across the Machair to the Bay at the Back of the Ocean. The Machair is a wide fertile stretch of flat, low-lying grassland that stretches from one side of the island to the other. Every winter the wind from the Atlantic Ocean blows sand across the flat ground, covering everything, and then in springtime grasses and small wild flowers push their way up through the sand creating a beautiful mat of flowers and grasses. We walk across the Machair into the wind and down to the wide beaches at the western side of the island. This is one of my favourite places, where all cobwebs are blown out of the mind. Here it is possible to gaze at the blue ocean, to find wind-sheltered spots to lie in the sun, to drift in the mind, to rest the heart and soul.

THEN, OF COURSE, given space for thinking, the problems in our community rise again in my mind. How can I/we resolve this? I think about mediation. I hear my beliefs that all that will do is to allow us to hear each other's point of view and disagree, or to hear the other's point of view and think it is resolved and then find out later that it isn't, as it wasn't, even though at the time it was.

Lady, I ask you to reveal the pathways of peace, peace for my own soul, peace for others. Forgiveness? When there is no remorse? When there is righteousness on my side as well as theirs.

It is a conundrum for me. I want to be/do something authentic. My feelings are hurt by the priestesses who attacked me, who attacked the Temple and by all who joined in. I can forget but I have a visceral reaction whenever I see any one of them. My body moves. I avoid them/run/turn away from them.

Ioua, Lady of the Isle, I ask for your help. I do not know how to do this. I do not know how to heal the wounds in our community. I do not know how to do it. Please help me/please help us. Show me the way. Beautiful Lady, you who know everything, please show me what to do.

Thank you Ocean, thank you Land, thank you Sky, thank you Earth, thank you Ioua.

NO-ONE in my own wounded blood family recognised me as a child, saw me, knew me as an adult. They were not capable of knowing me, knowing who I am. I see the family parallels in this community drama. No-one in this wounded part of our community knows me, sees me, but it is different in my life. Mike sees me, my children see me. Sally, Katinka, Erin, Sophie and others love me, do see me. The family has changed now and there is only a small part of the family that is unable to recognise me clearly.

LATE IN THE afternoon we meet as a group in the ruins of the Augustinian nunnery, with its truth-telling Sheela na Gig on the outer walls. She is old and weather-beaten, with legs akimbo, as She looks out from the convent walls. She has seen many people come and go. The ruins are always peaceful, as ruins often are, once the stories that were told within the walls, have died away. I stay there for a while, my eyes closed, drifting.

I see black skirts and the women's soft damp shoes, made of fish skin, seal skin, the occasional hide. Those belonging to the richer women are lined with rabbit fur, which is then stitched and re-stitched for the poorer sisters. The cloister is filled with women in black skirts, all standing in a great circle around the edge. There is noise, laughter, singing, dancing, as a great ceilidh is happening. Children are moving between the women, running in and out, holding hands, playing happily together. Candles are brought into the centre of the circle, lighting up the dark evening spaces as Sun Greine falls quickly to Her bed in the west on these short days and long nights. There is hot food and drinks, blazing fires in the corners, warmth against the rains, protection from the winds. Happiness flows through this holy place.

FOR OF COURSE, what were these remote nunneries for? As well as places of religious retreat for those called to a cloistered life, they also provided refuges for penniless women and their children, for women who had been abandoned, dispossessed, for women who had been raped, attacked, brutalised, gone mad with grief and anguish, the victims of tribal wars and the dominations of men. They were the only sanctuaries where women might feel safe. The Iona nunnery was one such sanctuary, built on the foundations of island care and hospitality. At one time all women were banned by the Benedictine monks from the Isle of Iona as a temptation of the devil. They were sent away to the nearby Isle of Women to eke out a living on barren rocky hillsides, waiting to serve the desires of their monkish neighbours.

As my mind floats I see images of earlier times of great circles of women and men coming together to dance in circles in round houses, with the Fire of Life in the centre, for the honouring of life, for the honouring of women and children, honouring the Motherline. For beyond all the suffering of patriarchal times there were earlier times of happiness and joy. There were the long ages when we lived in the Motherworld and we have those memories too, waiting to be re-membered when we have explored these troubled veils.

The next morning we share experiences of the Day of Silence which has helped each person in different ways to quieten and connect more deeply to themselves. Later we climb Dun I, the only high spot on the island. At 101 metres above the level sea it feels like climbing a mountain although it is not that high. It has wonderful panoramic views all around. To the west is the Atlantic Ocean, next stop America. On a clear day we can see the isles of Tiree, Coll, Treshnish, that make up the Hebrides – tHeBrides – the islands of Bride, for She is known everywhere here. And to the south there are more islands. To the east is Mull and the mainland of Scotland. Below the hill the land of Iona spreads out with all its hidden places, viewed from this eyrie.

To one side of the summit is the Spring of Eternal Youth. Here we make offerings to Ioua and sing a beautiful song which Kathy, one of our group, has composed for Her, sounding and resounding Her name. We sip the Holy Waters, dip our toes into the boggy edges of the small pool and some go in deeper. For it said that to enjoy these waters is to take eternal youthfulness into one's soul. Bride is said to come here every summer solstice at midnight, when it is still light in this northern land. She blesses the waters of the Spring so that they carry healing for all those in need who manage the steep climb. Up here the wind blows continuously, but there are small dips and gullies where it's possible to lie on the rock just out of the wind. The skies are wide and clouds race across from the west.

During the Retreat I give each person an individual Soul Healing or a Tarot or psychic reading. These healing sessions connect me more deeply to each person's energy field that I might understand them better. Iona also gives lots of massages and healing therapies. It has been a lovely retreat and our final goodbyes are filled with love and Ioua's blessings. We have each received something that we needed for ourselves – peace, relaxation, revelation, healing, recognition, deepening connection to the land and Ioua's mysteries. We are all grateful.

Chapter Twenty Four

The Process of Healing

READ A GREAT ARTICLE by Vicki Noble, the feminist, shamanic co-creator of the Motherpeace Tarot, which was first published in 1995 in 'Woman of Power' journal. It is called 'Authorizing our Teachers – Teaching in a Feminist Spiritual Context'. Vicki describes many of the challenges that she and others met in the US in teaching and in community, which we have faced as a feminist Goddess organisation in the last 2 years.

Vicki writes, *"The level of damage we have incurred in Western culture in the last five thousand years that separate us from our ancient foremothers in the Goddess cultures of Anatolia and old Europe is great, and, unfortunately, its experience has been felt in every workshop or ritual journey to retrieve the past that I have conducted. It appears that the recapitulation of that loss, at times toxic, necessarily becomes part of our experience together, but I have found that what looks like pure pettiness (and sometimes escalates into attacks) can be used to further our work of reclaiming our lost heritage."*

Vicki goes on to describe her own experiences and learning through working with groups of women over time. For me this is a really empowering article, which can still be accessed online.

See http://www.motherpeace.com/vicki_authorizing_our_teachers_1.html

It describes some of my own journey, the mistakes I have made and hopefully some of the learning.

I AM FINDING at the moment that the past and the present are becoming mixed up in my mind. I try to feel and work out my feelings, but they are confused. I see how my reactive feelings and projections move from person to person. They are my projections, nothing really to do with the people onto whom I have projected, although they provide the perfect hooks. I speak with Katinka and she talks about the Angry Women's Alliance. I see it more as the Wounded Women's Alliance WWA!! which is created through behaviours learned in school. In patriarchy we learn as girls to create alliances for survival, to disempower others in order to find power for ourselves. The patterns begin in childhood and are amplified amongst groups of girls. It is so different from the way that things once were between women.

A Delightful Memory Arises.

"We ride side by side into the surf on the southern shores of the Euxine Sea, our mares delighting in the coolness of the foam after the hot day. The sun is sinking beyond the mountains of Pontus as the full moon is rising, red as She lifts up from the horizon. Her blood light flows across the sea, ripple by ripple, towards us, gradually lightening as She rises gracefully in the sky. The beauty of Her radiance on this night is a wonder to behold.

Our Queen Orythia, She who Rages in the Mountains, and her sister Queen Antiope, ride ahead for a short distance into the tumbling waves, coming to a standstill in the salty waters. These are our Amazon Queens, for we are ruled by two equal Queens, who support and hold each other in love. Sometimes our Queens are blood sisters and sometimes they are lovers.

We sister Amazons halt in the foam a little way apart and watch as these two magnificent women of our company are outlined by Selene's growing light. From the girdle that snakes around her belly, Orythia takes her conch and placing it to her lips, blows into it, sending sound across the waters to Selene the Moon. The howling of the conch echoes long and far across the waves, calling to the waters of Euxine, calling to the sky, calling to the surrounding mountains, calling to all the creatures in the sea and on the land, to turn their attention to our Mystress Selene.

She is the one whom we love and adore as we follow Her cycle of waxing and waning, from the sliver of Her beginning at sunrise to the fullness of Her belly at sunset, as she swells with the souls of the dying, so that they might give birth to the living. Her horns are visible as She lies upon her back, the Boat of the Moon that leads travellers across the seas, fisher-folk to their catches, traders to their ports, warriors to their destiny.

We bow our heads in honour of our Mystress the Moon, for tomorrow we ride out against the foe that has invaded our lands. We are warriors, Amazons, and we defend our peoples against all who would come from the lands of forgetting, to rape and maim our mothers, our sisters and daughters, who would come to kill our brothers and sons. We are strong in word and deed, and none are stronger than our Sister Queens, who lead us carefully into conflicts.

We are said to be one-breasted, better to draw back the bow from which our arrows fly towards fleet deer, running mountain felines or human attackers. This is only true amongst those brave women, who have been sliced by a sword, damaged by a handheld knife and healed by careful sewing and poultices of herbs. These Amazons bare their wounded ribs for all to see, proud of their victory over death and the dangerous deeds of men.

Antiope leans down from her mare, dipping the beautiful shell she carries in her girdle, into the Euxine waters, filling the lustrous cup. She lifts it to the moon, raising it high above her head. She speaks the prayer to the Moon as she pours the libation. Between each phrase she bends down again and again scooping up the silvery waters into the shell, droplets of silver, red, green, gold and blue, sparkling back into the ocean.

> "Beloved Selene, Mystress Moon
> We call to you this night
> To come strengthen our resolve
> And fill us with your courage.
> With your Silver Light.
> We are your Maidens, Selene

Oh, Lady of the Shining Orb
Lady of the Wild, Untamed Lands
Virgin Queen, Mystress of the Hunt,
Protectress of Women and Children
Lady of Mountains and Woods
Lady of the Silver Sea
Hold us in your love.

On this special night
Bless your Amazons
We who ride out for you
We who storm the battlements
And bring the unworthy to justice.
We who hunt in your name
Protect our Warrior Queen Orythia
Protect me, your daughter Antiope
As we meet your enemy.

Protect the lands of the Moon
Protect the lands of Amasia
Protect us all, Lady Selene."

OUR HEARTS swell with love and adoration for Selene. Her Light floods our bodies, our horses dancing on tiptoes in the surf, excited by the prayer, excited by the strength of feeling that is arising amongst us. These horses are so sensitive to energy and to the touch of their women, bonded as we are, woman and horse, horse and woman. From the earliest days we make a commitment to the mare or stallion who will partner us. We become one, with no separation. Sometimes a horse will fall in battle and another will be needed to take her place and the process of connection must be made anew, but many horses and women are lifetime companions, for as warriors our lives may be shortened, until we return *again. Sometimes the Amazon may die and the horse live, but grief will shorten a horse's life.*

TONIGHT *we are excited as we watch Selene's rising orb, for the portents tell us that danger is on its way to us, and we are feisty women, always ready for a worthy fight. The smoke of the fires has been read by the Sybils. The Oracle has spoken and we know that some of us will not return home from the coming battle. But tonight we are held in our love for Selene and our love for each other.*

I love my Queen Orythia, who wears her girdle with such pride. She is so brave, her face now lit by the moon, light shimmering in Her dark hair. In profile she is like an animal, alert and watchful. As she feels the touch of my love, she turns to us, her sisters, and smiles. She smiles at me, and I am so happy. I feel her love for me. I know that we are all equal in our Amazon band, but I know that she and I have a sacred connection that extends through time and space, that extends through lives. I may not return on the morrow and neither might she, but our love for each other will continue through all adversity, through death and the great beyond.

I know that I have known her before in other lives. We were Amazons together, in another place further down the Euxine shores. We were together further back in the ancient Motherlands of Anatolia, before the onslaught of the warrior Gods. We lived in our mother families in times when there was no necessity for arms, no necessity to protect with violence those whom we loved. But the incoming horse masters of the steppes changed our peoples' lives and we have had to adapt. It is all there told in the stories by our evening fires, of the time before the Great Fall.

I wonder in these moments however this life ends, when new life comes again, will we recognise each other once more? Will we come back to this family, to this Amazon gathering? Will we come back together in our love for the Moon, for Selene, or for another of Her beautiful faces, in another time, another land, one when perhaps I am Queen and she is a daughter, a sister? As we change our relationship that we might learn from our experiences, how will we recognise each other? Will it be through a look, a smile, a glance of such depth that our souls touch, and we just know the truth of our relationship of love?

Some people see all with the inner eye. They see the scenes that enfold them and their loved ones, as they are lived out. Others like me, just have a knowing, at first uncertain, but then growing as synchronicities pile up, one on top of another, until the truth of our soul's connection can no longer be denied.

We, the women and our horses, begin to move again, first trotting through the surf and then rising to a canter along the sandy seashore. Then our pace quickens and soon we are galloping, whooping in delight, holding on to our horses' manes, shrieking, a howling band of Amazons, readying ourselves for the coming night and the next dawn's raid."

The following weekend I am running another *10 Hours – Exploring the Mountains of Avalon*. After introductions the journey begins, travelling gradually into the deeper layers of consciousness. We arrive on the Isle of Avalon and after securing our provisions, we make our way into the Field of the Ancestors. There I meet my beautiful soul sister Koko and I talk with her. I am so glad that I knew her in the flesh again. I wish that I had recognised our connection earlier and known for longer that she truly was my soul sister, my friend.

I feel deep gratitude towards my mother, my father, my grandmothers, for providing the perfect conditions for my remembering of who I am. I reach along the Motherline, through the eons of patriarchy, into the far past and the ancient Motherworld, when we all knew that we are children of the earth and we honoured you, our Mother Earth. This was a time of love and support and mutuality between women and men and children. This was important for survival and the future of a world, where nature was untamed and there were dangerous animals, diseases and accidents which could strike and kill more easily.

A river flows towards us along our incarnational lines from those times, as a ReSource of comfort and love and support. This river flows through the 5000 years and more of patriarchal wounding, a river of love and compassion, flowing into the present from the far past, bringing compassion for us in our difficulties now. The river is always here, but often unnoticed. As we open to the memory of Motherworld, so more love flows into now. Looking at the mess of the last couple of years I pray that the River of Love flows into and out of all the people involved and into my own awareness, healing my wounds, my resistances, my sadness, my reactions, my fears. All the fears that I carry, Lady, I pray that I will release these fears and pain, to heal them deeply and completely with no pretence. I pray for healing in an authentic, real, beautiful and loving way.

> *Grant me courage, ancestors, to meet these wounds and places of pain, and to see them from the deep perspective. I am a soul incarnate from those ancient times. I am come again to heal the past and remake the future. Bless me, Lady. Bless my journey. Bless my life. Bless everyone I know. Bless Mike, Iona, Torky. May their lives be filled with love and joy. Bless all priestesses who make/renew their dedication to you. Bless all who are awakening to you. Bless all who are asleep. Bless all that I have wounded. Bless all who have wounded me. Fill them with your love always.*

WHEN WE JOURNEY up into the Mountains to the Peak Sanctuary the Lady gives me a gift, a sparkling ball of light to place in my belly that can radiate light outwards, filling my body with loving light. My heart is filled already, but my belly needs this light, this radiance moving outwards, melting armour, calming, soothing others. Oh my Beloved Lady, how I love you and thank you for everything that you give to me. I am so grateful.

The day goes by so quickly, so fast. It should be 2 days at least. We need to stay longer in each place.

Oh my beloved lady, how may I serve you better? I pray to become more loving, less centred in myself, more aware of others.

At the end of the journey we have a final sharing. Nearly everyone has had deep experiences. One person is very displeased with the day and becomes angry.

"*Fucking Cunt! Who do you think you are? The high fucking priestess? You didn't want to listen to me because I didn't go along with the nonsense. Charging £50 for a day like this!*"

She becomes violent to other participants. We are all so wide open and vulnerable and then – Wack! Everything in my body reverberates with shock, as it does in everyone else in the room. It is interesting for me that in my journey to the Peak Sanctuary the Lady gave me the ball of radiant light to place in my solar plexus. Although I am shocked none of her accusations enter my solar plexus. I don't feel any personal reaction to what she is saying, she attacks repeatedly along many different tracks, a hungry ghost looking for a way in, to feed upon any fears, failings and insecurities. Something has definitely changed in me. Thanks to the process of the last year those cracks are now mended, healed and sealed.

The police are called and later find the woman in the High Street and talk to her. I understand that she acted as the extreme shadow expression of the group, saying things out loud, thoughts that might have passed through other people's minds at some point during the day, as we went on our inner journey of self-discovery. Some days later she sends a letter of apology for her behaviour.

THE FOLLOWING weekend is the final weekend of my Soul Healing course. As part of their practice I receive a healing from Agi. She says that she has removed lots of anger.

"*What anger?*" I say, in all innocence. It is still hard for me to find it within. As we are talking I begin to notice my feelings of anger towards a few individuals that have been just sitting there, hidden inside of me.

This weekend all my family are away, even the dog is staying with friends so that I can teach. I am here alone, my family shield is dispersed. I turn my anger to my own silly mind and its fears. I am fed up with feeling afraid of the unknown attacker. I just can't be bothered to do the whole routine of my mind games, to run through the endless pattern of fear. Actually this has changed since I retrieved the memory of the last incarnation in France. The pattern presents itself once again. It has been triggered by everything that has happened in the last year or so. It is the pattern I want to heal completely. The loyal soldier speaks in my mind,

"But once you let go of fear, then it will happen. You will be attacked. I am here to protect you. You must be vigilant and ready to defend yourself from all and any attacks!"

And I think about a woman who has hurt me.
>*Who are you that I place upon you my fear*
>*What role do you play in the unfolding of memory?*
>*For you must remind me of someone in this life*
>*Or of yourself in another time.*
>*Who is it, who flattered me and bought me gifts*
>*While undermining me behind my back?*
>*Building your powerbase among those who are disempowered*
>*Among those who look to you for sympathy*
>*Within their own places of fear?*
>*For you do not empower, but need others with you*
>*Muttering behind their hands*
>*Staying small so that you can be big*
>*Where did this begin for this is an old repetition?*
>*What did I do to you?*

IN THE FOLLOWING days I descend into a cauldron of despair and depression. I am on my own here. I am down amongst the stalks of the plants in the murky pond, searching through, hoping to find treasure. This descending is almost overwhelming, but I can see glimpses of golden light at the edges like I am plunging in the darkness of Her cauldron, but am not fully immersed.

I talk with Sue about forgiving all who attacked and hurt me. She says that there is something I have to forgive in myself. Is it that in the far past I took someone into our Temple who was not dedicated in the same way as I was/as we were? Did I make compromises that led to the downfall of Her Temple? Did I make compromises to keep things going, to make sure things happened? And this led to failure, to collapse? I don't know.

I HAVE A DREAM that Mike and I are in a harbour, waiting to get on a small cruise ship to go on holiday. The entrance is in the bow of the boat, like a ferry, but waves are crashing and the boat is rising and falling in the water. We see someone wading through water to climb aboard the boat, getting their legs wet as the surf crashes. The waves are getting bigger and bigger. We roll up our leggings and trouser legs, and then a big wave comes and swamps the boat, which is already full of people. Water rises along the sides of the boat and over the top. The boat sinks beneath the waves and disappears from view with all the people on it. Where is it?

The sea crashes and roars, and then calms. The boat slowly rises from beneath the waves as the seas sink back down. People crowd out onto the decks. Some are injured. The cruise will not be happening now. Are the people alright? What will happen? Will we get a refund of our money? Will we be able to get a holiday in the next two weeks? Then the sea calms right down and becomes flat like a millpond. I wonder how such a storm can have erupted so quickly, so that people got damaged, and once again all is calm.

I HAVE A great time at 5 Rhythms dancing the Shadow of Lyrical. Light, fluffy, out of the body, instead of, in the body, embodied in the unified field. It's a rhythm that I don't like. I don't like the music that goes with it much either. I wonder why. Often after Chaos my legs give out for a while and I sit down to recover, and kind of step out of the group into my little world. It was good to notice that. During the dance, in my mind's eye I see a black corner, which I extend into 3-D, then see that it is the corner of a glass case and in the case is a stuffed Wild Cat. It reminds me of stuffed wild cats we saw in glass cases years ago when Mike and I stayed near Loch Lomond in a very strange B & B, where someone walked around in the middle of the night. The feeling there was of loneliness, sadness, madness, grief.

So inside my glass box is a Wild Cat. As I dance my wild cat comes alive, snarling, hissing, baring her fangs. Wild, frightened, angry, claws out, ready to scratch anyone who comes near. It feels good to dance her and then go into what is the best I want to feel in my body, which is peace in my heart toward the abusers. I want to be released from thinking about them and projecting onto them.

Walking back home I realise that the Wild Cat is me, because that cat is in my consciousness. She is Wild Kat, Wild Kathy. She is the younger Wild Katie. The wild young girl child fighting in me, boxed up in rage in a glass cage, hurt, betrayed, defensive, angry, fighting anyone who comes near. Now she is liberated to express herself, and all her wounds.

I AM TRYING to understand the nature of the Shadow. I have just read Robert Johnson's book written long ago about the Shadow. Based in the Jungian model he suggests that the shadow – what is hidden, is always equal in size to the ego – what is in the light. It seems like a neat, but untrue equation.

I question the perceived wisdom about the Shadow. Is the Shadow in woman the same as the Shadow in man? There are so many unquestioned assumptions that are applied to women and our psychology from the pathologies of men. I have a sense that in this as in many other areas we, women and men, might be different. That Shadow in women which is built upon the wounding that comes from living in a misogynistic, woman-hating, patriarchal society that denies the talents and gifts of womankind, is different to the Shadow in men that comes from living in world where men are the main perpetrators of the wounding to themselves, each other and to women.

Robert says that accidents are an explosion of repressed Shadow material that has not been properly recognised/ritualised and integrated. I am thinking about my accidents in the last couple of years, where shadow material erupted suddenly and unexpectedly. He talks about holding paradox, a process that leads to revelation – holding the opposites, such as wanting to talk to someone/not wanting to talk to them. Deciding to talk to them/deciding not to talk to them, the place of holding both which is excruciating. I don't want to place my shadow projections upon anyone. I want to understand and allow the conflict to just be. I do not want to make anyone all bad.

I have a realisation that all this time I have not been asking the right question, or rather finding the right statement. I have been repeatedly thinking about what happened, thinking of all the things I want to say about what happened, all the details of *"I did this, but you did that,"* etc. Trying to work out how to forgive those who wounded me so deeply. How to forgive the unforgiveable and not being able to find the way through that.

People say I should repeat Ho'oponopono, the Hawaiian practice of forgiveness until it works: *"I am sorry. Please forgive me, I love you. Thank you."*

But this practice has not attracted me because in my reality abuse has been heaped upon my head, rather than me abusing others. I do not feel able to say sorry, until I feel I am sorry. When I feel sorry, I have no problem saying *"Sorry"*, but I have to feel it first. I have to know it in my body. I know that I am missing the point of the practice.

Now I understand a new way through the confusion of my feelings, that comes from a different tangent. It is completely unexpected and I always like that. I want to feel peace in my heart towards all those who have attacked and abused me. I want my heart to be peaceful for itself and to have a peaceful radiance for others. I felt this on Monday in the dance. My desire for myself, for my greatest good, is peace in my heart, like the feeling of peace that comes over me when I go to Iona, where peace vibrates in the land of Ioua.

IN WHAT FEELS to me like a great act of personal courage, (why is it so difficult, my fearful projection so strong?) on Tuesday I telephone one of my aggressors to ask to meet with her, but she does not answer her phone. I relax. It's almost like the very act of picking up the telephone, of daring to face my fear of meeting my projection, is enough of itself. Although I know I still need to meet and talk with her. The next afternoon I telephone her again and this time arrange to go to her house in three-quarters of an hour – not much time to worry or change my mind.

We sit in her sitting room facing each other and I tell her what happened for me in Monday's dance class and why am there – to be at peace with her. She talks about how she feels too. I am loath at this time to go anywhere near the difficult material of, 'You did this, I did that.' That is not the purpose of my being there. She understands. It is good. There is no hostility between us. There is sadness and a little discomfort, but I feel peaceful. I try to stay owning my feelings as mine. I name the consequences for me of what happened – that I have been attacked and abused over many months on the internet, by people whom I have taught, cared for, held in my loving embrace, and also by many that I do not know as more than acquaintances and by some I have never met. It has been a very painful time. I have been betrayed by women who were my sisters, and that has hurt me.

Many good things have also come out of that time. I am stronger. The Goddess Temple is stronger. We are all stronger. The implosion within the Goddess community has meant that the people who needed to find their own way out into the world have gone and those who stayed together are now a really supportive, caring group of people. We are looking after our Temple and we are looking after each other. Our conversation ends in a harmonious place and now hopefully we will slowly, slowly come back to an easier place.

I READ THAT Marion Zimmer Bradley, the author of 'The Mists of Avalon', has been publicly accused by her daughter, Moira Greyland, of child physical, emotional and sexual abuse against her. Marion Bradley died in 1999 and this news is very shocking for all those who have enjoyed her novels in the science fiction and magical reality genres, and especially those drawn to Avalon. 'The Mists of Avalon' has sold millions of copies worldwide. It describes the fictional lives of female characters within Arthurian literature and has inspired tens of thousands of people, mostly women, to travel to Glastonbury in search of living present day Priestesses of Avalon.

The vision of priestesses presented in 'The Mists of Avalon' helped inspire the idea of women and men becoming Priestesses and Priests of Avalon, in modern day Glastonbury. It was not the main reason for the creation of the Priestess of Avalon Training. This began with my personal desire to teach what I knew about

Goddess, about Avalon, about becoming Priestesses and in this day, Priests of Goddess, and about the deep processes of healing and transformation that can take place here. My desire is to change the world, to return Goddess to the centre of our societies and cultures, to return Goddess to the centre of our spiritual awareness, especially here in Glastonbury Avalon.

I also know that it is the desire of many to serve Goddess in Avalon as Her priestesses and priests. She is calling many of us to return here once again to learn about Her. We have been Her priestesses before and we are becoming her priestesses and priests again. Our Priestess of Avalon Training was created without any knowledge of Marion Bradley's personal life, emotions, thoughts or wounding. But many questions are raised by this disturbing allegation:

How can an inspiration that is so meaningful to so many, come from a woman who is so deeply flawed?

Should the works of such flawed writers be destroyed, reviled, ignored?

Do these emerging awful facts destroy the inspiring ideas that this deeply wounded woman wrote about?

Should millions of people who have read, enjoyed and been inspired by her writing, feel guilty by association with her?

Should her books now be destroyed or not recommended by us?

There are lots of questions to think about and debate.

ALTHOUGH Marion Bradley wrote about priestesses who lived in Avalon, the names *'Avalon'* and *'Isle of Avalon'*, and the titles *'Priestess'*, *'Priestess of the Goddess'* and *'Priestess of Avalon'* do not belong to her, or to any one person or any one tradition. One of the first times it was recorded that the Isle of Avalon was associated with Glastonbury, was in the 12th Century when the monks of Glastonbury Abbey claimed this as a fact. It is said that this was a publicity stunt by the monks, but it holds deeper echoes of truth.

CHILD PHYSICAL, emotional and sexual abuse is such a terrible transgression of our duty as adults to care for our children, who are the future. It is a deep sickness and inter-generational wound that rampages through patriarchal cultures. Men and women often become abusive to their children and families, when they themselves have been abused as children and young people. This abuse can continue through the generations, from father to son, grandfather to granddaughter, mother to child. This terrible abuse is now becoming revealed as victims find the confidence to speak up and are heard. All accusations by victims against abusers must be met with justice and compassion for all involved.

There are some who find refuge with us who have suffered abuse in their lives, as children and as adults, who are making their healing journey with Goddess. They take part in our trainings, and participate in the life of the Temple. We do our best to help such victims heal themselves, to bring justice to perpetrators and to have the courage to be the ones who end the repetition of abuse within their family lines.

Chapter Twenty Five

THE CRONE

E ARE PREPARING for the 2014 Goddess Conference celebrating the Crone Goddess. A memory arises in sympathy with my thoughts about Crone Nolava, the Death Goddess.

On the Isle of the Dead
Our home village of Brude sits upon the waters of the Lake of Mists not far from the Sacred Isle of Avalon. Brude is a small lake village, one of several to be found scattered across the large expanse of the inland sea. It is raised above the tidal waters on wooden stilts, laid over with brushwood, clay and rubble. It is connected in one part by a long narrow wooden trackway through the marshes to the sacred isle. Most of our travelling is done by small boat or barge, but sometimes we need to be able to get to the isle on foot and back again for sleeping, for no-one lives on the Sacred Isle. It is a temenos, a sacred enclosure, set aside for the souls of the dead to make their transitions. We, the priestess families of Brude, are soul midwives for the dying and those who have passed beyond life into Avalon.
On Brude there are twenty or so hearths, sometime swelling to thirty at the special seasons of the year. Each mother family has its own hearth and sleeping platforms, enclosed by walls of daub and wattle, with hazel and willow roofs to keep out the cold and rain. When the mud walls crumble as they can do after a harsh winter, we rebuild on top of the old hearths and so some homes lie higher

than others. We are all higgledy-piggledy, which suits us. The ancestral families who have served longest have the higher platforms and the better views, but we are also subject to more of the winds and rains.

Plants cling in profusion to the edges of our island. In springtime there are grasses and water irises, in summer tall reeds, bulrushes, and marsh marigolds. We are enclosed on one side by willow trees which love the pull of the tides. They dip their toes into the shallow fertile waters which are continually replenished by the streams and rivers that flow down from the northern ridges. These waters bring rich silt full of minerals down from the hills on which many plants and water creatures feed. The lake teems with fish and fowl and our diet is rich and plentiful. We also receive many gifts of food from the families who come every few days to partake of our services.

The Sacred Isle of Avalon with the outline of the high green Tor and the softer rounder Womb, both clothed with trees, dominate our view from this southern side of the island. Some days these familiar shapes are perfectly reflected in the mirror waters of the lake, still and calm. Other days the surface is ruffled as the breeze blows, as clouds scud across the Summerland skies, whipping up into waves in the southwesterly winds.

Today the tall wooden platform towers on top of the Tor are starkly silhouetted against a darkening sky, as grey clouds build from the west. It is on these platforms that the bodies of the dead are laid out in feast for Her ravens, hawks and vultures. Once the shroud is removed and the body uncovered, the carrion feeders swoop down and quickly pick away the flesh, cracking into the soft interiors of body and bone, heart and skull, cleaning each corpse of its flesh, until only the skeleton remains.

We are a village of ancestral priestesses and priests set apart for this sacred work, which has been handed down to us through many generations of matrilineal descent – grandmother to mother to daughter, sister to brother. Our priests are the ferrymen who steer the barges from the mainland through the mists to this Western Isle of the Dead. They carry the earthly bodies of those who are leaving this world across the Isle to the Death Lodge, and later in the correct *timing, on up to the top of the Tor, where they are laid out on the platforms.*

It is our work as Soul Priestesses of Avalon to accompany the dying and dead across the Lake and onto the Isle, to perform the ceremonies for their souls, helping them to make their final transitions, caring for their bodies and spirits as they meet death. We journey with them between the worlds, passing through the Veil to Avalon accompanying them on their return to the Lady, for none here dies alone.

My sister priestesses *and I are seated in the prow of the Barge of Avalon as it moves across the Lake towards the mainland. They are Enaj and Nire, and I am Nyrhtak. We are travelling to meet two souls who will be coming with us to the Isle of the Dead. As we reach the shores of the mainland we can see the processions of those who accompany the dying. There are two groups of people waiting, one larger, one small, each carrying a body on a pallet. It makes no difference to us how many come with the dying or the dead. We are here to be with the souls of the dead, although our empathy is also always with those who grieve.*

The smaller group accompany an old man called Jaran, in his sixtieth year. He passed away more than three days ago. His body is shrouded in a woven cloth of many colours. He was an elder in his clan, who know the importance of bringing him home to Avalon. His people have travelled with him for many miles, night and day, and his body is stiffening and softening into the familiar folds of death. His soul and its counterpart still cling to the corpse as if waiting until they have arrived at the Sacred Isle, to finally let go. This is common among those who know Avalon.

The larger group are crowded around a young woman, Elira, whose body has been irreparably damaged as she fell from a cliff edge, while she hunted for bird's eggs. Her body is broken without hope of repair, but she is still alive, just. Her family are with her and in such despair. Elira is a young woman, so full of promise, now snatched away by fate. Who can say what future this tragedy will weave into the lives of her family?

Enaj, the elder priestess, goes to accompany Jaran, and talks softly to his friends, who soon lift his body onto the centre platform of the barge, making it secure against the rise and fall of the boat as it crosses the lake. Enaj lights incense in the small clay pot and with the great feather fan she begins to cleanse the body. When the cleansing is complete she lights the great lamp and sits beside the body, holding Jaran's softened hand in hers. Beneath her breath she begins to chant the prayers for the dead.

Nire and I have moved to be with Elira and her family. She lies unconscious on a small pallet, her breath thready, but we know that she is still aware of the presence of her family. Surrounded by flowers her body is broken, the wounds bathed and covered in soft cloths. They have taken care of her as well as they are able. Elira hovers above her body in misty form, visible to the inner eye, still present, yet now out of pain. She can hear what is being said and we ask the family and friends to say their last words to her, to tell her how much they love her, how much she means to them, and to say goodbye. It will not be long.

Each person comes and speaks softly to her dying body, giving her their gifts of love and tokens of their affection — a rose, some herbs, a precious stone, a necklace, red ochre, a pot of honey. Her mother weeps as she kisses her daughter's face, and her father, a tall man with gold hair, rubs at his face as he bends to kiss her brow. These are such sad scenes of loss, which we witness many times. It is good that these tears of grief are shed, for they form the river on which the soul can ride more easily to the Otherworld.

It takes some time for the family to let go of their beloved daughter. Nire and I stand a short distance from the head and foot of the body. We have already begun to speak the prayers for the dying beneath our breath, to vision Elira's soul lifting out from her body, easily and gently, so that it might merge and become one with Goddess when the moment is right. Her body is lifted onto the barge, lying on its small pallet, just before Jarad. They are soul mates this day.

I take the incense and the feather fan and cleanse her body in great sweeping strokes, helping Elira to further release her hold on her body. She sighs and I know that her time is near. Nire and I sit on either side of her, hand holding *hand, touching gently, so there is no holding, no sticking to the physical, only the touch of deep care and compassion. We continue our prayers and the envisioning of Elira's release and return to the Lady.*

As the Barge moves out across the waters towards Avalon a huge wave of grief engulfs the people remaining on the shore, a great wailing, a keening arises from Elira's family that fills the air, echoing across the waters so that the lake birds are silenced by sorrow. As she hears the sound Elira moves just a little, enough to show she has heard. The breaking of the threads of physical contact can be so hard, like the snapping of the Thread of Life itself.

Tonight the wind is blowing and the Barge rocks as it moves across the water but we follow the usual practice. We begin to chant softly at first and then more strongly,

"Maiden, Lover, Mother, Crone
  Lady of Avalon, carry us home"

AS WE SING *well-known words in the secret language the wind dies down, the waves gradually subside and the surface of the lake becomes calm. This too is visible to people on the shore and the keening lessens as the sweet energy of the Lady radiates across the waters towards them. Enaj moves back to be closer to Jaran as Nire goes to stand in the prow of the Barge. Facing the Sacred Isle to the north she takes her wand in her hand and holds her arms out on either side of her body. She speaks the ancient words of power in the secret language, raising her arms upwards.*

"Lady of Avalon, Nolava,
  White Lady of the Lake of Mists,
  I call your mists to me."

AS SHE RAISES *her arms upwards strands of mist rise from the surface of the lake, swiftly weaving upwards, becoming more and more dense. Soon the Barge of Avalon and all its occupants are surrounded by damp cool violet white mist. Standing on the mainland the families and friends see the Barge disappearing* into the mist and once again a great wail of grief arises that echoes across the waters, taking minutes to subside as the knowledge that the bodies of their loved ones have now gone to Avalon and will not return to these physical forms again.

THE 2014 Crone Goddess Conference is awesome! In the Town Hall we create Her Temple and there we honour the Crone in ceremony and song, through performances and presentations, and workshops of many descriptions. We listen to amazing talks by Crones from within our Goddess community, who have journeyed with the Conference over many years, from artist scholar Lydia Ruyle, poet and Conference registrar Roz Bound, poet ceremonialist Rose Flint, photographer Ann Cook, international singing star Julie Felix and feminist witch Starhawk, amongst others. We hear their words of wisdom gleaned from their lives. We celebrate the Crone and Her Cauldron of Inspiration, Death and Rebirth.

Carolyn Hillyer, the gifted artist and singer/musician transforms the Assembly Rooms into *The House of Ancient Weavers*, a sacred shrine space which offers a journey into the tender, startling and mystical landscape of the Old Loom Women. The main installation, *The Loom of Ancient Weavers*, sits within the circle of Carolyn's new cycle of nine life-size paintings – The Shaman Weavers, who work around the rim of a vast bowl-shaped loom. The Ancestral Weavers of the land are WEFT – weaver of mountains; COPPER – weaver of rivers; ANTLER – weaver of forests (whose face is visible on all Conference literature); THORN – weaver of islands; DUSK – weaver of caverns; LICHEN – weaver of wild hills; SHARD – weaver of tundra; VESSEL – weaver of oceans; and BROKEN – weaver of deserts.

In addition to the main shrine the Assembly Rooms café area is transformed into the *Old Women's Weaving Room* for the duration. Through the week volunteers under the careful eye of Annabel du Boulay sew a *Death Road*, a ritual loom cloth formed from textile squares that all participants have been asked to bring in preparation for this Crone Conference.

We also have some wonderful singers/musicians – Carolyn, of course, and

Anique Radiant Heart from Australia who comes nearly every year to the Conference, Kellianna from the USA and Wendy Rule also from Australia. They are all amazing Goddess musicians who sing Her praises in their music.

In Friday's Heart of the Mysteries Ceremony, we, the Ceremonial Circle, covered in ashes and ancestral shrouds, process from the Town Hall to collect the Death Road from the Assembly Rooms. The women who have sewn the Death Road sing us a song they have composed together. We unroll the long cloth and everyone places their hands beneath it and helps carry it shoulder-high down the High Street and round the corner into the darkened Temple in the Town Hall. We lay the Death Road on the floor along the length of the Temple Hall. There is drumming, sounding and singing. The Ceremonial Circle Priestess who embodies the Crone of Death chooses all those who will die today, one by one, until all are chosen. Once a person is chosen, they symbolically rise into their light body and walk the Death Road towards Avalon, traditionally known as the Western Isle of the Dead, where they are greeted by waiting Soul Priestesses.

Once everyone has arrived in Avalon there is a sudden and transforming shimmering violet light in which a priestess embodiment of the Lady of Avalon Herself appears. It is a stunning moment of transformation. She tells us that now *is not* our moment to die. It is not yet time to let go of the material world, now is our time to return to life. In joy people walk, run, dance, skip back along the Life Road. It is a time of elation, of pure joy.

ON THE Sunday in the Thank you Circle after I have thanked everyone for everything that they have given in the Conference, Mike comes to the front of the hall and sinks down on one knee in front of me, in front of everyone. He takes my hand and asks me to marry him. I am completely surprised!

We have been together for 25 years and have talked on and off about getting married, sometimes we have been engaged and then not. We have talked recently about being the first to get married in the Goddess Temple once we are able to hold legal weddings there. Dawn Kinsella, our lovely Temple Melissa Mother, has been pursuing this avenue for some months. Mike and I have been reading and filling in pieces of paper for weeks, but now it seems like we are almost there and the Temple will soon be able to conduct legal wedding ceremonies. We have talked recently about getting married, but I said that he needs to ask me in a special way, not just sitting next to me on the sofa talking about it.

As Mike kneels in front of me, in front of everyone, and proposes, I am completely shocked, overcome and very happy. A gasp runs through the room, hands fly to mouths. This is a good proposal and something I did not expect at all in this way. Usually we can read each other's minds quite well, but the idea had only come to him an hour before, and I had been busy with other things, and had not read him.

Of course I say, "*Yes!*" That was a very good way to propose! The room erupts in happiness and laughter. Everyone still loves a good proposal of marriage, including feminists and anti-patriarchal Goddess-loving people. Romance is alive. It is wonderful and I love Mike for creating that wonderful loving moment.

THE FOLLOWING weekend Mike and I and Tork and friends go to the Glastonbury Musical Extravaganza. The evening begins with George Ezra the young man with the great voice. Then there is Robert Plant and his band who play fabulous music. He sings "*I need cooling…*", one of my favourite songs from the seventies. We dance and sing and dance and sing.

I AM TIRED after the Conference and we are not going on holiday just yet. One night I dream that one of my sister priestesses has my hand twisted up my back. It's the end stage of a ceremony in which I am supposed to be embodying the Lady for our students, but my sister has switched the lights on and revealed that it's just me in a veil. I don't understand what she is doing. She has me in a vice-like grip and I feel my bones are going to break. Suddenly I know that she has done this before. She has killed me in another life – out of competition, out of jealousy. She killed me. I am deeply shocked.

When I awaken suddenly as Mike gets up out of bed, I think I know this priestess. I am shocked by the feeling in my body, of the pressure of her strong arms holding me down. I think of her as representing a Shadow part of myself, from within my own psyche. Is she the part who is competitive, who will kill/hurt/restrict to get her own way?

BY THE END of August Mike and I are in Sardinia staying in a lovely hotel above Bitti, in the uplands. In the daytime it's very hot sitting by the unheated swimming pool, which is filled with freezing cold water, fresh from under the mountains. The views are lovely and we don't seem to miss the sea at all.

I am having ideas about healing the Goddess community Group Soul. We have been trying to approach the healing that is needed in our community on an individual level, but this does not seem to be working. I realise that there is also a collective Group Soul, which is desperately in need of healing too. We need to be working at a soul level as well as on a mind and emotional level. I think about the energetic work that I do when I am offering soul healing, which really seems to help people, and how we could do something similar for the Group Soul.

I want to talk to the Orchard Development Group about this, so that rather than working with Starhawk's manual, although we could use this as well, we really need to make people more aware of the Group Soul of which we are all a part. I reread Alice Bailey's *Esoteric Healing* to see what she says about group healing. I want to inspire people with our connection to our Goddess group soul, to the priestess group soul, which we are all a part of, from the most ancient times. I want to remind everyone that we are coming in together from an ancient lineage. In practice each person can connect to their own soul, to the priestess soul group, to Goddess, becoming aware of all the Goddess circles of which we are each a part. We can transmit healing energy from our soul spaces to ourselves, to others, to those who are part of our soul groups, including all the wounded people. Perhaps this will help solve the situation too.

✦ ✦ ✦

I HAVE a funny dream. I walk into a clothes shop in London.

The assistant is saying, *"Are you Kathy Jones?"*

I don't know the woman, but I say, *"Yes."*

She says, *"I have a present for you from a woman who is really grateful to you"*.

I've done something for the woman and she's grateful. The assistant shows me a large parcel. Inside is a small metal holder in which a large image of a standing woman is fitted. The woman has a flared skirt and a hat and is a bit of a stylish woman. She's not quite a Goddess figure, but I could see her as one. Looking around the shop I can see that there are some gorgeous embroidered long silk coats with matching trousers. I really liked one in blue, gold and silver. I try it on. It's beautiful. I ask how much it is. The tag says £384, but the assistant says that it is a gift. There is nothing to pay. I am amazed by this gift from someone that I can't really remember.

I WAKE thinking about love and that I want to be a more loving person especially to Mike, my love. I am thinking about the balance of love and clear boundaries. How can I be more loving, more conscious? I think about how to make him happy, for our wedding, but also in the everyday.

WE GO TO VISIT some of the sites of the Nuraghic culture in the interior of Sardinia. The Nuraghic culture was a strong stone-erecting culture that lasted from the late Bronze Age – 1900 BCE – to the 2nd century CE. Their characteristic monuments are big stone edifices with one, two, three or four high circular towers, which are called *nuraghe*. The remains of nearly 8,000 nuraghe have been found throughout Sardinia, which is not a large island. They also erected significant hypogea, stone circles, menhirs, betyls and Giant's Graves.

The weather is cold and windy on top of the high hill at Tamuli, where we see the remains of several Giant's Graves – like long barrows, with large entrance-blocking stones with tiny entrances, which only small people, children or fairies might crawl through. The forecourts are shaped like the horns of the cow/bull, like the original forecourt of West Kennet at Avebury, although there is only one unbranching corridor inside the grave. One of graves has three conical betyls – four foot high standing stones – on one side, which each have a pair of stone breasts protruding from the side. They are lovely to embrace. On the other side are three male betyls, without breasts and somewhat squatter than the female stones. The ancestors stand guard over the land.

We drive through beautiful landscapes of rolling hills, cork forests and scrubland to Santa Antine, where one of the most complete of the early Nuraghic Temples can still be explored. The oldest central tower was built around 1800 BCE and was about 24 metres tall. It comprised three levels, with beehive shaped rooms built one on top of the other. In later centuries this central tower was surrounded by an outer wall with three more smaller towers at three corners, creating a triangular building. Made from massive blocks of stone the top of the central tower was open to the elements and lower down on the first floor was a large opening to the south or southeast.

When we climb the big internal stone staircase to the first floor and look out through this opening we can see another nuraghe about half a mile away and an alignment towards the ridge of a mountain, over which the sun might rise at a significant moment – winter solstice? Or the moon or some special stars, that were meaningful to these people. This first floor room feels like a special sacred place. It's surrounded by an internal corridor in the walls of the tower with a couple of openings. A low bench runs around the edge of the circle, which archaeologists claim mean it was a meeting room, somewhere for the elders of the community to meet, or for the women? Although it's claimed that the nuraghic towers are defensive forts, they don't look or feel like that. Traces of red ochre were found on the seats and floors, perhaps this was the menstrual hut for the women of the community, a place where the dead waited for burial or dispersal. A line in some literature says that although the tribes had warriors and kings, the religion was probably woman-led. A short sentence that says much.

What made these people build such huge buildings so close to each other? The stones are very large and the buildings are high which requires people to work together for a common belief in something greater than themselves. No images of deities have been found from the nuraghic culture in Sardinia, apart from the betyls, and Goddess figurines that come from earlier Neolithic times.

I HAVE the idea that we should begin to teach longer Goddess Intensive Experiences for the Temple – one week, two weeks, one month, three months, nine months, so that people can really learn. That will take lots to work out and create. We will need lots of priestesses to help make it work.

WE GO for a walk up to the two breast mountains we can see from our bedroom balcony. We walk from the church outside Lula, where they are celebrating a saint's feast day. We climb the steep rocky path onto the saddle of Montalbo, which lies between Mount Caterina (Kathryn) and another mountain. We climb up between the trees to a precipitous edge and then we are on a long flat plateau area between two high white limestone mountains. Up here there are lots of trees and rocks, with flies and birds – jays, crows, buzzards calling. In the middle there is an obvious sacred tree circle but its energy feels a bit dark. We walk on along the track. There is no sound of human mechanical activity here. The silence is wonderful.

    As we sit in the stillness a faint breeze begins to blow across the mountain. Mike threw the I Ching earlier and got 'Wind over Mountain', and here we are. The environment of Her Nature has manifested before us. The hexagram was changing to Making Progress – like two birds flying, as they stay together longer, they will stay together for life.

> *And I shall write poetry of my love for my Lady*
> *For the curve of Her green gown*
> *For the fall of Her waters*
> *For the colours of Her earth skin*
> *For the swell of her bosom*
> *For the wetness of Her cleft*
> *I shall sing praises for Her beauty*

For the breath of Her air
As my heart swells in love for Her
As tears rise to my eyes
And drop over the rim of the fall
Rivulets flowing across the soft ground
Of Her beautiful body, into a stream
Descending a torrent, a force full of life
Of sorrow, of joy.
Crone of Tears, my beloved
I thank you for all that you have shown me
Slow-witted, dullard that I am
I have not appreciated
The Grace that you give me
Tears of Love, Tears of Compassion
For all those I love
Grace above me
Grace below me
Grace around me,
Grace within me
Your Grace, Lady, always
Your Grace.

Chapter Twenty Six

OUR WEDDING

ON OUR RETURN HOME from holiday there is another round of personal public attacks on me and on the Temple. Another open letter is sent out on Facebook, which is a revelation of feeling, of distress, of hurt, of disillusionment. It is based again in miscommunication. Those who tell an untruth to save their own skins, who cannot say, "*I did this. I made a mistake. I was confused*", open the door to a public firestorm. I am so tired of being attacked, blamed, resented. I can't resolve things. I don't want to think about it all anymore.

I AM IN a state of confusion. Mike and I are getting married in October. On Thursday we go to the Registry Office to sign some papers of intent. I notice that I have some resistance to the whole arrangement of the marriage. I am nervous, tense. I realise that it must come from the wound of my first short marriage to my children's father, which went wrong so quickly. In one moment I feel fine and then the next I'm not. I worry about what to wear, what do I want to look like at this age of 67? I feel mad, depressed, happy, elated. My emotions swing back and forth.

Today I ask a young dressmaker I have never met before to make me a dark red wedding dress. I am trusting her and giving her a chance to shine. It feels fine and bonkers. I can't settle to anything. I don't want to work. I want to stay on holiday. I feel confused by the weight of the first failed marriage, a weight that needs healing and letting go.

It is early October and I am in Portugal to offer a Goddess workshop near Sintra, west of Lisbon. Luiza Frazao, our Portuguese priestess, has invited me there to teach at Senhora D'Azenha, Centro de Artes e Ofícios do Mundo. The centre is organised by a wonderful young woman called Iris Lican and her partner, and is run by Iris, Lila Nuit, and Freya. Lieveke Volcke, one of our priestesses from Belgium, is also there.

I've never been to Portugal before and the language is new to my ears. It sounds like Eastern European mixed with Spanish, with a lot of swishing at the ends of words. This morning we walk five minutes down the road to the Atlantic Ocean, where big waves are crashing in, roaring in with force from across thousands of miles of ocean. We are waiting for a hot current, which is supposed to arrive this afternoon. The hot current does not arrive, but the sea is magnificent to be close to.

We drive a short way inland into dense forests which clothe steep hillsides. In amongst the trees are huge rounded ancestral stones. Some are many metres high. In places they cluster together and hold a magnificent energy. They feel like the places where ancestors can be called, from which they emerge at conception and to which they return at death. We climb up through the trees to a ruined ritual site, with circling stone walls and large stones. The energy is lovely there. As we walk I feel a strong connection with Luiza and Lieveke, as if we have been together before in this place, as young girls of the Goddess.

The next day Iris takes us through the forest to an amazing place. We walk along a narrow trackway to a high place of stones, where there are large faces of eagle and dragon carved by wind and weather and perhaps human hands, in the rocks. There is an enclosed circle where the women come in the evening to share their menstrual blood. I realise that these young women are a seriously devoted circle working together, out of their returned knowledge. It's very beautiful for me to behold.

I feel elated. I have experienced a new young generation of Goddess-inspired women here in Portugal and this makes me very happy. After all the troubles within our Goddess community I have been wondering how our work will continue when I am gone. I realise that I really don't need to worry at all. Goddess is awakening people all around the world, as She woke me. The great thing is that now young women and men are waking up to her earlier than we did, in part because of the energetic and practical gateways that we have already opened within patriarchal society.

BACK HOME in Glastonbury we hold the first Group Soul Healing meditation for the Soul Group who are connected to the Goddess Temple and the Orchard of Avalon. We have a need to recognise and nurture the Group Soul of which we are a part – all those who have incarnated to bring Goddess back into awareness again. We connect to our individual Souls, to each other and to the Group Soul in our centre. The experience is deep and powerful. When we look at the Group Soul it looks damaged and full of holes. We send in our collective love and healing energies to heal the Group Soul, to fill the gaps and smooth the energy field. It seems like a very good first step. I think of other ways in which we could work on healing the Group Soul, working in the same ways that I would work in an individual healing.

OUR WEDDING comes closer. My pre-wedding anxieties are expressed in the dress which is being made, which ends up costing hundreds of pounds, but is awful. It is not a special dress, it's badly made and generally, *"A disaster, darling!"* The young dressmaker has failed me completely. In the cupboard I find a dark red/purple dress that I wore at the Goddess Conference a few years ago. I'm hoping Mike won't recognise it. The idea is that I am in red and Mike is in white, the proper way round for Goddess wedding colours.

I go back and forth to Rosie Rose's house where she is making a red feather headdress with veiling for me. She is finding it hard to make as she broke her elbow recently and can't move her arm properly. I also bought red shoes which don't quite match the new colours. My wedding anxiety is being acted out. Iona gets a really bad cold and cough with flu symptoms and is really ill, suffering from great anxiety. She is shaking with fear and has begun to act it out with me. We are a mess.

On Monday we decorate the Goddess Temple in red and white. We open out the Morgen circle so that we can have a table there and chairs for the Registrar to sit. On Tuesday we decorate the Goddess Hall, where the reception will be held, also in red and white. It all looks beautiful.

On Wednesday my son Torquil and his girlfriend Lahla arrive from London. In the afternoon we hold Elemental Blessing Ceremonies in the landscape with everyone who is able to come. We have asked priestesses to lead four different ceremonies for us in the special places of Avalon. We arrange to meet everyone beside the Rural Life Museum, so that we can walk up Chalice Hill to the Air Ceremony. We gather beside the roundabout – Erin & Duncan, Katinka, Sally, Sophie, Lydia, Tork & Lahla, Luiza, Louise & Paul, Sharlea & Chris, Sue, Dawn, Angie & Rod, and Amber. On the way to meet us, Iona who is walking with Leigh, steps out into the road and twists her ankle. She can barely walk. Already feeling ill from the flu she has to turn round and go home. She is completely upset.

We climb the slopes of Chalice Hill walking through the gate towards the beautiful stand of beech trees where Michelle, Amanda and Heloise are waiting for us. They smudge us and call to Nolava of Air. As they do so the wind blows and gusts all around us. Each one of them says lovely loving words of blessing to us. My tears are rising. We walk down the other side of Chalice Hill to the top gate, which we must climb over. We have to lift Sally over the gate with her broken arm. We walk along Bulwarks Lane to one of the fields beside the Morgen Orchard. It is a lovely green and secluded spot surrounded by trees, where a Fire Bowl is waiting in preparation for the Fire Ceremony. Nolava of Fire is welcomed by Maiden Gabi, Mother Sophie and Crone Sally, and the fire is lit. We give away to the fire all that no longer serves us or Her. Each priestess speaks her words of love for us. It is very moving and we really feel their love and friendship for us. There are more tears. The blessing of the fire of love is given to everyone. We all feel very blessed and blissed out.

We walk back along Bulwarks Lane to the dark cave building which houses the White Spring. This sacred space is held by Katinka and Angie. Illuminated by candles the water twinkling in the dark central pool looks so inviting and because we are warm from walking I want to get into the pool. Mike and I strip off and climb into the round pool. It is beautiful and cold on the legs, but not deep. Holding each other in the centre of the pool our bodies warm where our skin touches, we sink down to kneel in the soft White Water. Ahhh! Ice cold on my vulva, Mike's member shrinks, but it's exhilarating. Then up again as everyone sings to us. We hop out of the water and dry off on the towels which Katinka has brought. The waters are blessed by Katinka and Angie and we drink the Red and White Spring waters. We are blessed inside and out by the Waters of Her Love. I am so happy.

We walk up Wellhouse Lane to the top end of the Tor and make our way to the Avalon Orchard, where Marion has laid out a lovely double spiral with small stones in the grass. Everyone walks the spiral and is blessed with the element of earth. This is our wedding on the land and we have been blessed by Her air, fire, water and earth. We have felt Her spacious presence and so much love for all these lovely people who are our true friends.

Later on we go to check that all is ready in the Goddess Temple for our legal wedding day tomorrow. The circle of flowers is laid out, the archway of flowers over the entrance is there. The flowers are on the altar. Everything looks beautiful.

IT'S THURSDAY 23rd October – our legal wedding day. Mike goes to Iona's flat with Tork to get ready. Iona comes to our house but she is still ill, poor girl. Jade arrives and puts red feathers in my hair. I am still deciding what to wear. Beautiful flowers arrive from Enchanted Florals – bouquets for me and Iona and buttonholes for Mike and Tork, and red and white splashed roses for my GIRLS. My lovely sister GIRLS (Goddesses in Real Life) arrive – Sue, Erin, Katinka, Sally, Sophie, Louise, Rose, Amanda, Heloise, Dawn, Michelle and Marion, the women that I love, who will escort me to the Goddess Temple.

We have a glass of champagne and go through the ceremony. Feeling the love. I try on the dark red dress I've now chosen, with red and white faux fur shawl, and do my face. I put the dark red flower headdress in my hair, with its dark red veiling. I go downstairs and there are lots of lovely responses. Phew!

Then it's time to go in Katinka's car. Iona is still unwell, but looks lovely in a long red dress, hobbling on her sprained ankle. We carry our bouquets. They are beautiful, mine has dark red and white roses with purple flowers and ivy drifting down. Iona's is round with red and white flowers. Each of the GIRLS have red and white splashed roses.

We park in the Abbey car park and walk all together along Magdalene Street, with drumming and singing to the Glastonbury Experience. We have to wait in the tunnel while Mike goes to see the registrar in the Avalon Room, before going into the Temple. Amber comes and takes me up the inside staircase to see the Registrar. It it turns out she is a good feminist too and is training Dawn to become our official Temple Registrar. I answer the official questions and then blow out the candles and return to the tunnel. We walk up the staircase to the Temple singing. I take my shoes off and pause as I go through the flower archway into the Temple. I am very aware of the Moment.

I turn to look at my beautiful man, standing there looking gorgeous in a white suit with red tie. My heart leaps. We have chosen a piece of music for this moment, Emeli Sande's *"I'll be your River."* It says it all. I feel so emotional and happy and present. I walk towards him singing the words of the song, gazing into his eyes, loving him so much.

"I'll be your river, river. Wherever you're standing I will be by your side...."

Tears well up as I come to stand with him in the centre of the circle of flowers in this holy moment. We are both completely blissed out.

Well, if we are going to do this wedding thing, we might as well really do it. I understand that there are personal ceremonies that life is made for, which need to be held and celebrated with total surrender – these are Birth and the Welcome to Incarnation, Baby-naming, Blood Mysteries, Marriage, Death and its accompanying Funeral, as well as lots more, but these are so important to do properly.

After a fantastic two hour ceremony conducted by Dawn, Mike and I are legally married. We have a lovely reception at Goddess Hall and after the next day's delicious Wedding Brunch made by Lahla, we set off to a secluded cottage in a valley on Exmoor for our love filled Honeymoon.... After 25 years together we find that being married makes a subtle and potent difference.

Chapter Twenty Seven

THE DUCKING STOOL

IN DECEMBER there is another flare-up towards me. I make a mistake by writing on our priestess group. I am surprised by a lack of commitment by priestesses who had said they would support a sister priestess in her Goddess project, and then didn't. I want everyone to know that I feel that this kind of behaviour is not OK for us as priestesses. If we don't help and support each other out in the world, then who will? It doesn't work if we let each other down.

But I didn't communicate it in the correct way and I upset people, who felt I shamed them in front of others, which isn't what I was trying to do. I reacted too quickly from my feelings within our private group, instead of writing to individuals personally, which would have taken me too much time. And I had wanted to communicate this to the whole group as well as to the individuals. The way I did it was a mistake – moving too fast, not thinking it through. I apologise to everyone.

I begin to think about what standards of behaviour we want for ourselves as modern day priestesses. The more visible we become in the wider world, the more our behaviour has to be filled with integrity. We are a new phenomenon, a new naming. How we are seen affects not only ourselves as individuals, but also our sisters and brothers in the wider group of priestesses. It's different when a group is small, but now we are becoming much larger and more visible in the world. How do we want to be seen to be as a group of aspirational people bringing Goddess alive in the world again?

Talking with other tutors we agree that we need to set up a new contact group, which is for Orchard members who willingly sign a Code of Conduct, an agreement to behave in supportive rather than undermining ways towards each other, and towards the public.

When the Priestess Training began in 1998 it was an expression of personal devotion to Goddess and expanding knowledge of Her in the world. Through many years of experience, our understanding of what it means to be Her priestess has grown and developed. Now it is not just about personal devotion to Goddess, it is also about being part of an ever-growing and visible community of devoted priestesses and priests. It is about the relationship of a priestess to a public Goddess Temple, and to the wider public, both local and international, who want to know about Goddess, about the Lady of Avalon and Her Priestesses, and who see priestesses as role models. People on the outside have high expectations of us – who we are, who we claim to be.

I AM WATCHING the full moon roll up the side of the Tor from our back garden. I have been ill for ages with winter viruses – sore throat, cold, fever, coughing, and illness takes me to the bottom of the Underworld. I feel so bad and it goes on and on. I lie in bed in a state of weakness and sleeplessness. I am on the floor of the Underworld, surrendering at last to my frustration and weariness. Tears rise in great waves. They are tears of fear and resistance to writing about everything that has happened in the last few years. I feel I have things to say that might help others, but I can't face going back and reading all the awful emails and facebook messages.

I wonder if any of us really descends willingly to the Underworld. I don't. It has taken me 6 months and a severe dose of flu virus to get to the place where I stop resisting the inevitable plunging down further to face the pain of what happened a year or so ago. I have been putting it off for months. It was hard enough to write about what happened in the first stages but now I must face the big betrayal – betrayal by my sisters. I don't want to remember, to feel it again and yet I must in order to heal it. I want to be lifted out of this fear of wounding.

As I lie in my sickbed I contemplate all that has happened. I have been dragged down, I have fallen, been catapulted into the depths of the Underworld. Here I squirmed, resisted, was broken, felt pain, sadness, anger, guilt, despair, nothingness, dullness. I have been taken into the pit of my own darkness, into my places of ancient wounding. In time, with Her grace, I would rise for a while to the surface dragging behind me strands of jewels, glittering rocks of memory, hauling complex chains, from which gems and nuggets of truth tumble out gleaming into the light of day.

I have fought with demons of inadequacy, competition, jealousy, fear – deep fear, anxiety, shock, disbelief. I have tried to persuade, assuage these demons and after each meeting with darkness, clarity has broken through for a time. I see that I/we need to have clear boundaries. I need to own what is mine and see what is yours, not mine. I feel my way beneath the surface of emotions held in personal memories of this life and previous lives, into collective memories, into the wounding which we all carry and share in streams of cognition, of knowing that we have done these things before. As painful memories arise and I re-member them, distorted energy is freed up and released into realisation and love. It is a painful process.

It is in the middle of the night as I am coughing and failing to breathe or sleep that tears rise to my eyes and I let go, let go into dying, into the darkness of your Underworld, Lady. Of course it's so much easier when I give in. I have not given in since I came to the time in my diary when I had to meet and write of all that happened. I want to say it in my truth and not as a justification for my feelings and actions. I want to follow the threads of truth so that I can see and feel and know and heal all that must be healed in myself and in our Goddess community.

I believe that everything that has occurred is the consequence of wounding that is carried in each of us as individuals and in our community of wounded souls returned to bring Goddess back into the world. We were all there – here before at the times of the endings of the Goddess Temples and each of us carries the marks of the wounds that took place at that time – fear, betrayal, deaths, rapes, cruelty, competition, survival of the fittest, those who could survive by any means.

Perhaps I can face it. I might be able to read what was written by others and feel again my own reactive responses. Time is the key and some time has gone by.

As I cough and sniffle with pressure in my lungs, when asked how I am feeling by a concerned friend I hear myself say, *"I have been underwater."*

I SEE a bright green light shining on the water. A scene with a ducking stool begins to unfold in my memory.

The village pond is not really the pretty pond of stories, rather the edge of the pond is covered in a patina of dirty scum, and the middle is brown and impenetrable. The recent rains and the kine who daily drink here have stirred up the muddy depths, leaving brown ruts and trampled vegetation around the edges.

Beside the pond is the ducking stool, an unnatural construction created by the evil minds of torturers. I am roughly dragged, poked and prodded into place upon the stool. I struggle but my body, arms, hands and legs are tied to the chair and a rope is tied tight around my neck to keep me in place. If I move too far forward the rope cuts across my neck, so I must sit still. I will strangle myself.

I am accused as a witch, a scold, of bringing death to children in my village, who died in the hot days of summer fever. I am accused of killing cattle who succumbed to unknown diseases. The need to blame is strong, especially to blame a woman who will not hold her tongue, who does not keep quiet about the mischief she sees going on about her. Too much talking, too much truth and too many lies. I am to be ducked in the pond to see if I am a witch or no. If I survive the ducking I am a witch. If I drown it is just as well; then my harpy's voice is silenced.

The people of the village watch, the men cursing, calling me names, the women shrieking, boiling to a frenzy, whipped up by the priest and his followers. The Magistrate is puffed up in his righteousness, because my witchcraft is seen as devilish, not the helping hand of a herbalist, healer, midwife and comforter. The need to blame and castigate, to rise together in mutual attack against a woman is strong in this man-led community, as it is throughout our country. Uppity women who speak out loud, who do not stay in their place, must be threatened, chastised, silenced and put back in their place. Heaven forbid that a woman's voice might be perceived to speak truth as she knows it.

There is a sudden jolt and in a moment pole, stool and hoist are flung up and out over the murky pool. Everything in my body cries with pain against this torsion – like riding the carts at the funfair, but now the restraints cut deep. I gasp for breath as my throat is squeezed. Suspended above the pool I look down into the dark eye of the water. I can see the shadow of myself and the ducking stool reflected there, the sky bright above me. The sounds of the baying frantic crowd grow louder and then recede as for a moment I sink into the great fear of my circumstances. I do not want to die.

My breath is short and yet I know if I am to survive I must take great gulps of air to hold in my body beneath the water. I breathe as deep as I can, filling my lings with blessed air. The voice of the black flapping priest whips the crowd further into their frenzy,

"Duck the Witch! Duck the Witch!"

Down I plummet into the dark water. Feet, clothes, belly, heart, arms, head, eyes, mouth, nose squeezed tight shut, into the water. The shock of the sudden cold, the pull of the ropes holding me to the stool, tearing into my body.

"Hold your breath! Hold your breath!" goes through my mind.

Wet rank vegetation floats across my face, water bubbles forcing their way into my nose and mouth. "Hold the breath!"

Mouth closed, nose closed, lungs full of air. Pressure building. Pain comes. I hold on until the moment I cannot hold any more and water seeps in. The ducking stool suddenly jolts and I am flying up into the air. Coughing I gasp for breath, clawing at the air. Around the pool the people clap and cheer like they are on a day at the seaside applauding a Punch and Judy show. Light sparkles in the sprays of water. Green slime covers my eyes and I have no free hand to remove it. Now I am muddied and dripping water.

Clunk! Down I go again into the watery depths. Not enough time to take a deep breath and I know that this time they will leave me longer in the water. Panic enters my whole body. I am in terror. My body writhes and pulls against its restraints, yet nothing moves. I cannot stop this hideous act. The water enters my lungs. It hurts so much – water, mud and bright green strands. My eyes are open looking desperately through the murky depths. Shall this be my death? A shaft of sunlight shimmers through the gloom and then is gone in a moment as mud flows back in.

Then up and out again. I cough up the dirty water, retching, gasping for breath. Pain floods through my body in great waves of wretchedness. Then over and over, up and down, up and down. I lose control of my breath, of life, of the desire to live. I step out of my body as it becomes too much to abide. I leave the pain behind and find myself viewing the scene from above. Below the swaying crowd are clapping as they watch my body, collapsed upon the stool, cord cutting into my throat – a clever trick to make the breathing even more difficult, to make survival impossible, for that is the mission in the torturer's mind.

The stool hovers above the pond and as my lungs feebly attempt to breathe I shoot back into my pain-wracked body. "Oh, let me go! Let me go!"

My body flinches and the crowd gasps,

"The witch survives! Kill the witch! Kill the witch!"

The chant rises through the summer air. This will be the final ducking. Time slows down. I look at the eye of the pond. This time Her eye is friendly, dark and welcoming. The stool, now become a stately carriage drawn by white horses, moves slowly down into the water. Splash, the refreshing spray of water, now clear and sparkling in the sunlight. Fresh water that washes away all sadness, all omissions, all regrets. I am riding a wave like a salmon in the river. I am going home, swimming through the death current. I am going home to my beloved.

Resistance is gone. I come to meet you, my Lady, Queen of my heart. Bless those who torture me. Bless them with love. Bless them with the understanding of what they have done. Bless all those I love. Now I am free, rising out of my poor shattered body into Her bliss. I rise again above the pond, rainbow lights *shining through the water spray. I see the ducking stool sunk into the pond. They will leave it there until they are sure I am gone.*

For I am a witch! That is what they are afraid of – that the powers She gave me will be used for good.

IT IS IMBOLC, the green spears of Maiden Brighde's snowdrops pierce their way through the frozen earth, their delicate white and green flowers unfolding gently – the first stirrings of colour and green beauty. I have not really thought about the troubles for more than eight months. I have not wanted to think about what happened between us. I wanted to just forget about it all, to be happy with my love, with my family and my friends. I cut off from all the horrible things that have happened in the last few years, as everything that we tried to do to make it different just didn't work and only seemed to create more antipathy.

KATINKA and I talk about approaching those who were once within the Orchard community, who have had any kinds of problems with us, with the Temple. We plan to meet them, one by one, taking time to hear each one, speaking our truth, clearing up misunderstandings, trying to reconcile and make things better. Our first attempt to approach the disaffected, trying to heal the situation, is a complete failure and only draws out more poison, as we are misunderstood.

LATER in February is the time of our four day Orchard of Avalon Gathering. Lots of priestesses, sisters and brothers of Avalon from Britain and all over the world are present. Thitis's clouds are scudding quickly across the sky, racing from west to east. We have a lovely Gathering with some excellent discussions about how the Orchard can move forward. We have unanimous support by those present and some proxy votes for three main proposals for the future of the Orchard of Avalon, which are offered by the Orchard Development group, who have been meeting for over a year to talk about ideas for the future of the Orchard, our community of priestesses, sisters and brothers of Avalon.

After long discussions we agree three proposals.

To open the Orchard to Priestesses of Rhiannon and Priestesses of Brighde, who successfully dedicate themselves to Goddess within the Goddess Temple Trainings. We are all the fruits in Her Orchard of Avalon.

All those who complete the First Spiral in any Training are asked to sign the relevant Training Code of Conduct in order to successfully dedicate as priestesses, sisters, brothers and daughters.

Finally the old Orchard of Avalon Yahoo group is to be closed and a new Orchard of Avalon Facebook group is to be opened. This group is for those people who sign a Code of Conduct, and who agree to express supportive and loving behaviour towards each other. This does not mean that we cannot disagree, as we do sometimes, but it's about how we disagree. We can always be respectful, loving and caring.

ON THE Saturday afternoon I lead a deep Group Soul Healing Ceremony that feels very strong and powerful. It is a magical act by this large group of sisters and brothers in Avalon sending loving healing energy to our group soul, that will also affect and heal our individual souls. I believe so strongly now that we are a group of Souls who were alive before, at the times of the endings of the Goddess Temples of the world, sometimes together and in different combinations at different times in different lands. We have returned together at this time to bring Goddess alive once again in the world. We carry our wounds from those times with us into the present with all the karmic consequences of those wounds, in other later lives and in this life. We are here to heal our Motherlines and to bring Motherworld into being.

WE CLOSE the old Orchard Yahoo group and open a new private Orchard of Avalon Facebook group for all who have signed one of the Codes of Conduct. Those who don't want to sign a Code are angry and hurt. Their reasons for not signing are varied – some don't want to be controlled by anyone else, seeing this Code as an attempt to control them, to make them part of our *cult*. We should just believe in their integrity, although their behaviour demonstrates something else. Some feel they are being silenced by signing a Code. Some who dedicated in the early days, who went through one year of training rather than three, feel excluded from the community by our actions.

Another Facebook group forms of those who don't want to sign a Code of Conduct and who now who feel excluded by us. There they vent their feelings. Several Temple people join but then withdraw when they find the main aim of the group is to attack the Goddess Temple and its people. The hostility from some of our sisters to what we are trying to do goes on and on. Several priestesses who have played important roles in the Temple refuse to sign. There is a split in our community and everyone can choose which group they want to be part of. Within the Temple itself and the Trainings there is now a strong dedicated group of priestesses and priests willing to love and support each other and the Temple.

Chapter Twenty Eight

SACRIFICES MADE

I HAVE BEGUN to reread the wounding emails from September 2013, which began the whole sorry saga. As I read and re-read them I observe my reactions. I can now read these emails in a really dispassionate way – the sting has gone out of them. I have changed. I have learned from these experiences and I feel grateful for all I have learned. I am grateful to them because my wounding was sitting there, hidden from my conscious self. I didn't know it was there and now it is healed or at least healing.

It's the first time for a long time that I've really been able to look at the wounding. I go to Five Rhythms and I dance and scream out everything that has been caught in my body. I dance out my resistance and fear. I release it and let it go. Before it was just too painful to remember, so I avoided it. I dance into a trance and breathe it out, releasing the harm. I will wait to see if this is a passing dream. I do feel that the Lady is leading me to my healing edge as is Her nature. She has/is taking me to a place of healing where Motherworld values can be expressed.

For that is the question – how to heal the wounds in ourselves, in women and in men, and in Goddess communities, and then in the world at large? We all carry these wounds and act from them. How can that healing process happen except through living the wound, doing it until there is some realisation, some kind of knowing where it comes from, what its causes are, and then letting it go and healing.

"Lady, I ask you to lead me to my healing."

I TALK with Mike and Katinka about our reactions to the negativity, to the hate mail. I can read it now in a dispassionate way, but when it first came it carried a huge energy of negativity, which came from people talking to each other in their homes, in conversations passing between people, gossiping, whispering in corners, behind private closed doors and in public. It's not just the words which are written down but all the emotion that is behind the words, which has been stored up and then erupts without censure into the world in a spray, a torrent of poison.

MIKE AND I drive north to Sheffield to visit first of all the Sheffield Goddess Temple. It's a long drive and I suddenly appreciate all the people who travel regularly to Glastonbury from great distances. Their calling to come to Avalon, their motivation, must be high to travel such long distances again and again. I am impressed by their dedication.

The Goddess Temple has been opened above a shop by a group of lovely people, which includes Ali and Brian Harrison who regularly come and help with the Goddess Conference, as well as Ann Staniland and Awen. The small Temple above a pagan shop is opened to the public each lunchtime by one of the group. This is the weekend of their Beltane celebration and they have a variety of ceremonies and events going on throughout the weekend.

We enter the Temple as Lynn Harling is giving a talk about the local Northern Goddesses that she has been re-membering. She is weaving the Wheel of Brigantia, the tutelary Goddess of Northern Britain. Lynn is particularly called by the River Goddesses, as the River Don or Goddess Don or Danu, flows through the middle of Sheffield, Her river flowing East for Eostra. Goddess Derwenna (Derwent River of the Oak Wood) flows south at Litha. Rhibelisama – River Ribble, flows west at Mabon, and Goddesses Isara and Edene (Etaine) are placed in the north at Yule, with the River Aire flowing north to south and River Eden flowing from south to the north.

Lynn places Bride, the maiden form of Brigantia, in the northeast. In the southeast is Nemetona, Goddess of the Sacred Grove at Beltane. In the southwest at Lammas is Gwenith, which is the Brittonic name for *grain*, meaning *blessed* or *golden*. In the northwest is Pen-Nain, where Pen is hill and Nain is grandmother, for the PenNine hills, which stretch through this land, meaning literally *Head Grandmothers*.

This is the beautiful beginning of Brigantia's Wheel and we feel privileged to hear Lynne speak about her discoveries. She also sings lovely simple songs which we can all join in with for the different Goddesses. She has created something unique and special. My heart is warmed to see these Goddesses being called once again into the world. In ways that I did not know when I began my own quest for Goddess, the creation of the Wheel of Ana, of Brigit-Ana and Britannia gives permission to everyone to invoke once again the ancient Goddesses of their own lands. It is an awesome gift whose reality took me many years to recognise. We also take part in Ali Harrison's lovely guided heart connection and feel the love flowing between ourselves and these devoted people.

The following day we go to Creswell Crags for a visit organised by Daniel Holmes, one of my current Third Spiral students, training to become a Priest of Avalon. Daniel has created the Pop-up Nottingham Goddess Temple, which opens for each of the eight festivals of the year in Nottingham, also connected to an alternative shop. Twice as many people wanted to come on this outing as Daniel had thought would come – we are 28 in number!

Creswell Crags are the site of the only known Ice Age cave paintings and carvings in Britain, dating from 11,000 BCE. The dramatic limestone gorge is tucked away within the gently undulating limestone landscape on the Derbyshire/Nottinghamshire border, which passes along the middle of the gorge. Archaeological and environmental evidence excavated from the caves show how the area witnessed dramatic changes in climate at the edge of the northern ice sheets and was populated by Ice Age animals such as hyenas, mammoths, woolly rhinoceros, and migrating herds of reindeer, horse and bison.

The caves provided shelter for nomadic human groups through a crucial period of human evolution between 55,000 and 10,000 years ago. Stone, bone and ivory tools from the caves reveal Middle and Upper Palaeolithic occupation, in addition to portable and recently discovered 13,000 year old engraved rock art figures of deer, birds, bison and horse. This evidence connects the Ice Age human cultures at Creswell Crags to other groups across northwest Europe.

Archaeologists first found the carvings in 2003 after deciding that there had to be some in Britain and looking for them at three possible Ice Age sites. At Creswell Crags as soon as they began to look closely at the rock walls they found many images, now faint or hidden beneath calcification, with loss of colour. Two groups of archaeologists examined the artworks – a British group and a Spanish group who knew what to look for from their experiences in looking at Spanish cave art. The British archaeologists found 20 carvings, while the Spanish saw 120 and claim that Church Hole Cave is the Sistine Chapel of Ice Age Art, anywhere in Europe.

On the day we walk first to the far end of the small lake created by damming both ends of the gorge, with a stream coming in at one end and another flowing out at the other end. This was a ploy by the Fifth Duke of Portland to prevent a railway being built through the middle of the gorge by 19th century coal barons. Daniel leads our motley band of Goddess pilgrims in a lovely ceremony in which we are marked as belonging to the Hyena Clan with ochre claw marks. The skull and jaw bones of spotted hyenas dating from between 40,000-22,000 years ago, were found in several of the caves that line the craggy sides of the gorge, as well as the bones of reindeer, woolly mammoth, woolly rhinoceros, wild horse and many other ancient creatures dating from 130,000 BCE. This gorge has been here from the earliest of times before, during and after the ice ages.

We don helmets with head-torches and go first into one of the low-ceilinged caves where people lived in the summer months on the fringes of the northern ice sheets. These people followed the reindeer from Europe across the Dogger Bank, when there was no North Sea. In this cave were found the remains of animals from long, long ago, and from later on, tools for skinning and cutting animals and stone needles for sewing skins.

Next we go into the painted Church Hole Cave where the guide points out to us the outline of a deer on a hanging rock. I cannot see it at first, but as I get closer and 'get my eye in', there the outline of the deer appears, with antlers and pointed feet, similar to the cave paintings of Spain and France. It is wonderful that here are marks made by our Ancestors. There are other images to be seen too with a little colouring of black and red ochre still visible 13,000 years after they were first carved and painted. There is an easily visible carving of an ibis and other creatures, as well as some rather indistinct shapes of the female form, that are found in many European caves, and two small pubic triangles, which usually symbolise the presence of Goddess for the ancient people. These paintings are all in the entrance to a deeper cave system and are naturally illuminated by the light of day, rather than deep in the caves, like our European neighbours. The cave entrance must once have been gloriously coloured, a place of magic and mystery, to which the ancestors returned year after year.

ONCE WE GET home to Avalon I feel a weight of depression descending on my body as another memory begins to arise within me. I can't put my finger on the feeling, but experience again the pressure in my chest/heart. A couple of weeks ago Sue woke from a dream of a time in which she and others, who are now present-day priestesses, were about to die in order that I might escape. When she said it I knew it to be true. And the memory returned.

> *"We are inside the Sanctuary of the Temple, the door to the outer Courtyard is bolted. There is noise and shouting outside. We, the Priestesses of Her Temple, are gathered together in circle. They are dressing me in an old cloak, hiding my hair and face beneath a hood. We sing praises to the Lady with tear-filled eyes and fear trembling our voices. I am the one who has been Chosen by Lot, to leave by the secret exit, to run from the invaders, to escape, taking with me the Lady's Treasures, all that we revere and honour, to hide deep in the land. These, Her most Sacred Objects – the Maiden Grael, the Sacred Cup of Love, the Mother's Chalice, the Cauldron of the Crone, Her Violet Flame, Her Mysty*

Veil, the Keys to Her Mysteries, all are wrapped in leather or hessian cloth to protect them through time, and placed in the basket I now hold. I shall guard these Treasures with my life.

Memory stirs, I have been in this place before. I have had to run before. I tremble as the past moves through my body, bringing its terror. Why me, Goddess? Why me?

My sisters will hold the Sanctuary secure for as long as they can while I leave through the secret exit. Fear flares up in my belly. Will the sisters who opened the Gate to the marauders also reveal this secret exit? It is only known to a few and I hope that they have never been told of its existence. In the Sanctuary there are paintings and tapestries, which hang on either side of the altars, covering the walls. On each side a wooden chest stands in front of the wall-hanging and behind the left hand one is the low doorway to a hidden stairwell. My sister Sarana pulls the chest from the wall, trying to make no sound as the chest scrapes across the floor, and lifts the hanging. The door handle is a little stiff. It has not been used since last autumn's Mysteries, when the Embodiment of Goddess came through the secret doorway to appear suddenly and mysteriously within Her Temple, veiled in mists.

This door leads down to the Cave of the Ancestors, where the bones of our Motherline are held in peace. In our Temple we pray and dance and make ceremonies upon the bones of our Foremothers, those Great Female Beings who are there, always encouraging us on our Goddess path, to be Her Priestesses, to be Free. A long narrow tunnel leads on to the outside world far over the hill. This tunnel is not often used and is lined with storage baskets and forgotten items.

Tearfully hugging each of my sisters in turn, I step through the narrow door into the passageway. I cannot believe this is happening.

"Farewell, my beloved sisters. I love you forever...."

The door closes, the hanging falls into place and I hear the wooden chest being pulled back across the floor. Beyond the Sanctuary walls the sounds of warriors beating the door rises. As well as the heavy basket I have a flickering torch in my hand to light the way. I cannot go immediately. I watch through *the small invisible eye-holes that allow the priestess to know the correct moment to enter the Temple for emanation.*

My sisters stand in circle around the Sacred Violet Flame, which sits within the bowl of Holy Spring Waters. They are holding hands. I see and hear their tears. I see them shudder with fear. It is unbearable. With quavering voices they sing the praise song of our beloved Lady. The force of the men attacking the door becomes louder and the door begins to bow beneath their hammers. Whatever they are using is strong and heavy and the wood begins to split under the rain of blows. I should run now, but I cannot bear not to see what happens.

There is a loud and thunderous cracking as the door breaks open. On the threshold stand warriors, weapons in their hands, shouting, tearing at the fragments of the door, faces contorted with rage, as they look in upon the beauty of the Temple and the soft bodies of the priestesses. They pour into the sanctuary, breaking the circle, roughly pulling apart my sisters – beloved Sarana, now taken into a corner, forced against the wall and raped in moments. My jewel Albita, stabbed in the heart, and Kejara, a great lick of blood pouring from her neck. Time draws out long and slow, but all is actually quick and brutal. In a matter of long terrible moments my sisters are decimated. They have no defences, no weapons. We are peaceful Goddess-loving people.

A scream rises to my throat, but I must not let it out. They are dying to save me, to save Her Mysteries.

"Beloved soul-sisters, I will never forget you!

Though time and eons pass I will remember this, your sacrifice for our Lady. I pray to be worthy."

I TURN *from the eye-holes and run fleet-footed through the underworld tunnels, the smell of death, of fire and the blood shed this day filling my nostrils. My sisters' cries of agony ring in my ears. As I run past the entrance to the Motherline Underworld, the smell of the recently interred bones of our ancestors also comes to my nostrils. The smells of this day will haunt my memory for lifetimes.*

> *"My Lady, My Lady, bless my sisters*
> *Hold them safely in your loving embrace*
> *Carry them on your barge to Avalon, to the Isle of the Dead.*
> *Swiftly heal all wounds.*
> *May their suffering be short and may they be held by you!"*

PAIN rips through my belly as I feel the cords break as each soul-sister departs from her physical body, their pain-racked screams echoing behind my fleeing footsteps. I retch as I run along the long path. After what seems like an age a gleam of light begins to show itself at the end of the tunnel where the Underworld path emerges through a narrow rocky entrance hidden behind bushes and close woven shrubs. This hidden opening lies beyond the Sacred Red and White Springs. Here too we could appear suddenly and unexpectedly in ceremony.

As I come to the exit I stamp out the torch. My breath is broken and wracked by silent sobs,

"My beloved soul sisters, you have given your lives for me this day. You too could have taken this route and escaped, but you wanted to give me time to get away, to take the Mysteries of Avalon into the future. My love is yours always."

And I know that there will be those who did not want to die today, those who were so terribly afraid, frightened out of their wits, whose resentment of my escape will haunt the corridors of our karma. Your fear and anger will play out in life beyond life. It is not just those who actively betrayed our sisterhood, who will have to deal with future pain, but those whose lives were given too quickly, who had not stretched into such challenges before, those made of simpler cloth.

Did you give your life that I might escape, and then hate me for it? Did you in your moment of agony cry,

"I don't want to die! Why is she the one to escape? Why not me?"

AND THE resentment and the competition are set in motion in that moment, to be repeated unconsciously through lifetimes and in future days, for that is the way of life. Guilt begins to flow in my veins for being the one chosen not to die, *for being the one who escapes while my sisters die. It is my fault that they are dying. I take on the Victim role, when I was not the one to kill them. In my anguish my mind distorts all meaning. Do I serve my Lady and protect the Treasures of Her Temple and live or is it better that I die with my sisters? Such decisions are impossible to encompass in the human mind. Sorrow, grief, pain, my desire to survive, overwhelm all certainty of purpose.*

I pause at the rocky entrance and peer out breathless between leafy shrubs. There is no sign from the outside that there is a hidden entrance here. It is invisible except to those who know of its existence, protected as it is by the magic of the Temple Temenos, which has imploded in other places, but not here. I slip out through the green entrance, the only sounds are of flowing water and birdsong, and beyond, over the hill, a low roar of agony.

I look around in all directions and cannot see another's gaze. There is no-one watching. I push out between the bushes and begin to climb the Sacred Hill of the Chalice, scrambling up the side of the Mother's Womb, towards to the Temple of the Trees. I bend low, grasping my dull cloak around me so that no-one might glimpse my shadow on the hillside. Across my back the small digging paddle presses into my flesh. At last I reach and enter into the circle of tall trees. There I am hidden from any human eyes. I feel the presence of the Watchers, of the Elementals and the Guardian Spirits of Avalon. I catch my breath, before I run on across the Sacred Hill and on over the Down of Stones to the farther edge. I pause in a more remote glade of trees.

Then I dig, quickly into the soft earth beneath the Mothertree, as deep as I am able, as quickly as I can. I dig until the hole is deep enough. Beneath my breath I chant the Sacred Words of undoing, of invisible planting, so that the Treasures will lie in this land undisturbed until I or another Rigan Sister returns. I open the basket and place the Treasures into the earth, into the beloved body of our Mother. My tears fall silently as I let go of them and hide their presence beneath ancient locks of power. Too quick I raise the small spade and tear my hand. Blood too drips into the hole, my life-blood flows as a blessing into the Sacred Hollow, a triple locking. Quickly I fill the hole with earth and pat down upon the priceless Treasures. Like a grave I raise a small mound above them that will sink with time. It is obvious, so then I cover the whole area with soil, leaves and twigs, so all looks undisturbed.

No time to rest, no time to dally. I must be gone, before I am found. Hiding the shovel in the basket I put it onto my back and run down the hillside towards the Lake. I cannot take the Barge, but must follow the hidden trackways out across the marsh following in the footsteps of the Fae and the Little People, as the sun sinks lower in the skies and the world darkens around me.

What shall become of me? Where shall I go? How shall I know friend from foe? How shall I travel? How shall I fend for myself? Where are my sisters now? Have all been cut down by the assassins' hands? Are any of them left alive?

As I run my body trembles, shakes with fear, shakes with fatigue. I must run on and on across the hidden walkways and muddy flats until the Temple and the Isle are a mere mirage on the horizon. Something once held so dear is now so far away. My heart is breaking! I feel cold and so alone. Who will comfort me as night draws on? Where will I rest this night? Who will lie by my side and speak of love with me, love of me, love of the Lady? So quickly light can turn to ashes."

Chapter Twenty Nine

Letting Go

I AM GETTING OLDER and so is Erin who teaches the first two Spirals of the Priestess of Avalon Training. We need to prepare so that the next generation of Priestess teachers can settle into place before we are too old to support them. It will be really hard to let go of this inspiring, joyful, time-consuming teaching, but my intuition tells me that this needs to happen. I want the Training and all that we have created within the Goddess Temple to continue when we are gone. I know that I have no control over the future, whether this happens or not when I am gone, but I want to make all the preparations that I can to ensure that this re-awakening of Goddess in Glastonbury continues when I have left my body.

Lovely sister Priestess Ruby Ward is going to take over as principal tutor of the First Spiral students. Another Priestess will teach the Second Spiral and I will continue to teach the Third Spiral for a while, as it's not so much work, and then hand that on to someone who is deeply connected into Avalon too. I am very happy that Ruby is taking the Training on. I feel she will bring renewed vision and ideas to our teaching. She has taken her own deeply transformative journey into the Underworld energies of Avalon and now hopefully she can help others on their journeys of transformation..

I HAVE ALSO decided that after 21 years as the Webster and Visionholder of the Glastonbury Goddess Conference, 2016 will be my final year of Conference

Weaving. The decision to let go of the mountain of work comes quite quickly and easily. I haven't been thinking about it and then it suddenly becomes clear. I realise that I am ready to let the Conference go. So far I have always wanted to be in control of it, to ensure that it is the fabulous, daring, Goddess event that it is meant to be. I have wanted this as Queen of my realm.

Now I want more time for myself just to be, to sit in my garden and watch the flowers grow, to have time even to garden. I want time to write. I want to make sure that new Motherworld ventures come into being. I want to create space for something new to come into my life, to allow new things to arise, also importantly to have time to be a grandmother to the baby who is on its way to my daughter and her partner.

I ask Katinka and Marion if they would like to take on the Weaving of the Conference and happily they agree. It is very exciting and scary for them. They have both been part of the Conference Ceremony group for many years and Katinka in particular has been a daring ally in going to the places that others might be scared of, in our ceremonies and embodiments. Marion has good skills as well and together they will make a great creative team. The Goddess Conference is now a world famous Goddess event, which people come to from all over the world. It has had profound and positive influences on the lives of thousands of women and men and has helped bring awareness of Goddess back into the world. It is an awesome event. I want it to continue after me, as well, to be the inspirational event that it is. I shall be happy to hand over the work to other people and I know that no-one really understands how much work there is.

AS I MAKE these decisions I feel a freeing up from my need to keep everything going. There are enough good people now to take things on. I am/we are Priestesses of the Leading Edge, who have breached the wall of patriarchy, and now allow other soul sisters/priestesses/priests who love Goddess in their souls to incarnate more easily once again. Younger women, younger men, girls and boys are now incarnating with knowledge of Goddess already in their hearts, because of the work that my contemporaries and I have done, with all the challenging experiences and struggles of bringing Goddess back into the world again, that we have encountered and lived through.

I feel change coming for me and don't know if this is just change for me or for everyone, or whether I might die sooner than I want to. I want to spend time with my grandchildren yet to be born, those beings I also carried when their mother was a baby in my womb. I want time to sit in the Temple with them. I want time to devote to your Temple, Lady.

I HAVE SAT beside the burning ghats of Mother Ganga. I have done my practice in the charnel grounds. I have taken the bodies to the high plateau in Tibet for their breaking with stone and mallet, for the tearing out of soft tissues, given to vulture, carrion crow. I have released souls to their destiny in the stars. I have gazed in wonder at the starfields of the heavens, at the womb spaces of the soul fields from which souls are reborn.

Over the interweb comes the image of the biggest photograph ever taken by NASA, of the Andromeda galaxy, and it is astonishing. One small portion of that galaxy, which is just one tiny portion of the sky, is filled with billions of stars, shining star souls in space, dwelling in the bardo state between death and rebirth, globes of light.

In 2015 we are celebrating the Mother of Air, of the Stars, of the Ancestors, in the North. We are exploring the space between death at Samhain and the letting go of the physical body and rebirth at Imbolc, with the renewal of physical life on earth. We are exploring the spaces between things, the spaces of the heavens and the heavenly bodies, the light-filled spaces and the dark matter that lies between and inter-meshed with the light-filled globes. As our ancestors did before us we are naming a star cloud, which is part of the Orion Nebula, as Stella Nolava. She is a Goddess shaped smudge of stars lying below Orion's belt. This is a creative star cluster from which new stars are continually being born.

We name this star womb as Stella Nolava, the birthplace of Anu, An Cailleach, She who is AnuDanaa, AnuBree, AnuUrs, AnuRhia, AnuOmnu, AnuKora, AnuBha, AnuWen and AnuLova. We will hold these nine faces of

Anu, circling spiralling through galaxies of time and space as a lens, through which we will call to the Cosmic Star Mother, the great being in whose Omniverse we are held. Our tiny lives are less than a milli-micron in the vastness of the Omniverse. How do we expand our consciousness to comprehend anything of the magnificence of the Goddess of whom we are each a part? This should lift us all out of the small details of interpersonal conflict.

In our Conference we are opening our hearts and minds to the vastness of our Universal Mother, who is the Womb of our life on earth. We expand our consciousness through spiritual practice, through connections made to the seen and unseen realms, with breath, with Her air in our bodies. As the birds fly in the air they show us how to lift off, to take flight, to soar upwards into the sky.

Symbolically the North is the place where Souls rest when they are out of incarnation, where seeds lie dormant in the earth in winter, where souls swim gently in the heavens, where we pause, take a breath, to sleep, to dream of the past and the future, to take stock, to recognise what we need for our future. It is a place of connection to other souls, to the larger group soul of which we are each a part. It is where we remember where we come from and our purpose in being, in incarnating again on the earth. We die to let go into the no-thingness, into the spaciousness She allows into our souls.

On our Avalonian Goddess Wheel Anu is Goddess of the North. We glimpse Her presence in Her Nine emanations, in the physical star cluster of Stella Nolava, and in An Cailleach, the most ancient Goddess. She is the one who has been here from the beginning in our land, honoured by our ancestors. She is the one to whom we return as Tomb, She who is made of stars!

MIKE AND I travel to Iceland again for a short summer holiday, while I am offering a workshop for a group of women brought together by Uni Arndisardottir, who took the First Spiral with us. With me I bring the elements of Avalon to blend with the Icelandic elements and I offer the Flame of Avalon to everyone. I feel my work is to inspire and invigorate certain people in the world – certain young women who are in their 20s and 30s, who are the initiates of a new generation. Uni is one of these young women moving into her empowerment. She has a pure energy and a lovely singing voice.

The following days Mike and I go to stay on Snaefellsnes where a cold westerly wind blows continuously, making it a challenge to leave the place where we are staying, even for a walk. Iceland is such a wild, harsh, unforgiving land, a Crone land, a Cailleach land, which forces me to sit still and go within. On the last day in Reykjavik Mike becomes quite sullen and moody and somehow it is my fault – I had done this, done that – his projection onto me. I watch my reactions as I am not doing anything that I can see. I can react or be compassionate. I decide not to react, but just to be aware of his unhappiness. His mood goes on and on and into the next day when he is still removed from me and unhappy. I don't react until we arrive back at Bristol airport. Then I get angry with him. He is my moody detached unfriendly father, not how a father, a husband should be.

I want to leave, to get away from him. If I could leave then I would do so, but we have one car in which to get back home again. By the time we arrive home I am feeling so angry. That's it, why be with someone so unloving, so unfriendly, so unwilling to see their moods and let them go? The drama resolves once I get angry.

Later we talk about projection. I can see how I have transferred my projections onto people and then transferred them from person to person. What is the best way to intervene when a projection is going on, either projecting oneself or being projected onto? The great question is how to break that magnetic spell. All strategies seem to fail – humour, stillness, non-reaction. When is it OK to react? There comes a point where I react and the dam breaks and something can then change.

Patriarchal belief systems aim to reach a place of emotional detachment and non-reaction to anything, but it's a very inhuman place. What is the Goddess way? To hear, to listen, to respond, to express and to react with awareness.

* * *

I WAKE this morning with the feeling that I must have been a betrayer myself. To see myself so often at the effect of betrayal, to be a victim so many times in so many lives, there must be an underlying opposite. My deepest darkest Shadow secret must be that I was once a betrayer myself. I shut this thought down quickly, I don't want to see it. But I can do this now. I am strong enough now. I give the thought light, I give it room and I flesh it out in my imagination.

"THRESHOLD Priestesses welcome the warriors at the Men's Gate to the Temple of Ishtar, a grand and well-established Temple within the city of Uruk. The Temple began in the ancient days when Inanna was worshipped and has continued to these latter days. The building is composed of a series of interpenetrating Courtyards and Sanctuaries, centred on Ishtar's holiest Huluppu tree, which rises up in the middle of the whole Temple complex, for Ishtar is the Sacred Tree and the Tree belongs to Her.

As is the custom at Her Temple, the warriors remove their weapons and leave them in the charge of the Guardians at the Gatehouse. Then each man is taken into the care of a priestess, who leads them into the Courtyard of the Bathing Pools. Here their travel-stained clothes are unbuckled, stripped off, as mothers remove the dirty clothing of children. Hard male bodies, chiselled by movement and action, sun-soaked and scarred, are unclothed, their nakedness revealed. Each man is led to the warm Releasing Pools, filled with soft soaps, where the dirt and smells of the journey are washed away. In the background soft music plays on the lyre, as songs in praise of Ishtar rise and fall. A warm soft breeze flows through the Courtyard, playing between the flowers, whose colours glow in sunlight.

When bodies are clean the men move on into pools of scented oils, softening, relaxing for the first time in weeks, months, years, here in the Temple of Ishtar, in the Temple of Her Love, where Her love and desire are shared with all who enter. Her Temple is famed through many lands as a Place of Pleasure where a man or woman might meet and experience the Beauty and Blessings of Goddess in incarnate form, in Her sacred Hierodules.

THE MAN *climbs out of the pool. He shakes his head, spraying water in all directions, rivulets running across his shoulders, his torso, down over his flat muscled belly and onto his strong thighs. In that moment he is caught by a shaft of sunlight and looks like a god, broad-shouldered, strong, enduring. The priestess watches – I watch – him through the shimmering veil. He is beautiful. I can see the ache in his shoulders, the weariness, the scars on his back, but he is beautiful. I see his playful eyes as he looks around him, taking in the surroundings of beauty. He smiles.*

He is laid upon the couch, his body softening further under the ministrations of the Melissa Healer who covers his body with oils and begins to massage away the harsh days of the journey, the memory of the battles, the weeks of travel which he has taken to be here in this moment, in the Temple of Love. So it is for many who come here. Each one is different, each one is the same, seeking, searching for something, else they would not have come here.

I step back into the Sanctuary of the Harlot. I am Dilbah, one of several Hierodules, whose blessing it is to embody Ishtar, for these Her supplicants. As I move through the Sacred Space, Ninmur, my assistant and friend, asks if there is anything that I need. I cast my eye about. The love nest is ready, the day bed prepared, the fruits and the cups are there on the side tables, the altar is shining with its bounty of glistening treasure, each gem an offering to Ishtar. The newest are laid at the front of the altar while the oldest lie at the back to be removed in time and used to provision the Temple. For this Temple to Ishtar is rich with offerings, as our service to Her is so highly valued.

I thank Ninmur for once again taking care of this Sacred Space for me and for beloved Ishtar. Ninmur has been with me for several years, since I was a younger woman, when she first taught me the secrets of this Holy Service to Ishtar, how to give and receive pleasure in the body, in the heart, in the Soul. In her time Ninmur was herself a Hierodule, until she moved on to become teacher and mentor of those coming after her. For we need to be taught these practices, as the men and women who come to the Temple are often wounded in body and mind, and need to be gentled and healed in Her love. Of course, our service involves the pleasures of sexuality, but the secret is that this is not really our main focus. We are here to soften harsh thoughts, to heal cruel hearts and minds, to lift the curses on body and soul, to inspire and invigorate the powers of life, through Her love.

As Ninmur leaves, I go to kneel at the altar, praying to Ishtar, waiting for the one who next comes to meet Her. I open my heart to Her, repeating the ritual phrases, offering myself in her service. In the next moments I hear Her voice inside of me,

"You are my Vessel of Love. I will change your life in ways you cannot imagine. Your Priestess journey is only just beginning. In the aeons that follow remember that you are my Vessel of Love."

Her words enter my heart and rest there, "You are my Vessel of Love." I shall be Her Vessel for all the men and women who come to Her Temple, whoever they are. This is my priestess path, this is my service, my passion, my pleasure and my testing ground, for I am not perfect, I am always a work in progress. Many days I love easily and wholeheartedly, sharing Her love in me. Other days I feel emotional, sad, angry, disturbed by fears. In these times I must put my personal cares aside to be Her Vessel of Love. Sometimes I really don't want to be available at all, and not just during my moon-time, when we can retreat to Her Moon-Lodge, although sharing Her love in the Red Days is the greatest of Her Mysteries. Sometimes I just want to be privately me. I am whole unto myself, but I have a secret longing for the one love, who will love me for myself, not because I am Dilbah, Priestess of Ishtar, but because I am me.

There is a gentle tap on wood, a rustle of curtains and Ninmur ushers a man into Her Sanctuary.

"Here is Daman, come to honour Holy Ishtar."

He could have gone to any of my sisters, but by chance, by fate, he comes to me, the man with the body of a god. "Daman", I turn his name silently with my tongue, "Daman".

He looks at me as if I am Goddess, his eyes widening, mouth opening, jaw relaxing, and beneath his loin cloth, his wand jumps and stiffens. He makes the *ritual offering of flowers and jewels and places them onto Her already bejewelled altar, beside Her shimmering image. For a moment I see this Sanctuary again through a stranger's eyes, filled with beauty and light. His eyes betray nothing as they pass over the abundance, the opulence.*

He is in Her Temple, the light is subtle here compared to the Bathing Pools, magic moves here in the beauty of these surroundings, in the scents of flowers, in the glittering altars, in my beauty, in the beauty of Her in me. I hold out my hand and taking his, I draw him towards me. His cloth drops away. I too, with swaying movement as She enters in, allow my body to become free of clothing, clasps opening, veils releasing. My long mane of hair falls down across my shoulders and I shake it back like a young filly. I look into his eyes. Is the God embodied in this man for me? Or does he come only as a supplicant to Ishtar? I live in hope always. (Ha!)

In Daman's eyes I see a glimmer, a spark of Soul, how much I cannot tell. He is looking down at my body now, not into my eyes. I feel my body rise to meet the desire that pours out of him. My vulva responds in power to meet his longing for surrender, for peace, for love. He looks into my face for a moment and I see conflict, but it passes quickly over and then is gone, as we both give way into this moment of Her pleasure. I surrender my body to Ishtar, and he surrenders to the presence of Ishtar in me. When our love-making is over we offer the gifts of love at her altar as is the practice in our Temple. And later he departs.

He returns the next day to the Temple and can choose the same priestess again, which is me, if he wishes. His worship of Ishtar is repeated. He comes to Ishtar's Temple every day and seeks me out. He comes again and again. He makes love well. He takes care of Her priestess. He is not a selfish lover like many, who are there only for their own pleasure. He can also give. I am taken into the House of Love by this man. I feel the God in him, coming to meet Goddess in me. This is unusual and I appreciate this gift from Her, for She has brought him to me. Is this what She meant by change? I begin to await his return, looking forward to the hour each day. I notice myself taking additional care over my preparations for love – longer in my bathing pool, a little more perfume, more oils for my body, more attention to my face and hair.

The Temple Priestesses have a hidden entrance to the Temple, a closed door that only opens from the inside, leading out into an invisible alleyway behind a street in the market. This is our private way in and out of the Temple so that we can come and go as we need to, and pass unseen among the throngs of people who walk in the bazaar around the Temple. We cannot only be on duty. We too need to be able to walk in the city and out into the wide spaces of the countryside around the city.

Daman asks if we can spend a longer time together, perhaps a whole night, if there is any way that he can come into the Temple, not only through the main entrance with its formalities and rituals. My heart skips a beat as I feel that he really wants to be with me. He often speaks words of love when we make love, but this I think is his love for Ishtar and I try not to take any of his words personally. I know that he is speaking to Ishtar, but he is saying that he wants to see me more. His words to me now are sweet and full of love. I am blinded by my own desire for love. He has proved himself over and over in these days and now weeks, coming almost daily, seeking me out. He has not always found me, but my sisters have helped our assignations of Her pleasure – we always help each other to spend times with the ones we can enjoy most.

One night once the business of the Temple is over I arrange to meet him in the cool air of the hidden alleyway, outside the secret priestess door. He will knock once and then three short taps so that I know that it is him and I can take him to my personal apartments for a night of love-making, that is for me, in surrender to Her. Perhaps then if all goes well I can one day leave the Temple and become a woman with a husband, a mother of my own children. I can grow fruit and vegetables, tend my garden, bake bread for my husband. Our children are the future after all. Temple children have many mothers and have happy carefree lives, but there is also the intimate life to be tended.

It is all in Her hands. I love my life as Her Sacred Hierodule and I have secret desires too, which She must know. She told me change was coming.

* * *

I AM STANDING waiting by the door. My heart is beating a little faster in anticipation of the night of bliss to come. I have risen into love with him. I look out through the spyhole. It is dark outside. I breathe slowly, calming myself. All is quiet, then there is movement in the darkness, a flickering light coming closer, shadows. Then comes the knock on the door. One loud knock followed by three light taps, on the thick wooden door. He is here! My hand moves to lift the heavy latch that holds this door closed, so that it cannot be breached from the outside.

There he stands, my beloved, my shining one, my god in human form. He looks at me, a strange half-smile on his face, then looks away. Something is wrong. The hairs on my body rise, alerting me suddenly to danger. In his hands he holds a knife that glitters with the light of the torch that he carries. He is not alone. Behind him I see in the shadows the shapes of five or six others. I recognise one or two who have also visited Ishtar's Temple. His arm clamps around my shoulders, across my mouth. He whispers hoarsely,

"Do not struggle, Dilbah! Do not cry out and no harm will come to you!"

Of course, I do struggle, I bite his hand, but force soon silences my voice as I gasp for breath. I am shocked beyond belief. Hands that were once softened by love, now drag me across the floor and into the Temple. The men, who I now see are all armed, move quietly through the passageways. They seem to know their way in. Have they seen a map? Did I give it to him? I cannot believe that this is happening. Where are our Temple Guardians? This is her Holy Inviolable Temple and now She is being violated.

They are going to Her Inner Sanctuary of Love, where he and I have made love on many days. I am dragged across the threshold and handed unceremoniously to another warrior, who cares even less. His rough hand clamps my jaw shut even harder and blood flows as I bite my tongue. Daman, whose eyes once flickered over bejewelled altars and looked away seemingly disinterested, heads for those very altars. Without hesitation he climbs the steps to the main altar and begins to pull from it rings, necklaces, pendants and bracelets of gold, bronze, emeralds, rubies, jasper, jade from the east, precious stones of all kinds. The men shout with excitement, unafraid to be heard. They throw the jewels into the bags they carry across their shoulders, filling them with treasure meant for Ishtar.

There is a movement at the door and Ninmar comes in to see what is happening, as she heard feet moving, rustling, heavy breathing, the shouts of delight. Her face falls as she encounters this terrible scene. I struggle and snatch my mouth free,

"Run, Ninmur, run!"

A knife moves swiftly to silence her scream, which falls away as a death sigh, a look of horror in her eye. My sister is dead! She is gone. She has died because of me, because of my longing for love. I have betrayed my sister, all my sisters. I have brought death and destruction to Her Holy Temple.

"Let me die, Ishtar, let me die in her place."

A sob rises in my throat, heaving through my breath. I know that he will not let them kill me. I must watch the destruction I have wrought through my desire for love. He looks at me and smiles, a sardonic smile. How did I not see who he was? How has this happened? How did I not recognise him for what he was? Was I so blinded by love, my need for love? I, who am usually so good a judge of character, did not see him at all. I was blind to his greed, his destructive nature. I saw only the side I wanted to see. Now I am shaking with fear and the horror of my friend's body draining of blood, draining of life.

The bags are filled and the men begin to leave, moving quietly along the corridors towards the priestess exit, taking the Treasures of the Temple with them. I am released from the warrior's grasp and slide to the floor in a faint of shame. As I slip downwards Daman comes close and looks me in the eye, his own twinkling. He whispers,

"Thank you, Priestess, for all the gifts of Ishtar."

And then he is gone. From deep inside of me a sound arises and I scream and scream with the pain of loss and shame."

I HAVE carried the shame of my betrayal of my sisters, of my Temple, hidden through the centuries, its consequences played out in other forms in other lives.

Its reverberations in this life have included excessive defensiveness on my part when under attack, denial of fault and strong resistance to being blamed for anything. Such default settings have played out in my life repeatedly, enabled by the conditions of my birth and childhood trauma.

The more positive effects of my failure include a strong intensity in my desire to serve Goddess in this life, completely and wholeheartedly. I have heard myself say on more than one occasion when we have been under threat, that I will be here holding our Goddess Temple open, no matter what, even if I am the only one left to do it. I will serve my Lady, no matter who else is here with me.

AFTER THIS memory has integrated into my awareness, my need to experience blame and shame seems to disappear from my life. And miraculously since then praise has been heaped upon me from all sorts of directions. Experience tells me not to take that too seriously either. I don't now need my ego to become over-inflated. Rather I can receive praise and let it be. Blaming and being blamed diminishes the ego and excess praise inflates it, so I'm just holding steady so that my soul's energies can flow easily through. I am very grateful however for this change in my day to day experience.

MIKE AND I go to see "*The School for Scandal*" which was written by my ancestor Richard Brinsley Sheridan, splendidly performed at Bristol's Tobacco Factory. This play was written by my great, great, great, etc, grandfather – my middle name is Sheridan, and I am named after him. The performance is hilarious and enjoyable. I have not seen the play before but it seems to perfectly describe so many of our recent troubles, including all the malicious lying and gossiping, the deliberate making up of untrue stories and scandal-mongering about myself and other Temple tutors, about the Goddess Temple, the Conference and all our activities.

The prologue to the play discusses the difficulty of preventing people from spreading scandal via tongue or written word (via email, facebook or Twitter in our modern age). Those of us who try to change the culture of undermining have a long road to travel. The play's final resolution in fact seems very MotherWorld – that people should be kind to each other, and not gossip and undermine each other.

The other thing that appeals to me is the naming of the protagonists with names which describe either who they are or how they behave. Examples are Lady Sneerwell, Sir Peter Teazle, Oliver Surface, Snake, Careless, Mrs Candour, Sir Benjamin Backbite, etc. I am so impressed that I almost feel to honour my ancestor by following in his footsteps, naming the protagonists in my own work of faction so as to disguise their true identities and confuse those who might seek to reveal the unworthy. After all I, as writer, am the only one who knows what is fact in this story and what is fiction.

THE Cosmic Star Mother Conference is awesome as we celebrate the many faces of Anu, An Cailleach. There is such a wonderful feeling amongst everyone attending of love, friendship and family. It is a palpable atmosphere from the first moments when people arrive.

The Heart of the Mysteries on Friday is one of my favourite kinds of day. It begins with a feeling of high anxiety (I don't like that part), then we dig in, going deeper and deeper into the energy. Katinka gives a great visual presentation about ancient Priestesses and early Temples, showing carvings and statues that demonstrate our presence through the ages. Then she speaks of and shows the Fall, the Ending, the Ruins of many Goddess Temples.

I read my re-membering of the ending of the Temple in Malta. Many people cry as they hear the story and feel its resonance within themselves. In the afternoon Katinka leads everyone into essence dance to find our places of wounding and to receive healing. A circle of embodied ancient Priestesses enters the Temple and transmits the energy of the ancient Motherworld, which is strong and resonant. Then we move into a Group Soul Healing for the large number of people who are here, all souls returned and connected into the one Group Soul. In the evening we offer music and blessings and a great embodiment of the nine faces of Anu, An Cailleach. It is a fabulous day.

At the end of the Conference I tell everyone that the coming year will be my final year as Conference Webster. It feels good for me and for everyone.

Chapter Thirty

RESOLUTION

IN SEPTEMBER I go to 13 Moons organised by Carolyn Hillyer at her home on Dartmoor. She and Nigel Shaw have created such a wonderful space on their land. I am interested to see how she/they hold the threads of their event, which is attended by hundreds of women, camping on the land or staying in B & B s for the weekend. There is lots of music, workshops and presentations as well as different held spaces on the land – a stone circle, White Horse Woman's cist, the Roundhouse, a sweatlodge, as well as tents for art and crafts.

On Saturday evening I lie on the ground looking up at the stars shining clear in the sky, listening to a beautiful concert by Carolyn. It's a very magical night. I go to the Deer Lodge under trees, lit by candles in jars hanging from the trees. There is a fairy glen with a mirror gleaming in the darkness. I go inwards, I go deep. I think about Koko. Where are you now? A woman walks by me on the right in the darkness – she has the gait and shape of Monica Sjöö, who died a few years ago now. I let her be Monica and communicate with her. It feels like a cycle is completing.

I journey with Tegwyn in the Moon Lodge, becoming eagle flying. I don't want it to stop I am enjoying my soaring flight so much, head turning, my eye seeing clear, my beak opening to cry. I want to journey for hours – for 10 Hours or double that. Can I lead such a journey for everyone at next year's Conference, which will celebrate the Lady of Avalon in the centre, at the end of our nine-year cycle of celebration?

I RECEIVE a telephone call from Mary asking if I would be willing to speak with Gwyneth, one of our distanced priestesses. Gwyneth and I meet a couple of days later in the Goddess Hall just after Equinox. Gwyneth tells me that she is very sorry for everything that happened two years ago and the part that she played in fuelling everyone's negativity. I am surprised by her words, but can feel that she really means what she is saying. She has understood. She has become more conscious of her part in all that happened and she regrets what happened. It is a deeply moving conversation for me. We talk for about an hour about many things. We talk about the woundings arising from the endings of the Goddess Temples, that have been played out in our community and she understands what I am saying. My heart is really warmed by our conversation. I am very grateful to her for her courage. I can see that it has taken her a lot to approach me.

A week or so later we hold a Resolution Circle for Gwyneth within the Morgen Circle in the Temple. We, the Temple Weavers, have agreed to create such Circles when someone who has attacked us wants to come back in towards the Orchard and the Temple. The Circle includes Luna, Marion, Mike, Angie and me, as well as Gwyneth. We begin with prayers and introductions as not everyone knows Gwyneth personally. Each person in the circle shares their feelings about what has happened from their perspective. Gwyneth tells us what has happened for her over the weeks and months, and that about two weeks ago the Lady of Avalon began speaking to her, calling her back to the Orchard.

Again the conversation is deeply moving for me, for all of us, as she names the part she has played and apologises. After our conversation last week she can see the repetition of the ending of the Temples scenarios. In fact she has been having dreams over the previous weeks about the endings of the Temples. Our Circle lasts an hour and a half. By the end, once again, I am amazed by the perfection of the Lady's transforming love. She takes us into the dark places of the Soul, into the Shadow places, into the wounding and then calls us through all the pain and suffering, to heal our wounds, to resolve, to become conscious of the bigger picture, to heal the ancient past as well as the present, to move into the future together.

Gwyneth signs the Orchard Code of Conduct agreeing to how we behave for ourselves and with each other, and in a few days we hold a special Ceremony for her. We give her a blessing of the elements and each priestess in the circle individually welcomes her back into the Orchard and into the Temple.

The Lady is beautiful and Her ways are full of Mystery. I have the same feeling now that I had when I resolved other deep wounds in relationships, in having cancer. The sheer beauty of Her ways is awesome! She is awesome!

IT IS autumn equinox 2015 and Angie and I go to view Somerset House on Magdalene Street which is for sale. We have been looking at possible buildings in the centre of Glastonbury for the last nine months, but haven't seen anything suitable until now. We have a vision to create a beautiful Goddess Healing Temple, because so many people in the world are in need of healing. We have held regular Ceremonial Healing days in the Goddess Hall for many years now, which are gifted by a variety of Priestess Healers and Melissas to people who freely receive healing. The Temple receives donations for this healing, or not, if people have no money. People are taken initially through a blessing of the four elements which helps them to ground into their bodies and begin to meet their need for healing. We have developed our own unique style of healing working for a short intense time in twos or threes on one person. The healing is hands-on and uses voice, sound and instruments – drums, rattles, bells, to move stuck energy. For me it is a vital part of what the Goddess Temple can offer to the world – healing in the name of Goddess, in the name of the Lady of Avalon.

The Georgian house was once a Nunnery next to a Catholic convent school. It looks quite imposing from the outside. It has been used in recent years as a telesales centre and is full of ugly desks, computers and electrical wires. The rooms however have lovely proportions and in one of the main rooms is a high frieze of mythical beasts. I don't know how we can find the money to buy it, but it would be perfect for a Healing Centre. Some people think that we or I have piles of money lying about somewhere, even though this is patently untrue. Everything we have done has been created step by step on a wing and a prayer, through Her grace, Her magic.

Amazingly the Glastonbury Experience has been looking to buy a building to expand its property interests and Somerset House seems to fit the bill exactly. The Trustees decide to put in an offer to buy the House, which is accepted, and the Goddess Temple will be the tenants.

How did that happen?

She moves in mysterious ways! Her wonders we behold!

We cannot move in for several months, but now we have to work out how on earth we are going to pay the very high monthly rent, plus all the other costs we are committing to. We have to trust that since She has provided this opportunity, somehow it will work out. Trust in the Lady! Trust in Her!

AT SAMHAIN we hold a great ceremony in the Goddess Hall where we honour the Dark Goddess, Crone Nolava, and our beloved dead. I light a candle for Lydia Ruyle who at 80 is having a hip replacement operation. Lydia is such an awesome presence in the ways in which she brings Goddess into the world through her GIRLS, her beautiful Goddess icon banners that fly all over the world. She only began creating them at the age of 60 and they have profound influence on many people.

> *Beloved Lady, Black Nolava*
> *You who take us down into the Underworld*
> *Into the Under Ground below the surface of everything*
> *Into the Dark Caves of Forgetting to the Places of Memory*
> *That hide beneath foggy blankets of unknowing*
> *Crone Nolava, Ancient Grand Mother*
> *I ask for your blessing*
> *For your loving embrace*
> *Heal me, hold me in your love always.*
> *I crawl through the tunnels of time, belly on earth*
> *Roots descending through mud*

Hanging in the tunnels of the mind
I ask for your blessing, Grand Mother
As I grow old I ask that your wisdom shines in me
For you are the strength of the ages
You are the One who holds us in empty space
As we die to the old, as we wait for rebirth, for the new
Show me your beautiful face, Grand Mother,
Your lines of age, your enduring hills and valleys
Your rocks and clefts, your mountains, your caverns.

AT OUR NEXT Temple Weavers meeting we tell people about our plans for the newly named Goddess House, a Goddess Temple Wellness, Healing and Goddess Educational centre. It is to be a Motherworld enterprise, with healing treatment rooms and workshop spaces. People are happy with the idea and it's all very exciting.

IONA WANTS to give birth in a birthing pool in our sitting room as there is more space there than in her own flat. Mike and I practice putting the pool together, which is a good idea, as it's a bit complicated. I can't quite believe that this is going to happen. I am praying to the Lady that all goes well and easily for her.

A telephone call comes at 12.30am on December 1st in the night and Mike and I leap out of bed. Iona is in early labour. Stumbling out of sleep we make space for the birthing pool and set it up. Iona arrives with her partner Leigh and is pausing every few moments to breathe through her contractions. We fill the birthing pool, two midwives arrive and we all calm down. The lights are low and there is soft music and my beautiful girl labours through the long night. Leigh and Mike and I are a great support team for Iona, massaging her back, giving her drinks and later gas and air, but by morning she is very tired. This first baby is coming slowly. As dawn comes there is a change of midwives and contractions slow down through the morning.

By late morning Iona is exhausted and has no strength to push, although we can just glimpse the crown of the baby's head. It's decided that she should go to hospital to have something to help with her contractions, which have almost stopped. We follow the flashing light of the ambulance to Taunton and into the brightly lit hospital, where now there are seven midwives in attendance. A drip is attached and contractions begin again. In an hour or so we can see baby's head emerging. It is one of the most wonderful moments of my life, along with me giving birth to Iona and Torky. It is so amazing to see Samba Ziggy Jones emerging from his mummy. Iona pushes hard through the pain again and again, digging deep into her determination. His head comes first, he turns and his shoulders are released and then the rest of his little body, all arms and legs. We are all crying, sobbing with love for Samba and for Iona. He is laid skin to skin on his mummy's breast. His head is elongated from its journey through the birth canal and he looks like a Nubian/Egyptian prince.

I am so proud of my beautiful girl. She has come through her initiation of giving birth, of journeying through fear, meeting the possibility of death and the creation of life. It is an extraordinary moment with my daughter that I am privileged to witness. Iona was a caesarean birth, creating patterns of needing to be rescued when things get tough. Now the pattern is met and changed. She has fought through her place of wounding and altered the pattern by giving birth naturally to her baby boy. Samba is perfectly formed, so tiny, so lovely, so gorgeous. I love my girl so much and something changes now between us as mother and daughter. And I love that little boy so much.

ON MARCH 1st 2016 we take possession of Goddess House, our newest Goddess Temple Motherworld adVenture. It's very exciting and lots of people come to help paint and decorate. I have named each room after one of the Goddesses on Bridannia's Wheel and chosen the colours. We paint and decorate them in their colours accordingly – the Nolava Room is violet, the Rhiannon Room is red, the Brighde Room is green and white, etc. Miraculously within three weeks the energy and feeling in the House completely change and it becomes a place of great beauty. Wendy Andrew's Wheel of Britannia wall hangings grace the entrance. Tiana Pitman has given us some of her paintings to hang on the walls and to sell. I bring in paintings of the Lady of Avalon that I own. There are lots of other paintings given or lent by friends.

At the Spring Equinox we have an Open Day and welcome visitors into the House. We all crowd into the Nolava Room and call the Lady of Avalon into Her House for the first time, asking that She blesses everyone who comes through our doors, and that She helps us offer care and healing to all healers and all visitors.

ON MARCH 26th we hear the sad news that our Soulsister Lydia Ruyle died from a brain tumour, which came a few months ago and then aggressively took her. Her husband Bob and niece Katie Hoffner, with other family members, looked after her as she became progressively weaker. Lydia's colourful GIRLS have flown every year in the Conference since 1998 and she came to the Conference many, many times, giving inspiring presentations on her world travels and the Goddesses she found and painted, walking with the GIRLS in our Sunday procession. I love her and I miss her. We light candles for her in front of her photograph in the Temple and pray for her soul, praying too that a little of her essence will rest here in Avalon.

BY BELTANE Samba is 6 months old and is a gorgeous little boy, who brings us so much joy. I wake one morning from an amazing dream which I believe is about Goddess House, as well as obviously our lovely grandson. I dream Samba is my baby asleep in a pram. Someone asks me how the baby can be mine as I am too old to have a baby. I say, *"It's just a miracle!"* and laugh. Mike and I are a few metres away as Samba sleeps in his pram. I go to look at him and he is peacefully sleeping. I leave him and then go back a few moments later and he is hidden by blankets. I lift the blanket and there is a mother hare and a leveret, and Samba has also changed into a hare. The three of them hop out of the pram and into a field of high grass. I wonder how I will find him in the long grass.

A man comes along with a mower to cut the grass and I am frantic that the mower will chop up the hares. I beg the man to stop mowing and to find Samba. Then I see a couple of men coming with a box and inside is Samba, still in the form of a hare but wearing a woollen waistcoat, which is how they know he is Samba. To change him back into a baby all I have to do is feed him from my breast, which I do. He changes into Samba.

GODDESS HOUSE continues to grow and develop supported by lots of good people – healers and therapists, priestesses and melissas and assorted partners who come to help. It is a dream in the making and gradually more healers and therapists come to join us. Priestess Bee Helygen does a wonderful job gifting her time and energy, holding the House together as head receptionist as we find our way forward. I am creating a Goddess library in the new Bridannia (Britannia in another form) Room, transferring many books which I have had for years, from home to the House as the focus for our Goddess Educational centre, which is on its way to being realised. We are receiving books on Goddesses of the world, on feminism, on landscape, on Glastonbury/Avalon and on healing and wellness. From small acorns great oak trees grow.

THE Conference Ceremonial group spends the year designing and creating the ceremonies and shape of my last Goddess Conference as Webster. We have a circle of eight Priestesses of Avalon with the Lady of Avalon, our Goddess, in our centre. We are Sally Pullinger, Katinka Soetens, Marion van Eupen, Sue Quatermass, Michelle Patten, Sharlea Sparrow, Anna Saqqara and me. We will each begin in one of the eight directions and move around the Wheel changing every day. I begin on the Tuesday in the northwest as Crone Nolava, then move to Nolava of Air on Wednesday, Maiden Nolava on Thursday, Nolava of Fire on Friday, Lover Nolava on Saturday, and Nolava of Water on Sunday – when I will probably have some tears to shed. We will all be circling. The thirteen Trove Priestesses who look after the participants in the Conference are also dedicated Priestesses of Avalon, who love our Lady.

I feel happy that I am handing on the mountain of work it takes to create the Conference. It is the right time for me to let go. I have been very happy organising everything for the last 21years and now is the right time to stop. This year I am putting myself forward to take a bigger priestessing role, both in the Opening Ceremony, and in the Heart of the Mysteries, sharing what I have learned through the Goddess Conference and leading a special 10 Hours ceremony. I give myself lots to do, worrying a little that I might be being self-indulgent, but my sisters reassure me that it's OK and people will want my offerings. There is also to be special ceremony handing the Keys to the Mysteries on to Katinka and Marion.

BEFORE the conference I begin to feel very anxious about the whole event, for no particular reason except that it's my last in charge. It happens sometimes as the energy builds before an event of power, but it's almost unbearable this time. The teachers who are leading the Fringe workshops – Starhawk, Alisa Starkweather, Ruth Barrett and Falcon River, come into town over the weekend to give their workshops. Marion leads a large group around the Kora of Avalon, taking them along the edge of the land between ancient lake/sea and the rising isle.

On Monday we decorate the Town Hall as the Lady's Temple and it's very beautiful. By Tuesday morning it's the start of the Conference and am in such a state of anxiety I am really tempted to leave then, as people are beginning to register. I walk to the door and tell sister priestesses Alexandra and Joan Cichon that I am thinking of walking away. They say they will join me and something about the way they are willing to just go with me, breaks my fear and I start to laugh. The anxiety flows away. Thank Goddess!

Our Opening Day goes really well. Participants enjoy the Preparation Ceremonies in which they receive the blessings of earth, water, fire and air in four different locations in preparation for the evening's Opening Ceremony and the whole of the Conference. These ceremonies are held by our wonderful Conference Melissas and other Priestesses who want to contribute to the Conference.

In the evening participants enter the ceremonial space as if they are coming through the reeds at the edge of the Lake of Avalon. There is a wonderful musical soundscape created by Sally Pullinger and her son, Jerome O'Connell, which helps everyone to enter an altered state of reality as they journey across the Lake to the Isle of Avalon. A magical image of the Isle is projected onto misty material. Mike in his role as the Ferryman guides the Barge across the waters taking the people into the mists, and beyond to Avalon. The Priestess parts the mists to reveal a scene from Ancient Avalon where a circle of priestesses are in the process of welcoming the Lady of Avalon into their Ceremony. They speak in an ancient secret language and together support one of their circle to become the embodiment of the Lady of Avalon. As we create this ceremony it feels like this is how it's meant to be in an embodiment, that everyone in the circle is creating the embodiment together calling Her into the priestess who steps forward.

Her priestess is adorned with a beautiful purple cloak created by many hands – by Anna Saqqara, Alejandro and Mandie. An amazing antlered headdress created by Sue Quatermass is placed on her head. Standing tall she becomes the Lady of Avalon in the centre of the invocation, turning in the circle towards the people who have journeyed across the water to enter Avalon.

The Lady speaks to Her ancient priestesses and to all the people, asking them to bury the symbols of Her natural powers, Her Treasures, in Her land of Avalon, from where they will emanate Her energy through aeons of time. These Treasures will be shared with future generations of pilgrims, who will come seeking Her in Her Sacred Land. The Treasures include the ochred bones of swan, deer antlers, crystals, stones, comb and dark mirror, feathers, fire and fur, and beads of earth that the Lady wears around Her neck. For those of us who priestess the ceremony, it is very powerful and very real. We are there in the ancient Motherworld. We are re-membering some truth which we all recognise as part of our collective memories. In the ancient world we bury Her Treasures deep in the earth of Avalon. We shall return again in the future to retrieve them.

WEDNESDAY is a beautiful sunny day and in the afternoon we make a long Pilgrimage from the Town Hall out into Her nature, across the hillsides to some of the sacred sites of Avalon. We walk in procession singing and drumming to Avalloka, a field beside the top end of the Tor. There we sing and encircle a central altar, before following an intuition, a thread of memory, for we are the priestesses of old returning. We cross the field to a spot in the earth where a violet rose once bloomed. There we dig down into the earth, first with our bare hands, then with help from our men with spades. We retrieve and celebrate a large wooden box containing the Treasures of Avalon, revealing them to Her people. It is such a magical powerful moment when Her Treasures of Avalon are released from the earth where they have been buried for long ages. There is a huge energetic flow out from the land, radiating out to the whole of the Isle and beyond, and up into the sky. She is returning fully to the earth, to our human consciousness.

Our participants place their prayer sticks into the hole in the earth, which was left when we removed the Treasure chest. It is a beautiful and prayerful time for everyone as Oshia Drury and Heloise Pilkington sing softly of Avalon. These prayers will continue to resonate through the land for many years to come. Katie Hoffner places a small amount of her Aunt Lydia's ashes into the ground. Part of Lydia has returned home to Avalon, as was her heart's desire.

Different Goddess singers – Kellianna, Julie Felix, Jana Runnalls, lead everyone in singing and drumming at Avalloka. We eat food and relax in the sunshine, before wending our way down Wellhouse Lane to Chalice Well. We bless the Lady's Treasures with the Waters of Avalon at the vesica pool and Iris Lican and Lila Nuit from Senhora d'Azenha in Portugal offer us an amazing dance, dipping deep into the freezing cold waters of the pool. After a time in the gardens we walk to the foot of Chalice Hill and then climb to the top where we are greeted by Priestesses of Brighde, who sing to us and invite us to lie down belly to belly, on the Great Mother's belly, as we feel the Air of Avalon flowing all around us. We offer Her Treasures to the Air for blessing. We sing more songs as we lie upon Her body in the balmy air.

As the sun begins to slide down into the western sky we walk down the hill to Bushey Coombe where the Lammas bonfire is waiting to be lit. The Ceremonial Circle enters, bringing eight long burning torches to the eight directions.

"We light the Fire, the Lammas Fire. We light the Lammas Fire!"

We plunge the torches deep into the large stack of wood and a huge flame rises quickly through the well-prepared bonfire. We have some awesome Conference Melissas, many of them men, who work tirelessly to support the Goddess Conference through the week. I am deeply grateful to them all. Everyone cheers wildly. We offer Her Treasure to the Lammas Fire and feel truly blessed by the heat of Her Flames.

Then there is much singing and dancing offered by the various groups who have come to the Conference from around the world – with Dov Ahava from Israel, with Kellianna and Ruth and Alisa from the USA, with Jana from Spain, with Stephanie from Switzerland. There are so many talented people at the Conference.

It has been an amazing day retrieving her Treasures from the land and blessing them with earth, water, air and fire. We are all blissed out!

THURSDAY is a day of great talks, workshops, and a lunchtime concert from Heloise and Julie, to inspire and entertain. In the evening there is a special musical performance of Goddess songs, which have been composed and offered to the Conference over the last nine years by the amazing musician priestess performer Sally Pullinger. The evening is narrated in the most wonderful way by Gabi, Sally's granddaughter, in her own words. For the last six months priestesses and singers have been forming a new Goddess choir to prepare for this special evening, which is their gift to me, and to everyone. It's a very moving experience listening and joining in with all these well-known and well-loved songs, which are sung in a cycle following the Wheel of the Year. A wonderful photo presentation created by Marion van Eupen goes alongside the songs with images and memories of many Conferences. Mike and I are sitting in the middle of the Hall, loving the whole experience. It's only when we get round to the south and the water year, and there are photos of Koko and me, and Lydia and me, and other Conference friends who have passed away over the years, including Evelien from Holland, that tears fall down my face in buckets – so much love for my beloveds.

It takes a few more songs to recover, but the cycle continues until we reach the centre where we sing one of our great favourite choruses,

> *"O-oh, Lady of Avalon*
> *Creatrix of these sacred Isles*
> *Nolava, Goddess of Annwn*
> *Oh Apple Queen of Paradise.*
> *Oooh, Lady of Avalon*
> *Your Creation goes on and on*
> *Violet Lady of the Summerlands*
> *You are the Source and the Return!"*
>
> Sally Pullinger

IT IS A wonderful evening and I am so grateful for all the time and effort that has been given to create this memorable evening of song and dance and poetry.

THE NEXT DAY in the morning I give a talk about my experience of twenty-one years of the Goddess Conference. I begin with a song by Norwegian singer Ane Brun – *You lit my fire*.

> *I will never ever, I will never ever forget*
> *I will never ever, I will never ever forget*
>
> *They changed our game*
> *I want to kiss the feet of all those women*
> *Spray my body in gold, engrave myself with their names*
> *Stand tall in awe to the freedom, that they gave to us*
> *And never ever forget, No, I will never ever forget*
> *Now, we are all alone. Now, we are all alone in that*
> *And nothing can hold me back.*
> *You're lighting my fire*

We take their struggle for granted
We are blinded by this taste of power
Forsaking our sisters and brothers
Oh, this fight goes on for the freedom that we can't give up

And never ever forget. No, I will never ever forget
Now, we are all alone. Now, we are all alone in that,
And nothing can hold me back
Oh, you're lighting my fire
And nothing can hold me back
Oh, you're lighting my fire – [repeated]

WITH SUE'S HELP I have written in gold on my skin the names of the women who have inspired me and had a big influence in my life – *Alice Bailey, Jane Roberts, Virginia Woolf, Mary Renault, Evangeline Walton, Mary Daly, Merlin Stone, Asphodel Long, Jane Harrison, Marija Gimbutas, Monica Sjoo* and more.

I am nervous as I begin to speak and then get into my stride. I talk about the beginning of the Conference 21 years ago with Tyna Redpath, my first experience of breast cancer and my gratitude to Mike for his unwavering support for me and all that we have created for Goddess from the beginning. I talk of the people who have contributed to the Conference, the many talented presenters, performers, poets, artists and musicians. I talk of the inspiration of the Lady, of the challenges and the triumphs of the Conference, of the things I have learned, the nuggets of Her wisdom I have received over the years. Once I get going I realise that I can just go on and on talking. I observe myself and find it humorous that I seem to like the sound of my own voice so much. I hope I am entertaining the audience too.

I manage to stop talking – a bit over time. We have a short break and then the room fills again with about 250 people for the 10 Hours Journey into the Heartlands of Avalon. There is barely room for everyone to sit or lie upon the floor, to be comfortable for the next 10 hours. I ask everyone to refrain from talking as I lead the journey in a state of Her embodiment. I am assisted in making sounds and music by musicians Heloise Pilkington and Sophie Pullinger. And the Ceremonial Circle holds seven more Priestess Embodiments of the Lady, whom everyone can visit during the 10 Hours when they are ready.

We begin the journey and soon we are moving into a completely altered state of reality, absorbed into a process of deep inner work, women and men journeying together into the Mysteries of Avalon. It is an amazing experience for everyone as they meet unknown parts of themselves, descending into their Shadow material as well as rising to the heights of the Lady's inspiring Presence, meeting Her in the Heartlands of Avalon, and in Her embodied priestesses.

We have two short breaks part way through for light food created by Yamuna Wynn. As usual when 10 Hours begins it seems like it will be a long time to sit or lie upon the floor, but once again it's over all too soon. I think how to create longer journeys and how to make them work practically, with sleep and food. It has been an amazing experience for me and for us all. We are all grateful for all we have received.

ON SATURDAY morning Kay Dayton gives a very funny talk about her experiences within the energies of Glastonbury. This is followed by Luciana Percovich, an Italian Goddess scholar who talks to us about *"Quintessential Connections"*, with a tribute to Mary Daly, and the inspiration of one of her final books *"Quintessence: Realising the Archaic Future"*.

Luciana indicates that what we are doing in Glastonbury and in the Goddess Conference is an example of,

"Quintessence… the Fifth Dimension, the Fifth Province, the Fifth Spiral, which is the realm of Nolava, who inhabits and rules the core of the reign of Avalon.

The Fifth Essence, Quintessence, is the substance that vibrates in the centre of any Circle of Awakened Women, the centre which holds the four directions and the four elements together, allowing the living plan of ordinary time/space to shift into another dimension. In fact, every time you open a Circle, you create an extra-ordinary space/time, you do the magic of entering another dimension. Provided that this is your strong intention, your shared will."

LUCIANA'S TALK is completely inspiring to me. Tears are running down my face. I am overwhelmed by her recognition of all that we are doing here in Glastonbury and in the Conference. I am personally grateful to Mary Daly, our Foresister, who had a huge effect on my thinking in the 1980s, through her marvellous capacity to deconstruct patriarchal language, to name the forbidden and hidden, and to expose it in her searchlight thinking. As a consequence of reading her books and those of other women, I did not read any books written by men for the following 20 years, as I was sure that men were so entrenched in patriarchal thinking that they knew nothing that was interesting to me.

I want to read Mary Daly again. I just took some of her books from my shelves to Goddess House. I want to retrieve them and read them again. I am in a state of bliss.

THE FOLLOWING DAY we walk in procession, singing and drumming up to the top of Glastonbury Tor, with Lydia's colourful GIRLs flying in the wind. We call in the Wheel of Nolava on top of the Tor, turning to the eight directions and sending the Lady's blessing out across the land. As usual we share a Fruit Feast and then sit and talk in the sunshine.

On the way back to the Town Hall there is a moment as we reach the bottom of the Tor when I feel completely overcome with grief for this ending. My body is tired and I feel very sad. Katinka and Marion come and hold me strongly on each side as we walk along the road. We begin to sing and the emotion lifts and the sadness dissolves. My strength returns.

IN THE AFTERNOON we hold the Give Away ceremony where everyone gives and receives gifts in a random exchange. We give all the participants a small key, representing the Key to the Mysteries of Avalon, which they have all experienced in the Conference. I lead the circle of thanksgiving, as usual thanking everyone who has given of their talents and energy to the Conference. I give the Ceremony Group bouquets of flowers. I receive a bouquet of flowers from Mike. Then comes the final ceremony.

I had wondered how to create a meaningful ceremony to hand the Conference on into the care of Katinka and Marion. What came to my mind was to create something about lineage. In the Goddess world our lineage as priestesses, which comes from ancient Neolithic times when Goddess was last really loved and adored by the whole world, was cut. At some point the handing on of knowledge of Her ways from older to younger priestesses ended. Now it is time to re-establish lineage, not in the sense of ownership of tradition, but in the sense of visible commitment and dedication to Goddess.

As the person who initiated the Conference and other Goddess ventures in Glastonbury I am a lineage-holder, and I give value to this lineage of the Lady, which is being newly established. Our Ceremony needs to reflect the handing on of the lineage of the Conference. I have found a set of really old keys, two of which I want to give to Katinka and Marion, as a symbol of the Keys to the Mysteries of this lineage of Avalon. As the day of the ceremony draws closer I am in a panic. I have lost the keys! It is so crazy and somehow symbolic. I have lost the Keys to the Mysteries! Fortunately there are two more, which I can use in the Ceremony.

As the Ceremony begins we attach violet threads from all parts of the Conference furniture, from the altars, doors, sound equipment, etc, and I gather the ends of all the threads together in the centre of the Temple Hall. I am supported by Michelle, who carries the beautiful embodiment cloak of the Lady of Avalon, and Sue who carries the Lady's magical deer headdress. Katinka and Marion, in front of me, are supported by Sally, Sharlea and Anna Saqqara. We come together in the middle of the Temple and I place my hand first on Katinka's heart and then on Marion's. I transmit the Lady's palpable energy to each of them in turn, consciously establishing Her lineage into the future. I hand them each a Key to Her Mysteries. Then with great joy I hand them the threads of the Conference and the Temple erupts into cheering. Katinka and Marion ask everyone to come and help them hold the threads of the Conference. Everyone pours towards them to help hold the threads. I turn away and climb to the main altar.

It's an amazing ceremony. I feel so light and happy. I have let go and it feels so good. Later when we are clearing up everything out of the hall I find the original Keys to the Mysteries in the bag where they were supposed to be. I had not been able to find them when I looked. It seems that I still need to keep my own set of Keys to Her Mysteries...

Finale

GRATITUDE

I AM SO GRATEFUL to so many people for your presence in my life. I am blessed by knowing you.

I am especially grateful to Mike, my true love and husband, to my lovely daughter Iona, my gorgeous son Torquil, and my joyous grandson Samba Ziggy, and to partners Lahla and Leigh, for being in our family. I love you all so much.

I am so grateful to all my sister priestesses who are remembering, reclaiming, restoring Goddess to the world. I am so happy that we found each other again in this life, that we have incarnated together at this time. I am especially glad that we are committed to healing our individual wounds and to creating MotherWorld together.

My thanks especially are to my Soul Sisters Erin McCauliff, Sally Pullinger, Katinka Soetens, Marion van Eupen, Ruby Ward, Sue Quatermass, Rose Flint, Roz Bound, Sharlea Sparrow, Katie Player, Heloise Pilkington, Sophie Pullinger, Anna-Saqqara Price and all those who have played a part in the Temple and Conference Ceremony, Priestess, Melissa and Admin groups in past years. These include Amanda Baker, Louise Tarrier, Tegwyn Hyndman, Annabel Du Boulay, Lydia Lite, Tina Free, Mary Bruce, Alexandra Cichon, Joan Cichon, Geraldine Charles, Peter Wood, Brian Harrison, John Reeves, Kai Rawnsley and so many many more – too many to mention.

Thank you to my Soul Sisters who inspire me in the inbetween spaces of international travel, whose love and sharing is a great joy to me – Anique Radiant-Heart, Apela Colorado, Ava Park, Leona Graham, Sarah Perini and all those I meet on the road.

Thank you to all the wonderful Melissas who hold the Glastonbury Goddess Temple open every day for the public to enjoy, and to all who are helping establish Goddess House, our newest Motherworld adVenture. Thank you to Temple Melissa Mother – Dawn Kinsella, Melissa Poppa – Trevor Nuthall, to Angie Twydall, Bee Helygen, Nandini Gibbins, Mandie Thorne, Mary Bruce, Marisa Pi, Iona Jones, Stephanie Mathivet, Beth Twydall, Ann Pelsmaekers, Anna-Saqqara Price, Carmen Wattana and Rachel Harris.

Thank you to those who read the earlier drafts of this book, giving me your helpful opinions. In particular my thanks go to Katinka Soetens for pointing out that I did not need to write all the detail of 'who did what to whom' to communicate what I want to communicate in writing this book. Thank you also to Tressy Driver for casting an editorial eye over the final draft.

My special thanks go to all those who are characterised anonymously in this book as critics, attackers, underminers, betrayers, all of whom are my Shadow projections. You are all part of my healing, my learning and I am grateful to you for bringing to light those painful wounded places in me that needed so much healing. I would not have found them without you. I am very sorry if my words or actions hurt you in any way. I did not mean to do anything to upset you. If the things which happened then were to happen now I would not react in the same way. I would hopefully act from much less pain and with much clearer boundaries. Thank you all.

MEMORY comes not only from the past. Like my foresister Mary Daly, I too have travelled into the future and on my sojourns I have met some of our future selves. I have been there and am there in the future, in the times when MotherWorld is fully alive and is lived and enjoyed by human beings on Her beautiful body the Earth. I am inspired by these future memories as much as I am inspired by memories of past peaceful times.

Finale: Gratitude

We are on our way to the Parliament House in London for the inauguration of our new Motherworld Prime Minister, Ana of Avalon. She is the first woman politician to be elected who has trained as a Priestess in Avalon and she is part of our Goddess community. We have great hopes for her although we recognise she will have to deal with sometimes conflicting partners. We are a group of sisters and brothers who have travelled from Avalon to the capital for this special day. There have been Motherworld representatives in government for some time now as it is recognised how effective our ideas are in making Brigit's Isles a better place to live and work in, but this is a first, where we are in power.

Life is so different now from the early days when the Motherworld Vision first came. Climate change really began to bite and the weather and seasons altered. Radical change was forced upon governments worldwide. However once change began then it only took a relatively small shift for people to understand what Motherworld people were calling for – a complete overhaul of everything that had been taken for granted – that money was the centre of everything, that violence, war, starvation, destruction of the environment are inevitable, and all those out-dated patriarchal notions of what life is meant to be. It was the hundredth monkey syndrome in action. Once a few people woke up, lots of others followed.

It has helped massively that thousands and thousands of souls have incarnated with Motherworld values embedded in their souls. We the young, inspired and informed by our elders, know it from the inside rather than having to be persuaded or convinced of the need for change. It's a great blessing from Goddess that the times of awakening are upon us. We have seen the effects of the past six, seven, eight thousand years of patriarchal power-over rule and while taking the positive outcomes of those years, we can let go of the negatives. There are no longer the rich few whose wealth outweighs the incomes of the majority. There have been changes in nearly all countries to bring people's value and incomes into balance, and where they have not changed yet, people are uprising as they see on the Motherweb what is possible in other lands.

Now Mother Earth, mothers and the values of mothering, love, care and support are placed in the centre of most societies. As people experience being loved and giving more love themselves all sort of old unconscious behaviours are changing. We are all learning nonviolent practices for the resolution of conflict, which are taught in all schools and there is less violent conflict between people and between nations. We are learning to get along with each other.

Great strides have been made in changing practices which oppressed and abused women, children, and men. The 51% of the planet who are women have stood up and are being noticed. We are leading the revolution with the help of our awakened brothers, fathers and sons. Female genital mutilation is now outlawed in all countries of the world. Child sexual and emotional abuse is considerably reduced as it has been recognised as a disease and perpetrators are helped to meet their wounding passed usually from generation to generation, and thus the repetitious cycles are healed and ended. Rape is dying out as men come to truly honour women.

Every law, every decision can be referred to the basic ideal – does this action support Mother Earth, does it support mothers? Does it uphold the values of mothering? Of course all this requires lots of discussion and coming to consensus, which can take an annoyingly long time. But we are slowly learning to trust each other again as the bonds between women become so much stronger and thus the bonds between women and men, and men and men strengthen too. It has actually become simpler to make decisions as we align with Motherworld values through multitudinous different expressions.

Of course there is still much to be done and for at least seven generations there is a tendency to lapse into old once familiar ways, but we are vigilant, and can help each other to overcome our failings. At least now in every town and village there are support and healing circles for those who want to face and meet their wounding. The old national health service has become a much more open and flexible health service that is no longer in the thrall of drug companies. It offers all kinds of medical and complementary health advances, from acupuncture to deep soul healing, herbal medicine to laser surgery, immunotherapy to sound healing – whatever is in the patient's best interests.

FINALE: GRATITUDE

There are much improved services for the great transitions of life – the important care for mothers who are birthing, for their babies and for fathers. There is a much greater understanding of the importance of a peaceful letting go of life in conscious dying. This is one of my favourite subjects – the care of the soul into and out of incarnation.

We are travelling across London by electric taxi – the battery problems of the turn of the 21st century were eventually solved and now electricity from solar, wind, wave and geothermal power can be stored for use everywhere when it is needed. Brigit's Isles are fuelled by Her nature at last. The other blissful consequence of Motherworld initiatives is that the factories and people that once worked for the defence industry, manufacturing weapons of war to sell to impoverished nations, have become the places where 'ploughshares' are manufactured – all that is needed to build the infrastructure to help us be self-supporting in energy, in healthcare and in exporting our innovative life-affirming technologies to other countries.

EARLIER IN OUR visit to London we went to pray and make offerings at the London Goddess Temple, a large beautiful building with a central Sanctuary with lots of glass, and many smaller colourful healing and meeting rooms. It is based on a similar design to the great Temple of Avalon in Glastonbury. The London Temple began as a dream between a few Priestesses who had trained on the Sacred Isle. They began by creating pop-up Temples above alternative bookshops, holding them open for a few days at a time in each season, offering ceremonies. At that time with so many distractions on offer in London they were a small but vibrant presence. But gradually the nascent Temple grew stronger. As the Lady's violet stimulating energy continued to stream forth from Avalon, from Glastonbury, everyone who was connected to that energy gained in confidence – from 'con fide', with faith.

Now the London Goddess Temple is a light and bright space that pulses with life and colourful energy in the heart of the capital. Hundreds of Londoners and visitors from all over Britain and the world come into the Temple each week, seeking a peaceful place to worship Goddess as Tamesis of the River Thame, as Bridannia, ancient Goddess of these Isles – Bridannia to distinguish from but not remove Her connection to Britannia, the Romanised form of our tutelary indigenous Goddess. She is celebrated through Her seasons as Brighde, Artha, Rhiannon, Domnu, Ker, Banbha, Keridwen and Danu, and many other of Her faces in London. And all around the capital there are smaller local Goddess Temples held within neighbourhoods by people called to love Her. There is one for Isis who was worshipped in London over 2000 years ago in Roman times and one for Brighde, near to the site of the old St Bride's Church in Fleet Street, which had claimed Her name. And so many more.

In Glastonbury the Temple of Avalon itself, the Source Temple for the Lady's energy for this new radiation of Goddess love, has also grown in size. What began as a pop-up Temple in 2001 is now a great beautiful vulva-shaped Goddess Temple in the centre of the town. It is placed on the edge of the sward of green grass that also houses the ruins of the old Glastonbury Abbey, where Christianity first entered Brigit's Isles, with all those consequences. There is also a special Goddess Healing House and Educational Centre, with a great MotherWorld Library full of Goddess, Feminist, Sacred Landscape, Mysticism, Environmental and Healing books. The world needs the education that we can offer. There is a Goddess Arts Centre, Bookstore and holistic Café and Goddess shops where you can buy statues and priestess ephemera.

In the Goddess Temple we offer regular public seasonal Ceremonies and Ceremonies for the Dark, New and Full Moons, conducted by dedicated Priestesses of Goddess and Avalon. There are also many personal and smaller group ceremonies as needed, for special occasions, Conception, Birth, Naming, Menarche, Manning, Guardianship, Weddings, Mothering, Fathering, Midlife, Menopause, Croning, Saging, Death and all the other special moments of life which need to be ritually marked.

The Circle of Priestesses and Priests who first created the first legal Goddess Temple in Brigit's Isles are now legendary, moving from real-time memory into the mythical dimensions, as their foresisters, the Nine Morgen Priestesses did *long ages ago, becoming inter-dimensional dakinis. They worked together through lots of challenges to create the first Motherworld community, and are honoured in Avalon as First Ancestors. We communicate with them in our ceremonies and receive their wisdom and blessings for our progress now. We feel deeply connected to them as they speak to us in dreams and in the Inner Sanctuary of the Mysterium. They are always present to us, holding our backs, as they learned to hold each other through difficult times. We learn so much from their experiences even though it is now quite long ago. Some of us are those Ancestors returned, again and again, in each life healing more of the wounds of patriarchal times. I know that I am one of those who has come again to serve the Lady and Her people. She communicates with me through dreams and visions, heart to heart. I am so grateful for my life.*

WE ARE coming closer to the Parliament building, another large circular building (MotherWorld loves circles) built close to the old Houses of Parliament, now a museum to past ideals. They were so out of date with their adversarial seating arrangements and lack of office space, and it took ages to convince everyone of the need to come into the modern age with a purpose-built, cooperative building where members can all see each other as part of the circle. We have become much more adept at creating public and private spaces which enhance communication, rather than impede it. This shows up in private housing, which is no longer isolated boxes with two parents and 2.4 children per box. Shared communal buildings have developed with zero energy consumption. Streets of houses remain, not everything can change overnight, but communal kitchens and relaxation areas have been added, where people can meet and share meals, childcare, creative and leisure activities, friendships and love relationships. Things have really changed.

We leave the taxi and walk towards the Parliament building. The streets are crowded with people, who look like they are really enjoying themselves. We can hear people singing the anthem of Avalon, composed all those years ago, by Priestess Sally of Avalon. The crowds are calling in the Lady of Avalon, to work

Her magic here in our capital. We have seats in the gallery in our own Avalon section with some of our elders, who travelled here too for this momentous day. The great circular Hall is alive with sound, people talking, laughing, faces smiling.

The great Conch is sounded and everyone settles. The play of light and sound changes as the Ceremony begins. Drummers beating in Journey Rhythms enter the central open space, spreading out to either side of the circle, shifting dimensions, altering mind spaces, their drums rising to a crescendo and then stopping, Boom! Led by two Guardians, a woman and a man dressed in ceremonial garb, Priestess Ana of Avalon enters the circle. She wears violet, shimmering from head to foot in pale to deep purple. On her head is a beautiful headdress of fresh flowers picked from the gardens of Bridannia's land. It's almost as if we can smell their scent drifting up to where we are seated, keenly peering over the balcony edge.

Nine Priestesses and Priests from Avalon and from the London Temple enter the circle moving to stand in the nine directions. Look! There is Priestess Garielle and Priest Jaron from the Avalon Temple. We in the gallery feel so proud of our sister and brother, proud that they are here on this day and are recognised as Priest/esses of Power from the Sacred Isle. The Invocation of Goddess begins, with the recognition of Her Presence and gratitude to Her in Her many different forms, here in London and also throughout the whole of Brigit's Isles. Each Priestess and Priest offers gifts of the land to place on the main altar, seeds, grains, flowers, herbs, fruit, vegetables, earth, water, feather, bone, all naturally found on Her land from Her mountains to Her valleys, Her fields and gardens, to Her streams, rivers and lakes. The abundance of the gifts that She gives to us always becomes visible.

Two priestesses, two priests enter the circle, with great feather fans, wafting clouds of incense to cleanse the ceremonial space – the smoke alarms are turned off. They ritually cleanse Priestess Ana, and we can see her body visibly relax as she lets go of anticipation and any anxiety about this day. Then comes the Sacred Fire, a Flame rising in the centre of the circle. Ana is led close to the fire and holds her hands out to the heat, blessing herself with fire. She lights the Flame of the New Time, which is her time to lead the circle. Beside the fire is a large bowl of water which begins to bubble upwards as a fountain. Great swan feathers are dipped in the water and Ana receives the blessings of emotions, each of her chakras are sprinkled with water. Then the bowl of earth is brought forward, earth collected from all corners of Bridannia's Realm and mixed together. This is the Sacred Earth, the soil which feeds and supports us all. Soil too is placed upon each of Ana's chakras, blessing her earthly body.

Everyone watches with great attention not wanting to miss a moment of this anointing and blessing. Forward come the painters, who quickly and expertly begin to paint the symbols of Goddess and Motherworld on Ana's face, arms and legs. She already carries her priestess tattoos, but this is the paint of empowerment. Her whole demeanour becomes more emphatic, as energy spirals through her body and she enters into the empowerment and embodiment of Goddess. For as our Prime Minister she will be called upon to embody Goddess, to speak for Her in the different forms in which She reveals herself through Bridannia's Wheel of the year. The traditions first renewed at the turn of the 21st century have developed over the intervening years. Who knew when they first appeared that they would become so beloved by people, that they held such potency?

The Song of Dedication begins, a single beautiful voice calling to the powers of earth and sky, fire and water to bless our new Prime Minister. We join in with the chorus, voices rising in crescendo. There is an ecstasy in these moments as we lose ourselves in the sound and the generous power of now. Then Priestess Ana moves to the centre and speaks, offering her human body as vehicle for the desires of Goddess. Her embodied voice resounds through the space as She speaks the words of Goddess and gives Her blessings to the elements of Her nature, to the land, to Her people, to Her Motherworld. These are the intentions which matter, not procedures and platitudes, but focus, purpose, love and gratitude. Then all shall be well.

The ceremony continues with more singers, dancers, artists and musicians, poetry and prose, all the cultural gifts of the people. We are filled up with hope and joy. There are so many gifted people in our lands which we need to honour and celebrate. Hours do pass in this beautiful ceremony until the final moments of blessing. As we slowly make our way out of the building we are feeling high as birds, elated and inspired by these new days. Motherworld is firmly anchored into the psyche and physicality of our land and its people, as is happening throughout the world. We are part of a great movement of change. The Dream that was received long ago has become real in the world. Blessed be!

THE VISIONS that we have in the present are the visions that create the future and we too are there in the future we created when we were the ancestors. We will be with each other again and with others we are yet to meet and greet anew. In each life lived we heal our wounds empowering ourselves to live the life we know to be the best and the truest for everyone – the best for the earth Herself, for Her continents and oceans, for Her fires and airs, for all plants and trees, for all of Her nature, the best for all Her animals, for all who live in rivers, lakes and oceans, for all Her birds that fly in the air, and for all human beings everywhere. We are the future that will come. We are Her MotherWorld. Trust in this prophecy!

*May the Lady of Avalon's
many blessings fill your life with
love and gratitude.*

KATHRYN OF AVALON

Ariadne Publications

BOOKS BY KATHY JONES

Priestess of Avalon, Priestess of Goddess; A Renewed Spiritual Path for the 21st Century

Join Priestess of Avalon Kathy Jones on this inspiring and exhilerating journey into the Heart of the Goddess, learning of the Mysteries of Avalon and the renewed Priestess and Priest of Avalon tradition. Share Kathy's experiences of living in Avalon for 40 years, learning of the ways of the Goddess in the sacred land. This book is the foundation text for the Priestess of Avalon Training, now in its twentieth year of teaching.

544 pp   pbk illust.

The Ancient British Goddess: Goddess Myths, Legends, Sacred Sites and Present Revelation

An inspiring journey into the bounteous and abundant nature of our native British Goddesses, revealing Her as Maiden, Lover, Mother and Crone, as Mother of Earth, Water, Fire and Air in landscapes and legends. Also exploring Her present day revelation in the lives of Goddess-loving artists, writer and performers. Lavishly illustrated with original photographs and artwork.

256pp   pbk illust.

Chiron in Labrys: An Introduction to Esoteric Soul Healing

A book about transformation and the healing of disease in the patient and the wounded healer within the context of the natural cycles and energies of our Mother Earth. A reworking of Alice Bailey's classic teachings on Esoteric Healing based on Kathy's 25 years healing experience.

212pp   pbk illust.

In the Nature of Avalon: Goddess Pilgrimages in Glastonbury's Sacred Landscape

Beautifully illustrated Goddess pilgrimages in Glastonbury's sacred landscape providing an excellent guide for those who wish to journey through the Veil into the magical Otherworld of the Isle of Avalon. With detailed route directions, maps, Goddess historical and mythic information, and suggestions for prayers, rituals and visualisations all designed to bring you into closer contact with the Goddess.

224pp   pbk illust.

Breast Cancer: Hanging on by a Red Thread

A strong story based on diary extracts of Kathy's journey through the experience of having breast cancer, looking at the physical, emotional and spiritual aspects of this dangerous disease. With ideas on how to help yourself.

124pp   pbk illust.

On Finding Treasure: Mystery Plays of the Goddess

An autobiographical account of the transformative work of Ariadne Productions which regularly presented original sacred dramas in Glastonbury. Includes five performed playscripts.

264pp   pbk illust.

To buy:
www.kathyjones.co.uk

For Goddess Trainings:
www.goddesstempleteachings.co.uk